ASK NOT

MAUREEN CALLAHAN

ASK NOT

THE KENNEDYS AND THE
WOMEN THEY DESTROYED

MUDLARK

Mudlark
HarperCollins*Publishers*
1 London Bridge Street
London SE1 9GF

www.harpercollins.co.uk

HarperCollins*Publishers*
Macken House, 39/40 Mayor Street Upper
Dublin 1, D01 C9W8, Ireland

First published by Little, Brown and Company 2024
This edition published by Mudlark 2024

1 3 5 7 9 10 8 6 4 2

© Maureen Callahan 2024

Maureen Callahan asserts the moral right to be
identified as the author of this work

A catalogue record of this book is
available from the British Library

HB ISBN 978-0-00-847324-2
PB ISBN 978-0-00-847325-9

OVER THE RAINBOW (from *The Wizard of Oz*) Music by HAROLD ARLEN,
Lyrics by E. Y. HARBURG © 1938 (Renewed) METRO-GOLDWYN-MAYER INC. © 1939
(Renewed) EMI FEIST CATALOG INC. All Rights (Excluding Print) Controlled and
Administered by EMI FEIST CATALOG INC. Exclusive Print Rights Administered by
ALFRED MUSIC All Rights Reserved Used by Permission of ALFRED MUSIC

Book interior design by Marie Mundaca

Printed and bound in the UK using 100% renewable
electricity at CPI Group (UK) Ltd

This book contains FSC™ certified paper and other controlled
sources to ensure responsible forest management.

For more information visit: www.harpercollins.co.uk/green

For inconvenient women everywhere

They were careless people . . . they smashed up things and creatures and then retreated back into their money or their vast carelessness, or whatever it was that kept them together, and let other people clean up the mess they had made.

— F. Scott Fitzgerald, The Great Gatsby

CONTENTS

CONTENTS

AUTHOR'S NOTE

History, to paraphrase the adage, is typically told by the victors. But what of the other side? This book tells the stories of women whose lives were upended by Kennedy men, but whose collective history has never been captured in total. In my attempt to do so, I relied on methods common to nonfiction writers and historians: years spent in archival research; original interviews conducted with surviving family members and friends; preexisting biographies, memoirs, personal journals, and contemporaneous news reports. All informed what I believe are the closest, most accurate approximations of their thoughts and feelings. I would often ask those closest to these women if my assessments sounded fair, and only those agreed-upon conclusions—those thoughts and reactions—are the ones you'll read here. Even the emotional fortress that was Jackie Kennedy Onassis shared her most intimate horrors with historians, relatives, and friends. What these women endured, I learned, is accessible, if only one looks hard enough. My subjectivity is, I believe, no less or more than that of any other historian drawn to their subjects.

PROLOGUE

T his book is not ideological or partisan. It's about thirteen women and a piece of American history hiding in plain sight. Kennedy men have been valorized and lionized for nearly a century, but the women they've broken, tormented, raped, murdered, or left for dead have never really been part of their legacy.

They must be. None of this is history. As William Faulkner wrote, "The past is never dead. It's not even past." The Kennedys remain a powerful and frequently destructive force, both in our politics and our culture. As of this writing, Robert F. Kennedy Jr., a prominent conspiracy theorist and anti-vaxxer who has made racist and antisemitic comments, is running for president of the United States. He has raised tens of millions from big donors, almost all based on legacy. He remains unbothered and unquestioned about the circumstances leading to the suicide of his second wife, Mary Richardson Kennedy, in 2012 — a fragile woman whom he tormented toward the end of their marriage and in the lead-up to her suicide, cheating on her, cutting off her credit cards and access to cash, trying to forcibly hospitalize her, telling her she'd be "better off dead." He continues to smear her reputation, telling the press in December 2023 that yes, he had flown on the late pedophile Jeffrey Epstein's private plane not once, as he previously claimed, but twice, and that was only because Mary had a "relationship" with Epstein's chief procurer, the convicted child sex trafficker Ghislaine Maxwell — an assertion that several people who knew Mary well told me is impossible, given her character, her morality, and her devout Catholicism. RFK Jr. also, incredibly, has been given a huge pass for his false accusation that the savage 1975 sexual assault and murder of fifteen-year-old Martha Moxley was committed not by his once-convicted cousin Michael Skakel but by two teenagers from the Bronx, one Black, one mixed-race — teenagers he publicly named, endangering their lives. RFK Jr. wrote that one of the teens was "obsessed" with Martha's "beautiful blonde hair" and that both young men decided to go "caveman" on her.

Imagine anyone but a Kennedy leveling such racist, baseless accusations. The media would, rightly, be aflame with indignation. Yet all these decades later, the Kennedys benefit from a perverse double standard — in the press, in the justice system, and in the court of public opinion.

It's a double standard that is clearest and most insidious when it comes to the crimes that Kennedy men have committed against women and young girls. What was done to Mary and Martha are only two recent examples. Any victims who dare to fight back will find themselves confronting the awesome power of the Kennedy machine, one that recasts any woman, no matter how wealthy or famous or powerful, as crazy, spiteful, vengeful; a drug addict, a viper, a seductress. Whatever grievous harm a Kennedy man may have done to her, the message remains clear: She was asking for it. It was her fault.

Thus Camelot, that fairy tale of Kennedy greatness and noble men, still stands.

The late Ted Kennedy, vaunted "Lion of the Senate," drove off a bridge and left a twenty-nine-year-old woman to die in three feet of water — his passenger Mary Jo Kopechne, whose life could have been saved. Yet that criminal act has successfully been transformed into "Ted's tragedy," an awful event that unfairly kept him from ever becoming president of the United States. Ted Kennedy served out the rest of his life in Congress and was given a statesman's funeral with wall-to-wall news coverage, while Kopechne's name was barely mentioned. He was memorialized by Ellen R. Malcolm, the founder of EMILY's List, as "a true champion for women." Cecile Richards, then-president of Planned Parenthood, lauded him as "a true champion of women's health and rights." Neither woman mentioned Mary Jo Kopechne.

This well-known drunk and serial sexual assaulter has been the glorified subject of two recent biographies, both by men: a two-volume treatment hyperbolically titled *Catching the Wind* and *Against the Wind*, respectively, by prize-winning author Neal Gabler, and *Ted Kennedy: A Life,* by prize-winning historian John A. Farrell. The latter describes Kopechne as "attractive but not gorgeous"—that observation, why?— before noting that she had the bad luck to be in a vehicle that passively "left the bridge," as if, like the car in Stephen King's *Christine*, it had a mind of its own. As if that car hadn't been driven by a drunken Ted Kennedy, his driver's license expired. As if Ted hadn't sped down an unlit dirt road and careened off a small bridge with such force the car flipped and landed on its roof, the windshield smashed in.

Ted escaped. He left Mary Jo in that car upside down, forced to crane her neck at an awkward, painful angle as she struggled to breathe through a tiny pocket of air, surrounded by dark water, waiting for help that never came.

After the accident, guess who was at fault? Not Ted but his victim, Mary Jo, for being a single woman in this married man's car late at night.

The Kennedys have a way of quashing anything or anyone—a book, a miniseries, an interview—that contradicts their golden image. They typically do this through power or payoffs. Caroline Kennedy and Maria Shriver personally lobbied the History Channel to kill *The Kennedys*, a 2011 miniseries that one family loyalist called "vindictive" and "malicious" in the *New York Times*, and were successful.

In one of the saddest ironies, even the most powerful Kennedy women would like this history erased. And such efforts have allowed this lie, this cancer in the American body politic, to further metastasize. It's time to do right by the women and girls—and ourselves—by excising it.

———

Their stories are not told chronologically. Some women are paired throughout and some stand alone, but their unique experiences resonate in ways that link them across twentieth- and twenty-first-century America politically, historically, culturally, and socially. Some—such as Jackie Kennedy Onassis, whose life progressed along the path of modern American feminism, going from high-society debutante to First Lady to trophy wife to sexually liberated New York City career woman—will reappear; other girls and women have shorter stories, shorter lives.

Through deep reporting and interviews with many who have never spoken before, this book seeks to understand what being a woman among Kennedy men felt like over the years. I have taken some creative license here, but each of these stories is anchored by years of research. Many of these women are complicated; they, too, were attracted to money, fame, power—and that's okay. We have made great strides in realizing that few girls and women ever make perfect victims. No one in these pages, despite what the Kennedys might have you think, deserved what happened to them. Not one deserves the stains on their legacies wrought, with great deliberation and zero remorse, by the Kennedys. This book is intended as a corrective, a new take on some women we think we know and some we've never really met, neither in full nor in fact.

Think about this: Jacqueline Kennedy, a thirty-four-year-old widow and mother who held the nation together after narrowly escaping the assassin's bullets that killed her husband—who signaled to the world that America would not only survive this trauma but emerge stronger—was, upon her remarriage five years later, castigated as a whore who had sold herself to the highest bidder. That mantle hung over Jackie's fascinating, difficult, creative, controversial life until the day she died. A man would never have been so denigrated. What happened to Jackie would be unthinkable today.

The Kennedys remain very much with us. But what is the Kennedy legacy, really? How should we define it? Do the Kennedys deserve to remain a power center in American life and politics? Or should we relegate them to their inglorious past? If not, what should we now demand of any Kennedy who seeks power?

We can answer only by fully reckoning with how the Kennedys have brutalized women throughout generations. The pattern originates with the ruthless patriarch, Joseph P. Kennedy Sr., a financially and sexually rapacious man who fathered nine children. His path to power would be through his sons; his daughters were bred for marriage and babies, worthless as anything else in his eyes. Ever the overachiever, Joe committed two original sins. The first was political, and it would keep him from ever becoming president: his open admiration, as United States ambassador to the United Kingdom, of Adolf Hitler and his bloodless acceptance of the looming death of Western democracy. That was followed by his personal original sin: the unthinkable act he committed against his beautiful young daughter Rosemary, who suffered a fate worse than death. These are the poisonous roots from which all Kennedy misogyny and violence — psychological, physical, political, and personal — has flourished.

This book's title comes from the most famous line of John F. Kennedy's 1961 inaugural address: "Ask not what your country can do for you..."

"Ask not" has also forever been an admonition to women in the Kennedy sphere: Ask no questions. Don't ask for help or respect, for fairness or justice.

This book takes that as a dare. Ask not?

Let's.

—January 2024

PART ONE
ICONS

CAROLYN BESSETTE

The minute she said yes, she regretted it.

Carolyn could say that about so much of her life recently, but nothing felt quite like this. She was going against her gut, trying to keep her husband happy — really, trying to keep up appearances, their marriage at its most tenuous — by agreeing to fly with him in the small plane he was still learning to pilot, to a Kennedy wedding on the Cape. His flying was a point of pride for him and fear for her.

"I don't trust him."

Carolyn said this to family members, friends, the waitress at their favorite restaurant in Martha's Vineyard. She didn't think her husband had the patience, the diligence, the attention span, and, really, the humility to be a good pilot. To know when he shouldn't get in the air. He was still a student, but he had so much hubris. He didn't take his training seriously. He hadn't banked nearly the hours in the air, in daylight and at night, to pilot alone. He would break the rules, sneak in solo flights when he was supposed to have an instructor fly with him, but not one person admonished him or threatened to take away his training certificate. Nope, it was just John being a Kennedy, a rogue and rebel like his father, risk in his blood.

"To Flight Safety Academy, the bravest people in aviation," John wrote to his instructors, "because people will only care where I got my training if I crash."

John thought it was funny. Carolyn did not. John, unlike Carolyn, thought there was no way he'd ever have an accident — even though he'd had a cast on his ankle for the past six weeks, having broken it in crash-landing a contraption called "the flying lawnmower." He'd needed surgery on the ankle. John's doctor had just removed the cast the day before, and even though John needed a cane to walk and would need months of physical therapy, he swore the doctor had cleared him to fly.

Not likely. But John was so confident. Overconfident, as usual.

Carolyn couldn't fully blame him. No one said no to John F. Kennedy Jr., heir to Camelot, the only living son of the beloved slain president, with movie star looks and charm to match. "America's Prince," the media called him, and whenever John wanted to do something — to become a lawyer, start a magazine — hell, run for president of the United States, everyone knew that was coming — the answer was always yes. Sure, yes, of course Mr. Kennedy, and you know what? Let's start you at the top of your field.

Sometimes, Carolyn would say no to John just to say no, to habituate him to real life. It always stunned him. When they first started dating seriously — after he had ghosted Carolyn, the formerly accommodating, easygoing Carolyn of a few years before — she recalibrated. She suddenly wasn't so available. She wasn't so understanding of his lateness, forgetfulness, entitlement. She was forcing him to realize that other people were important, too.

She stood him up once. This was before everyone had cell phones, no way for her to reach John F. Kennedy Jr. as he sat in a darkening Broadway theater, all eyes on him and the empty seat next to him, to say she had to work late. Carolyn expected John to be furious with her, but it only made him want her more.

And Carolyn realized her superpower. She became the only woman in the world to tell JFK Jr.: *No, not okay, don't behave like that, I won't put up with it, say you're sorry, do better.*

Don't take me for granted.

And he got off on it. There was a picture that went around when they were going public, Carolyn on a boat in a thong bikini, John bent down in front of her, helping her into a wrap. That was their dynamic: Carolyn was the dominant, John the submissive. He liked to be bossed around by the women in his life. And Carolyn liked bossing him around. She got off on denigrating him, calling him a "fag" in front of her fashion friends, taunting him with the male model she kept on the back burner, her explosive temper keeping him unsure and on edge.

She should have known that her power over him would be fleeting.

He's under so much pressure, Carolyn's sister said.

It was 1997, and John's magazine, *George*, barely two years old, had gone from being one of the most successful launches in industry history to a spectacular failure, teetering on the brink of insolvency. Worse, no one read it.

John, as editor-in-chief and face of the magazine, not only didn't have the esteem of his publishing peers — he was a laughingstock, called the worst thing anyone could call him: Dumb.

It was a label that had plagued him since he failed the bar exam twice in his twenties — an exam he never wanted to take, forced by his mother to pursue a respectable career in law — tabloid headlines all over New York City screaming some variation of the same headline: "THE HUNK FLUNKS!"

When he did finally pass, his mother having arranged special circumstances for his third test and the esteemed Manhattan District Attorney Robert Morgenthau arranging a plum position for him, John's new colleagues were unimpressed. John would take his lunch hour shirtless in the park, playing football. His first case was prosecuting a robber who had fallen asleep while committing the act and was awakened by the cops.

JFK Jr., Himbo. He was painfully aware of his reputation. But he didn't seem to realize how his narcissism played into it.

George, meant to upend that image, was instead a failure on three fronts: commercially, critically, and as an intended triumph of public relations — one meant to give JFK Jr. the gravitas for a run for governor of New York or US Senate.

The most respected satirical publication of the age had, within months of *George*'s launch, put John on their cover, chin resting on hand, brow furrowed as if in serious contemplation. The headline: "WHAT WILL HE THINK OF NEXT?"

The piece that ran in *Spy* magazine mocked his professional failures, beginning with his first business idea — a quixotic attempt to sell handmade kayaks that would somehow be mass-produced. That was followed by an ill-thought-out rent-a-dog scheme, inspired by the people who stopped John all the time when he was walking his own dog. Surely there would be a market, right?

It took Matt Berman, his business partner, to explain. *John*, he said, *they're probably not stopping you because of your dog.*

John had to concede: Matt had a point. It was on to the next idea, one far more glamorous, high-profile, and unexpected — a magazine!

How hard, he asked, could it be?

John and Matt enrolled in a two-day course called "How to Start Your Own Magazine," and despite their teacher's warnings — most start-ups fail, and magazines about religion and politics are surefire losers — John decided to become the founder and editor-in-chief of a magazine that would mix politics and pop culture.

How was unclear. But no one — not his mother, not his longtime friend Jann Wenner, the founder and editor-in-chief of *Rolling Stone*, and certainly not Carolyn — could talk him out of it.

At his mother's request, her friend Joe Armstrong, a former ABC News exec and magazine publisher, tried to offer John advice. Go slow, Joe said. Keep your plans to yourself. Learn the answer to every possible question you could get in a pitch meeting.

John sailed into those meetings without due diligence and met headwinds he'd never experienced or expected. One executive couldn't believe John's gall in asking for a $20 million investment without being able to answer the most basic stuff. Such as:

Who was the magazine's audience? What was the brand identity? Who would John hire to write? What stories would the magazine break? Who would make ideal profile subjects? Why would their as-yet-unnamed magazine be successful when political magazines, by definition, were small and lucky to break even? How would they attract advertisers once, let's face it, the novelty of being associated with JFK Jr. wore off?

Carolyn knew all too well about that novelty wearing off.

John was like *Seinfeld*'s Bubble Boy, so coddled and spoiled that he didn't know what he sounded like to others. He could be prickly and impatient and something of a brat, really. John didn't live in the real world and never had; he lived on Planet Kennedy, where he was king, and his main experience was a feedback loop of awe at his looks, his lineage, his fame, his *politeness*.

He's so down-to-earth — give him a gold star! That was the line on John, from waitresses to movie stars, paparazzi to presidents. But he wasn't down-to-earth, not really. Anyone who knew him behind closed doors knew that.

Even his close friend Steve Gillon, an eminent historian, gave up trying to educate John on the realities of the Vietnam War and his father's back-room decision to escalate troop levels rather than, as post-assassination myth had it, end American involvement.

Gillon had taught John, who'd previously failed a Vietnam seminar, at Brown. Still, Gillon was shocked when John informed him that he, as the president's son, knew more about the war. The day after a tepid debate that saw Gillon stand down, John informed his former professor that one of his father's prime Vietnam advisers, his secretary of defense, had weighed in.

"I talked to Bob McNamara last night," John said, "and he said you are completely wrong."

Gillon let it slide. What was the point?

John didn't know what he didn't know and was sure, as throughout his life, that others would take care of the details. So what if he was planning a political magazine devoid of a political point of view? That, he thought, would be its strength.

His mother, herself now a book editor, was doubtful.

"John," Jackie asked, "is it going to be the *Mad* magazine of politics?"

By which she meant: Are people going to laugh at it? At you?

"John has never shown the slightest interest in the magazine business before," Jackie told the journalist Ed Klein. "And he has no experience in journalism."

But her skepticism was John's fuel. No one doubted Jackie's intellect, or his sister Caroline's, and certainly not his father's. Why couldn't he be taken as seriously? Carolyn had tried to tell him: If that's what you want, treat other people and things with the respect you crave.

But John's habit of being careless with his own things and those of others was his defining character trait. Responsibilities were for other people, not him. He rode around the city on his bicycle and never locked it up. He spent thousands of dollars replacing bike after bike.

When it came to his public image, however, John was nowhere near as thoughtless. He was always in the tabloids with his shirt off, running out of the surf or playing touch football in Central Park, displaying his perfectly sculpted body. The truth was that John was a terrible athlete, totally uncoordinated. But he looked the part.

At the gym — any gym — he'd strip off his towel after showering and slowly, pointedly examine his genitals. This was well before the era of smartphones and social media, but John's peacocking was innate: he presented himself as just another guy — no at-home gym to avoid the hoi polloi, no request for a private shower or bathroom — yet he was different, special, a rare specimen even among the protected class.

No one would ever have guessed he'd taken so many risks, had come close to death so many times in his teens and twenties. No one would have believed that the kind, humble, gorgeous John Kennedy had a habit of putting others in danger, too — most often his closest friends and girlfriends. Speeding, swimming too far out into the ocean, driving recklessly onto sidewalks or while high on pot, skiing in whiteout conditions, acting like an expert in all sports when really he was just an amateur — there was little John wouldn't dare, and he bullied almost everyone in his life to be as wild as he was.

He'd nearly killed his first serious girlfriend, Christina, at least three times. John had met her in high school. Christina was part of his social set yet she was mesmerized by John's mother, by the palatial apartment at 1040 Fifth Avenue, by the gravitational pull this awkward-yet-beautiful boy exerted and the unbelievable notion that *he* had chosen *her*. His emotional lability added an exquisite tension to their romance.

John's moods could darken instantaneously, without warning. *Don't talk to my mother, why won't you walk with me in torrential rain, call her Mrs. Onassis, my ex means nothing to me.*

Her? She's just some stupid actress.

I've been bossed around by too many women.

If you won't ski with me we'll have to break up.

When I die, I want it to be sudden. Fast. Boom.

Easter 1986. John's aunt Lee had invited them to Acapulco, but John had another idea: roughing it in Jamaica and kayaking in the open sea.

John knew nothing about kayaking in the open sea. Neither did Christina, and this idea terrified her. She had badly broken her foot in February, and after a six-hour operation—his cousin Anthony by her bedside all night, John sending flowers but otherwise unable to tear himself away from whatever he was doing—her doctor had warned her: Nothing extreme. A shower, a bath, a gentle swim in a pool, nothing more. She was still on crutches. Kayaking was against doctor's orders. John hadn't been able to bring himself to even look at Christina's foot, let alone hear about her pain. Telling other people to "suck it up" was his way of avoiding what made him uncomfortable.

Even Jackie had tried to encourage Christina not to go. She told her about hurting her ankle years back, when she was engaged to Jack and playing touch football, trying to fit in with all those rambunctious Kennedys. "That was the last time," Jackie said.

But as was John's way, he pushed and pushed Christina till he got what he wanted, and off to Jamaica they went.

"Nothing to be afraid of," he told her.

Sure enough, before they knew it, John and Christina were swept out to sea, the strong current pushing them quickly toward a giant boulder. Christina's poor foot would be broken again. Their kayak was about to split apart. John had forgotten to pack life jackets and the spray skirts that would keep water out of the kayak.

They were going to die.

And then, suddenly, a rogue wave. At the very last second they were lifted up and over the boulder, and when it was over, with both of them pushed to a beachhead and marooned, Christina sat in shock while John paced and muttered aloud to himself: *"Don't tell Mummy. Don't tell Mummy."*

So much for the fearless John Kennedy.

The weird thing was the look in his eyes, like he was turned on. Dying, getting that close to it, was a high for him. No wonder the other near misses — almost smashing into a forty-nine-foot-long whale in Baja or kayaking straight toward the Staten Island Ferry or swimming far out into the ocean, way past shore — hadn't stopped him. If anything, they electrified him.

If he wanted to keep risking his life, fine. But why was he so insistent on risking Christina's? Why did he have to pressure other people into going along with his crazy ideas? Christina was a house cat, a girl who loved books and the theater. She was no athlete. But John told her: If she wanted to be his girlfriend, she had to do all the things he loved to do. Otherwise it would never work.

She tried. After all, there were any number of girls, a lot of them famous and glamorous and sexier and more beautiful than she, waiting in line to date JFK Jr. Even after John had asked her to share an apartment for a summer in DC, Christina had her misgivings. One day she made a list of what she didn't like about John:

He doesn't always tell me what his plans are.

He can be tardy. He is a slob.

He is spoiled. He gets annoyed when he misplaces things and expects me to find them.

But he had floated the idea of marriage. He teased Christina with a story about his recent visit to his mother, at her weekend home in New Jersey, and how she was so convinced John would propose that, John said, "she got some things out of the safe."

"What things?" Christina asked.

"Her engagement ring."

Would that proposal ever come?

———

After that near miss and their crash-landing on the beach, Christina refused to get back in the kayak. She and John had come upon a group of fishermen who had offered to take them to the mainland the next morning, to share their food for dinner. Christina, for a moment, allowed herself to calm down. It would be okay.

No, John said. They would kayak back that night.

Christina was near tears. John was stubborn enough to go without her and leave her alone with these strange men.

"What if a wave hits us?" she asked John. "What if we capsize? I can't swim in that."

John brushed her off. "It's our best shot," he said.

What were they, in an action movie? Their best shot was waiting for these experienced fishermen who knew this water to sail them back. "No way we'll wreck," John said. "I know I can turn the 'yak."

So off they went, exhausted and traumatized. John pushed off using his paddle, steering and counting seconds between wave breaks, but the swells were so much bigger than John had anticipated. The current was so strong. They were losing control.

Suddenly, they were underwater. Christina felt extreme pressure; the brace on her leg was going to burst. She opened her eyes and found herself looking up at a blurry ray of sunshine penetrating the deep. They must have been fifteen feet down. *This is it,* Christina thought. *We are going to die.*

Her paddle was swept right out of her hand. She watched it float away. Her crutches were gone, too. The weight on her bones was like concrete. Somehow, miraculously, the kayak spun and broke the surface, only to be pushed underwater by another sudden wave, then back up again. John was screaming instructions.

Bail! Bail! Find the bailer now!

The kayak was taking on water. Christina was crying.

"There is no bailer, John!" she exclaimed. "How could you not pack a bailer? We're in the goddamn ocean!"

"Fuck, use anything! Use your hands!"

Her hands?!

She looked over at John, who was using a cotton baseball cap.

Later, years after his death, Christina was still unable to remember how they ever survived. When they finally reached land, John tied up the boat like nothing had happened. Christina was shaking.

"John," she said. "We could have died."

"Yeah, Chief," he said. "But what a way to go."

John had given Christina valuable information that day: He had a death wish. It was strong, in his DNA. She didn't know if he was even aware of it, and she couldn't allow herself to fully admit it to herself. John could be so tender with her, so sensitive. That was the John she could never leave. And so disasters kept happening.

On Martha's Vineyard, John took Christina sailing one raw February night to a remote island. They camped at night and the next morning Christina saw the sign: "DANGER."

He had brought them to a navy bombing test site.

When Jackie found out, she was furious. "You were with *Christina*," she kept saying to John. But nothing landed with him, not even his mother's anger. And lo and behold, later that very afternoon, John insisted Christina get on top of a Jeep while he spun it around at high speed, just for kicks.

Christina hadn't planned for this.

She was wearing a brand-new camel coat she'd just bought at Bergdorf's specifically for this weekend. It was the last one left, two sizes too big and way too expensive, but Christina loved it. Jackie would approve, and she wanted to impress Jackie—no longer Mrs. Onassis to her now. This was not the stuff of a genteel weekend with the refined Jackie O.

"I can't," Christina said.

John pushed. He leveraged her fear that this would be their last time together, having told her that he needed to see other women before he married her, then telling her that she was too good for him, that she had a calling—acting—and he did not, and that he needed to find direction on his own. Alone. But then she would hear and read about the movie star he was seeing, Daryl. John and Daryl were all over the tabloids.

But he'd always come back to Christina and sweep her off somewhere glamorous and talk about baby names.

"Flynn Kennedy," he said to her. "It's got a good ring. What do you think of Flynn?"

How could Christina say no to John in this moment? She wanted to but she couldn't. After all his hemming and hawing, his push-pull with her, he was once again talking marriage and babies.

This will only work if you do the things I want.

And so John lifted her up in her brand-new camel coat and put her on the roof of the Jeep and revved the engine, spinning it around, faster and faster, Christina laughing and clinging on for dear life.

He never really broke up with her. One of their last times together, on the Vineyard, John waxed rhapsodic about birds.

Hawks mate beyond life, he told her. *When the male finds his female, he flies in circles around her until he locks his talon in hers and they lock in a death spiral, crashing to the ground.*

Christina was sure he had made that up. True or not, it didn't really matter. John was telling her something else: *I'm too dangerous for you. For any woman, really.*

The line on John was short and spiky: *Momma's boy.* He did whatever Jackie told him: He gave up the dream he shared with Christina, acting, because his mother was grooming him for politics. Then he became a lawyer, but this bored him, and anyway John, with his ADHD and constant need for physical excitement, was unsuited for it. He drifted and dated a lot but everyone knew he would only marry a woman his mother approved of. Actresses, for many reasons, did not meet with Jackie's approval.

Daryl Hannah, whom John was seeing while still with Christina, was a movie star. Nothing softened Jackie's stance. It didn't matter that Daryl came from real money, or that the director of her latest blockbuster was married to Jackie's sister Lee, or that her family had deep connections to the Democratic Party. Daryl was flashy and bedraggled and in the news for all the wrong reasons, her relationship with singer Jackson Browne among them.

John thought about marrying Daryl. When, years later, they finally broke up, everyone assumed it had to do with Jackie.

Not so. The truth was *Daryl* dumped *him.* It was early 1994, and Jackie was suddenly battling a very aggressive cancer. John had an even tougher time focusing now. And so one day, John took Daryl's dog for a walk and, when John wasn't looking, the dog wandered into traffic, got hit by a car, and was killed.

Other people's things. Other people's pets. Even, once, his own.

John once had a German shepherd, Sam, that he refused to train. Sam had a habit of biting people, including one of John's young female assistants, who got it in the face. John put Sam down and got another dog.

In sum and substance, the message was: He was JFK Jr. and everyone else — well, frankly, everyone else was not. He could board any domestic flight he wanted without showing his ID. He was often without his wallet anyway, or whatever ticket he needed for whatever gala. He was an editor-in-chief who had trouble with spelling and grammar, who had never managed employees or run a company. When *George* was at its most vulnerable, hemorrhaging ads and money and cultural capital, the publisher getting ready to pull the plug, John took off for three weeks. He left his Number Two, a magazine veteran named Biz Mitchell, to handle it. She had no idea what to do. Why would she? Salvaging a struggling magazine wasn't her purview.

She tried calling and calling John, but he never answered. And when he came back he threw a fit that Biz, in way over her head, hadn't fixed everything. He said it was best if she left. Biz was dealing with a boyfriend who was fighting leukemia — and she never once used that as an excuse, never asked for special treatment, was nothing but a top-tier professional who had worked her heart out for John — but she agreed to go with six months' pay and a noncompete clause.

This was the John the public never saw.

————————

Even when they were dating, Carolyn saw the warning signs. John was well loved by his friends and had great qualities — he could be generous to a fault, loaning money or offering access to the best doctors or lending his name to a cause. *This* John allowed Carolyn to excuse what could be his arrogance, his thoughtlessness: When they first started dating seriously, his shower was so filthy that Carolyn had to put a face towel under her feet. When they moved in together, there were the nights he insisted she make dinner only for him to come home at midnight, never calling to say he was working late — if that's what he was really doing — or going out for drinks with colleagues.

Soon Carolyn was constantly picking up after him, John too lazy to hang up his wet towels or put his dirty laundry in the hamper. He was such a heedless driver, speeding and switching lanes and, when stuck in traffic, driving on sidewalks. No wonder his closest friends refused to get in the plane he was learning to pilot, assuming — rightly — that he would fly the way he drove.

There was the time Carolyn and John got pulled over on the Massachusetts Turnpike, the car reeking with the smell of pot, a starstruck cop letting them go without even a warning. "There's an unwritten rule in Massachusetts," John told her, "whereby members of my family can commit murder and mayhem" — after all, decades earlier his uncle Ted had left a young woman to die in three feet of water — "and nobody bats an eye."

That heartless remark was a huge red flag. Carolyn ignored it.

When John was shopping *George* around town, his name got him meetings with the most powerful people in publishing. Carolyn had experience in this world, with these kinds of people, and she knew that if John didn't perfect his pitch for *George*, word would get around. And it did. One executive was brutal in his post-pitch assessment. "'I'm JFK, so there you go,'" the publisher recalled. He deemed it "the worst presentation I had ever seen in my life."

Carolyn knew this was John's Achilles heel. It was the thing he feared most, that despite the fancy education and the storied lineage, he really was dumb. Entitled. Overindulged. Carolyn was smarter than he was; they both knew that. Hipper, too. John was a square, once tossed out of the legendary Patricia Field boutique for mocking the kids who worked there as freaks. Those freaks were her people.

Carolyn had been a real asset to *George* in the beginning, bringing her exacting eye to covers, models, and layouts. She courted advertisers with him and was a hit with Donatella Versace, Giorgio Armani, the fashion elite. For once, people were paying less attention to John than they did to his wife, the cool and charming Carolyn, the former Calvin Klein muse who knew her stuff.

———————

When she had first gotten to Calvin, Carolyn Bessette was no longer the most beautiful girl in the room. High school in Greenwich, college in Boston — it was no match for the competition in New York City. She'd confess, in her more vulnerable moments, to feeling *jolie-laide,* ugly-pretty: Her eyes, more aquamarine than true blue, were beautiful, she knew, but her nose was too long and pointy. When she smiled, which she tried to avoid in pictures, her face could take on a witch-like cast. Her smile was too gummy.

But Carolyn had something very few women her age had: self-possession. It was how she bagged the job with Calvin. With zero experience in fashion, fresh out of Boston University with a degree in early childhood education, Carolyn Bessette sat across from the greatest American designer ever and acted as though she could take this job or leave it.

Oh, how she wanted to take it. To get it. To be chosen.

So there Carolyn sat, wearing a borrowed black crepe Calvin suit, no shirt underneath, hair shiny and face scrubbed, just as a kindly female Calvin executive had suggested. She got the job.

Carolyn was preparing for a big life, bigger than dating the C-list actors or club owners or male models or star athletes of her past. She excelled at pretending not to care about famous men but pretty much exclusively dated famous men.

Carolyn never really talked much about her biological father. Her mother had divorced him when Carolyn was little, only about eight years old, and he was around but not really a presence. Was this why she wanted the affections of a big man, an important one? Would it fill that hole, validate her as worth something? Really, there was no one more famous than John F. Kennedy Jr., and when he walked into the Calvin Klein showroom for the first time, Carolyn knew exactly what to do. She ignored him.

———————

That was the key to hooking him—she knew it instinctually. Calvin's wife, Kelly, on the other hand, would practically pant and drool whenever John came in. *Jesus, Kelly,* Carolyn would say. *Get it together!* The truth was, Carolyn was just as starstruck.

Underneath Carolyn's simple, unfussy presentation was a very complicated woman. She was always assessing, teasing apart someone's psyche and figuring out what made them tick, what would make them happy or upset, and using that to get what she wanted. She could hone in on someone's most painful insecurity and weaponize it. But she could also be extremely kind and warm. You never knew which Carolyn you were going to get; even her closest friends were kept at a remove. If you crossed her she'd drop you flat, just cut you off with no way back. It was a trait she shared with John's mother.

Carolyn was so good at reading people, the mercurial Calvin especially, that soon she was styling his big clients. The models, the movie stars, the network news anchors, the socialites. And after each wealthy female client left, Carolyn's diffident mask would drop. She'd turn and drill down every colleague in the room: Where do you think that woman gets all her money? How did she land that guy? Where do you go to meet rich men? Famous men?

Carolyn was serious. That was her endgame.

She studied Calvin's models harder than any subject in school: How did they stay so thin? What did they do to their hair? Their skin? Who did their waxing, plucking, dyeing, manicures? Polish or no polish? Nails short or long? She studied their high-low aesthetic, the way they'd match a white Hanes T-shirt with Prada or low-top Converse sneakers with a floor-sweeping silk skirt. The trick was to look like you threw it all together without thinking, when really you spent hours trying. All that effort had to look effortless.

It wasn't easy to pull off at Calvin. He was so micromanage-y, so obsessed with detail and order and cleanliness, that he'd installed floor-to-ceiling mirrors in the offices and kept the lights always on and bright so his staff would be looking their best, always. But somehow, some way, Carolyn had figured out how to lower the lights in her office. She'd sit there and secretly pluck stray hairs from her brows or her chin. She had this in common with John, a sense that the rules didn't apply to her. She was special, and she knew it. The way to get John was to make him think she was the prize, not him.

Carolyn could be in a room full of supermodels and still make John Kennedy want her. And when he finally came around and asked her out, she'd just as often say no, that she had other plans. Really, Carolyn never had anything better to do. She'd just hole up in her crappy studio apartment all weekend, hoping that people would assume she had this fabulous, mysterious life full of wealthy suitors. She'd say, loudly, that she was not waiting around for JFK Jr. to call, but really she was waiting around for JFK Jr. to call. As they grew closer, she would insult him just to keep him back on his heels, off-kilter, but quietly she'd marvel at his beauty. She wanted him so badly.

More than anything, she wanted to be Mrs. John F. Kennedy Jr.

———————

May 24, 1992.

There was a big gala that night for the Amazon rainforest, the hippest cause going. Carolyn's friend Narciso Rodriguez, an up-and-coming designer at Calvin, strolled by. You're going to *die*, he told her. John Kennedy was going. He had the seat of honor at Calvin's table, in fact. This was a shock. Carolyn was again seeing John, but they were off and on. He clearly hadn't invited her. What was happening? Was he bringing someone else as his date? Or was he planning to go solo so he could shop around for other women — celebrities, models, women of his social strata?

Carolyn's ultracool force field dropped. She made a beeline for one of her closest friends at Calvin, a young woman whom she knew had three extra tickets.

"I need that ticket," Carolyn said.

Her friend refused.

Carolyn begged. She badgered, she bullied, she nagged, and she whined. *Give it to me. This is important. I'm your friend, I need the favor, what is wrong with you?* But her friend had zero patience for this. She'd already been distancing herself from Carolyn ever since the night she had to rush home to see her sick father. Carolyn seemed full of concern, but her questions were weird: How long was she going for? When was she planning to be back? Was her boyfriend joining her?

That last one made her queasy. And lo and behold, the next day, that co-worker's boyfriend called her. "Your friend Carolyn," he said, "is really fucked up."

Carolyn had made a move. Her friend hadn't been surprised so much as hurt, and though she never said a thing to Carolyn — well, karma could be a bitch. No ticket for her.

John Kennedy Jr. was Carolyn's white whale, but snagging him long-term seemed unlikely. Everyone in their circle had watched Carolyn treat so many boyfriends terribly. It was emotional abuse that sometimes turned physical. There was the actor who was totally in love with Carolyn, who'd meet them all at the Noho Star and sit there, humiliated, while Carolyn talked about how pathetic he was and how she wished he'd stop calling her all the time. She'd insult him while refusing to even look at him.

Then there was the underwear model, head over heels for Carolyn, and oh how she tormented him. This was a guy with his own billboard in Times Square, the new face of Calvin Klein, and Carolyn just ground him down till he felt like nothing. After seeing him light another woman's cigarette at a party, she tore up his apartment one night and attacked him in the street. The truly messed-up thing was that they weren't even together at the time, broken up yet again. The male model had done nothing wrong, but Carolyn always had to be right.

"Date them, train them, dump them," she'd say. To the young girl at Calvin who idolized Carolyn, so sweet and impressionable with her nice, down-to-earth boyfriend: "Break up with him," Carolyn said. "He's not good enough for you." What Carolyn meant was: He doesn't make enough money.

Later, at the gala, her friend with the three extra tickets and the true-blue boyfriend saw Carolyn leaning against the bar, tossing her long blonde hair and laughing loudly, oh-so-casually introducing everyone she saw to "my friend, John Kennedy."

Being John's exclusive girlfriend, when it finally happened, was a full-time job. Once they got serious, Carolyn began transforming herself from a downtown hipster with unwashed, dirty-blonde hair and an extra fifteen pounds to a sleek Upper East Side white-blonde ice queen.

She treated herself like an art project, a sculpture defined by removal: The weight. The small lines erased with Botox. Her face grew hard and angular, with hollows under her cheekbones. Her once unruly hair was heated and ironed straight, her scalp scorched and pulsating under the bleach, the burns cooled into hard, raised scabs underneath that platinum mane. Her thick eyebrows were plucked into wisps. That so-called effortless style was full of suffering.

Gone were the days of showing up to the Calvin Klein office hungover, wearing dirty clothes and cheap Egyptian musk bought off the street. Now she secretly took barre classes at Lotte Berk on the Upper East Side, even though she hated exercise, just hated it. Cigarettes and cocaine helped kill her hunger. She studied John like a Talmudic text and kept the *People* magazine issue from 1988, John on the cover with the headline "SEXIEST MAN ALIVE," stashed under her kitchen sink.

When her friends saw paparazzi pics of Carolyn in a kayak, paddling alongside a shirtless John in the Hudson River, they laughed so hard they cried. Carolyn's natural habitat was the bar at Rex, a banquette at Odeon, the Barneys warehouse sale.

Kayaking? Wow, did she want this.

When John proposed two years later, Carolyn waited three weeks before saying yes. Part of that was manipulation, sure—torturing the boy who had everything was fun. But Carolyn also wanted to sit with the question. Did she want not just to be John's wife, but JFK Jr.'s wife? As she well knew, these were two different people: JFK Jr. was a persona, a character he played in public: affable, humble, all-around-regular-New-Yorker-who-just-happened-to-be-the-most-wanted-man-on-Earth. The private John, Carolyn had learned, was a moody and complicated person, not nearly as low-maintenance as his public image, a mystery to others and most often to himself. Carolyn would be marrying someone who, at thirty-six years old, was still in search of his identity.

And she would not just be a Kennedy wife—she would be *the* Kennedy Wife, married to a legacy and a future that would surely mean children, political campaigns, a life of endless public scrutiny, quite possibly the White House and life as a First Lady.

Could she handle the attention? Did she even want to?

She was only twenty-nine years old, enjoying a fast life in high fashion. She didn't want to give that up quite yet. As it was, she was already a paparazzi target, followed on the street, into boutiques, walking their dog, picking up his poop. What if they had kids? Would John be okay with them living in a fishbowl? Because Carolyn would never allow that, and that would be a deal-breaker. She loved the fame and hated it and didn't know what to do with it.

I've lived with this my whole life, he said. *Once we're married they'll lose interest. They'll leave us alone.*

July 16, 1999.

John's cousin Rory was getting married in Hyannis and John expected his wife to go, even though he had recently moved out of their loft, been photographed with an ex-girlfriend, had yelled at Carolyn to *Get the fuck out of my life!* from his office phone at *George*, where everyone on staff could hear.

Come to the wedding, he said. *I'll fly us up there.*

He had just had that cast removed from his ankle. He was still in flight training. He wasn't licensed to fly alone at night. He didn't care, and Carolyn didn't trust him. She told almost no one, but Carolyn was so terrified of her husband's piloting that she would often fly commercial rather than get in his plane. Or drive the four hours to Massachusetts—six if there was traffic—and take a ferry to the Vineyard. Or fly up in a separate private plane piloted by a licensed professional. But John never stopped hounding her to do what he wanted, and so two weeks prior, on the Fourth of July weekend, Carolyn caved. She had flown to the

Vineyard in a plane piloted by him, on one condition: John's flight instructor had to be on board.

Now he was insisting on flying the two of them and Carolyn's sister Lauren up the coast for a Kennedy wedding. She didn't want to go and didn't want him flying. But everyone — that is, the few who knew what was really going on in her marriage — told her to give John a break.

If you don't go, his assistant RoseMarie told her, the tabloids will say you're getting divorced.

That was uncomfortably close to the truth. But why was it on Carolyn to keep up appearances?

———

Her sister Lauren, rooting hard for their marriage, offered to fly with them. She thought the wedding could be therapeutic, and Lauren was looking forward to meeting up with John's cousin Bobby Shriver, whom she'd begun seeing. And then there was RoseMarie, who handled all of John's press. There was truth to RoseMarie's warning: The press wasn't going to blame John for his wife's absence at a Kennedy wedding on the Cape. And they would certainly never blame him for what Carolyn suspected was his infidelity. Oh no — if this marriage failed, they were going to blame Carolyn for not being caring enough or docile enough or attentive or appreciative of the gift she'd been given, being a Kennedy wife. John F. Kennedy Jr.'s wife.

Nothing made Carolyn more anxious. She wanted out of her marriage but also felt trapped. "I can't get a divorce," she'd say. "I'll wind up living in a trailer park, out of my mind, going 'I used to be married to JFK Jr.'"

That quote wound up in the *National Enquirer.* It was hilarious and mortifying.

Now, with this latest Kennedy family wedding three days out, John was begging her to come, even though he'd done worse things than cheating. For someone so obsessed with his own privacy, he was spilling all their problems to his friend group, intimate details — like her five-times-a-week therapy sessions and her drug habit and her refusal to have sex with him.

Him! The guy who, as one of his friends so memorably said, could "order it up" anytime he wanted.

Now John was telling everyone that Carolyn was crazy. But if she was, in fact, so unhinged, wouldn't she be a liability at this wedding? Wouldn't he have wanted her, this druggy, frigid, wild woman, to stay home? The truth was, John needed Carolyn. His magazine was failing. His cousin Anthony, truly more like a brother, was dying. John and his sister Caroline, once as close as twins, were now barely speaking, fighting about their late mother's estate.

The last thing John needed was the press speculating over his marriage. And to be fair, from John's perspective, this was part of the deal. This is what it was to be a Kennedy wife.

Once again, for Carolyn — three years into a marriage that never felt equal — it was all about John. And he was insisting on flying his brand-new aircraft, one far more powerful and complex than any he'd regularly flown before.

Carolyn really, really did not want to get on that plane.

JACKIE BOUVIER KENNEDY

Later, when the history books were written and the documentaries made and the anniversaries marked, that trip—for her, not him—was never inevitable. It wasn't fated. She hadn't agreed, as with so many things before, out of obligation.

She'd gone because she wanted to. Because it meant so much to him, and because he needed her. She needed him, too, in a different way but just as much.

Her greatest regret was telling one historian, one she'd trusted, that she and her husband had had sex the night before. At the time, full of sedatives and vodka, she wanted the historian and all those other inside men who'd worshipped her husband, who thought his compulsive womanizing meant that theirs was a marriage of convenience, or political theater, or that worse, she wasn't enough—she wanted them to know: They were in love. Theirs was a real marriage.

They were equals.

Where had this need for validation come from? It's not as though the world knew the truth about her husband and his constant philandering. It's not as if she wasn't writing history, or rewriting history herself, coronating two of those "bitter old men," as she called all those jealous chroniclers—those who lived through her husband, the Great Man, vicariously—to tell a larger story. To craft a great myth that the country, she knew, would swallow whole.

Besides, everyone only wanted to know one thing: What had it been like in the back of that car?

———

The day had felt hot and wild, the sun so strong. Jackie had gone to put her sunglasses on but Jack said no, please don't, they really came to see you. The convertible had been left open for just that reason. God, was he a charmer: John F. Kennedy, the youngest elected president of the United States, lavishing Jackie with praise for her star power. How could she say no? Ahead was a small tunnel. Soon it would be cool and dark, just for a few moments, all the screams of Jack's supporters lining the streets and the sounds of the motorcade muffled.

Jack turned to her, puzzled. He held his hand out and then it just dropped and a chunk of his head came flying off, white, not pink, and then he was slumped in her lap, his blood and brains all over her—her face, her legs. Her pink roses and white gloves were soaked through with blood. It was so thick, almost neon. It kept gushing and gushing, just an endless supply.

"My God, what are they doing?" she screamed. "My God, they've killed my husband! Jack! Jack!"

She had no memory of leaping out of the car and crawling on the trunk. When she later saw the photos and the Zapruder film she could never recognize the woman in the pink suit or what she was trying to do. Escape? Get help? Grab a piece of Jack's skull? His brain?

Jackie would have fallen off that trunk and onto the road, the car going seventy miles an hour and approaching eighty, if not for her favorite Secret Service agent, Clint Hill. He ran toward her, nearly falling himself if not for Jackie reaching out and grabbing him. Hill saw the terror in her eyes and was just as scared. "Get us to a hospital!" Hill screamed. "Get us to a hospital!" He used his body like a canopy, pushing Jackie back into this bloody cavern, chunks of bone and brain splattered everywhere, the car moving so fast that Hill's sunglasses flew right off his face.

Jackie huddled over Jack, cradling what was left of his head, frantically tamping brain matter down into his skull as if this could save him. "Jack!" she said, yelling over the sirens and the screams and the motors gunning all around them. "Jack! Can you hear me? I love you, Jack. I love you!"

Hill saw clean through to the back of the president's skull. Now Jackie realized it, too. "My God!" she screamed. "They shot his head off!" She never once asked if she had been hit. She never asked if any of the blood was hers. She never flinched from the sheer carnage in that back seat. Her only concern was Jack. He had to know he wasn't going to die alone.

———————

"You come with us." Big men in white surrounded the car, ordering Jackie out. She was on top of Jack, shielding him. No one was going to see him this way.

"Mrs. Kennedy. You come with us." She couldn't look up. The more she was told to get out of the car the farther down she shrank, the tighter she held him.

"Mrs. Kennedy." It was Clint Hill, speaking softly. "Please let us help the president." Jackie couldn't understand: Why was no one accepting reality?

"I'm not leaving," Jackie said. "You know he's dead."

"Please," Hill said. He was begging. "Let us get him into the hospital."

Jackie looked up at Hill, keeping Jack's head, what was left of it, hidden against her chest. Hill realized: She didn't want the world to see the president this way. If she couldn't save his life, she could at least save his dignity. Hill shook off his suit jacket and placed it over Jack's head. Finally, reluctantly, Jackie let the Secret Service agents pull her out, but she held Hill's coat over Jack's head the whole time as she ran with his stretcher, clutching its side.

Then the whoosh of the emergency room curtain. Jack was on one side, Jackie the other. He wasn't alone, but she was. Coming toward her was Dave Powers, one of Jack's closest aides. He was practically part of the family, known jokingly as Jack's "other wife." It was Dave who woke the president in the morning, who tied his necktie and smoothed his feathers and was always able to defuse the tension in any given room. Jackie really loved Dave, and this was largely because she had no idea what he really did for Jack Kennedy.

Dave had been riding in the car right behind theirs when Jack was shot. He burst into tears as Jackie, dry-eyed, oblivious to Jack's blood all over her, sat on a folding chair and smoked. Nurses and doctors rushed behind that curtain. It was pointless.

No one comforted Jackie. They stared, though. One nurse had tried to strip Jackie's gloves right off; others tried to move her to a bed. A doctor rushed by and Jackie slipped something into his hands.

It was a piece of Jack's brain.

Nellie Connally, who had been riding up front in the same car with her husband, John, the governor of Texas, was suddenly next to Jackie. John Connally had also been shot. He was in Trauma Room Two. Nellie said nothing. Softly, Jackie asked Nellie how her husband was.

Silence. Then, after a few moments, a brusque reply: "He'll be all right," Nellie said.

Jackie motioned to Powers. "Dave," Jackie said, "you better get a priest."

All around her, men—big Texans, orderlies and interns, Secret Service and police—were losing their composure. She sat there, in her folding chair, quiet yet watchful, shooing away the doctors who kept telling her she needed to be taken off and drugged. Like Jack's personal physician, whom she and Jack called Doc Burkely.

"Mrs. Kennedy," Burkely said. "You need a sedative." Burkely was heaving with sobs. If anyone needed a sedative...

"I want to be in there when he dies," Jackie told him. Jack was still taking shallow breaths. His heart was still beating—irregularly, but still beating. "I'm going in there," she declared. Suddenly the nurse who had tried to take Jackie's gloves was standing in her way. Doris Nelson.

"You can't," Doris told Jackie. Doris stood, soldierlike, between Jackie and the curtain.

"I'm coming in," Jackie said. Everyone thought she was so demure, but Jackie was tougher than anyone knew. She hated this nurse. Who was she? How dare she keep the First Lady from the dying President of the United States? Move!

Jackie shoved Doris. "I'm coming in and I'm staying," Jackie said.

There had been a time when Jackie listened to doctors and nurses, all those years ago when Jack, one year into their marriage, was in a top hospital in New York City, near death and calling for her desperately. His cries had broken her heart. In his anguish she heard the little boy who'd been left in one too many hospital beds by his mother and father. But back then Jackie did what the doctors said and stayed in the hallway, trusting they knew best. She had sworn that she would never leave Jack alone like that again.

———————

The night before, the last time they would ever make love, they had been hoping for another baby. Jackie had woken that morning to her period, the first she'd had since losing their newborn son only weeks earlier. She hadn't thought she could survive that loss, but Jack got her through the worst of it.

Now she was drenched in blood, his and hers. Chunks of his hair were stuck to her dress; bloody strands were encrusted on her face. The last thing she wanted to do was clean any of it off. As they came to take Jack away, his body under a white sheet, Jackie noticed his foot sticking out. She cradled it in her hand and kissed it. The closest she came to losing control was in the hallway afterwards, nearly passing out, a nurse rushing to her side with a cold compress, pressing it to Jackie's forehead.

Father Thompson, one of the priests who had just prayed over Jack, approached Jackie. If ever a moment called for him to summon grace, compassion, to offer God's assurances that all would be all right, this was it.

"Mrs. Kennedy," he said. Then, on the verge of tears, he fled.

Jackie watched as her husband's body, naked and seeming so little, was placed into a bronze coffin. Burkely was at her side, clutching her, shaking her. Was there no man in this hospital who could keep it together?

Jackie summoned Kenny O'Donnell, a member of Jack's Irish Mafia. "You've got to get me in there alone before they close that coffin," Jackie said. "You've got to get me in."

Jack couldn't travel back to DC in that coffin with nothing. In the trauma room, she'd slipped her wedding ring on his pinky finger, but she wanted to give him more, something from Patrick, the baby they'd lost. She thought of giving Jack the medal of Saint Christopher, the patron saint and protector of travelers.

Oh, the irony.

Jackie had recently bought a new Saint Christopher medallion to replace the one he'd lost, her wedding gift to him. She had tried not to read too much into Jack losing that medal. Jack could be careless, not just with things but with people. Women. His own wife. Even his own baby daughter.

———————

It was August of 1956. Jack was about to make a last-minute run to be the vice presidential candidate, vying for the spot on the Democratic ticket next to Governor Adlai Stevenson of Illinois, and Jackie was expecting. This was the first pregnancy she was carrying successfully after two miscarriages, her most recent the year before. She had grieved those losses alone. No one understood, especially not her in-laws, whose credo had always been Just Get On With It.

None of Jack's sisters had problems getting or staying pregnant or giving birth and then getting pregnant again, immediately. Jack's mother Rose had nine children. Jackie's sister-in-law Ethel was on Rose's track — she and her husband, Bobby, already had four and Ethel was expecting her fifth in five years with not a single complaint.

Jackie knew the Kennedys were judging her as a woman, and no one judged her more harshly than the Kennedy women. Anything else she might bring to her marriage — her erudition, her looks, her class, her bearing right out of central casting as a future First Lady — none were as important as giving her husband children. And the Kennedys blamed Jackie for losing her pregnancies. Why couldn't she stop smoking? Why did she have such a sensitive disposition? They wouldn't hear of stress, the rigors of campaigning, the pressure to look perfect and never misspeak, to quietly abide a Kennedy man's wandering eye.

Jackie wasn't naïve. She knew Jack wouldn't be faithful. But she hadn't known just how promiscuous he was or how little he'd do to protect her. Later she'd learn, along with the whole world in news reports too numerous to bear, that Jack had likely infected her with his own constant sexually transmitted diseases, the asymptomatic chlamydia among them, and this was quite likely why she'd had so much trouble carrying her first two pregnancies to term.

So when Jackie got pregnant a third time, she was rightfully nervous, waiting until she was safely into her seventh month to create a nursery at their new home in Virginia. She felt so confident, in fact, that she would defy her doctor's orders and campaign for Jack at the Democratic Convention in Chicago. Jackie hated politicking, but she worked her heart out for him that mid-August week, rising early to attend ladies' breakfasts, standing shoulder to shoulder with her sisters-in-law under hot spotlights, her feet aching in heels, worried that her mascara was running or her hair was frizzing, shaking sweaty hands and saying all the right things, fighting nausea—she had wanted to do all of that for Jack.

It wasn't enough. Jackie was inconsolable when Jack fell short of the VP nomination. She knew how anxious he was to reach the White House. He was sure he wasn't going to live a long life. Losing three siblings, two to violent deaths and one simply gone missing, could convince someone of that. So she sat beside Jack at a postmortem family dinner, dressed in a fine black dress and pearls, and openly wept.

It was that rarest of things for Jackie, an unguarded display of emotion. But she wasn't just sad about his loss; she wanted him to stay with her until the baby was born. She was nervous and afraid and she wanted her husband. But Jack was headed to a trip to the Mediterranean, off to lick his wounds, sailing with his brother Teddy and fellow senator George Smathers—and everyone in DC knew what Smathers and Jack got up to together.

"Won't you stay with me?" she asked.

Jack left the next morning. She hadn't wanted to beg, to be the needy wife of an important man. And Jackie could rationalize his decision; it was the done thing in their world. Jack and Jackie's fathers, compulsive womanizers themselves, found nothing wrong with Jack's assignations, no matter the time or place or woman. Jackie had been bred to tolerate it, warned about whom she was marrying. Friend of the family? Have her over to dinner, seat her across from the wife, slide your hand under her dress. Staff member? Part of the job. Movie stars? Impossible to resist, don't even ask.

There had been other humiliations, and they had cut to the bone. But baby Arabella was the first time Jackie thought she might divorce her husband.

In those last few weeks, when Jack was sailing on the Med, Jackie was at her mother and stepfather's estate in Rhode Island. She hadn't wanted to be there, but it was the best of bad options. Her sister Lee was married and living in London, and Jackie had no one else. That was partly by design and partly who she was: Jackie was always happiest alone, even as a small child, preferring her dolls, her horses, and her books to actual company. As a teenager, she couldn't bear for anyone to see her imperfections, her faults, her black moods.

Now she couldn't bear for anyone to know the truth about her marriage.

Her mother knew some of it, of course. Why else would Jackie be with her, waiting out the last weeks of her first viable pregnancy? The media bought the line about Jack needing rest, but all those men in the press had a bit of a hero-worship complex about Jack. She understood. Jackie did, too. She'd had no shortage of suitors, and in fact, when she met Jack Kennedy, she had been engaged to John Husted, a successful stockbroker. Jackie was "so terribly much in love," with Husted, as she wrote to her priest three years prior. "I KNOW I will marry this boy . . . It's the deepest happiest feeling in the world."

Then Jack Kennedy came along and two months later, Jackie silently slipped her engagement ring in Husted's pocket and walked away. Husted thought it was the coldest thing anyone had ever done to him, but to Jackie, who hated messy emotional scenes, it was the cleanest, kindest cut she could deliver.

Jack was hardly a sure thing, but Jackie was laser-focused on landing him. The handsome, charismatic, witty, intelligent, popular, powerful, wealthy Jack Kennedy, on track to become senator and, with his father's machinations and money, president. Jack Kennedy, who could, and most often did, have any woman he wanted.

Jackie wanted to marry him. She knew that early on. It wasn't just his family's wealth — though that was something, the importance of marrying rich having been drummed into Jackie and Lee at a young age — but many things. She admired the Kennedy clannishness and loyalty, so unlike what she had growing up. They were already a famous family, one resistant to outsiders—and that meant boyfriends, girlfriends, anyone who married in or had a seat at their table. And Jack was so much like her father, who was named John but went by Black Jack—both were cocksmen and rogues and renegades. People were drawn to Black Jack and Jack Kennedy, with their movie-star looks and fizzy insouciance that floated above a darkness below, a darkness few would ever know. Her father eventually slid into alcoholic ruin, but Jack was one of life's winners. He was an optimist, a brilliant conversationalist who, like Jackie, relished history and literature as much as gossip and badinage. He had that *thing*, that magnetism that turned every head in the room his way.

Jack was a challenge. Jackie loved a challenge.

If she became Jack's wife, she might succeed where her mother had not, taming an infamous womanizer. And Jack was a passport to a bigger life. That was one of the reasons Jackie rejected John Husted: Her life with him would have been comfortable, sure, but safe and simple, leaving her to wither in some leafy suburbia with all the other decorative housewives. She would be the equivalent of wisteria, beautiful but sagging under the weight of low expectations. Jack Kennedy, though! This man lived among power brokers and princes, aristocrats and actors. His life was only going to get more exciting and unpredictable. Big. Enormous.

Jackie didn't just want that life—she wanted that life with *him*. To get it, she had to pursue Jack without seeming to: it wasn't ladylike and it wasn't going to work. Jack Kennedy was nothing if not a hunter, so Jackie had to lure him in while being just unavailable enough. In the beginning, she'd miss his calls or not return them right away, but it turned out that Jack was just as elusive, which made Jackie want him all the more.

Slowly, she began making herself indispensable, hand-delivering homemade lunches in pretty baskets as Jack worked in his Senate office; traveling to other states to hear him speak and watch him woo a crowd; happily accompanying him to rubber-chicken dinners and engaging in all the requisite mind-numbing small talk; gamely participating in all that Kennedy roughhousing up on the Cape, until a broken ankle—and the clear adoration of Old Joe, Jack's father—left Jackie in her favorite place, alone with a book.

She translated ten books in French for Jack, just so he could have a more nuanced take on Indochina. And also, she joked, to force a proposal. Only to herself would she admit: It wasn't a joke. She was dying to marry him. They were, as Jackie put it, "twin icebergs" — impenetrable on the surface, with all the messy, interesting stuff submerged and quietly breaking apart deep, deep below.

Jack had never heard such an apt description of himself. His childhood trauma, even by Irish Catholic standards, had been repressed: the maternal neglect; the domineering, unfaithful father; the mysterious fate of his sister, beautiful Rosemary, who was only twenty-three when she disappeared, the remaining siblings understanding they were never to ask where Rosemary was or what happened to her. Jack had lost his twenty-nine-year-old brother Joe Jr., a navy pilot, in a midair explosion during World War II; four years later, in 1948, Jack's beloved sister Kick died in a plane crash. She was only twenty-eight. Jack himself had nearly died many times and was a bona fide war hero.

Yet to look at him you'd never know any of it. Jack Kennedy, on the surface, was placid, easygoing, dashing, always a good time. And of all the women he'd been with, Jackie Bouvier, twenty-three years old to Jack's thirty-five, was most like him. Neither had ever been much of a joiner. They were both self-sufficient, self-sustaining, stoical, their independence forged in lonely and often terrifying childhoods. Jack had been a very sick little boy. Jackie knew all about that. At two years old he'd already survived measles, whooping cough, chicken pox, and then scarlet fever, which almost killed him. He'd spent a month in the hospital, then a few months recovering in Maine, a little boy alone, his parents never visiting.

Bronchitis, appendicitis, tonsillitis, upper respiratory infections, jaundice, ear infections — on and on it went, little Jack terrified and often near death while his father, who glorified health and robustness above all else, was away with other women. And his mother? Jack was sure she didn't care. How else to explain her complete absence from Jack's bedside? Rose pumped out baby after baby and left her growing brood for couture shows in Paris or six-week vacations in California. The help gave the hugs. "You're a great mother to go away and leave your children all alone," Jack told his mother once. He was five years old.

Jackie understood. Black Jack, for all his devotion to Jackie—his namesake—was a drunk, a gambler, and a playboy. He was never home. The party, the real fun, was all outside the house, with other people. No wonder her mother was so prone to rages. Black Jack, like Joe Kennedy, had a habit of cheating with his wife's friends, holding their hands or groping them right in front of Janet Lee Bouvier, American socialite and daughter of a wealthy Manhattan real estate developer. Janet, of course, was expected to maintain her ladylike decorum: smile, ignore Black Jack's humiliations, swallow each one like a cold cocktail.

Jackie was five when Janet first smacked her across the face.

Jackie learned to take it. She knew her mother didn't like her very much. She looked just like Black Jack and had his independent, rule-breaking streak, her own dark magnetism and aloofness. She didn't much care what other people, including her own mother, thought—except when it came to men. Janet really did want the best for her daughters, and in the 1920s, flappers and sexual liberation aside, that had meant marrying well. Money was the only real protection a woman had in this world, Janet told them. Love was nice, but it wasn't enough, as her girls could plainly see. She worried particularly about Jackie's prospects.

What man would want a woman like Jackie? She was extremely bright, sharp, and funny—cutting, even—and she had real goals. Janet told Jackie to tone herself down, to hide her intelligence lest she scare off the best available men. But Jackie wasn't sure she could hide her smarts, mainly because she didn't want to. She needed a man who could keep up with her and let her shine. Her mother had hung her entire identity on being a wife and mother—and look how that turned out. Janet tried to hide her depression, but Jackie knew her mother drank and took pills and sometimes slept the day away. Neither one of her parents had healthy coping mechanisms. They were all id, their emotions wild and explosive. Little Jackie learned to shrink herself down while growing up fast.

By the time she was ten, Jackie was the real adult in the house. Black Jack was gone by then, weary of his wife's outbursts and violence. Janet had once shoved her husband during an argument; he hit his head and bled in front of Jackie, who had stopped playing with her stuffed animals. It was one of the few times Janet ever saw her daughter cry.

Normally Jackie wouldn't give her mother the satisfaction, especially when she became the object of her mother's rage—the slapping of the face, the hitting that continued well into Jackie's early twenties. "If something unpleasant happens to me," Jackie said later, "I block it out. I have this mechanism."

Jack had that, too.

———

On August 23, 1956, Jackie woke up from a nap in great pain and bleeding heavily. She was rushed to Newport Hospital, where she underwent an emergency cesarean section and gave birth to a girl. The baby was stillborn.

When Jackie came out of anesthesia hours later, at two in the morning, it wasn't her husband at her bedside but her brother-in-law Bobby. It was he who broke the news, who held Jackie's hand, who told her he would take care of everything—by which he meant the baby's burial—and who made the excuse Jackie wanted to believe: Jack was still at sea, unreachable in the Med.

Of course, Jack was reachable in the Med. Bobby knew, because he'd already spoken to his brother.

"What's done is done," Jack told Bobby over the phone. "The baby is lost." Jack saw no point in cutting his vacation short.

Her husband had given no greater rejection. Mourning a child she never got to see or hold, Jackie lay in the hospital absorbing the message that her husband's absence, the lack of so much as a phone call, had sent.

I would rather be off with random women than comforting you.

I'm not sad about the baby.

Someone else can take care of the funeral. What does it matter? She's dead.

That, she would read much later, was what Jack had said to his own father.

I don't care how much pain you're in.

I don't care about you.

Really, what else was there to understand? Meanwhile, anyone who had ever seen Jackie nurse Jack back to health in those early days of their marriage, Jack nearly dying after one of four risky back surgeries, would never have doubted her love for him. And had Jackie ever complained that she'd been sold a false bill of goods? That she'd been led to believe she was marrying a healthy, vibrant young man? That she had been lied to?

"It's best if you don't go into my medical problems with Jackie," Jack had told his private physician, Dr. Janet Travell, before their wedding in September 1953. "I don't want her to think she married an old man or a cripple."

And indeed, Jack's illnesses, when Jackie finally learned of them, were overwhelming.

He suffered from colitis, ulcers, prostatitis, urinary tract infections, frequent headaches, stomachaches, upper respiratory infections. One leg was shorter than the other, a congenital defect. He had Addison's disease, a rare endocrine disorder that left him dependent on cortisol injections and hormones secreted through an implant in his thigh. The Addison's was so serious that Joe kept Jack's meds locked in safety deposit boxes all over Europe in case Jack had an attack abroad.

Jackie never even had a honeymoon period with her husband. In fact, days into their actual honeymoon, Jack suggested she fly home alone so he could travel with "friends." Jackie declined. She later felt ashamed that she'd even considered his request.

He was hardly in a position to be so callous now that Jackie needed him. It was as if his own body waited for him to have a partner before it broke down. Jack's back was such a mess that he couldn't bend over to tie his shoes, or climb stairs without help, or tolerate riding in a car. He walked with crutches, an obscenity to him. They both knew a wheelchair was next.

There was a surgery that might help, but it could very well kill him. Joe begged him not to have it; he had already lost three children and he couldn't bear the idea of losing Jack, his favorite.

But Jack was never cowed by risk. In fact, he craved it, and to Jackie, this was one of his sexiest qualities. After all, his family was selling him to America, deservedly, as a war hero who had swum four miles with a badly injured soldier on his back, a strap clenched between his teeth to tug him through the choppy ocean. If Jack could survive that, why couldn't he survive this?

And if he didn't — well, Jack told Jackie he would rather die on the table than be disabled for life. She understood. So in October 1954, when Jack was wheeled into New York City's Hospital for Special Surgery on a stretcher, the press gathered out front, she was by his side, holding his hand. Throughout his four-hour operation, Jackie waited and prayed. Afterwards, she sat with him in the hospital, hours each day, mopping his brow, spoon-feeding him, helping him go to the bathroom, putting on his socks and slippers. She canceled a promised appearance for a Boston charity fashion show at the last minute, even though it was just a ninety-minute flight and she could have done the trip in a day and been back at Jack's bedside that evening.

"I just wouldn't want to leave Jack for the day or so," Jackie wrote the chairman, "as he's not allowed any other visitors — that would mean he'd spend a whole day alone, which in that morbid hospital might really lower his morale . . . Even if I did come it wouldn't make any sense because I'd just be worrying about Jack."

When he slipped into a coma days later, Jackie was there. When the priest was summoned to administer last rites, she was there — all three times. When Jack fought his way back only to spend the next two months in the hospital, Jackie rallied him, bringing stacks of newspapers and magazines and reading aloud to him. His curiosity, she knew, was key to his recovery: as long as he remained interested in the world, in what was going on outside this hospital room, he was fighting.

So she brought him games, made him laugh, encouraged his friends to visit. She shrugged off the Marilyn Monroe pinup, which he'd turned upside down above his bed, positioning Marilyn's crotch in his face. She even ignored the private hospital visit from Grace Kelly, although it made her nervous.

Where was Jack for her now?

———

Jackie was so weak and depressed that she couldn't even attend her daughter's burial. Bobby stood over the baby's coffin while Jack was still sailing with his starlets and bikini babes off the south of France, drinking, smoking cigars, having fun. She knew he was cheating on her. What kind of narcissist had she married? A week went by, and Jackie was still in the hospital with no word from Jack. He intended to keep cruising around the Med till September—and as soon as he got home, he was going off to campaign for the next three months. So really, Jack was leaving her for the foreseeable future.

Jackie wanted an annulment. Divorce was not enough. She wanted the Catholic Church to nullify this marriage, negate it, treat it as a great nothing just as her husband had done. "I'm never going back," Jackie said. Jack's self-preservation must have kicked in, because three days after the baby's funeral, he was suddenly in her hospital room. Ten days had gone by. Any suspicions Jackie had about why he was there, why the change of heart and the great sacrifice of yet another bacchanal, were well founded.

Her nemesis, the equally lecherous George Smathers, was the one who got Jack back home to her. It was hardly the stuff of romance. If you ever want to be president, Smathers said, "you better haul your ass back to your wife." When Jack finally landed in the States, he told a reporter that Jackie had not let him know about the stillbirth because she didn't want to ruin his vacation. Her mother was disgusted. "He is unconscionable," Janet said.

Everyone in DC knew the truth. Jack's womanizing had always been off-limits with the press—but how much longer would they abide by that gentleman's agreement? If a fraction of Jack's sex life made the papers, it wouldn't be Jack left humiliated. When Jackie was finally released from the hospital, she stayed with her mother at Hammersmith Farm, where she mourned her baby and her marriage.

"How could I have been so stupid?" she'd ask through tears.

Janet couldn't stand to hear Jackie blame herself. None of this was her fault, but it was obvious why Jackie felt this way: Rose and Joe Kennedy were already making snide remarks about Jackie's smoking having caused the stillbirth. If the marriage ended, the Kennedys, too, would blame Jackie. The press would blame Jackie. Society on the whole laid the success or failure of any family—but especially one with this much luster—on the woman; it was Jackie's performance as a wife (dutiful, domestic, sexual) and a mother (if she could even successfully give her husband children) that would determine the success of their marriage. Not Jack.

Janet told Jackie to get a divorce while she was still young and beautiful and could make another life for herself. That November, physically stronger but emotionally still a wreck, Jackie left for London to be with Lee and her brother-in-law. Jack could spin all the stories he wanted to his adoring press, but Jackie's silence, her decision to put three thousand miles between them, spoke louder than anything he could say.

Jackie had left him, likely for good. In Virginia, she confided in her neighbor Walter Ridder, the famous newspaper publisher. If anyone knew how this would play out in the media, it was Walter. She asked him to go for a walk and give her advice: What would happen if she filed for divorce?

"It's not a decision you can make on a personal basis," Ridder said. That this came as no surprise to Jackie—product of a broken home, a prominent wife considering divorce precisely because her husband had depersonalized and abandoned her and their stillborn baby—was as much a reflection of her dutiful nature as it was the times.

"If you should leave him and divorce him, there is no way he can be president," Ridder said. "And I doubt you want that mark on your life."

"I know," Jackie said. She couldn't see that this was not something she was doing to Jack, but something Jack was doing to himself.

Jackie had Ridder's sympathy—up to a point. "We have all known Jack is difficult in the ways of women," Ridder said. "But A), you knew that from the beginning"—you signed up for this, do not complain—"and B), I'm sure there are many moments that make up for it."

That was true, Jackie had to admit. Despite everything, she was still deeply in love with Jack. He was the smartest, the cleverest, the best gossip, the brightest light in any room. When she had his attention there was nothing like it.

"When he's around," Jackie told Ridder, "he's just an enchantment."

So think hard, Ridder said. "Now you're in the public domain, and the decision you have to make involves a great deal more than your personal relationship with Jack."

"I know that," Jackie said. "I know that, and that terrifies me."

It was a terrible weight for a twenty-eight-year-old woman, the idea that her needs could cost the country a potentially great president. Couldn't she just tolerate it, as so many women of their class did? Sexual promiscuity did not necessarily mean anything. So much of being Mrs. John F. Kennedy made up for that.

Didn't it?

After all, her life's ambition, as she wrote in her boarding school yearbook, was "not to be a housewife." Then again, what was becoming First Lady if not becoming America's preeminent housewife?

This was Jackie's conundrum: her best chance at a great life depended on maintaining a smart marriage. Faithful husbands did not necessarily make the most interesting or enthralling ones.

If anything, the more successful Jack was, the crueler he became. "I suppose if I win, my poon days are over." Jack had scribbled that note to himself back in 1960 while on the campaign trail. But that hadn't been true — not after winning the White House and certainly not before. Jackie had caught Jack getting a blow job in his Senate office, a young girl under his desk, just after they were married. He didn't even try to hide his affairs.

Now, with Arabella gone, no one asked Jack how he could have left Jackie alone for over a week, or how he could have left it to Bobby to bury their baby. Maybe if there were more women in the press corps things would be different. Maybe not. There was little surprise that all Jack's fans in the nation's newsrooms would happily print and reprint the rumor that old Joe Kennedy paid Jackie one million dollars not to divorce Jack. Little surprise, too, that they wrote Jackie Kennedy off as bought-and-paid-for. In their estimation, Jackie Kennedy was the problem here: shallow, self-absorbed, and willing to sell her soul for the right price.

What had she gotten herself into?

———

Privately, even during their engagement, Jackie agonized. In Jack, she had landed America's most elusive bachelor. And to her surprise, Jack admired her mind. He loved how smart she was. He loved that her dream job was, as she said more than once, to be Overall Art Director of the

Twentieth Century. Jack had not known that he had bad taste, or no taste, until he met Jackie. He let her style him, order his designer suits, furnish their homes, renovate and landscape. Jackie was showing him the elemental pleasures of beautiful things. She elevated his taste level, and he was her eager student.

As Jack and the Old Man said more than once, Jackie really classed up the Kennedys. It irked Jack's sisters to no end. Igor Cassini, a high-society gossip columnist and younger brother of Jackie's favored designer, Oleg Cassini, talked about a particular Kennedy picnic on the Cape: The dressed-down Kennedy sisters had packed beer and hot dogs, while Jackie showed up immaculate in a white Christian Dior sheath dress, toting a basket filled with foie gras, caviar, and cold champagne. "Pat Lawford and Eunice Shriver never got over that," Cassini said. "Years later, they were still jabbering away about it."

For Jack and Old Joe, that level of refinement was Jackie's superpower. Their only concern was whether the average American woman was ready for a First Lady like her. Would such a young beauty, a well-traveled sophisticate, become a symbol of aspiration or aspersion? Would women feel talked down to and looked down upon, or would they see in Jackie a point of pride, a representation of America's own youth and futurism? Jackie let the Kennedy men fret. She wasn't about to focus-group herself into becoming mumsy or relatable. She could not be anyone other than who she was.

———

Doris pushed the First Lady back and away from the curtain. This nurse was about to meet the real Jacqueline Kennedy.

"I'm going to get in that room," Jackie said. She had another voice, not the airy high-pitched one she used in public but the one she used in private, deep and resonant. It had real power, both in its sound and ability to surprise.

Doc Burkely intervened. "It's her prerogative!" he yelled at Doris. "It's her prerogative!"

"It's my husband," Jackie said. "His blood, his brains are all over me."

The curtain parted. Jackie dropped to her knees and prayed before

Jack. In came Dr. William Kemp Clark, the hospital's chief neurosurgeon. One look at the president and Clark knew: He was dead. He turned to Jackie. "Would you like to leave, ma'am?" he asked. "We can make you more comfortable outside."

"No." Jackie's voice had gone; she mouthed the word. There were tubes and catheters and blood transfusions and beeping and sucking sounds. Clark performed CPR for ten minutes anyway. Blood from Jack's head wound pooled on the floor. His flesh had gone cool and alabaster.

Before calling the time of death, Clark spoke to Jackie. "Your husband," he said, "has sustained a fatal wound."

"I know." Again, the words did not come out. She made her way to his body and pressed her cheek against Jack's.

Burkely called for the room to be cleared, then stayed with Jackie as she caressed her husband. The hole at the base of Jack's throat was gaping, the tubing from the tracheotomy pulled out. The stiff corset he had worn for his bad back, which kept him upright after that first shot, had been cut off his body. His thick head of hair remained, even though the bloody undersides of his scalp had been shorn backward over his skull. His eyes were wide open. He was as handsome as ever. Jackie stared at his mouth and thought how beautiful it was.

Two priests came in to deliver last rites. They were both in shock, both struggling to maintain their composure, as was Doc Burkely. Jackie prayed with them, her voice stronger now. "Let perpetual light shine upon him," she said. The priests left.

Alone with her husband, or so she thought, Jackie kissed his naked body everywhere: His mouth, his chest, his leg, his penis.

For all of Jack's women, she was the last to possess him.

PART TWO

The Girls

MIMI BEARDSLEY AND DIANA DE VEGH

O n her fourth day at the White House, Mimi Beardsley got a call at her desk, inviting her to drinks with the president. Sort of a welcome party for new staffers.

"Where do I go?" she asked. Dave Powers, JFK's unofficial "First Friend," had proffered the invite. He said he'd be back later to bring her upstairs.

Mimi looked around at the other women in the secretarial pool. None appeared to have been invited; no one was checking their makeup or dashing to the ladies' room. Mimi's hair was still damp from her afternoon swim—another wild, unexpected treat, asked to join the president for his regular midday dip in the pool—and she felt awkward and underdressed.

But what could she do? She couldn't say no.

It was spring 1962, and Mimi was fresh off the train from Farmington, Connecticut, where she had just graduated from Miss Porter's School— Jackie Kennedy's alma mater. Mimi felt every bit of her nineteen years: unsophisticated, unglamorous, inexperienced with grown-ups. With men.

Powers swung by at 5:30 that afternoon to escort Mimi to the White House's private residence. She felt the eyes on her back as she followed him. Mimi could barely type.

The doors opened on the second floor, and instantly Mimi felt relieved. There, seated on sofas and surrounded by bookshelves, were Jill Cowan and Priscilla Wear, two girls around Mimi's age. They had also joined President Kennedy in the pool that afternoon. This was an unusual White House, but then again, this was an unusual president: he was young, good-looking, cool. Of course things would be looser. Maybe this was how the president kept in touch with the youth of America. Maybe this was how he liked to unwind—light chatter with pretty girls. Why not?

———

"Have a daiquiri." Powers was filling a large glass from a pitcher. Mimi wasn't a drinker.

"Thanks," she said.

The daiquiri went down sweet and easy. Powers refilled her glass.

Mimi had a nice little buzz on. She sat and listened to Jill and Priscilla as they talked about the absent Jackie Kennedy. Mimi had an affinity for the First Lady. Actually, she was kind of a fan. She had even written a story about Jackie for the school paper. That had been her first time at the White House: the First Lady's social secretary had shown Mimi around and introduced her to the president. Apparently, Mimi made an impression, because one year later she got a cold call from the White House asking if she would like to work there. But what was Mimi doing *here*, in the First Family's private residence, with the president's inner circle? She couldn't even make small talk.

"Would you like a tour of the residence, Mimi?"

It was President Kennedy, standing over her.

Wow. Yes, yes, of course she would.

It wasn't so much the president who interested Mimi—it was Jackie. No one was chicer. No one had better taste. Her mother idolized Jackie, too. And Mimi could be forgiven for seeing a bit of herself in the First Lady, or vice versa. She may not have been as beautiful or stylish, but Mimi had the same background and breeding, the height and bearing, the private school diction, the rounded vowels and soft voice. She shared the First Lady's obsession with interior design and French culture. Well into her teen years, Mimi had painstakingly renovated her Victorian dollhouse with new wallpaper, paint, furniture, and electric lighting. Mimi had a family of five dolls living in that house, and she made them all French. The parents were Marie and Paul Perot, and Mimi worked out all kinds of interfamily difficulties and dynamics—all the emotions and conflicts never addressed in her own WASP household — with that fake French family in that perfect miniature mansion.

Along with eighty million people the world over, Mimi had been riveted by the televised tour Jackie had given of the newly renovated White House back in February, an undertaking the First Lady had spearheaded. So many in the press — hell, even JFK himself! — had initially dismissed it as frivolous, exorbitant, the result of female boredom run amok, yet it was immediately seen for what Jackie had intended all along: the White House as an institutional reflection of and for the American people, representing the nation's dignity, philosophies, and heritage to all who would ever pass through, be they statesmen or civilians.

Now Mimi had the chance to see what the First Lady had done to the private quarters — to see how she lived! It was thrilling. She stood up to join the president, who was already making his way toward the residence.

There was a curtness to this tour. The president showed Mimi the dining room, which Jackie had redone in wallpaper depicting scenes from the American Revolution. Mimi wanted to linger, but the president spoke peremptorily, noting the distinctive features of the residence and leaving no time for questions before moving quickly to the next. He was the world's least enthusiastic tour guide.

Until.

"This," he said, opening the door, "is Mrs. Kennedy's bedroom."

Did they not sleep together? Mimi didn't understand.

She looked around. The room was exquisite. An ornate chandelier divided the First Lady's seating area from the bed, which was dressed in soft white linens and baby-blue blankets. The headboard's blue and white floral matched the floor-to-ceiling curtains, and a canopy of what looked like blue silk hung above the headboard. The color, the draping — it looked like the Virgin Mary's veil by way of Marie Antoinette.

A bench at the foot of the bed was neatly piled with books. Mimi noticed that the bed was actually two twins pushed together. "This is a very private room," JFK said. The president was behind her, his breath on Mimi's neck. She felt woozy. Was it the drinks? Was this really happening?

He moved to face her, put his hands on her shoulders and pushed her down onto Jackie's bed. Mimi froze. She was left half-sitting, half-lying down, propped up on her elbows. Now the president was undressing her. Mimi was wearing a shirtdress and he undid the buttons, played with her breasts, slid his hand between her legs and pulled off her underwear. He pulled down his pants but did not undress. Suddenly the president was inside her.

"Haven't you done this before?"

Mimi had been kissed once, in the eighth grade.

"No."

"Are you okay?"

Mimi said yes. But she knew she was in shock. He finished, got up, and redid his pants. The whole thing lasted less than three minutes. He never kissed her.

The president pointed to Jackie's bathroom.

"If you need it," he said.

Then he was gone.

Mimi walked into the bathroom. It was cool and graphic, the lower walls black against cream tile, the white sink wide-lipped on either side for Jackie's brushes and perfumes and makeup.

Mimi didn't really wear makeup.

There were flowers, cotton balls in a pink ceramic jar, setting powder and moisturizing cream, Jackie's bottle of Joy perfume — the most expensive in the world — on the windowsill. Mimi could smell the president's cologne on herself, citrusy and warm. What would Jackie make of her, this nineteen-year-old intern whose husband had just — what? What had he done with her? Mimi hadn't said no, but she hadn't said yes either. When she thought about it, days and weeks and years later, well into her sixties, she still didn't know how to define it.

She had taken her dress off, hadn't she? Wasn't that consent? But the way the president moved, grabbing her so fast, pushing her down on the bed so forcefully — she could never have stopped him. Short of screaming, she'd later write, there was nothing she could have done to get him off of her.

He wanted her and he was going to have her. And what about that?

The president of the United States had wanted her, Mimi Beardsley, a teenage girl from New Jersey with nothing to offer him. Yet here she was, washing off blood and semen in the First Lady's bathroom.

———

"Would you like to come for a lunchtime swim?"

It was Monday at the White House, the Monday after a long weekend Mimi had spent alone, so anxious that she saw no one, obsessing over what, if anything, was going to happen next.

Dave Powers was on the phone again, inviting Mimi to join the president. Word around the West Wing was that President Kennedy had just returned from spending the weekend with his wife and children at Glen Ora, their country house in Virginia. That meant Mimi had been on the president's mind all weekend. How could she say no? Besides, it was clear that Dave Powers wasn't asking. The president was. And an intern could not refuse the president.

So Mimi rose from her desk at lunchtime and made her way to the locker room, slipping on one of the many bathing suits, all different styles and sizes, ever at the ready. Why were there so many women's bathing suits? His cabinet was all men. The only women in the White House — well, girls and women — were secretaries. But this was treated as totally normal, the president needing company for the afternoon swims that soothed his bad back. Still, Mimi felt so self-conscious. Who else would be in the pool? Would they be able to tell she was no longer a virgin? Would they see her reaction to the president and know that they had been intimate?

Would they laugh?

When she arrived, the president was floating on his back, barely acknowledging Mimi. Two female White House staffers were splashing away. Apparently they were regulars. Dave Powers was there, too. Mimi stepped into the pool and made her way toward the group. She hoped her face betrayed nothing. After a few moments, the president turned toward her.

"Did you have a nice weekend, Mimi?" he asked.

Was he kidding?

"How are you enjoying your job?"

Mimi didn't understand. Was he being distant to throw off suspicion? Or was Friday night a fluke, a one-off, something the president regretted? Or worse, had Mimi been so bad, so frigid and immature, that the president had no desire to have sex with her again?

She wanted him, but she also felt relief. She hoped it would happen again but wasn't sure that was true either. She didn't know what she thought or how she felt. Was sex this confusing for every woman? She wished she had someone to talk to, but whom could she trust with a secret like this?

Who would even believe her?

Later, around 5:30, the phone rang.

Once again, Dave came to get Mimi and took her upstairs. This time it was just the two of them waiting for the president. A pitcher of cold daiquiri was set out, along with some cheese puffs.

Clearly the First Lady wasn't home. Jackie Kennedy would never abide cheese puffs.

A few minutes later, the president entered. Idle chit-chat with Dave, *blah blah blah, laugh laugh laugh*, then Dave got up to leave.

"Stay for supper, Mimi," the president said. "And have another daiquiri."

This second encounter would set the tone for their relationship. Mimi would be welcomed upstairs only when the First Lady was away, and it was her job to remind him of simple pleasures: small talk, shared bubble baths, and sex, hasty though it always was. They never discussed the big stuff, the pressures of the presidency or the state of his marriage. He didn't seem to care whether she slept over or not, but when he offered she always did. Wearing the same dress to work, two days in a row, never embarrassed her. It was Mimi's nonverbal way of letting all those other women in her department know: she had special privileges. She was the president's favorite.

The White House was her dominion.

———————

"Well, my dear, you have the advantage here. You know that I'm Jack Kennedy, but I don't know who you are."

It was 1958, and twenty-year-old Diana de Vegh was a junior at Radcliffe. Until that moment, she had been bored to tears at a fundraising dinner in Boston. James, her date, was the one interested in politics. He had been volunteering for then-senator Jack Kennedy's reelection campaign in Massachusetts; Diana was merely his plus-one.

"Give me your seat," Kennedy said to James, "so a tired old man can sit next to a pretty girl."

The self-deprecation! Jack Kennedy was far from old. He was young, vital, charismatic. He understood the value of youth. "This is the table I need to be at," Kennedy said. "You young people will set me straight. The rest of these guys just tell me what I want to hear."

He swiveled toward Diana.

"Who are you?" he asked. "What's your name?"

Say something smart, she thought to herself. *Do not be an embarrassment.*

"I've read your book," she told him.

She hadn't, but flattery would probably be enough.

"And?"

"And . . . it's wonderful."

Jack Kennedy liked what he heard, liked what he saw. He waved to summon an aide-de-camp and ordered him to make sure Diana was at his next event.

"I'm going to count on seeing you," Jack Kennedy said. "Dave here will give you the details."

One week later, Dave Powers stood at the front door of Diana's off-campus house, ready to ferry her to the senator. James, Dave said, would not be making it to tonight's appearance; instead, he would be working for Senator Kennedy elsewhere. Besides, Diana was precious cargo.

"The senator doesn't want you driving around the back roads with some kid who might get lost or drink too much," Dave said. "He'll feel safer having me drive you, okay?"

As cultivated as Diana looked—she was of Jackie's world and wore her hair and makeup in similar fashion—she was a nervous wreck. She couldn't figure out what Senator Kennedy was doing with her. Soon he'd be inviting her to rally after rally, Dave and other staffers tending to Diana's every need, Jack taking off with her after each event and cracking that same joke:

"I'm working pretty hard for just one vote here . . ."

He would sit with her in his car, side by side, his arm slung over the back seat above her shoulders.

Was he making a pass? Diana couldn't tell. She hoped he was, but at the same time she didn't. Girls like Diana — good girls with prominent, successful fathers and expensive educations — didn't have sex before marriage. Certainly not with other women's husbands. Even though Diana knew Jack Kennedy was speaking in clichés when he told her she "had a spark" and was "something special" and would grow up to do "great things," she wanted to believe him. She wanted to see herself the way Jack saw her, as an intellectual, someone whose opinions on politics and campaigning mattered.

He sat with her on those drives back to her dorm at Radcliffe, listening to her talk about the Middle East or the books she was reading, treating her as if she were twenty years older and a foreign policy expert, a beautiful one at that. Her opinions mattered to him. He was having Diana chauffeured to all his events, and after each one, he wanted to know what *she* thought. Jack Kennedy made her feel as if she really were something. Diana was so young that she didn't even know herself yet, and the world was telling young women that they weren't worth much without a man. But Diana had *this* man! And this man saw things in her she could not even fathom.

Diana could be more than what she was brought up to be, more than the only option in her future: a girl with good breeding and a good education who would use those gifts in service of one thing, making a respectable marriage and bearing beautiful children.

Couldn't she?

And so she continued, rally after rally, cheering him on in that back seat — his hype woman, cupping her mouth with her hands and yelling, "By overwhelming majority, John Kennedy sails to victory!"

He was her romantic hero. But after months of this, Diana still had no idea what was going on. They had never discussed his wife. Did Jack and Jackie have an arrangement? Or was Jack's interest in her platonic? After all, he had yet to make a move. Was she little more than a convenience, a pretty girl who was always available, who glowed in his presence, who reflected what he wanted to see? Who he wanted to be? Or was that enough? Was that not, in a sense, power?

One night Jack asked Diana back to his apartment. He was hungry and tired. "We'll find something to eat," he said. His place was hardly the setting Diana anticipated, so dismal that it felt, on some level, like a joke. It was dim and cramped, with hardly any good furniture, just a crappy TV and a cheap plastic football from the five and dime. Only the bed was nice.

The single clue that JFK lived here was his small personal library, books on economics and history mixed with *Lolita* and *Call the Lady Indiscreet*. Eclectic taste, to be sure.

Jack stood in front of Diana now in his sad little kitchen, the look on his face different. Serious. He put his hand on top of hers. She froze, even though this was what she had wanted from the beginning. Why was this so confusing? She was sure she was in love with him and now she was sure he was in love with her. That neither had ever said it didn't matter. As for her reputation: Who would ever know? Their relationship was all about secrecy. Diana was safe.

Jack gestured toward the bedroom.

"Let's go," he said.

She went.

There were no kisses, no professions of love.

If he hadn't known she was a virgin before, he knew now.

Mimi didn't know about Diana, but she quickly realized that Jill Cowan and Priscilla Wear, his frequent playmates in the White House pool, were also among his favorite young female staffers. Nor was Mimi the only young woman to administer one of his daily scalp massages, rubbing ointments and conditioner into his thick brown hair before his press conferences, senior male staff often walking in on them and trying to act as though this was all perfectly normal, a teenage would-be typist performing such intimate caregiving.

Mimi never set foot in Mrs. Kennedy's bedroom or bathroom again. She tried to put Mrs. Kennedy out of her mind entirely; she was hardly ever at the White House anyway. Maybe they had an understanding, she told herself. After all, the Secret Service agents never blanched. Maybe everyone saw how good Mimi was for the president — how she helped him relax at the end of a hard day, how she only ever sought to please him, how she demanded nothing in return.

When Dave called, Mimi answered. She never made plans after work — never made any friends, really — because this was too big a secret. She only cared about being available to the president. It didn't seem like a sacrifice; if anything, she felt special. Of all the women he could be with, the president of the United States had chosen nineteen-year-old Mimi Beardsley. So on those workdays when Dave called, Mimi would wait to be taken upstairs. Sometimes Dave would stay for a bit, and at these times Mimi would feel superfluous, invisible, silly. She had no idea what Dave and President Kennedy were talking about, and she had nothing to add. It made her feel self-conscious, as though her silence underscored her only real use: sex.

Other times, Dave would leave Mimi upstairs alone — Dave really trusted her, it seemed — and Mimi would wait for the president, for however long it took. Sometimes she would go into his *en suite*, draw a bath, take a soak, and wrap herself in one of his bathrobes, then sit and wait some more.

Sometimes they would bathe together and he would charm Mimi with his boyishness, playing with the rubber duckies he said belonged to his children.

Mimi tried not to think about his children, either.

The president, it turned out, was compulsive about showering, sometimes up to five times a day. He changed his dress shirts as frequently, if not more. It never occurred to Mimi that this was something other than hygiene. Obsessive-compulsive disorder never crossed her mind. Nor was she aware of his hyper-promiscuity, that he was often washing away the smell of sex. She was too young and inexperienced to wonder even further, to ask herself if the president, despite his compulsivity, even liked sex all that much, or liked women that much. He only ever really came alive, in a sustained way, in the company of men. She was too much in the throes of hero worship to ever wonder if he found sex dirty.

If he found women dirty.

After bath time they would go into the kitchen and dine on whatever his staff had stocked in the fridge: leftover roast beef sandwiches, shrimp, chicken. The staff never cooked dinner when Mrs. Kennedy was away. In these moments, Mimi wondered what an actual sit-down dinner with the president would be like, hot meals elegantly plated on the gleaming dining room table, multicourse servings amid candlelight and conversation. She wondered what the rest of the residence looked like; her access was limited to the sitting room, the president's bed and bathrooms, and the kitchen. As if she were a concubine or a house pet.

Mimi convinced herself that none of this mattered. Just as it didn't matter that the president never kissed her. Just as it didn't matter that she only ever called him Mr. President, even though they were regularly having sex. Just as it didn't matter that he never told her to call him anything else, that he never told her he loved her or cared about her. It was okay, really. Mimi was nineteen and a college student; he was forty-five and the married leader of the free world.

Who was she to complain?

Diana would find herself in the White House too, in due time. But in 1960, as Jack Kennedy ran for president, he became remote to her. It was surreal to see this man who had seduced her in his tiny apartment on TV and magazine covers, photos of him at campaign events with gorgeous actresses.

What if he forgot about her?

But then he would call, and it was like Diana had been plugged back into a wall socket, her adrenaline soaring and warming her up.

Come see me at the Carlyle, he said one night. It was all so furtive and elegant. This was the stuff of secret romance: Manhattan's Upper East Side, cold martinis, a famous man waiting on the other side of a door for her. The future president of the United States. Could it get any more glamorous?

So on that night, dressed up and made up, Diana took the elevator to the thirty-fourth floor and knocked on Jack Kennedy's door. He swung it open and hugged her.

"Great timing!" he said. "There's good news. We've — "

That was it. The phone rang and Jack was off to grab it, his mind already elsewhere: on the next vote count, the next endorsement, the next fundraiser. It went on like this all night, and it was the first time Diana had ever seen how distractible Jack was. He was all over the place, one minute paying attention to Diana and the next deep in another phone conversation, mouthing, "Sorry," but not being sorry enough to hold all calls.

Why had she come here?

"Don't make that face at me," Jack said.

He had just ended his fourth or fifth phone call since she'd arrived.

"You of all people can understand what a campaign is," he said.

Diana, of all people? She was a college girl. It seemed like his wife, of all people, would understand what a campaign is. Maybe that was the problem.

Jack kept trying to placate her.

"We've been together in this from the beginning," he said, and for all Diana's starry-eyed infatuation, this struck her as glib. Jack was just trying to get her into bed. There would be no wining, no dining, no romance — his attention was on other things, more important things. There would only be fast, technical sex with Jack Kennedy, man on the move.

For all their growing knowledge of Jack's faults, neither Mimi nor Diana knew that he could be a real sadist. Humiliation and sex went hand in hand for him. He was at his best during the chase, but once he seduced you, he seemed to think less of you.

These humiliations were never sudden; they were subtle at first, and easy to explain away. Like the way he would joke with Mimi about what she got up to with the other students in her all-girls boarding school. She knew he wanted to hear about furtive couplings and whether she had ever experimented, but no matter how many times she said, "Nothing," he kept bringing it up. Mimi could always brush that stuff off as the president joking with her. Besides, what was she going to do — pick an argument with him? Who was under more stress than he was? What kind of woman would demand more of him, especially with his bad back, his multiple ailments, his clearly unhappy marriage?

These girls would serve, more than they knew, at the pleasure of the president.

So it was that, in 1962, Mimi found herself on a cruise around the Potomac, an after-work treat the president hosted on the *Sequoia*, his yacht, in the late days of summer. Her presence was always explained away as one of Pierre Salinger's aides in the press office. She wasn't even old enough to vote, but most people went along with it.

Most, that is, except one. Mimi wasn't sure of her name, but she looked older. Word was she was the mistress of Senator Smathers. She pulled Mimi aside during cocktails on the upper deck.

"You are too young to be here."

Mimi was stunned. Humiliated. She thought she had become so sophisticated, keeping such a dangerous secret with élan. But this woman had seen right through her. Who else knew? She had to recover quickly.

"I have no idea what you're talking about," Mimi said.

"You're going to regret it," the woman said. "All of a sudden you'll turn around and you'll be twenty-five and you won't have a life." Really? Mimi took offense. John F. Kennedy had chosen *her*. *Name one other nineteen-year-old*, she thought, *who is sleeping with the president of the United States.*

Jack Kennedy had decided: He could not live without Diana de Vegh. Would she come to Washington? Please? He would get her a job, a high-status one on the National Security Council staff. He was the president now; he could make anything happen for her.

Maybe she should go. It wasn't as if Jack Kennedy had a complete hold on Diana. She wasn't in danger of becoming subsumed by him — hadn't paused her life or given up her studies or even stopped dating other men. In fact, the only other person who knew about their relationship was Diana's current boyfriend, a journalist at *Time* named Billy Brammer.

Billy asked her why she was involved with Jack. Diana was beautiful, young, educated, wealthy. Her father was a famous economist. Didn't she want more for herself than to be the president's plaything? Jack Kennedy did, after all, have quite the reputation among the press and politicos in DC.

"Nothing will come of it," Diana told him. "But he has a hold on me."

She was hardly the only woman he had a hold on. There was Pamela Turnure, Jackie's newly appointed press secretary; Judith Campbell Exner, who had been involved with Frank Sinatra and mob boss Sam Giancana; and Helen Chavchavadze, first cousin to Jackie's spurned fiancé, John Husted.

And then, of course, there was Marilyn Monroe, whose ongoing affair with Jack dated back to 1955.

That was supposed to be a secret, too.

PART THREE
THE BOMBSHELL

MARILYN MONROE

Marilyn Monroe was the world's biggest sex goddess when she met Jack Kennedy, the rising star of the United States Senate. It was the summer of 1954 in Los Angeles, Jack's favorite place for what he called his hunting expeditions—and Marilyn was his latest prey.

He had been angling to meet her, and finally got his chance at a Hollywood party with Jackie on his arm. Marilyn was with Joe DiMaggio, her husband of six months, who also happened to be one of America's greatest ballplayers, more famous than Jack Kennedy.

"I think I've met you someplace before," Kennedy said to Marilyn. It was hardly the most original line, but Marilyn played along. Certainly possible, she said. They had friends in common, especially Kennedy's brother-in-law Peter Lawford, a film actor of some renown. Marilyn was wary of Peter; she thought he was secretly gay and not just envious of her, but very much wanted to *be* her. Clearly, Peter also wanted to be Jack. Marrying his sister, Patricia Kennedy, hadn't been enough for Peter; he quickly became Jack's shadow, his pimp, his fixer, drug supplier. Anything or anyone Jack wanted, Peter made it happen. This was a new psychosexual dynamic for Marilyn. She found it compelling.

Marilyn slipped Jack her phone number. A few months later, Jack was in the hospital recovering from back surgery, at death's door, Jackie tending to him 24/7 underneath that upside-down poster of Marilyn Monroe.

To Jack, who had always felt rejected by his mother, who had repelled her with his tears as much as his sickly body, the orphaned Marilyn vibrated on a different frequency than his other women. They were both self-inventions, damaged people who had willed themselves into super-human stratospheres: he, the physical embodiment of postwar America, vibrant and youthful and much too cocksure; she, pure carnality softened by kittenish innocence, a symbol of the culture tip-toeing its way to the sexual revolution, women on the verge of second-wave feminism.

Jack Kennedy and Marilyn Monroe, two personas built on damaged foundations, casting their dark magic. People wanted to have sex with them, be them, or bask in their orbit, for however long, at whatever cost. But Marilyn had a neediness that Jack did not.

She wanted two things: to be loved—a deep, full love that she believed could heal all her wounds—and to be smart. She wanted powerful and famous men to see past the sex symbol and realize that Marilyn Monroe had substance. She always carried a book with her, a serious one. A big one. *Ulysses*. She didn't understand it but didn't realize that almost no one did.

By the spring of 1955, Marilyn thought she was happier than she'd been in a long time. Her brief marriage to Joe DiMaggio had ended in divorce after just nine months. Once DiMaggio had won Marilyn, he—like so many men before him—wanted her to snuff out her light, to exist only in relation to him. Her testimony in a Santa Monica court-house, fifteen minutes in total, gave America another look at its most worshipped athlete.

"My husband would get into moods where he wouldn't speak to me for periods of sometimes ten days," Marilyn testified. She was twenty-nine years old. "If I would try to reproach him usually he wouldn't answer at all. When he would, he would say, 'Leave me alone.'"

Marilyn said that DiMaggio isolated her and wouldn't allow friends to their home. "I hoped to have out of my marriage love, warmth, affection, and understanding," she said. "But the relationship was one of coldness and indifference. I voluntarily offered to give up my work in hopes that it would solve our problems, but it didn't change his attitude."

That testimony won Marilyn her immediate freedom. She did not testify to the physical abuse she'd suffered, did not reveal that DiMaggio had left her right arm black-and-blue after he watched, in a rage, Marilyn film her most famous scene for *The Seven Year Itch*: standing above a New

York City subway grate, her white dress billowing up, an exuberant Marilyn covering her groin and laughingly preserving her modesty.

After that, they were done. The announcement that they'd broken up left America siding at first with Joe. She emerged a wicked woman who had pained a wholesome sports hero. Days later, back in California, someone passed her an envelope containing a piece of toilet paper; human feces spelled out the word *whore*.

Marilyn didn't need any of it. Getting away from DiMaggio, with the judge believing her testimony and granting her the divorce immediately, had left her feeling euphoric.

Her subconscious, though, told her something different. In one of her most upsetting nightmares, so terrifying in its literalism that she wrote about it in her diary, her acting teacher, the famous Lee Strasberg, was colluding with the psychiatrist she was seeing five days a week, Dr. Margaret Hohenberg.

Both Strasberg and Hohenberg, whom Marilyn called "Dr. H," were pushing her to investigate her early life, insisting that it was the only path to becoming both a good actress and a fully realized human being. She didn't want to. Marilyn had so much trauma in her past: she'd been abandoned her whole life, passed from adult to adult, used and abused, sent from foster home to foster home, violated and molested and raped and made to feel worthless. But hadn't she vanquished that? By shedding Norma Jeane Baker, the shy, stuttering, unwanted child and creating Marilyn Monroe, hadn't she won? Why couldn't she keep forging ahead?

In this dream, Strasberg and Dr. H were in agreement. They were leaders in their fields, the greatest minds applying themselves to the impossible case of Marilyn Monroe, and so, like the obedient girl she was, she followed their prescriptions. As Marilyn wrote of her nightmare, "Best finest surgeon — Strasberg to cut me open which I don't mind since Dr. H has prepared me — given me anesthetic and has also diagnosed the case and agrees with what has to be done — an operation — to bring myself back to life and to cure me of this terrible dis-ease, whatever the hell it is — "

Strasberg makes his incision, and it leads to the actor's worst fear realized — that the thing that sets them apart, that makes them so able to become other people and mimic emotions, is due to what they lack: a sense of self.

"There is absolutely nothing there," Marilyn wrote. "... He thought there was going to be so much — more than he had ever dreamed possible ... Instead there was absolutely nothing — devoid of every human living feeling thing — the only thing that came out was so finely cut sawdust — like out of a raggedy ann [*sic*] doll — and the sawdust spills all over the floor & table and Dr. H is puzzled because suddenly she realizes that this is a new type [of] case. The patient ... existing of complete emptiness. Strasberg's dreams & hopes for theater are fallen. Dr. H's dreams and hopes for a permanent psychiatric cure is given up — Arthur is disappointed — let down."

The Arthur in her dream was the playwright Arthur Miller. They had first met in 1951, on a movie set, and he had made a strong impression. "Met a man tonight," she wrote in her journal. "It was ... bam! It was like running into a tree. You know, like a cool drink when you've had a fever." He had captivated her by suggesting she act on the stage, that she clearly had the chops for it. When Arthur said that to her, on set in front of everyone, people laughed. But he hadn't. He meant it.

Was this the man to finally see the real Marilyn? To appreciate her gifts?

They reconnected, and as soon as her divorce from DiMaggio was final, they threw themselves headlong into a serious relationship, marrying on June 29, 1956. She hadn't heeded the warnings about writers, how everyone in their world was material — fair game for their work. And why would she ever doubt Arthur? He was so kind, so adoring — worshipful. He was also a genius, the most celebrated and revered living American playwright. She wanted him to be proud of her.

That he'd pursued her, even left his first wife to marry her, should have been enough, but it wasn't. Some of Marilyn's best performances were before his crowd, at gatherings with the writers and intellectuals who intimidated her. The women especially were terrifying, accepted by their male counterparts as equal talents, if not better and smarter. Carson McCullers. Isak Dinesen. The photographer Eve Arnold, who always captured Marilyn as she saw herself: an avid reader, a seeker, a student.

Marilyn especially admired Harper Lee and Greta Garbo, two women who lived alone and on their own terms. They were originals, artists in full control of their careers and creativity. No studio boss was going to make decisions for them — tell them when they'd aged out, gained too much weight, needed plastic surgery. No one to tell them they were no longer necessary.

These women had it so much better than Marilyn — than most women, really. Marriage and children wasn't all there was. Marilyn wanted to level up and be like them. She wanted to be as smart and together. Marrying Arthur was part of that. As with DiMaggio, she was willing to dampen her blazing career as the biggest movie star in the world. Maybe it would be a short-term sacrifice. Maybe, if they had a child, a longer-term one. "She will be my wife," Arthur told the press around the time they were married. "That's a full-time job."

Yet Marilyn could never shake the fear that, for the playwright, she was merely the ultimate trophy. He loved her, of course, was crazy about her, but still. It was in the letter he'd written to her shortly before they were married, five pages of rambling about his guilt, his children, his divorce, his parents, and how gratifying it was for them that their son had landed Marilyn Monroe. Their hope that her fame would uplift him, making him the most envied man in America. He wrote to Marilyn of his ex-wife Mary Slattery's anger — a violation of her privacy. Arthur and Mary had been married for sixteen years, and Mary's humiliation was compounded by the fame, beauty, and sexual vibrancy of her rival.

He wrote of his Freudian struggles with his mother — oh yes, The Dumb Blonde was a student of Freud and devoted to her psychoanalysis — and the metaphorical slaying of his father by saying, without saying: I am with Marilyn Monroe and you are not. "In effect I say — I am a lover," Miller wrote. "Look, I say, look at my sweet, beautiful, sexy wife. I can see my father's pleasure at the sight of you..."

Where was the real Marilyn, the person, in all of this?

Despite it all, she loved the playwright. She was out-of-her-mind crazy about him, ignoring the cynics who thought he'd married down and she'd married up, that he gave her class and she only gave him sex appeal. The Egghead and the Hourglass — that's what the press called them.

Arthur looked nothing like her leading men, had none of the magnetism or animalism. But to Marilyn he was the sexiest man in the world, and as vulnerable as she.

"I am so concerned about protecting Arthur," she wrote in her diary. "I love him — and he is the only person — human being I have ever known that I could love not only as a man to which I am attracted to practically out of my senses about — but he is the only person . . . that I trust as much as myself — because when I do trust myself (about certain things) I do fully." Her marriage would not be a casualty, she wrote, of what was done to her as a child, of the shame she still carried, of the sense that somehow she had deserved that abuse, had invited it. "I will not be punished for it or be whipped or be threatened or not loved or sent to hell to burn."

But the playwright, like the ballplayer before him, soon came to resent Marilyn. She was too careerist, too comfortable with commodifying herself. Too beautiful for the geeky, gangly likes of him.

Then came Jack Kennedy.

Marilyn did not have this problem with Jack. He loved those qualities. He luxuriated in her carnality. He reveled in sitting next to her at fancy restaurants, at big dinners with friends, aides, other stars, and pinching her rear end, whispering dirty jokes, caressing her under the table.

Oh, the fun they had in the years to come. The night at Puccini in LA during his 1960 run for president, Jackie at home six months pregnant, Marilyn seated with Jack, Peter, and Kenny O'Donnell, Jack's hand moving higher than usual and his shock at realizing Marilyn wasn't wearing underwear. Jack turned bright red. So maybe even he could be scandalized. She loved it, found it so funny.

And when Jack became the leader of the free world, Marilyn would be at his side — how was that for smart? She delighted him, even as her own husband found her tiresome, uninteresting, and intellectually lacking. She knew this was true, because Arthur wrote as much and left his notebook for her to find while they were far from home, in London. Marilyn was shooting a movie with Laurence Olivier, the first for her new production company. Arthur knew how insecure she was working opposite the greatest actor alive. Had Arthur subconsciously wanted her to know what he really thought? Had he lacked the guts to tell her to her face? What would Freud say about that?

Olivier, too, had made his disdain for Monroe clear. He was dismissive of her on set, which was bad enough as her leading man, even worse because he was also her director. He told the cast and crew that Marilyn was a trifle, a bauble, a nothing. She wasn't an artist or a real actress. She was just a starlet with a shelf life, out of her league with all these Great Men, and Olivier knew just how to humiliate her.

"Try and be sexy," he said.

It was almost two years since she'd first met Jack Kennedy. Marilyn and Arthur were living in a rented manor in the English countryside, Parkside House, and it was a sanctuary, her haven from the cruelty on set. They spent her time off bicycling through town, stopping at pubs, lazing away gorgeous summer afternoons. People left them alone. She had been so content with Arthur — until she read what he had written. One word in particular jumped out.

EMBARRASSED.

She embarrassed him. His notebook was full of ugly feelings: He worried that his own work would be compromised by this "pitiable, dependent, unpredictable waif." He was ashamed to be her husband, especially when they were around his friends, the intellectuals. Had he done the right thing leaving Mary, the mother of his children, for Marilyn Monroe? What would it do to his career? Would the august Arthur Miller become a laughingstock? The only one he would ever truly love, he wrote, was his daughter.

Marilyn had been his wife for two weeks.

Jack Kennedy hadn't made her feel this way. Here was a man known for surrounding himself with the best and the brightest. His was a first-rate mind that loved Hollywood gossip. He never assumed that Marilyn's affectations—her compliance with men, the baby-doll whisper she shared with Jackie—meant that she was dumb. Jackie certainly wasn't dumb.

Only Marilyn's shrinks had any inkling why she spoke that way, why some women who were abused as children sometimes adopt a child's voice. It was a way of saying: *I'm smaller than you. Please don't hurt me.*

She never thought Jack Kennedy would hurt her.

PART FOUR
THE LONELY GRAVES

MARY RICHARDSON KENNEDY

All her life, she had wanted only one thing: to be a Kennedy. Mary Richardson had been starstruck by the whole family, but no one more so than Robert F. Kennedy Jr., son of the martyred Bobby Kennedy and nephew of the late JFK. Bobby was an alpha Kennedy, and she had won him.

For a time, anyway. The gorgeous, smart, talented Mary Richardson Kennedy — mother of four, married to the most famous Kennedy man aside from JFK Jr., living in a million-dollar house she'd redesigned in the wealthy suburb of Bedford, New York, a woman everyone wanted at their charity galas and dinner parties — was now on the verge of losing everything.

With her thick, dark hair, large brown eyes, and perfect pale skin, Mary was the Kennedy wife who, more than any other, evoked Jackie Kennedy. She worked hard at it; her husband, after all, had been counseled by the family to find a wife like Jackie — a wife who could get him to the White House. She never really knew Jackie, who'd died one month after she and Bobby were married, but Mary — like Jackie, a highly visual person — emulated the former First Lady's style and affect. She wore preppy tennis sweaters during the day and minimal black shift dresses at night. She spoke in a similar manner, using a synthetic accent that sounded Long-Island-by-way-of-London. She was as comfortable talking to presidents as she was to PTA members. She was more charismatic, more coherent than her husband, especially when speaking in public.

She was even good on television, as she had proven in 2008 when PBS star Bob Vila brought a camera crew to tour the family home in Westchester. Mary, an architectural designer, had gutted and redone the entire house after discovering mold on all three floors. Her work was masterful. She had turned a basic old Georgian colonial into a cutting-edge green home, honoring its original bones while buffing her husband's environmental bona fides.

As they were being interviewed, Mary displayed her original renderings while Bobby sat back in his chair, arms crossed, frowning.

It didn't matter. Vila was more interested in talking to her.

"Mary," Vila said, "you have had a huge job here, because part of that job was breaking the news to your family that the house had become a sick house."

A sick house.

It was still, even though the mold was long gone. Only the people who lived there knew it.

Now, three years after that triumph, she could barely get out of bed.

On the days when she summoned enough energy to take the kids to school, Mary was often in ratty pajama bottoms, her hair unkempt. "You have to pull yourself together," the other mothers told her. "You're a Kennedy. You can't go around looking like this."

In those moments, Mary would think: *None of you could do what I do. None of you could hack being a Kennedy wife.* It was something Mary had in common with Carolyn Bessette, married to Bobby's cousin John Jr. Almost every day, Mary dealt with the assumption that came not just from other women, but also from tabloids and esteemed historians: that being a Kennedy wife—especially the wife of the namesake, the eldest son of a beloved, martyred leader—meant you were special. It was never the other way around—that you'd chosen *him*, that you'd chosen *this*. That behind the scenes, you were the brains. The mover, the shaker, the one who got things done.

And if you failed in any way, everyone, including your husband, would let you know, their contempt sometimes hidden but mostly not: *Look at the world I brought you into, the wealth and fame and admiration handed to you on this family's silver platter.* How hard could it be?

As Carolyn said every time her husband asked her that very question, "I didn't get the fucking employee handbook."

It was cutting and true. Kennedy men tended to treat their women as afterthoughts. Even the adored John Jr., the *ne plus ultra* of Kennedy men, could be guilty of this. He was hardly like his father and deserved credit for that; he took his marriage seriously and, as he said at the outset, had every intention of being faithful. But he and Bobby Jr. had that male Kennedy entitlement, the expectation that their wives should be mind readers, hostesses who could throw together a dinner for twelve at the last minute — the uncomplaining Cool Girl. If her husband didn't come home when he said he would, if he was an hour or a day or a week late? The good Kennedy wife just brushed that off. And, of course, a wandering eye, Bobby's wandering eye, was just part of the deal. Congenital, generational, baked in — the original recipe Kennedy.

For all the comparisons she drew to Jackie, Mary was really most like Carolyn.

Both were from upper-middle-class Catholic East Coast families; both had worked in creative fields — Mary at the famed Parish Hadley Design firm, Carolyn as a top adviser to Calvin Klein; and both were habitués of the downtown New York scene, Mary running with the Warhol crowd and Carolyn with actors and models at exclusive, twelve-seat SoHo night-clubs. Both had far more edge than their husbands. More style. They were cooler and smarter and quicker, though everyone told them that *they* were the lucky ones, *they* were the ones who had married up.

Not so. Mary and Carolyn gave their husbands a sharpened eye, a sense of the new and modern. Both women, like Jackie before them, introduced their men to beauty for beauty's sake. They shared a high emotional intelligence and their own streak of danger. It was never a good idea to be around either Mary or Carolyn when one of them was angry; their explosive rages, often coming out of nowhere, could be terrifying. There were times when Mary hit Bobby hard, punched him in the face. She pushed him down the stairs once. But he'd always come back to her.

Their relationship hadn't always been this abusive. Mary was still deeply in love with Bobby. Sometimes she'd say she was addicted to him, and the alcoholic in her meant it. They had met when she was fourteen and he was twenty-one, and though she'd gone on to have a great romance with the heir to a Greek shipping tycoon—a man Bobby knew well—and another with the son of a famous novelist, neither stood a chance against the Kennedys.

Long before Mary and Bobby ever met, Mary had befriended his younger sister Kerry at Putney, a progressive boarding school in Vermont. There, they were roommates and quickly became best friends. Soon she was subsumed into life at Hickory Hill, the Virginia home base for the Robert F. Kennedys, spending weekends and holidays there, going on vacations with them, volunteering to work for any Kennedy sibling who needed help. She was ensorcelled. This was a tight clan that brooked very few outsiders, but they had welcomed Mary—brilliant, suffering, complicated, charismatic Mary, whose own home life in New Jersey had been upended by her father's unexpected death when she was young. Here she was in the bosom of America's First Family, themselves no strangers to grief. She never wanted to leave.

Bobby's mother, Ethel, called Mary her fifth daughter; Kerry became another sister to her. But Bobby, beautiful, long-haired, wild Bobby—well, her feelings for him weren't familial. He was only five years older than she was, but at seventeen he may as well have been an adult. Girls fought over him. Boys wanted to be him. When he married his fellow law student Emily Black in 1982, Mary resigned herself: Bobby would never be hers.

And then, one night at an art gallery in Manhattan, it was as if Bobby truly saw Mary for the first time. It was 1993. Bobby was a father now, with two children both under ten, a boy and a girl. He was recently divorced from Emily, he said.

Would it have mattered if Mary knew that he was lying? That he and Emily were not, in fact, divorced? Would it have mattered if Mary knew Emily's side? That Emily loved Bobby and had stuck with him through his heroin addiction, his overdose and arrest, the rehab stint in New Jersey, the serious health issues to follow, the five-months-long hospitalization? That in 1992, after ten years of marriage and two children, Emily and Bobby had separated over none of those issues but over his constant infidelities?

Probably not. Mary had always been in love with the Kennedys. Now she had the chance to be one. She had liked JFK Jr., but there had been no real interest on his side. Besides, JFK Jr. was kind of a square, in her opinion. Dull. There was nothing dull about Bobby, and there was nothing cynical about their romance. They found solace in each other, these fatherless children who had struggled so, Bobby with drugs and, as Mary would learn, with an absentee, often rageful mother.

Soon, Mary would realize all too well that the family she so idealized had its own secrets, and that Bobby wasn't exactly the favored son. He had been kicked out of famous boarding schools and fobbed off to Lem Billings, his uncle Jack's best friend, himself so desperate for proximity that he used drugs with Bobby Jr. This namesake son spent his formative years fairly crying out for maternal attention, but nothing could rally Ethel—not his alcoholism, not his heroin use, not his expulsion from boarding school because his friends feared he was one overdose away from dying. Not even the incident where he'd spat ice cream in the face of a cop on Cape Cod—ground zero for the Kennedys—could compel Ethel to pay attention to her very troubled son.

On the other hand, all Mary wanted to do was pay attention to Bobby. In her way, she understood him. Bobby Jr. was nine when his father died; she was twelve when her father went into the hospital with colon cancer. His death after surgery was a shock; he was only fifty-seven. Like Bobby Jr., she'd never had the chance to say goodbye.

Mary's mother vanished into her own grief, and Mary developed an eating disorder. She was haunted by feelings of abandonment and low self-esteem. She drank and used drugs too, and when she was twenty-two her anorexia became so severe that she wound up in Boston's famed McLean Hospital for three months. She'd tried to commit suicide twice, once at twenty-five and again at twenty-six.

In Mary, Bobby had found that most elusive partner: someone who needed help, and someone whom he could possibly save. Or maybe they could save each other.

———————————

Their courtship was heady and fast, not the advisable thing for two people newly sober and working their steps in AA. Within months, Bobby had whisked Mary off to Ireland, and she got pregnant. He proposed right away, and that was when Mary learned the truth, that Bobby and Emily were still married. She didn't care. She was that much in love.

Like Carolyn Bessette, her future cousin-in-law, Mary chose to ignore these blazing warning signs. Like Carolyn, she imbued her Kennedy man with all the qualities he lacked—self-awareness, humility, and intelligence. Mary was brilliant, always top of her class, a voracious reader and generator of ideas. Bobby, not so much.

Years before his cousin John Jr. came up with the idea of mass-producing custom-made kayaks, Bobby—who was trying to carve out a career as an environmentalist with Riverkeeper, a nonprofit dedicated to protecting New York's Hudson River—wanted to sell bottled water branded with the foundation's name. That the bottles would likely be plastic didn't seem to matter to him.

Bobby was soon making enemies and embarrassing himself as a self-branded environmental expert. His book *The Riverkeepers*, which he co-authored with John Cronin in 1997, was meant to burnish his reputation in a field relatively new to him. It had the opposite effect. James Gorman, deputy science editor of the *New York Times*, noted the book's multiple inaccuracies, including the assertion that DDT had eradicated entire bird populations. "This is not a trivial mistake," Gorman wrote. "The environment is Kennedy's claimed field of expertise, after all, and the DDT disaster is a famous one." Nor was Gorman impressed with Bobby's accounts of his addictions and recovery, or his tone-deaf hosanna to his Costa Rican nanny, whose "heavily accented versions" of fairy tales and folk tales, Bobby wrote, inspired his environmentalism.

But nothing could stop his ambition, his unerring belief that he was always in the right. Not even that bad review—in a newspaper that usually covered the Kennedys favorably, no less — gave Bobby Jr. pause. And Mary was always proud of Bobby.

His divorce was a quickie obtained in the Dominican Republic, granted days before his and Emily's twelfth wedding anniversary. Uncle Ted, the only other Kennedy man to divorce, suggested Bobby ask a close family friend down there, a priest named Father Gerry Creedon, to make it happen. Creedon had married Bobby and Emily. What Mary knew of this didn't ruffle her; Emily was as unhappy as Bobby and wanted out just as much.

Mary never truly sat with the big question: Why? What had made marriage to Bobby so unbearable? It was far easier to accept what other family members said: Emily didn't care for the responsibilities of being a Kennedy wife. Mary could. She was born for it. So three weeks later, in April 1994, Mary and Bobby were married on a simple boat in the Hudson River, with no frills and no celebrities. A big life awaited her as a senator's wife, a governor's wife, and maybe, someday, First Lady. She gave up her job, would have three more children, and six years after the wedding Mary Kennedy found herself in a million-dollar house alone.

Bobby was never around. Ever. He didn't have a job that required travel, yet he traveled all the time. It was like a compulsion. Some days he'd be in three different states, giving speeches or taking meetings or . . . really, she didn't know what he was doing. His packed schedule signaled status, but it was all a façade. Bobby gave paid speeches and appeared on television and hobnobbed with the elite, but he was prone to outlandish beliefs. He could be a snob, even within the family itself. It mattered so much to him whether Ted, more than any other aunt or uncle, liked their children and made time for them. It mattered whether John and Carolyn liked him. It mattered that *he* mattered to the A-list Kennedys. Mary understood. It mattered to her, too. But the more her looks and smarts and elegance redounded to Bobby's benefit, the more he seemed to resent her.

Now her husband would rather be anywhere but with her. And when he did swoop in, he'd take one or all of the children off on some adventure and leave Mary behind. She was never invited. Mary had somehow become persona non grata, despite hosting all the dinner parties, the Fourth of July barbecues, the fundraisers, the celebrity-studded games of capture the flag. Uninvited, despite writing all the thank-you notes and RSVPs. Despite doing the day-to-day work of raising their children.

Despite pretending not to notice when she'd see the look on another woman's face, that look that said, *Oh my God, Mary, your husband is touching me under the table*, or *I've slept with him but it's in the past, it meant nothing*, or *It's still going on but let's all be adults about this.*

Mary didn't handle it well. You could say to yourself, *Who would?*, but of course there had been the dignified Jackie. There was Ethel, there was Rose. The question was never: *Why can't Bobby be faithful?* The question was always: *What's wrong with Mary?*

———

Gaslit. That's how Mary felt.

The more pain she was in, the worse Bobby treated her. Some days he wanted a divorce; others, he wanted to bring another woman into their bed, an idea that left her humiliated. She rejected him outright. One day Mary had a female friend over and Bobby sauntered in, right out of the shower, and dropped the towel around his waist, exposing himself.

Mary had long suspected he was cheating on her, but he would always deny it. He'd tell her she was crazy, that she was the one destroying their marriage and driving him away. Was it any wonder he never wanted to be home?

Then she found the diaries. Oh, the diaries. It was as if he was writing for posterity, for some future biographer. In Bobby's writings, Mary was either the perfect wife or an unhinged monster. There was no in-between in these pages, no nuanced portrait of his complicated, funny, observant wife, one who saw and understood far more than her husband knew. He accepted zero accountability for her anger. In fact, Bobby used it against her.

"Mary is being impossible," he wrote in one entry. "She refuses to do anything fun with me like snorkeling...and is deeply resentful when I do it myself."

She had been pregnant with their fourth child.

"Mary is out of control. She is angry now every day...She is not even remorseful but is filled with venom and retribution."

"Mary is continuing in her resolve to deal with anger and control...I am discovering the well of resentments I have against her."

"Mary on a rampage...She is really possessed by some terrible demon."

Not once did Bobby link her rage to his constant cheating, which was all over these pages. Had he left these diaries somewhere she was bound to find them? In the back pages of each book, under the heading "cash accounts," were lists of women, delineated by month, that Bobby had been with. He ranked them from one to ten, as if he were a teenager. Ten, Mary knew, was for full-on intercourse.

"My lust demons," he wrote, were his greatest failing.

He used the word "mugged" a lot — women who, he wrote, just came up to him on the street and said, *How about it?* If they had sex, he considered himself mugged, a passive victim of aggressive women.

There were so many — astronomical numbers, Mary said, and she knew a lot of them: The celebrated actress who came to their house and went on vacations with her family. The older model who was always around. The socialite whose husband was one of Bobby's good friends. A gorgeous royal. The wife of a very famous man. A lawyer. A doctor. An environmental activist. All these beautiful, accomplished women. How could Mary compete?

It wasn't just the womanizing. It was the way Bobby described being away from Mary as both respite and a constant battle to control his sex drive. The thirty days he spent in a maximum-security Puerto Rican prison for protesting navy exercises, he wrote, were among the happiest of his life. It was the summer of 2001, and Mary had just given birth to their fourth child, Aidan Caohman Vieques. The "Vieques" was for the Puerto Rican island where Bobby had been arrested for trespassing.

"I'm so content here," Bobby wrote of prison. "I have to say it. There's no women. I'm happy! Everybody here seems happy. It's not misogyny. It's the opposite! I love them too much." Not misogyny? Could have fooled Mary.

———

To stay married to Bobby would be self-abnegation. To stay would be to grind herself down into a woman with no needs or wants, without dignity, without equality in the relationship. And even then Bobby wouldn't be happy. He'd probably just have more contempt for her. But if they were to divorce, Mary would lose her entire identity—not just as a Kennedy but as person of importance. She had left the workforce when she married Bobby, and as their children grew older she found herself with entire school days to fill. What would she be without the fundraisers and the Kennedy summers on the Cape?

And so she clung to him. And the harder she clung, the more he pulled away. And the more distraught she became, weeping and drinking and struggling to get out of bed, the harder he turned on her. In 2012, after nearly twenty years of marriage, Bobby said he had enough and was moving out. Mary was nuts, Bobby said. Mentally ill. In need of serious psychiatric help.

Mary panicked. She worried that Bobby was beginning to lay the groundwork, to set her up as an unfit mother. It was what Kennedy men did—turn on their women when they were done with them, call them crazy. Dispose of them. And what would become of her? Money was tight. He'd taunt her with threats: *I'll take the house. You're going to be poor.*

The Bobby Kennedy Juniors weren't nearly as well-off as people assumed. Bobby had been one of eleven siblings, and the bulk of his father's money had been spent on the 1968 campaign for president. Bobby Jr. was augmenting his salary at the Riverkeeper Alliance with work as an adjunct law professor at Pace University, and he had his book deals and those speaking engagements, but none of it was enough to raise four children in the manner of senior Kennedys—let alone pay child support for the two children from his first marriage, or the gut renovation of their home.

When Mary gave interviews about that project—a creative and environmental triumph for her—she described the redone house as powered by geothermal energy, heat gathered from the Earth. It was a metaphor for the home Mary had always wanted: a self-sustaining, deeply rooted ecosphere, warmth spreading from the bottom up, an ever-renewing source of comfort. She had told Bob Vila that the decision to gut the home had been devastating for the children and for Bobby. To ease them through, Mary reframed it as "a process of salvage."

She was still trying.

Mary, though, would come to hate that house. Bobby had managed to get most everything done for free, but it still cost $40,000 per month to run and staff it. What was meant to be a private sanctuary had become a display case for fundraisers and events—and, ostensibly, their perfect family.

When Bobby had a film he wanted to show about Earth Day, a project that was a real point of pride for him, Mary arranged for a big party at the house. "A Conversation with RFK Jr.," she called it. Bobby would give a speech and they'd show the movie and he'd sign his books and be in his glory.

If only he had bothered to show up on time. If only he hadn't all but forgotten about it—all the work she'd done, all the luminaries and Kennedy admirers in their home. If only he had cared about how this would reflect on Mary. Those guests who knew her well could detect her anxiety: she was furtively looking at the door, then her watch, then the door again. When she finally got Bobby on the phone, he showed up and did what he did best: glad-handing, accepting praise, pocketing money, ignoring his wife.

It wasn't as if he were the only one to blame here. Even those close to Mary—much like those close to Carolyn Bessette—would admit she could be difficult. Very, very difficult.

Bobby was trying to rein in Mary's spending, her compulsive shopping. But she was trying to fill an emotional black hole with clothes, trips, private yoga sessions with a local teacher who was becoming one of her closest friends. That should have been a warning sign to Mary—that she was becoming so alienated from her actual friend group, from the social circles she usually moved in, that she'd come to rely on someone who provided paid services to her, with all the inequality that entailed. But Mary couldn't stand the idea of the Bedford moms or Bobby's other women, some of whom lived quite close by, knowing how undone she was.

So it was the yoga instructor who, one spring day in March 2012, came by the house to find Mary alone in the dark, curled up on her window seat, inconsolable. She seemed to have been crying for hours, just ugly-crying, and in her anguish Mary divulged Bobby's cheating. Her friend wasn't shocked. Everyone in Westchester knew about Bobby. The first time Mary's friend had met him, at the house with Mary, she could tell Bobby was sizing her up, seeing if she might be receptive to a flirtation right then and there. Maybe more. Her friend shut down, refused to engage on that level. Had Mary seen it? Her friend had no idea.

It wasn't just the cheating that had Mary so upset. She confided that after finding evidence of yet another affair, she'd become so hysterical that she'd run out of the house, gotten in her car, backed out of the driveway, and accidentally run over and killed Porcia, the family dog. Was she as bad, as hopeless, as Bobby seemed to think?

"I don't think I can go on," she said.

Mary had been seeing a therapist in the city—sometimes alone, sometimes with Bobby. Her name was Sheenah Hankin and she specialized in high-profile patients. When Bobby asked for Mary to be diagnosed as mentally ill, Hankin refused. Bobby had already tried to institutionalize Mary, driving her, at first without her knowledge, to the psychiatric wing of a local hospital. When Mary realized where he was taking her, she jumped out of the car, and Bobby followed. He tried to restrain her. Someone called the police, and when they showed up, Mary explained what was going on. Bobby argued he was afraid Mary would harm herself, and the cops said, in sum and substance: Take your wife home.

Your wife isn't mentally ill, Hankin told him. *She is angry and depressed and emotionally immature, but she is not ill. Do you have any idea what could be upsetting her?*

Of course not.

Hankin explained to Bobby that Mary likely suffered from borderline personality disorder, its origins Mary's deep fear of abandonment, probably stemming from her father's death when she was still a child. Mary's chronic spending, her constant insecurity and need for reassurance, her bouts of rage, were all hallmarks. Mary had never really grown up, and latching on to the Kennedys so soon after her father died, becoming part of Bobby's family as a teenage girl, had left her profoundly vulnerable to him. Mary needed Bobby much more than he needed her.

Her drinking, which was among Bobby's big complaints, was situational, Hankin said — another by-product of being left alone so often, for long stretches, by a husband who didn't come home when he said he would. Mary was trying to self-soothe, she explained, while punishing herself for not being the wife Bobby wanted. Hankin knew more about Bobby than she let on. She had another client, a woman, who had been at an event with Bobby and Mary, who'd said Bobby had come on to her very strongly. Yet another client, also a woman, had been seated next to Bobby on an airplane; they were strangers, but he came on to her, too, and fast. This client had embarked on a brief affair with him. So Hankin knew well Mary's torment.

When it was only Mary in session, Hankin tried to advise Mary. Gently but firmly, she would say: "You know, Mary, I don't think this is ever going to be the marriage you want. I don't think Bobby is ever going to be the husband you want."

Really, Hankin was saying: *Get out.*

It was the affair with an actress that tore Mary apart.

Bobby had filed for divorce in May of 2010 and had moved into a nearby house in Mount Kisco, New York. Mary couldn't bring herself to accept that Bobby was really leaving. He was the sun, the person she talked about all the time, "Bobby" this and "Bobby" that. Sometimes she wanted him back and others she reviled him. She told one friend that Bobby said the ugliest things to her — that she'd be "better off dead" and that things would be "so much easier" if she committed suicide.

Now she was seeing pictures of Bobby with Cheryl Hines, the star of *Curb Your Enthusiasm* and an age-appropriate match. When Hines was in New York, she was staying with Bobby and building relationships with their kids. No more parties at the Kennedy compound in Hyannis for Mary. No longer was she the fifth Kennedy daughter, as Ethel had called her all those years. And how could she consider Kerry her best friend now that Kerry was happily socializing with Bobby and Cheryl?

"They could destroy me." Mary said this about the Kennedys more than once. She had found what she thought was even more proof of his womanizing, the names of over forty women, some from Canada and Europe, stored in his cell phone. Not that it mattered. Cheryl, it became clear, wasn't going anywhere.

And so Mary drank, so much that she got arrested twice for driving under the influence. Her mug shots made the news: The once-refined Mary Richardson Kennedy, glassy-eyed with wild hair, in police custody. She was withdrawing from her everyday life, canceling her regular yoga classes. All but two of her friends had abandoned her. One accused Mary of being status-conscious of her own children, using their first and last names in conversation so that people would know she was a Kennedy. It took Mary aback; people wouldn't have dared speak to her like that if she and Bobby were still together.

Everyone knew what a mess she was. She could hear the other Westchester moms now: *Poor Bobby. Look what he's had to put up with all these years. No wonder he strayed—can you blame him? That Cheryl sure seems to have it together. Works with Larry David, no less! What a great couple. Well-matched.*

———

There was a story about Bobby. After he'd filed for divorce from Mary in May 2010, he had gone into the city for a deposition with her divorce lawyers. Someone brought in lunch, and when the day was done, Bobby got up and walked out the door, leaving his leftovers and crumbs and dirty napkins for someone else to discard. The trash bin was three feet from where he had been sitting.

One of the lawyers in that deposition thought it said everything about Bobby Kennedy Jr.: Entitlement. Arrogance. His trash was something for the help to take out, and that was how Bobby was treating Mary now. Mary's divorce lawyer echoed Hankin's advice.

"Get out," he said.

———

By April 2012, Cheryl was looking like the next Mrs. RFK Jr., and Kerry seemed all for it. She had posted a picture of Bobby, one arm around the actress Glenn Close and the other around Cheryl, taken at Glenn's birthday party. Mary had considered Glenn a dear friend, but for Kerry to share that on social media—that was thoughtless at best, cruel at worst.

The day before that, on April 14, Cheryl tweeted about dining at Mary's favorite haunt, a place she'd often taken her children. "At Armonk's Burgers & Shakes in Armonk, NY," Cheryl wrote. "So, soooo good." Then there was the gala in California, with Kerry tweeting a picture of Bobby and Cheryl with Jackson Browne, writing that the latter two "were amazing on stage and off." It was as if they were all saying to Mary: *Good riddance. You don't belong anymore. You're not missed,*

Bobby was making ruthless moves now. He cut off Mary's credit card, court-approved for $20,000 a month in living expenses. She owed $32,000 to American Express and had a balance of zero in her checking account. Her card was getting declined at the drug store, the supermarket, even her child's doctor's office. She was reduced to asking other moms at the school run if they had an extra $20 so she could get gas and groceries. The whole town knew she was broke.

Mary Kennedy, American royalty, had been dethroned.

One evening, not long after that California gala with Cheryl and Jackson Browne, Kerry came by to visit Mary. It was May 14, 2012, the day after Mother's Day. Whatever was said during that house call left Mary in tears.

———

Two days later, on Wednesday morning, Mary put on her yoga clothes and sandals, walked out to her barn, stacked three metal crates atop each other, then used a metal ladder to tie a hangman's knot around the rafter.

When she was found that afternoon, Mary's fingers were stuck inside the rope around her neck. She had changed her mind. She had tried to save herself.

———

The Kennedy Machine kicked into overdrive. Laurence Leamer, the famous Kennedy historian, was given access to Bobby's side of the story.

It ran in *Newsweek* just four weeks later, a radiant Mary on the cover, one of her toddler boys in her arms, the headline reading:

BEHIND THE MARY KENNEDY TRAGEDY.

Even the font size minimized her. This was a Kennedy story first, another family tragedy second, and Mary—well, Mary herself was something of a footnote.

The story inside, of course, absolved Bobby of any responsibility.

"Here was the womanizing Bobby," the story read, "always described as a former heroin addict, leading his innocent wife to her death, yet another victim of an overweening male ego—and he did so while flaunting his affair with actress Cheryl Hines, who played Larry David's wife on 'Curb Your Enthusiasm.' It was a juicy tale, lacking in nuance. But perhaps Bobby wasn't guilty. Perhaps nobody was guilty. Perhaps Mary Richardson Kennedy was, and had been for some time, a desperately sick woman. That's the portrait that emerges from a sealed, sixty-page court affidavit filed by Bobby during divorce proceedings, which I have reviewed in detail, and from interviews with those who were closest to Bobby and Mary, including medical professionals who treated her and said she suffered from a psychiatric disorder."

All of Mary's siblings, four sisters and two brothers, insisted that these claims were lies, that Mary's depression was a direct result of her husband's cheating and neglect, his threats to take the children and leave her with nothing, bringing the full weight of the Kennedy family to bear against her. Sheenah Hankin hadn't said that Mary was mentally ill. Nor had Mary's lawyer. Under circumstances like the ones Mary was under, you'd have to be crazy not to be depressed.

Two days after Mary hanged herself, Bobby and Kerry gave an interview to the *New York Times*. They said Mary was a disconsolate alcoholic. They spoke of her arrests and her suicidal ideations. "I feel like I've lost half my body," Kerry said, "half my soul."

"A lot of times I don't know how she made it through the day," Bobby said. Mary's siblings had been aware of her lifelong battle with depression, and in 1997 her brother Thomas sought to assuage Bobby Jr.'s fears.

"I know you think Mary's going to kill herself," Thomas reportedly emailed Bobby in 1997, "but I guarantee she won't. I may regret those words one day, but that's how I feel."

Yet Mary's siblings were infuriated by Bobby's talkativeness. There was no reason to defile her in death. There was no reason to give that sealed affidavit to a journalist if not to save Bobby's reputation at the cost of Mary's. Her brother wanted to take Mary's remains and bury her in Westchester, but Bobby fought them. He wanted her buried in the Kennedy family plot in Massachusetts. He took the matter to a judge and brought along one of his teenage sons as support for his argument, and he won.

And so there was a Kennedy funeral, with famous people there, of course, such as Chelsea Handler and Julia Louis-Dreyfus and Susan Sarandon. Mary's siblings stayed away. Bobby and Kerry gave eulogies. Three hundred people listened as Kerry spoke of Mary's demons, of Mary having lost her fight. Kerry also talked to the media in the parking lot outside St. Patrick's Roman Catholic Church in Bedford, where the service was held.

"I just think about the story of Michael the Archangel, who had to battle the forces of evil, had to battle Satan who was trying to enter paradise," Kerry said. "And that's what Mary did her whole life. She was battling, battling those demons and keeping them out of the paradise that was Mary."

In his eulogy, Bobby said he would never feel about another human being the way he felt about Mary. He said that Mary blamed him for "taking her away from her profession" to be a stay-at-home mom. "I know I did everything I could to help her," he said. In Bobby's telling, in the church and in the press, the real victim here was Robert F. Kennedy Jr., enduring such a mentally disturbed wife all these years, a depressive and a drunk who had been hospitalized for anorexia as a young woman, who had two previous suicide attempts in her past, and who, at a low point in their divorce, was found passed out at the dinner table, face down in a plate of food.

The funeral, though — that was elegant. The service ended with everyone singing "America the Beautiful," a nod to all that the Kennedys have sacrificed for the nation and their unique and enduring suffering. Outside the church, Bobby blew kisses to the press and the crowds.

———————

Mary's casket was loaded into a hearse and driven four hours from Bedford, New York, up to the Kennedy plot in Centerville, Massachusetts. Sixty-five mourners, including an aging Ted Kennedy, gathered at Mary's grave as the sun went down. Each of her children touched her coffin as Bobby looked on. Mary Richardson Kennedy was buried near Eunice Shriver, JFK's sister — given pride of place among the Kennedys, a public acknowledgment of her station.

One week later, in the middle of the night, without telling Mary's siblings or obtaining the required legal permitting, Bobby Kennedy Jr. had Mary's coffin dug up and moved seven hundred feet away. When reporters found out and asked why, Bobby, through family spokesperson Ken Sunshine, said, "The grave" — *the* grave, not *her* grave, another depersonalization — "is now on a sunny hillside, shaded by an oak tree with room for her children and other family." Bobby also said he failed to realize how crowded the Kennedy family plot was, a claim that strains credulity.

Mary was left to face traffic, no headstone marking her grave, buried alone.

KICK KENNEDY

Kick Kennedy was already famous when she arrived in England in 1938 at age eighteen, she and Jack the stars among US ambassador Joseph P. Kennedy's nine children. Old Joe favored her openly. "All my ducks are swans," he said. "But Kick is especially special."

When Jack met Jacqueline Bouvier some twenty years later, he was astounded at the similarities she had with Kick: the youthful stubbornness, the determination, the snobbery, the love of fashion and horseback riding and swimming. Kick, like Jackie, had gone from Debutante of the Year to a career in journalism. Like Jackie, Kick was distant from her mother but worshipful of her father. Her easy wit, her vivaciousness, made her the star of high society wherever she went, from Paris to London to America. Kick was Jack's equal in every way, except when it came to sex: her father left porn magazines on Jack's bed, open to particular pages, but her mother had a fit when Kick, still a virgin at age twenty-three, fell in love.

Kick and Billy were opposites in every way: he was tall, she was tiny. He was slow in thought, speech, and movement; Kick was electric. He had an aristocratic bearing and regard for politesse; Kick had no use for any of that, showing her affection through jokes and gentle mockery. She was American, he was not. She was Catholic, he was Protestant.

Kick was born Kathleen; he was born William Cavendish, Marquess of Hartington, heir to a mansion in London, a castle in Ireland, descendant of a seventeenth-century namesake who had helped to dethrone a Catholic king.

Together, they fit. He quickly became her Billy.

Kick was the American empress of the Jazz Age, a screwball heroine out of the Hollywood movies she adored, fond of throwing parties in her father's new residence, a crumbling old pile with fifty-two rooms and a basement where Joe stashed two thousand bottles of champagne. Her days were spent shooting grouse, cheering at the races, playing tennis, and attending garden parties at Buckingham Palace or luncheons at St. James's Palace. Her nights were spent in London's poshest clubs, theaters, restaurants; at cocktail parties in castles, with maids attending to tasks grand and small, squeezing toothpaste onto waiting toothbrushes that were angled just so.

Kick was among the beautiful and privileged youth of England partying at the edge of the world, losing themselves in midnight strolls through grand topiary mazes on even grander estates, young women in gowns of the finest silk or gossamer chiffon strolling through damp, verdant grass, swinging champagne bottles in one hand and lit cigarettes in the other, the shimmering stars strewn against a velvet night sky in a quiet that would not last. Each night they were drinking away the looming specter of Hitler and the approaching horrors. "All you can hear or talk about at this point is the future war which is bound to come," Kick wrote in September 1938. "Am so darn sick of it."

War would mean going back to the States. It would mean losing Billy.

Before Billy, Kick had a singular kinship with her mother, Rose; no other Kennedy child defended Rose from Joe's constant womanizing. Now, that loyalty seemed to mean nothing. Kick knew her mother might not approve of Billy's religion, but she never anticipated her mother's cruelty. She never anticipated her mother disowning her. After all, Rose's own parents hadn't approved of Joe Kennedy, but she'd married him anyway. Was this some particular grievance that Rose had against Kick? Was Kick too much like the boys — Jack, especially?

How could Rose believe in a God that would judge another based on mere denomination? And Billy's father was as aghast at the romance as Rose Kennedy. The Devonshires were anti-Catholic; Billy and Kick were, in essence, a Montague and a Capulet. How could their parents care about such things now, with their young lives at stake, the world as they knew it careening toward the abyss? For there was no question that when war came, Billy would serve in combat. There was also no question that Ambassador Kennedy would order his children back to the States, adults or not, once war broke out.

———————

In fall 1939, eighteen months after docking in England, Kick was back in America. Her first salvo was a thank-you letter to her father, "for giving me one of the greatest experiences anyone could have had." She did not reference the terror she'd experienced: in anticipation of the Blitz, London began going dark in September 1939, a zombie city at night, aerial bombings imminent. There was still nowhere she'd rather be, her London still a place where, as she wrote, "the moon shines through."

The moon was Billy.

Kick bided her time in New York, returning to her former life as "just a Kennedy girl"—no longer the brash American whose worldview had been broadened and deepened by her British friends, all of whom were won over by her *joie de vivre*, her unpretentiousness, her willingness to learn and change her mind.

Kick's greatest conflict with her father had nothing to do with Billy at all, but with Hitler and America's role in the war. Joe, as US ambassador to the United Kingdom, had sought to meet with Hitler and had encouraged appeasement with the Nazis; he thought democracy, in Western Europe and America, would soon be dead, and that Germany would establish a new world order—one that he in fact agreed with. Joe Sr. blamed the "Jew media" in the United States, as he wrote to Viscountess Nancy Astor, condemning their coverage of Hitler and his atrocities for setting "a match to the fuse of the world."

Kick's oldest brother, Joe Jr., admired the *führer* as well, writing that Hitler was smart to seize upon "a common enemy, someone of whom to make the [scape]goat . . . too bad it had to be done to the Jews. The dislike of the Jews, however," he continued, "was well-founded. They were at the heads of all the big business, on law etc. It is all to their credit for them to get so far, but their methods had become quite unscrupulous . . . The lawyers and prominent judges were Jews, and if you had a case against a Jew, you were nearly always sure to lose it . . . As far as the brutality is concerned, it must have been necessary to use some."

Kick's father was grooming Joe Jr. to run for president of the United States. But he would barely stand up for her and for Billy against Rose. Should she have been surprised? Catholicism wasn't their one true religion. Power was.

Kick returned to America believing, unlike her father and brother, that Hitler must be defeated. She was proud of Billy for enlisting, and frantic to see him. "At the moment it looks as if the Germans will be in England before you receive this letter," she wrote to Old Joe in May 1940. She reiterated her belief in Britain's moral and military supremacy.

"In fact, from reports here they are just about taking over Claridge's now," she continued. "I still keep telling everyone 'the British lose the battles but they win the wars.' I have received some rather gloomy letters . . . Billy's letter was written from the Maginot Line. Daddy, I must know exactly what has happened to them. Is Billy all right?" France's Maginot Line, a miles-long triumph of fortification, had been overrun by the Germans.

Jack, equally convinced that democracy would not survive World War II, wrote to their father on Kick's behalf. "Kick is very keen to go over," he said, "and I wouldn't think the anti-American feeling might hurt her like it might do us — due to her being a girl — especially as it would show that we hadn't merely left England when it got unpleasant."

Kick was no girl. She was a woman, braver than her brothers. But she took what she could get.

Kick couldn't just wait around like some incipient war widow. She dabbled in schools in New York and in Florida, and in 1941 got a job at the *Washington Times-Herald* as a research assistant. She found herself drawn to John White, a thirty-year-old reporter and inveterate debater. He was also a minister's son with a snake tattoo on his arm.

This guy was Kick's speed. Another rebel. Another apostate. White liked Kick a lot, but her dogmatic opinions surprised him. "Birth control is murder," she'd say. Premarital sex—that was out, too. How could such a firebrand be so...dogmatic? Everyone knew what the Kennedy boys got up to. Birth control was the least of it. White was even more surprised at how deferential Kick could be toward Old Joe, that she wasn't outraged when he ran background checks on her friends and suitors—something White knew about firsthand, because Old Joe had hired someone to investigate him.

Kick's brother Jack was allowed to date whomever he wanted, including their friend and colleague Inga Arvad. Rumor had it Inga—Inga-Binga to Jack—might be a spy for Germany, but did Old Joe care about that? No. He cared that Kick remained a virgin till marriage. And oh, how that frustrated John White. After they went out for dinner or a movie, Kick would sometimes allow John back to her place. She'd let him sit on her bed, rub her back, but nothing else. When White would press for more, Kick would only say: *That's the way it is.*

White tried to kiss her once. Kick shied away. "I don't want any of this, John," she said. "You must understand. Please don't try. I don't want the thing the priest says not to do." Whether because of her childlike affect or despite it, John fell in love with Kick. They shared newsroom banter right out of *The Front Page*. He called her "an ignorant, thick-headed mick," and she'd call him "a shrinking, bald-headed, irritable old man."

White often said that Kick was the most fun to argue with because she was always wrong. Kick kept circling back to that birth control argument, and that led her to thoughts of her friends back in England, who told Kick in cables and letters that sex was now the most defiant, life-affirming thing one could do. It led her to thoughts of Billy, and what sex might be like for them, what it would be like to see him again. "I am nearly going mad," she told her father.

Jack, now as pessimistic as his father, tried to talk Kick out of it. "I would advise strongly against any voyages to England to marry any Englishman," Jack wrote Kick, "for I have come to the reluctant conclusion that it has come time to write the obituary of the British Empire."

Yet by March of 1942, Jack was off to war. It took Kick another fifteen months, but her stubbornness paid off: on June 23, 1943, she boarded the *Queen Mary* as a new member of the Red Cross, headed to London. To Billy.

———————

They married on May 6, 1944, in a seven-minute-long civil ceremony. Kick wore a knee-length pink crepe dress with tea-length sleeves and a high neck, a copy of one of her own black dresses. Everyone she knew in England, even her milkman, had given Kick their clothing ration coupons for her modest wedding dress—a testament to how much they loved her, this young woman whose wealthy family was so withholding.

On her wedding ring Billy had inscribed, "I love you more than anything in the world."

Only one member of her family was present—her brother Joe Jr., who was serving in London. He had to defend himself for smiling in Kick's wedding pictures. "I saw no point in looking extremely grim throughout," Joe Jr. wrote the family, "so I looked as if I enjoyed it." As far as America was concerned, Joe thought Kick was now royalty, on her way to "dizzying heights of glory and power" as the next "first lady of the realm."

None of it impressed her mother. Rose had taken the advice of one of New York's top newspaper publishers and, as a means of boycotting Kick's wedding without seeming vengeful, had herself hospitalized for two weeks. And just in case anyone failed to get the message, Rose issued a statement that she was too "physically unfit to discuss the wedding with anyone."

When the news reached Kick, it devastated her. She didn't recognize this as histrionics, a temper tantrum meant to shame her. The day after the wedding, Joe Jr. sent his parents a one-line telegram meant to convey Kick's sorrow: "THE POWER OF SILENCE," he wrote, "IS GREAT."

———————

A sort of evil influence. So it was that Billy's father, the Duke of Cavendish, described Kick, even as she promised to raise her future children Protestant. But her beloved brother Jack was thrilled for her. Shortly after the wedding, he wrote to his best friend, Lem Billings: "As sister Eunice from the depth of her Catholic wrath so truly said, 'It's a horrible thing — but it will be nice visiting her after the war, so we might as well face it.'"

Kick had married the love of her life and, as Jack noted, Britain's most eligible bachelor. She was profiled in *Vogue* and approached by *Life* magazine for a story hailing the nuptials as "the greatest gesture for Anglo-American relations since the Atlantic Charter." It still wasn't good enough for Rose — status-conscious Rose, straining to be taken as more than mere lace-curtain Irish.

Kick and Billy had just a few weeks before he would be called back to duty. Their wedding night was spent at Compton Place, the Devonshire mansion adorned with Titian's Venus and Adonis — the armed warrior escaping Venus's embrace, Cupid asleep under the trees. A suite was ready and waiting for them, and Kick watched as Billy looked at the twin beds that had been pushed together and hastily pulled them apart. Kick later confided to two friends that her wedding night had been a disappointment, that Billy was terribly inexperienced. Oh, Billy. The soldier who ran in fear; the dashing bachelor who was probably a virgin.

They moved into a hotel while awaiting Billy's orders. Kick was going to make this marriage work, and she wasn't going to give Rose an inch of satisfaction; she wrote home of the peace that had come over her. "I am feeling better now than I have since I left America," she said. "This is the first really good rest I have had for a year. Have put on some weight" — a dig at her parents, who vocally detested the slightest weight gain — "and am getting plenty of sleep. MARRIED LIFE AGREES WITH ME!"

They had a brief honeymoon at the legendary Swan Inn, where they were given the best room — running water, a fireplace, dinner set out every night. They luxuriated in picnics and bike rides through the country, and fantasized about their lives after a war that was escalating beyond their summer fields, beyond comprehension.

Billy would die just four months after the wedding, killed in action by a German sniper. Rose was not sorry. Kick had returned to the States on August 16, upon learning that her brother Joe had been killed while flying a combat mission. Jack met her at the airport, and Kick collapsed in his arms. Now, not one month later, Billy, too, had been killed in combat, shot in the heart in Belgium. She grieved this fresh, unbearable loss keenly and mostly alone, her siblings acting as though nothing was amiss — except Jack. He sat up with her in a New York City hotel the night she learned of Billy's death. Jack said he'd never experienced a worse night.

"So ends the story of Billy and Kick," she wrote in her diary. "Life is so cruel." She treasured a letter Billy had written to her and reread it often.

"I have been spending a lovely hour on the ground and thinking in a nice vague sleepy way about you & what a lot I've got to look forward to if I come through this all right," he wrote. "I feel I may talk about it for the moment as I'm not in danger so I'll just say that if anything should happen to me I shall be wanting you to try to isolate our life together, to face its finish, and to start a new one as soon as you feel you can. I hope that you will marry again, quite soon — someone good & nice."

President Roosevelt and Prime Minister Churchill sent personal condolences, but these were small comfort. Even as a grieving young wartime widow, she was still, in her mother's eyes, a sinner. Rose's rejection stung all the more after Kick received a beautiful letter from Billy's mother, somehow strong enough to console this shattered young woman.

"I want you never, never to forget what complete happiness you gave him," she wrote. "All your life you must think that you brought complete happiness to one person. He wrote that to me when he went to the front. I want you to know this for I know what great conscientious struggles you went through before you married Billy, but I know that it will be a source of infinite consolation to you now that you decided as you did. All your life I shall love you — not only for yourself but that you gave such perfect happiness to my son whom I loved above anything in the world. May you be given the strength to carry you through these truly terrible months. My heart breaks when I think of how much you have gone through in your young life."

So Kick returned to England, to the bosom of Billy's family. She described herself as a small cork tossing around the ocean. Her eighteen-year-old sister-in-law Elizabeth slept on the floor beside Kick's bed for many nights.

Her father, in his way, tried to console her, lavishing Kick with gifts and even encouraging her to write a book. "Mother and I were talking it over last night," Old Joe cabled her, "and decided that nobody in the world twenty-five years of age has had the kind of life you've had or as interesting. If you haven't kept a good diary of all this material, you've robbed yourself of another thrill and that is writing a book. I'm sure you could make enough out of that to buy all the clothes and jewelry you want in Paris for many a year and, in addition, have a most interesting contribution to make to our literary field."

He sent her a diamond and sapphire watch. He bought an airplane so he could see Kick more frequently. And he gave her his ultimate gift: his blessing for her to stay in England, among Billy's family and friends, without guilt. She was free — finally, and at great cost — of the Kennedy directive. She was the lone daughter Joe encouraged to be independent and rebellious, ineffably herself, perhaps because he saw his best qualities reflected in her. Kick was unlike any of the Kennedy girls, Rosemary especially with her needs and limitations. Above all, Joe wanted Kick to find love again.

So London it was, and with that decision Kick embarked on her life's second act. Two days after what would have been her and Billy's first wedding anniversary, the war ended, and one year after that she met Lord Peter Fitzwilliam at a ball given for the elite wartime unit known as the Commandos, established at Churchill's request after the evacuation at Dunkirk.

Fitzwilliam eyeballed Kick, slim and elegant in a soft pink gown, then asked her to dance, his wife Olive's presence notwithstanding.

Kick and Fitzwilliam's connection was instant and intense. Her father and brothers had no problem dating married women; why should moral standards for her be any different? More importantly, whether she was conscious of it or not, for Kick, a dalliance with a married man meant a natural end: she could give of herself only what she could afford to lose. There would be no chance of devastating heartbreak, as with Billy.

Billy. Kick was still living with her in-laws, clinging to her old life. There were days, she said, when she felt Billy had been dead six years; others, six seconds. She was actively grieving still. But Fitzwilliam sparked something in her. Tall, dark, and ten years Kick's senior, he was a star in London's social set: convivial, stylish, brave—a war hero!—exceedingly wealthy. Dangerous. He liked fast cars, fast boats, and fast women. His family owned mansions in England and Ireland. He had a private plane. He bought racehorses and summered on the French Riviera. He could provide Kick with the travel and luxury to which she was accustomed.

And Fitzwilliam was more like her father and Jack than any man she'd ever met. He had infamously abandoned Olive on their honeymoon for another woman. He brought his mistresses home for dinner or shooting weekends and paraded them in front of his wife, whose job was to make sure they were well fed and cared for. And when Olive decompensated and became an alcoholic, she was blamed for making Fitzwilliam's life a misery, not the other way around. Really, who could blame a wealthy, dashing war hero for his many love affairs and one-night stands when he had such a difficult wife at home?

————————

Kick was supposed to be just another fling, but as it turned out, she was different. She was in thrall to Fitzwilliam, intellectually and sexually. As their affair deepened, Kick confided only in Jack, who listened raptly and came away thrilled for Kick but sad for himself: he had never been in love like that. He doubted he ever would.

Kick's friends and confidants, however, were alarmed. She was beginning to openly talk about marrying Fitzwilliam, which no one thought was a good idea. Their mutual friend Evelyn Waugh, the esteemed writer and himself a devout Catholic, tried to talk her out of it. "If you want to commit adultery or fornication & can't resist, do it," he wrote her. "But realize what you are doing, and don't give the final insult of apostasy." Her brother-in-law Andrew Cavendish was against it, as was the aristocrat David Ormsby-Gore, who would one day go on to romance another young widow named Jackie Kennedy. Ormsby-Gore told Kick that marrying Fitzwilliam would be a terrible mistake, that he was far too selfish and would make Kick's life hell. And to Rose, well — Fitzwilliam was an even worse choice than Billy. He wasn't just a Protestant but a soon-to-be-divorced one. If Kick married him, Rose said, she would consider her daughter well and truly dead.

Her mother's threat, the ugliest yet, did not have the desired effect; if anything, Kick drew closer to her father, certain that he would never abandon her. And indeed, Joe agreed to meet Kick and Peter in Paris, at the Ritz, on a Saturday afternoon in May. To celebrate, she and Peter decided to fly to Cannes before Paris. Kick was so excited that she packed two suitcases for three days, a wardrobe reflective of the sexual sophisticate she had become: expensive negligees and lacy underwear, heirloom jewelry gifted by the Duke and Duchess of Devonshire, a black garter belt, a douche, her birth control. No longer did Kick think contraception was murder or that sex, as the Catholic Church and her mother believed, was only for procreation. Billy's death and her mother's hypocrisy — just how Christian was it to disown your daughter for falling in love? — had dislodged all that doctrine. Kick knew how fragile life was now and had no intention of sacrificing a thing. She had been through a crucible and emerged a woman of the world so well regarded that she hosted Princess Elizabeth, the future Queen of England, and her sister Princess Margaret at the Cavendish estate. In a round-robin letter to her family back home dated October 20, 1946, Kick wrote:

"The two Princesses arrived last nite just before tea. They are very sweet but Princess Elizabeth is very royal and very hard to talk to. She has a sweet face but dresses so badly. Her evening clothes make her look much fatter than she really is."

For all the Kennedy ways of being that Kick shucked off, her obsession with weight and looks was not among them. For the plane ride to see her father in Paris, she chose a sleek, dark-blue suit, a strand of pearls, her rosary beads, and her wedding ring. As in love as she now was, Billy was always with her.

May 14, 1948. Upon landing in Paris at 12:45 p.m., Peter whisked Kick off to an impromptu lunch at the Café de Paris. They returned to the airport nearly three hours later, flushed and buzzed from their leisurely, boozy meal. To Fitzwilliam's consternation, Peter Townsend, their pilot, was refusing to fly. A massive storm had grounded all commercial flights; Fitzwilliam's plane was a tiny thing, a twin-engine ten-seater with two recently repaired propellers.

Meteorologists had forbidden a takeoff. Fitzwilliam insisted.

The last twenty minutes of that flight were so terrifying that everyone on board likely knew they were going to die. Their pilot lost communication with ground control and flew into the storm's eye. He couldn't tell if the plane was upside down, right side up, pulling toward the skies or plummeting to earth. A wing was shorn off. One engine fell, then the other. The tail detached. The little plane gained speed as it headed straight for a mountain.

It took first responders four hours to reach the crash site. Kick's high heels had flown off her feet and landed near the wreckage. Co-pilot Arthur Freeman, who had heroically tried to pull the plane out of its death spiral, had nearly lost a finger in the attempt; he was found, like Townsend, with devastating head wounds and a handkerchief stuffed in his mouth, a final desperate act meant to preserve the tongue upon impact.

Fitzwilliam was unrecognizable. Kick was found strapped into her seat, her back, her legs, pelvis, and jaw smashed. The wedding ring from Billy was still on her finger.

Joe Kennedy immediately took a train to the small French region of Ardeche to identify Kick. Before leaving, he memorialized his beloved daughter in his diary, which he doubtless knew would be published after his death.

HOTEL GEORGE V, PARIS {MAY 14, 1948}

> No one who ever knew her didn't feel that life was much better than
> that minute. And probably we know so little about the next world

that we must think that they wanted just such a wonderful girl for themselves. We must not feel sorry for her but for ourselves.

File JPK on Kick

Written by me 1/2 hr after notified of Kick's death

The Kennedys made no arrangements to bring Kick's body home. Her in-laws, with whom she had still been living at the time, offered to bury Kick in their own family plot. Joe agreed and was the only Kennedy to attend Kick's funeral. Jack was too distraught.

Rose took Kick's death as proof that she had been right. God had struck down her daughter — the sinner, the sexual savage. Rose flat-out refused to attend Kick's funeral and said Kick would be denied heaven and stuck in purgatory. Lem Billings was perhaps the only non-Kennedy to know Rose's true feelings.

"For her," he said, "that plane crash was God pointing his finger at Kick and saying, 'No!'"

Kick was buried alone in the English countryside. Her gravestone reads:

IN LOVING MEMORY OF KATHLEEN
1920 — 1948

She was given no last name.

PART FIVE

TED'S BLONDES

MARY JO KOPECHNE

He didn't even know how to spell her last name. While he stood behind Police Chief Jim Arena's desk — to Arena's surprise, Ted Kennedy was already running this investigation, making calls on his phone — he struggled to formally identify the young woman whom he had left in his car the night before, a car he'd left upside down in three feet of water after careening off a bridge.

Her name was Mary Jo. Ted could pronounce her last name, kind of, but he didn't know how to spell K-O-P-E-C-H-N-E. So Ted, in writing out his statement, just left that part blank.

It wasn't important, really. Ted knew that some other police officer or administrative clerk would figure it out and fill it in. He had one other, equally pressing question for Chief Arena: Would he go back down to the pond? Ted wanted to be sure that his black Chevy "got out and cleared okay."

The news reports to follow would only prove Ted right: in headline after headline, this would be called Ted's accident, and how lucky America was that Senator Ted Kennedy survived, narrowly escaping the Kennedy Curse. The young woman whom Ted left to die would be identified as "the blonde" or "the victim."

Decades later, even into the new millennium, historians and journalists and pundits would call this scandal, this callous disregard for human life, not by the dead woman's name but by its location: *Chappaquiddick*, a small Massachusetts island off the coast of Martha's Vineyard.

Before Ted calmly reported himself to Arena that morning, he had first called Mary Jo's parents. It was Saturday, July 19, 1969, a momentous weekend for the Kennedys. Three American astronauts were hurtling toward the moon, a seemingly impossible goal set forth by JFK in his 1961 inaugural address. If they survived, they would land on the moon's surface shortly before 11:00 p.m. that night. The eyes of the world were glued to live broadcasts, with 53 million Americans watching. The goings-on at some tiny shack on Martha's Vineyard were, at this moment, inconsequential. Mary Jo's mother Gwen answered the phone. Ted wanted to talk to her husband instead. Joe Kopechne wasn't home, but no matter. Gwen knew something was very wrong. She would not be getting off that phone.

"Mary Jo," Ted said, "was in an accident."

"Was it in a car?"

"It was an automobile accident," Ted said. "Mary Jo was returning to take a ferry back to the mainland when the accident occurred."

This language was too passive. Too officious. Gwen cut right to the point: Was her daughter dead?

Kennedy paused. "Yes."

Gwen remembered nothing else other than screaming. "Mary Jo's been killed! I'm alone here!" Gwen's cries were so loud that she woke a neighbor, who came in and found her in such hysteria that she smacked her in the face, more than once. Gwen did not feel a thing.

Mary Jo had been her only child.

Ted Kennedy gave Mary Jo's parents no details. They didn't know that Ted had been driving. They didn't know he had an expired license, had been drinking heavily, and had pitched his car, their daughter inside, into the shallow waters of Poucha Pond ten hours before. They didn't know that he had emerged from the water and walked over a mile, passing by several houses, at least one with the lights on, never knocking for help. Or that he had passed the local firehouse. Or that he had bypassed pay phones and never called the police or 911.

Her parents didn't know that the very next morning members of his staff could still smell alcohol on Ted's breath. Or that their daughter had been alive for hours, tossed upon impact into the back of the car, contorting herself upside down in the rear footwell, clutching at the back seat and craning her neck to breathe through a small air pocket.

They didn't know that John Farrar, the diver who pulled her body out of the car, quickly determined that she'd probably lived for at least an hour after the crash, and that had Ted gotten help, Mary Jo could have been saved. Or that, later, Farrar would describe Mary Jo as having been alone in the dark water, "re-breathing her own air," the oxygen turning to carbon dioxide, her "emotional trauma" overwhelming.

Mary Jo, even in death, was immaculate. She was found in her dark blue pants and long-sleeved white shirt, her jewelry—a ring and two gold bracelets—intact. She was not wearing underwear. Only her chain-link belt came apart as Farrar pulled her body from the car, her eyes and mouth open, her teeth clenched. Farrar would later describe that last hour of Mary Jo's life in unpitying detail. "Try putting a plastic bag over your head and breathing," he said. "Then try to imagine that bag being held over your head by a 300-pound wrestler and think of having to struggle to get out of that situation knowing you might be breathing your last . . . The anxiety that sets in is just unbelievable."

Gwen and Joe Kopechne didn't know that Mary Jo waited, in agony, for help that never came—and why wouldn't first responders be on the scene? Who would leave a young woman to die that way?

Ted Kennedy would.

After leaving the scene, the married senator went back to his hotel room in Edgartown, where he made seventeen long-distance phone calls to friends, advisers, his brother-in-law Steve Smith—known as the Kennedy family "fixer"—and Helga Wagner, whom friends described as the love of Ted's life. Around 2:30 in the morning, Ted complained to the front desk about guests in a nearby room who were having a party. The noise, he said, was disturbing his sleep.

Gwen and Joe Kopechne didn't know that the men in suits who quickly descended on their modest house in New Jersey were tried-and-true Kennedy men, the cleanup crew, there not to protect the Kopechnes from the press, as they claimed, but to make sure that Ted Kennedy emerged from this disaster with his bright future intact. Ted needed to walk away from this with no felony charges, no criminal or civil trial, no prison time, and no reputational damage whatsoever. He needed a clean path to his rightful inheritance: the Oval Office.

The Girl, as Ted would continue to call her—well, she was collateral damage.

Mary Jo had thought little of Ted Kennedy. As everyone on the Hill knew, Ted was a legendary drunk and womanizer who cheapened high office and degraded the slain president's legacy. She deeply admired Jack Kennedy, but it was Bobby whom she had really come to DC for — Bobby, she loved. Mary Jo had worked for him in the Senate, babysat his children, and went to Hickory Hill, his and Ethel's famed house in Virginia, for pool parties and speechwriting. She loved his children, Bobby Jr. especially, and Bobby Jr. loved Mary Jo, too.

She was so good with the children and so conscientious that Ethel asked her about taking on a nanny role. But Ethel had miscalculated. Yes, there was a part of Mary Jo that was deeply old-fashioned: she was a devout Roman Catholic who comported herself with modesty. She barely drank. She didn't smoke. She didn't appreciate bawdy humor. But she was also ambitious and independent, determined to carve a path that felt right for her. She had been the first in her family to graduate college — Caldwell College for Women, where married students were not allowed to graduate, where literal interpretations of the Old and New Testaments were taught, where premarital sex, indeed any sex outside of marriage, was considered a mortal sin that would damn you to hell for eternity.

Sex was a mystery to Mary Jo. Her church made it something to fear. She didn't have siblings — there was no one older to guide her, no one younger to rebel with. She didn't talk about sex with any of her friends. There was one boy in high school she was crazy about, probably her first real boyfriend, but when her friends tried to warn her that his preppy good looks masked a devious nature, she refused to believe it. And when she did finally break up with him, her friends never knew why — they could guess, but they would never dare ask. There were lines you didn't cross with Mary Jo. For all her enthusiasm and good nature, she held herself at a distance. No one she worked with knew her well. Neither did her friends or her boyfriends.

To look at her, a sunny blonde pixie in the trendiest clothes, you would never guess at her stubbornness, her seriousness. Mary Jo knew that she was pretty. She liked a party and loved to dance, and that was the only time anyone saw her out of control and un-self-aware: her dancing had a ferocity to it, as if everything she suppressed—her anger, her fears, her desires and sexual energy—used that single, socially acceptable expression to escape.

It was a burden, at times, being an only child, especially a girl. Her parents worried over her as if she would break. When she told them she wanted to teach on an Indian reservation, they begged her not to go. When she changed her mind and got a job teaching at a Catholic high school in Montgomery, Alabama—a flashpoint of the civil rights movement—her parents, again, begged her not to go. Every time they came to visit, they harped on every reason she should come back to New Jersey with them. It could feel infantilizing.

Mary Jo was twenty-two years old, and like so many young American women of her generation, she was a study in contrasts. She seemed meek but was driven. She was humble and grounded yet drawn to the glamour of the Kennedys, a family and a world to which she wanted to belong. She had a sharp mind and a lacerating wit but knew to hold back in polite company. Mary Jo was fearless when it came to her beliefs, and remaining a virgin until marriage was paramount among them, no matter how many men broke up with her over it. Not long after her move to DC, she had begun seeing a young law student named Owen Lopez. They were together for a couple of years, long distance, but when she would visit, Mary Jo would always insist on staying anywhere other than with Owen. Her devotion to God, the Catholic Church, and Bobby Kennedy, in that order, meant there would be no sex for this single girl who otherwise, in so many ways, was ahead of her time.

And anyway, men, for the moment, were a lesser concern: Mary Jo was building a foundation for her future as a working woman, actively contributing to bettering life for those who suffered—the poor, the minorities denied basic human rights, and, if she thought about it, women like herself. She considered her year teaching in Montgomery a kind of tithing, a gift of service and self-sacrifice before moving on to her larger goal: working for social justice on Capitol Hill. Ideally for Bobby Kennedy. And someday in the White House, after she helped make him president.

Bobby, to Mary Jo, was the country's best hope. It was he alone, of all the Kennedys and all the politicians, really, who cared about the things she did: poverty and racism and social inequity. Mary Jo called Bobby "The Answer."

Late summer 1963. Mary Jo's year of teaching had left her emotionally depleted. She had trouble creating boundaries with her students, and she found herself trying to solve all sorts of problems that extended beyond the classroom. She told her mother that she hadn't yet figured out how to help others while protecting herself. How could she share her talents, her essential goodness, without giving other people her entire being? When was it kind, to herself and others, to say no?

When she arrived in Washington that summer, she had hoped to work for President Kennedy, but Mary Jo didn't have the upper-class sheen, that boarding school, world-traveler hauteur that so appealed to JFK's snobbery. Mary Jo wasn't like Mimi Alford or Diana de Vegh. She didn't give off a knowing vibe, much less an available one. So instead she was offered positions with two other congressmen. One was with George Smathers, JFK's great friend in the Senate and at sea. Smathers, the one who had broken up Jack's party cruise in the Med after Jackie's stillbirth, telling her husband that he'd never be president if he stayed on that boat.

Mary Jo knew that Smathers and President Kennedy were close. So she went to work for him as a way of getting to the president, and when the president died, Mary Jo, heartbroken, persuaded Smathers to let her go work for Bobby instead. She had kept a framed photo of Bobby on her desk that whole time. How could Smathers say no?

His mission consumed her. Mary Jo worked harder for Bobby than she had for her beloved students, rising quickly from secretary to advance woman in charge of staging campaign stops to speechwriting aide to one of six so-called Boiler Room Girls, toiling in a windowless chamber as they tracked delegates around the country, worked up policy positions, and gathered and synthesized the kind of data that Barack Obama's team would use, much later and with much greater technology, to win the presidency.

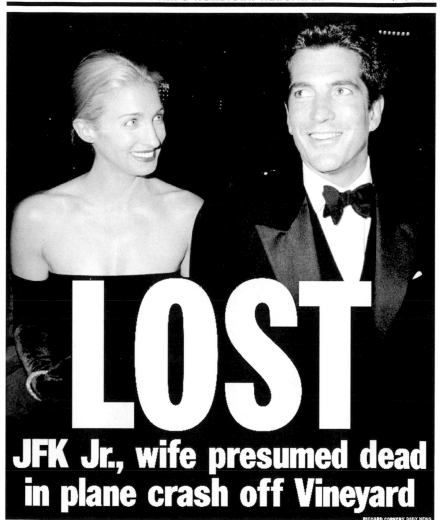

SPORTS ★ ★ ★ ★ FINAL

DAILY NEWS

$1.00   www.nydailynews.com   **NEW YORK'S HOMETOWN NEWSPAPER**   Sunday, July 18, 1999

LOST

JFK Jr., wife presumed dead
in plane crash off Vineyard

RICHARD CORKERY DAILY NEWS

(New York Daily News Archive/Getty Images)

A glowing John Jr. and a downcast Carolyn leaving a Kennedy family party in New York City, October 10, 1996. *(Douglas Healy/ Associated Press)*

A furtive Carolyn on the payphone at Martha's Vineyard airport; undated photo. *(Kevin Wisniewski/ Shutterstock)*

A young Jacqueline Bouvier—maybe fourteen years old—with her father, John "Black Jack" Vernou Bouvier III, and grandfather John Vernou Bouvier Jr. *(CSU Archives/Everett Collection/Bridgeman Images)*

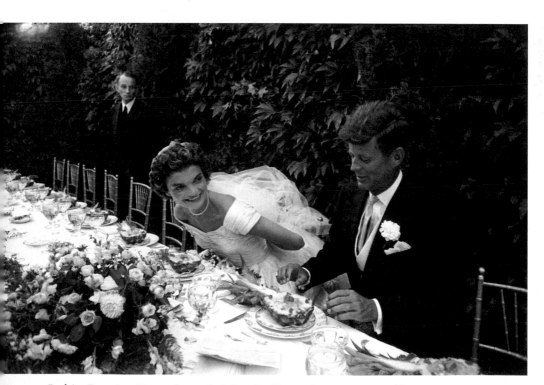

Jackie Bouvier Kennedy and John F. Kennedy at their wedding reception at Hammersmith Farm, her mother and stepfather's Rhode Island estate, September 12, 1953. *(Lisa Larsen/The LIFE Picture Collection/Shutterstock)*

Jackie, blood-spattered and in shock moments after JFK's assassination, stands next to Lyndon Johnson as he takes the oath aboard Air Force One. The repeated suggestion that she change into a clean white dress for this photo op outraged her. "Let them see what they have done," she said. *(Cecil Stoughton, White House)*

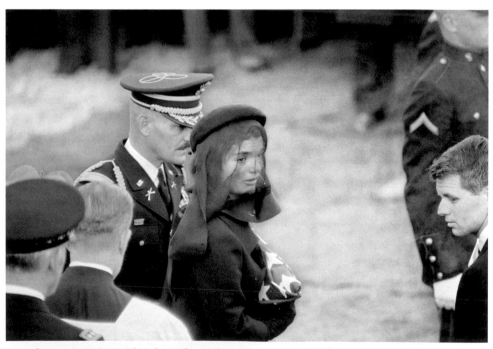

The formerly sphinxlike, beatific Jackie Kennedy lets the nation see her devastation at JFK's funeral. It was a rare moment of vulnerability for a woman who otherwise described herself and the president as "twin icebergs." *(Elliot Erwitt/Magnum Photos)*

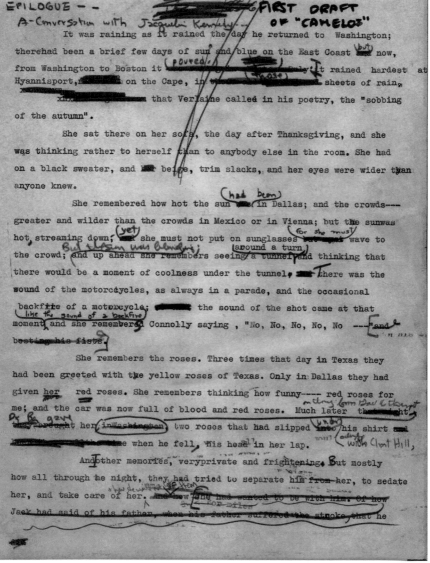

The first draft of "Camelot," Jackie's largely fabricated account of her husband and his administration, just one week after the assassination. She summoned presidential historian Theodore White to interview her for *LIFE* magazine with the caveat that she would have final edit. Her strikethroughs and notes are testament to a woman sick of history as told by men; an underestimated mind with a keen understanding of mythology; and the savvy New York City book editor she would become. (*Estate of Theodore H. White*)

A flirtatious Jackie says goodbye to brother-in-law Robert F. Kennedy, who casts a look back next to wife, Ethel. Years after Bobby's assassination, his lengthy affair with the newly widowed Jackie came to light — too scandalous for the Kennedy-loving media to report then, it was a relationship that today would be considered a trauma bond. *(Bettman/Getty Images)*

Jackie's 1968 marriage to Greek shipping magnate Aristotle Onassis scandalized the world — as she hoped it would. It also liberated her to reinvent herself, and this new incarnation, Jackie O., was a jetsetter in Chanel who began to truly enjoy her fame. Nothing says luxury, after all, than a bespoke limousine carpeted in fur. *(Left: Bettman/Getty Images. Right: Bridgman Images)*

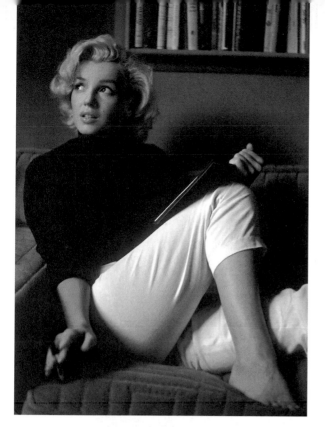

Marilyn Monroe, the world's most famous sex goddess, wanted more than anything to be considered smart. Her simultaneous affairs with President John F. Kennedy and Attorney General Robert F. Kennedy gave her more validation than she could have dreamed—for a time. Their use and abuse of Marilyn, seen here in the only known photo of the three, led to her premature death, under mysterious circumstances, at age thirty-six. *(Top: Alfred Eisenstaedt/The LIFE Picture Collection/Shutterstock.*
Bottom: Cecil Stoughton, White House)

A somber Marilyn, seeming to restrain herself from speaking, shot by the legendary photographer Bert Stern weeks before her death at thirty-six years old. As a book editor decades later, Jackie Kennedy Onassis, aware of JFK and Monroe's affair, excitedly suggested bidding on Stern's book of Monroe photos called *The Last Sitting*. She was likely unaware that Monroe had also posed in a dark wig that recalled Jackie as First Lady. (*Marilyn Monroe, Black Dior Dress,* The Last Sitting® *1962 ©bertsterntrust*)

For her work, which extended to nights and weekends, Mary Jo earned $7,500 a year. Her male counterparts were earning twice that.

Mary Jo was Bobby's star, the sharpest and most dedicated of his junior staff. She was so pretty that her office nickname was Twiggy, like the ultra-mod, doe-eyed model. Behind her back the other women called her a prude. Yet as Bobby's profile ramped up and his candidacy for president was announced, rumors circulated, in New York and DC, that he and Mary Jo were having an affair.

It wasn't that outlandish: Mary Jo and Bobby did travel together while campaigning and they did stay in the same hotels. It was no secret that Mary Jo was in love with Bobby. The men she dated knew they couldn't compare. For Mary Jo, Bobby Kennedy and whatever he or his family needed came first.

She'll never marry me, one boyfriend told Mary Jo's father. *She's married to the Kennedys.*

The boyfriend was right.

If Mary Jo heard the rumors about her and Bobby sleeping together, she never said a thing. Whispers like that were just another way to discredit women who were outperforming men. Mary Jo knew her value, and she knew that if Bobby won the White House, there was no doubt he'd be taking her with him. How many junior male staffers did Bobby hold in similar esteem? *She* was the one weighing in on drafts of his speeches. *She* was the one who could mock him and get away with it. "Everything you've ever wanted," she told him after his staff gifted him a globe. "The whole world."

Bobby laughed. He loved it.

Mary Jo's irreverence and self-deprecation delighted him. She knew she wasn't one of the cool kids and didn't try to compensate; instead, she would joke about how square she was. This endeared her to Bobby, who by turns could be shy, mean-spirited, compassionate, vengeful, empathetic, religious, unfaithful, ruthless, a marvel with little children, and the most attentive listener one could hope for. He gifted Mary Jo a framed photo of herself at her desk, the back of her head to the camera.

"You work so hard," he inscribed, "this is the only way I ever see you."

Mary Jo had a guileless view of the world: There was right and wrong, good and evil, heaven and hell. She still kept dolls and stuffed animals in her childhood bedroom, right under more photos of JFK and Bobby. Bobby, to her, was all good. In turn, he spared Mary Jo the worst of himself.

Yet she was also born for politics and understood all that came with it: compromise, moral and otherwise; the massaging of inconvenient truths; the power of images and how to manipulate them. She was drawn to the counterculture and obsessed with the musical *Hair.* On an advance trip to Wilkes-Barre, Pennsylvania, in the fall of 1966, it was Mary Jo who figured out that Bobby's designated speaking location needed to be moved so that television cameras would capture even a small crowd looking like ten thousand fans.

Bobby was the Beatles. Mary Jo understood how to make him so — how to cut through his earnestness, his tragic legacy and self-seriousness. When he announced his run for president of the United States on March 16, 1968, it became her mission to get the American electorate to see Bobby as she did: The Answer.

———————

June 5, 1968, Los Angeles, 12:02 a.m. Mary Jo was at the Ambassador Hotel when Bobby finished addressing his supporters in the Embassy Ballroom. The California primary results were in and Bobby was the leading Democratic candidate, ahead of his nearest rival by 7 percent. Lyndon Johnson, who had succeeded Jack after the assassination, had announced he would not be seeking a second term. The nation had been further traumatized by the escalating war in Vietnam and the assassination of Martin Luther King Jr. on a Memphis hotel balcony on April 4. Bobby was poised to be a bookend of healing, the younger Kennedy brother who was preaching unity and grace.

It was Bobby who had broken the news of MLK's death to a largely Black crowd of thousands in Indianapolis, and who, despite his inordinate privilege, helped ease the collective shock. Wearing a black overcoat that had belonged to Jack, Bobby quoted a passage from Aeschylus that meant a great deal to him. "He once wrote: 'Even in our sleep, pain which cannot forget falls drop by drop upon the heart, until, in our own despair, against our will, comes wisdom through the awful grace of God.'

"What we need in the United States is not division; what we need in the United States is not hatred; what we need in the United States is not violence or lawlessness; but love and wisdom, and compassion toward one another, and a feeling of justice toward those who still suffer within our country, whether they be white or they be black . . .

"Let us dedicate ourselves to what the Greeks wrote so many years ago: to tame the savageness of man and to make gentle the life of this world. Let us dedicate ourselves to that and say a prayer for our country and for our people."

It was a speech Bobby himself had cobbled together on the fly, yet it was the most heartfelt and impactful of his political career. It was that kind of humanity that was going to make him the next president of the United States.

———————

"So my thanks to all of you," Bobby said in his LA victory speech, "and on to Chicago and let's win there." It was his last line of the night, the crowd at the Ambassador going crazy for him, chanting "We want Bobby!" over and over. He was meant to be safe among his people, yet two of America's most prominent Black athletes, friends of Bobby's, had volunteered to bodyguard him that night: Rafer Johnson, the two-time Olympic decathlete, and former NFL lineman Rosey Grier. Despite what had happened to Jack, presidential candidates were still not afforded Secret Service protection. Bobby had mentioned both men in his speech.

"To my old friend, if I may, Rafer Johnson is here," Bobby said. "And to Rosey Grier, who said that he'd take care of anyone who didn't vote for me."

Bobby began making his way to the Ambassador's back exit through the kitchen. Ethel, who had been by his side as he spoke, was trailing just behind. Reporters, busboys, and kitchen staff surrounded him, as did photographers and television cameras. The dispersing crowd outside could hear what sounded like a thump, but no one blanched. "RFK!" they chanted. "RFK!"

That thump had been the first of three gunshots. Now Bobby Kennedy lay on the kitchen floor, bleeding, as Johnson and Grier subdued the gunman. A seventeen-year-old immigrant busboy from Mexico named Juan Romero cradled Bobby's head as he struggled to speak. His lips were moving but no words came out. Romero lowered his ear to Bobby's mouth.

"Is everybody okay?" Bobby asked. His blood was pouring through Romero's fingers.

"Yes," Romero said. "Everybody's okay." He took his rosary from his shirt pocket and wrapped it around Bobby's right hand while holding Bobby's head off the cold concrete floor.

Bobby turned his head slightly. "Everything's going to be okay," he said.

On June 6, at 1:44 a.m., after one day in intensive care at LA's Good Samaritan hospital, Robert F. Kennedy was pronounced dead. He had been shot three times, the fatal bullet through his head. His assassin, Sirhan Sirhan, later said that he killed Bobby for his pro-Israel views and for contributing to the persecution of Palestinians.

Bobby's death was yet another national trauma. His campaign itself, which prioritized civil rights and the eradication of poverty, had been a balm after the assassinations of JFK and MLK. Bobby Kennedy had allowed—encouraged, really—America once again to look to the future with hope, to reject the carnage of the 1960s.

Now Bobby was another victim of that carnage. His body was flown back to New York City; thousands lined up to view his casket at St. Patrick's Cathedral before it was taken by train to Washington, where thousands more stood along the route and saluted. Ted Kennedy, the last surviving Kennedy brother, eulogized him—a eulogy written not by Ted himself but Kennedy speechwriters. This eulogy came to define Bobby's legacy:

"My brother need not be idealized, or enlarged in death beyond what he was in life; to be remembered simply as a good and decent man who saw wrong and tried to right it, saw suffering and tried to heal it, saw war and tried to stop it . . . As he said many times, in many parts of this nation, to those he touched and who sought to touch him:

"'Some men see things as they are and say: why?

"'I dream things that never were and say: why not?'"

———————

Mary Jo's grief in the wake of RFK's death was even more paralyzing than when JFK had been killed in 1963.

She traveled on Bobby's funeral train. She helped packed up his office, a task that, in its enormity and finality, took months. One day she sat at her desk for hours, staring straight ahead and not moving, not saying a word, leaving her colleagues to ask if she needed help getting home.

When all that work was done, Mary Jo Kopechne, rising star, moved away from DC.

She didn't want to be there without Bobby Kennedy. "I just feel Bobby's presence everywhere," she said. "I can't go back because it will never be the same again." She still loved politics, but there was no longer a future for her on the Hill. Whom would she work for? Certainly not Ted. He was unserious, the runt of the Kennedy litter, kicked out of Harvard for cheating. He was a sybarite whose sweet, beautiful wife, Joan, served two purposes for him: as a stay-at-home mother to their three young children and as a campaign prop. Mary Jo knew Joan and liked her and thought she was so kind and pretty. Poor Joan. Surely she had heard the stories about Ted's other women. Then again, even Kennedy wives were a bit starstruck by their husbands. Why would Joan be an exception?

As it was, everyone thought Mary Jo, too, was worshipful around the Kennedys. Even the family thought so — and this wasn't specific to Mary Jo. They had a phrase they used for their most devoted staffers: "Honorary Kennedys." Like it was special dispensation to be in their orbit, even more so to be considered one of them. But anyone who wasn't blood would never truly be one of them, no matter how many sacrifices they made, no matter how many injuries to their own egos, their own dignity. It was a lesson their most ardent loyalists would learn for themselves, often in unique and brutish ways.

The truth was that most of the Kennedys weren't that special. After Bobby died, their true stars — save Eunice, who had a political mind to rival her brothers, but who, alas, was a woman—were gone. As for the wives? Jackie was the most famous, but she'd shed her widow's weeds, and with Bobby dead—oh, how Jackie loved Bobby—she seemed hell-bent on getting out of the family and out of America. No: power was for the Kennedy men exclusively, and now only Ted was left—the youngest of all Rose and Old Joe's children, the son with the least potential. Mary Jo didn't want to work for him or advise him. She certainly didn't want to date him.

———————

Martha's Vineyard, June 19, 1969. The Boiler Room Girls, along with some older male Kennedy loyalists, were gathering to mourn Bobby and commemorate all they had done for him. Mary Jo had been working for another politician and was due in South Carolina, but at the last minute found someone to take her place.

She called her mom before heading to the Vineyard. She had big news to share, she said, three major life decisions she'd just made: First, she had been offered a job at Matt Reeves Associates, the top political consulting firm in the country. They were doubling her salary to $15,000 a year and she was taking it. Her career was heading exactly where she wanted it to go.

Then Joe picked up the phone in another room, and suddenly the dynamic was off. Whatever else Mary Jo had to confide, her other pieces of news—was she marrying the man she'd been seeing, the foreign service officer they'd yet to meet? Mary Jo and Owen had broken up before Bobby was assassinated; for Owen, the distance was a hindrance, as was Mary Jo's refusal to have sex. Whatever else Mary Jo had to share, she kept it to herself once her father joined the call.

The party on the Vineyard that Saturday night was sad all around. Later, when it became the subject of news reports and speculation, much would be made of all these young, single girls drinking and carousing with older married men. So many questions as to the character of these women, and Mary Jo especially: Were they drunk? Sleeping with Ted Kennedy or his staff? What was Mary Jo doing, going off alone in a car with Ted Kennedy, midnight approaching, leaving her handbag and hotel room key behind? What could Ted and Mary Jo possibly have been doing between the time they left the party and the time an eyewitness saw Ted's car heading toward the ferry—an hour and a half later at around 11:20 p.m.? Why was alcohol found in her system—after all, hadn't everyone who had known her said that Mary Jo hardly ever drank? Which was it, then? Was Mary Jo a perfect Catholic angel or a secret party girl with a Kennedy fixation? Ted said she had asked to leave with him, so clearly she was after one thing, right? And when the detail some-how leaked that Mary Jo's body was found without underwear—well, didn't that say it all? No matter that tests for sperm came back negative.

All these contradictions led the Massachusetts Southern District Attorney Edward Dinis to request, in August 1969, an exhumation of Mary Jo's body for an autopsy.

Mary Jo's mother was horrified. "I don't want my little girl's body dug up," she said. "My tiny, lovely baby.

"Mary Jo was left in the water for nine hours," she said. "She didn't belong there."

———

Ted had been drinking the afternoon of the crash, sailing in a regatta. That evening he had taken a bath, had his fourth rum and coke, and then began making his way over to the small, two-bedroom rented cottage in Chappaquiddick where this gathering was in effect, the mourners drink-ing and smoking cigarettes in this spartan, dingy house. The grill was so tiny that everyone settled for sausage and cheese hors d'oeuvres. There wasn't even any music—one of the girls had to venture into town to find a radio. Really, it was a bunch of sad, middle-aged men moping around and drinking heavily—hardly the kind of grand affair one would associ-ate with the Kennedys, but to Ted, as always, a party was a party.

And a pretty young blonde was just another pretty young blonde, like this one who had asked for a ride back to the inn.

Or had she? That was Ted's testimony, delivered in grandiloquent ver-biage at the inquest on January 5, 1970: "She indicated to me that she was desirous of leaving, if I would be kind enough to drop her back at her hotel." Mary Jo's close friends doubted that; they thought it far more likely that Mary Jo, who had said she felt queasy from too much sun that day, went into the back seat of the black Oldsmobile to nap, and that Ted, drunk and unaware she was in his car, took off. That, they said, was the more likely explanation as to why her handbag and hotel room key were left behind; Mary Jo, a stickler for detail, had not intended to leave.

Then again, maybe Mary Jo *had* asked for that ride. The last ferry from Chappy to Edgartown left at midnight. Maybe she looked around and saw that no one else was in the mood to leave and hadn't wanted to crash on a hard, dirty floor. Maybe in her haste she simply forgot her bag and key, and those could easily be recovered the next day; the front desk would surely give her a spare.

And who better to hitch a ride with than Ted, who knew the island so well? It could be confusing and scary at night — few street lamps, unpaved roads, no lit signs, no way to know where you were going, really, unless you already knew where you were going.

On the way back to the ferry that night, Ted was going way over the twenty-mile-per-hour limit, flying down Chappaquiddick Road before veering onto a dirt path called Dike Bridge Road. It was rough and narrow, a road to nowhere. Ted was gunning the car so fast that by the time he felt the road give way beneath him, tires rolling over the planked-wood bridge, no guardrail on either side, he had steered his black Oldsmobile Delmont 88 off the right side and plunged into the water, where the car landed upside down. The force of impact caved in the windshield.

At the inquest, Ted detailed the moment before losing control. He put Mary Jo in the passenger seat.

"I recall . . . the movement of Mary Jo next to me, the struggling, perhaps hitting or kicking me. And I, at this time, opened my eyes and realized I was upside down, that water was crashing in on me, that it was pitch black. And I was able to get a half gulp, I would say, of air before I became completely immersed in the water. I realized that Mary Jo and I had to get out of the car.

". . . I can remember the last sensation of being completely out of air and inhaling what must have been a half a lung full of water and assuming that I was going to drown. And the full realization that no one was going to be looking for us until the next morning, that I wasn't going to get out of that car alive, then, somehow, coming up to the last energy of just pushing, pressing and coming up to the surface. I have no idea in the world how I got out of that car."

Mary Jo was still alive. If Ted — strapping, athletic six-foot-two inches, an excellent swimmer — could get himself out, surely he could rescue Mary Jo.

He tried, he said. The water only came up to his waist, and he said he dove again and again. "I was doing everything that I possibly could to get the girl out of the car," Ted said.

The Girl. The Blonde. The next day's headlines:

"TEDDY ESCAPES; BLONDE DROWNS."

Those words were buried under the top story, JFK's dream realized, the front pages of every newspaper in America with astonishing images:

"MEN WALK ON MOON."

The American flag had been planted there. All the astronauts survived. The country was turning toward futurism again, and hope. What was Brand Kennedy if not those very things? If Ted could tap into the regard felt for Jack and Bobby, could lean into his promise as the last Kennedy brother and the bridge, as it were, to a new decade — well, maybe he had a good shot at getting out of this. Better than good, actually.

"My head was throbbing and my neck was aching," Ted testified. "I was breathless and, at that time, hopelessly exhausted." Ted said he gave up and floated the fifty or so feet to shore, then rested for about twenty minutes before jumping back into Poucha Pond — not to rescue Mary Jo, still struggling to breathe, but to swim the length of two-and-half-football fields, through a tide he later called brutal, back to shore. Once there, he passed several cottages, their lights still on, and ran all the way back to the party house. There he stood, dripping wet, issuing one command.

"Get me Markham!" This was Senator Paul Markham, a former US prosecutor for Massachusetts. He was Ted's other fixer.

Ted's cousin Joey Gargan was also summoned. "There's been a terrible accident," Ted said. "The car's gone off the bridge down by the beach, and Mary Jo is in it."

The three men piled into a Plymouth Valiant parked outside and raced to the scene. Gargan and Markham stripped down and went into the pond while Ted stood on the bridge and watched as they tried to save Mary Jo. But they weren't trained first responders; they had no idea how to execute a water rescue.

"Oh, my God," Ted said, looking up at the night sky. "What am I going to do? What am I going to do?"

Against the advice of the smartest Kennedy advisers, current and former, Ted decided to deliver an emergency televised address one week after the crash. For most of these men, it was a real reckoning with the Kennedys: to a one, they had been repulsed that Ted asked why he couldn't say Mary Jo had been driving that night. JFK's most venerated speechwriter, Ted Sorenson, wrote Ted's address to the nation. It went, in part:

> I made immediate and repeated efforts to save Mary Jo by diving into the strong and murky current but succeeded only in increasing my state of utter exhaustion and alarm. My conduct and conversations during the next several hours, to the extent that I can remember them, make no sense to me at all.
>
> Although my doctors informed me that I suffered a cerebral concussion, as well as shock, I do not seek to escape responsibility for my actions by placing the blame either on the physical and emotional trauma brought on by the accident, or on anyone else.
>
> I regard as indefensible the fact that I did not report the accident to the police immediately.
>
> Instead of looking directly for a telephone after lying exhausted in the grass for an undetermined time, I walked back to the cottage where the party was being held and requested the help of two

friends, my cousin, Joseph Gargan, and Paul Markham, and directed them to return immediately to the scene with me — this was sometime after midnight — in order to undertake a new effort to dive down and locate Miss Kopechne. Their strenuous efforts, undertaken at some risk to their own lives, also proved futile.

All kinds of scrambled thoughts — all of them confused, some of them irrational, many of them which [*sic*] I cannot recall, and some of which I would not have seriously entertained under normal circumstances — went through my mind during this period. They were reflected in the various inexplicable, inconsistent, and inconclusive things I said and did, including such questions as whether the girl might still be alive somewhere out of that immediate area, whether some awful curse did actually hang over all the Kennedys, whether there was some justifiable reason for me to doubt what had happened and to delay my report, whether somehow the awful weight of this incredible incident might in some way pass from my shoulders . . .

Today, as I mentioned, I felt morally obligated to plead guilty to the charge of leaving the scene of an accident. No words on my part can possibly express the terrible pain and suffering I feel over this tragic incident. This last week has been an agonizing one for me and for the members of my family.

Ted Sorenson forever regretted writing that speech, which did little to help Ted's case. After its broadcast, polls showed that 51 percent of Americans did not believe him.

———

At the inquest, John Farrar, the diver who recovered Mary Jo's body the next afternoon, testified that Mary Jo had not drowned but had suffocated to death. He said she had been alive for at least an hour in the water, maybe longer.

That didn't matter to Ted. He was sticking to his story.

"Was there any particular reason," prosecutor Edmund Dinis asked Ted, "why you did not call either the police or the fire department?"

"Well," Ted testified, "I intended to call for assistance and report the accident to police within a few short moments of going back into the car."

"Did something transpire to prevent this?"

Ted dodged the question. Instead, he became most talkative about his own physical pain, self-pity, fear, and a childlike belief that the whole problem — Mary Jo's death and his responsibility for it — would just go away. He was afraid, he said, to call Mary Jo's mother. "I just couldn't gain the strength within me, the moral strength, to call Mrs. Kopechne at two o'clock in the morning and tell her that her daughter was dead."

Instead, he called Helga Wagner.

Then he went back to his room at the inn, and despite being seen by multiple witnesses at breakfast the next morning, freshly showered and shaved, neatly dressed, composed and with a healthy appetite, Ted insisted he had not slept the night before, tossing and turning and pacing, overwhelmed by "the tragedy and loss of a very devoted friend" whose last name he was unsure of and whom he had left at the bottom of a pond.

In the immediate aftermath of the crash, Bobby's widow, Ethel, was deputized to call Mary Jo's parents. Ethel told them, as a recent widow and fellow Catholic who had welcomed Mary Jo into her and Bobby's home many times, that she knew loss, that faith was a comfort, and that — rest assured — the Kennedys would be attending Mary Jo's funeral.

On July 22, 1969, hundreds gathered to watch Mary Jo's funeral procession in Plymouth, Pennsylvania. In Catholic tradition, hers was an open casket. Mary Jo was dressed in a long blue gown, reminiscent of the Virgin Mary. A rosary was laced between her hands.

In the front pew sat Ted, wearing a neck brace he did not need, and Joan and Ethel Kennedy. Joan had been told by her doctors not to fly, that her pregnancy was too fragile, but she defied them. What would the press think if she didn't go? Her absence would only fuel the rumors that Ted was having sex with Mary Jo or had planned to that night.

Yet Mary Jo, in American media, was still nameless. She was "The Victim Drawn to Politics" (*New York Times*), "The Girl in Ted Kennedy's

Car" (*Ladies' Home Journal*), "The Blonde Who Drowned" (*New York Daily News*), the expendable woman whose death "made Ted a man" (*New York Times*) yet might keep him from becoming president.

Ted had promised to tell Joe and Gwen Kopechne what happened that night, when he was ready. Her parents were dissuaded from exhuming Mary Jo's body and from suing Ted Kennedy, afraid of what it would do to all of their reputations. As the years passed with no explanation or answers, and no justice for their daughter, Gwen began self-medicating with Valium. Her father, who kept all his anguish bottled up, eventually developed stomach cancer. They spent their lives tending to Mary Jo's grave and her memory while fielding calls from Ted Kennedy every few years, asking them to quietly support his latest election bid. As ever, Ted would hold out the empty promise that someday, one day, he would tell them the truth.

The Boiler Room Girls refused to talk to Gwen and Joe about Mary Jo's last weekend alive, or what they saw and heard in the aftermath. None told Mary Jo's parents why some of them remembered seeing her leave the party that night at different times, or not at all, only to recall in official testimony, one by one, seeing Mary Jo leave between 11:00 and 11:15 that night.

No other media outlet picked up an explosive report in the *Washington Post* by Bob Woodward and Carl Bernstein, fresh off Watergate, that the surviving Boiler Room Girls may have been targets of blackmail, possibly by Ted's enemies. The exposé focused on a New York City apartment rented by a former White House secret investigator named Anthony T. Ulsewicz, which he claimed was for establishing a private detective office to conduct confidential investigations.

"However," the article read, "sources said that the apartment was furnished with velvet wallpaper and fur rugs, hardly the décor for a private detective agency. Government attorneys have been told that the apartment was to be used to seduce female friends of the late Mary Jo Kopechne...

"The scheme involved hiring a good-looking man to seduce the women in the apartment, have pictures taken secretly, and then blackmail the women into revealing details about Miss Kopechne and the party that took place shortly before the Chappaquiddick accident."

What, if anything, resulted from that scheme remains unknown.

———————

For their silence, the Boiler Room Girls were rewarded with Ted Kennedy's contempt. Years later, Mary Jo's roommate, fellow Boiler Room Girl Nance Lyons, said Ted never spoke to her professionally because she was a girl and once claimed that it was Nance, not Ted, who wanted to say Mary Jo was driving the car that night.

Not that any of it mattered. Ted had been protected from the beginning. The judge presiding over Ted's hearing, in which he pled guilty to leaving the scene of an accident, was a longtime Kennedy family friend. Ted's crisis managers had all worked and written speeches for Jack and Bobby. The bulk of the on-scene reporters were men. The first historian of Chappaquiddick, Jack Olsen, whose book was published two days before the inquest began in January 1969, was secure in his book's premise.

What *had* Mary Jo been doing with Senator Ted Kennedy that night? "The obvious answer was that they were playing around in the weeds," Olsen said. "She's had a few drinks. She's very giddy and excited. She's with a Kennedy—a lifelong dream."

"He's probably been loving her up a little," Olsen continued. "Just to be in the car with him in the middle of the night on a deserted island... She must have been beside herself with excitement, a spinster girl. What was she, twenty-eight?"

Mary Jo had been a week away from turning twenty-nine. In the Kennedy version, Mary Jo died a temptress, a seductress, a slut, and a groupie.

In all likelihood, she died a virgin.

JOAN BENNETT KENNEDY

She always said that this was what broke her—not the fame or the drinking or the other women, but Chappaquiddick. That's when she gave up. That is when Joan Kennedy became a true alcoholic—a hardcore, dawn-to-dusk drinker, food stains on her designer blouses, broken bones and falls, once in a gutter in Boston, rehab after rehab after rehab.

Ted was an alcoholic, too, and a cocaine addict, but he always pointed to Joan and her addiction as his albatross, his cross to bear, another liability that might keep him from becoming president. When Joan was at her best and clearest, Teddy and his advisers loved putting her front and center, on the cover of *People* or any number of women's magazines, selling her story of pain and redemption while minimizing her husband's role in her misery: his lengthy absences, his cruelty and neglect when he was home, his drinking and self-pity and verbal abuse and constant, barely concealed womanizing. He would mock her looks, even as his face and belly puffed up from the booze and his voracious eating habits. The media followed Ted's lead: Joan was the loser, the drunk, the weak one.

When Joan suffered her first miscarriage in May of 1963, Ted was nowhere to be found. When, six months later, his brother Jack was assassinated, Ted kept Joan away from the wake in Hyannis Port. Neither she nor her grief was welcome. Her exclusion was all the more painful because she really loved Jack, and she was one of the few people he trusted with his torment after baby Patrick died thirty-nine hours after his birth that August. Jack was moved by Joan's sincerity, by her ability to just let him talk, and especially by her lack of Christian piety. Never once did Joan say that Patrick was better off, or with the angels now, or that God had a plan and that this longed-for baby's premature death, Jackie having held

Patrick's hand for all of ten minutes before he died, was in any way logical.

"You know," Jack said after one of her nightly talks with him, "she's a great girl."

If only Ted felt that way. He was so cold and dismissive. "Take a pill or something," he would say to her.

This was not meant to be her life. Joan Bennett, the smart, gorgeous blonde debutante from New York City, college-educated at Manhattanville, had been bred for good things. She was a golden girl, a pageant queen, and then a Revlon spokesmodel earning thousands upon thousands of dollars, guided by her ad-exec father. But modeling had never been her dream; she was in it for the money, which would allow her to travel the world and pursue her love of piano, which she might someday play professionally. The modeling gave her independence.

Joan was a star in a famously unforgiving industry, never made clearer than the day she was up at her agency's office with her latest beau only to hear someone ask, "Who's that fat kid with Joan?"

It was none other than Ted Kennedy. They had been introduced by Ted's sister Jean at Manhattanville, during a dedication of a gym named for their late sister Kick, in October 1957. Joan hadn't known much about the Kennedys but her father sure did, and he was impressed. After a few phone calls and sporadic dates over the next twelve months, Ted asked Joan's father for permission to marry her.

Getting fast-tracked into the Kennedy family was a coronation. This would be the most high-profile Kennedy wedding since Jackie married Jack in 1953. But as for the looming fame that came with this marriage—well, Joan wasn't built for it, wasn't after it. She was marrying Ted in spite of the family he came from, not because of it. She had been in love with him at first sight—Ted so tall and athletic, his insatiable lust for life so like her own *joie de vivre*.

And Ted couldn't believe his luck. If he was going to follow his brothers into the White House, he needed the perfect wife—and here she was. Joan was Catholic, respectable, drop-dead gorgeous, a virgin. She never complained. She was willing to overlook Ted's shortcomings: his drinking, his unavailability, his bluster, his crassness, his intellectual laziness.

Joan was a people pleaser, the default setting of so many young women raised in respectable postwar families where, say, alcoholic moms and abusive dads such as hers weren't discussed. Joan hadn't the wherewithal then to understand that Ted and the Kennedys were like her family of origin on steroids—that she was drawn to them for that very reason— but she understood, innately, that her most important role would be to please Ted and her in-laws.

Of course, as a future First Lady, Joan Bennett Kennedy would also need to please America.

For all her wealth and beauty, Joan hadn't been popular in high school. Not in college either. Boys called her a prude. She was shy and often happiest alone: painting, reading, playing her piano. She didn't attract attention, because she didn't want it. The historical figure with whom Joan identified most was Eleanor Roosevelt, whose intellect and rich inner life she aspired to. She could see herself like that—not just the wife of a great man, but a woman of substance standing apart in her own right. In her own power.

Yet Joan was surprised when Ted Kennedy proposed. Maybe she should have known that those weekends in Hyannis were tests, that she was being submitted for Rose and Joe's approval: Get eyes on her, try her on for size, like any important acquisition. Make the best assessment: Is this woman going to be a liability or an asset? Could she be in it for the long haul? Could she get Ted to the Oval?

Joe and Rose, as it turned out, loved her. Joan was light—cheerful and sunny. Ted marveled at her disposition. "Nothing gets her down," he would say. "She's perfect for my family."

In June 1958, as soon as Joan graduated from Manhattanville, Ted proposed on the beach. He didn't have an engagement ring, but Joan said yes anyway. The announcement would be made to the media that September and the wedding would be in November. The only decisions Joan had to make were choosing the flowers and her dress. She settled on a long-sleeved satin gown with a full princess skirt, its sweetheart neckline bordered in lace, and a long bridal train, purchased off-the-rack in Bronxville.

It was all so exciting—until it wasn't.

ASK NOT

Joan wanted the former president of the University of Notre Dame, a close family friend of the Bennetts named Father John Cavanaugh, to marry them. Old Joe insisted on Francis Cardinal Spellman, the archbishop of New York and informal chaplain to the Kennedy family. At their engagement party, the first time Joan had seen Ted since he proposed in June, Ted showed up very late and handed her an unwrapped box. Inside was a diamond engagement ring. His father had bought it. Ted hadn't even seen it till Joan opened the box—she could tell.

None of it felt right. Ted wasn't acting like a man in love. He wasn't in the throes of a grand romance. This, Joan realized, was a merger. She was a casting coup. The wedding Old Joe was planning was out of her control, and her father was all too happy to play along, paying for sound design and lighting worthy of a Hollywood set. Her role would be to look pretty and produce children as if she were an assembly-line worker—like Ethel, the family's shining example of that and so many other idealized Kennedy qualities. Joan would need to campaign dutifully and look the other way when it came to Ted's many, many women.

Joan knew. She may have been sheltered but she wasn't naïve. Before their wedding, her friends would tell her of seeing Ted out on dates and openly kissing other women. But Joan found it all too easy to blame herself. After all, she was a virgin, and she was refusing sex with Ted until their wedding night. Meanwhile all these beautiful young women were throwing themselves at him. Technically, he was still single and one of the most eligible bachelors in America. How could she complain? It went against her very upbringing: be good, don't cry or get angry, don't show how you feel. Ladies don't do that. Otherwise the brush—the beribboned hairbrush her mother kept on the wall, the one she beat Joan and her sister Candy with when they misbehaved or otherwise displeased her—would come out, and their mother would ask: How many smacks do you think you deserve?

Marrying Ted was feeling like a smack in the face.

Joan barely knew him, but what she was learning she didn't much like. She wasn't so sure she wanted him or the life that came with him anymore. He hadn't taken time to really get to know her; she simply ticked the right boxes and came along at the right time. She was only twenty-two years old. What would her life become?

Was being Mrs. Ted Kennedy worth it?

Joan wanted to stop the wedding. Maybe not call it off exactly, but at least postpone. She couldn't talk to Ted about it — he was never around, for one thing. And he was so passive. Joan couldn't talk to Joe Kennedy either — who was she, after all, to approach the Kennedy patriarch with such an insolent request? She was just some girl from Bronxville, a very confused one at that. She had become awed by the Kennedys, whom she called "really the big time." Could she handle them? Was this what she really wanted? Or was she crazy to turn this down? How many other women would kill to be in her position, marrying into America's First Family?

So Joan did what women of her class and station did: she talked to her father, who then took her worries to Joe and Ted in a face-to-face summit.

It didn't go as she had hoped.

"They're not going to write in the papers that my son has been tossed over," Joe thundered. "This wedding is going to happen, whether Ted or Joan like it or not."

Her father would not defy Joe Kennedy. That was that.

Her mother tried to be of some comfort, but all she could do was manage Joan's expectations. "He may be a little raw," she told Joan, "but Ted can finance a marriage . . . and he likes children. You want children, don't you? Keep him happy, whatever you do."

The wedding was grand, the bride looked beautiful, and the newlyweds made the front page of the *New York Daily News*. The groom did not so much as touch his bride during the reception. Off they went on their honeymoon, a lush and secluded spot in the Bahamas, and, for the first couple of days, it was paradise. Then one night, Ted suddenly leapt out of bed and began packing. He had to leave. He had forgotten, he said, that he had an essay due for law school, and he had to catch a flight home immediately. Joan began to cry. She knew this was an excuse, a lazy one at that.

Not long after, Joan was watching the film of their wedding. All the main players were wearing microphones — which was how she could hear Ted's best man, his brother Jack, lean over and whisper some last-minute advice: getting married, Jack said, didn't mean Ted had to give up sleeping with other women. Despite that, Joan still liked Jack, and Jack instantly liked Joan, too. He had nicknamed her "The Dish," but she didn't feel minimized by it. Joan sensed Jack's pride in her beauty, and she was allowing herself to feel that, too. Her looks were currency. Power. She could walk into a room and outshine even Jackie, whom she so admired and wanted to be like, and who kept her at arm's length because Joan's allure was a threat.

Jackie's wariness extended to the strangest things. In the early days of her marriage, Joan had gone to lunch with Jackie in DC, some fancy French restaurant that Jackie loved. Joan was looking her most stylish, or so she thought until she walked toward their table and saw Jackie in a simple white shift dress and minimal makeup, flipping through the latest copy of *Paris Match*. Here was Joan, with her big, cascading pageant hair and hot-pink miniskirt, her effort to impress practically shouting itself across this hushed dining room. Joan was tacky, but everything about Jackie was elegant and understated—except the smoking. Jackie smoked three packs a day but joked that it was her sister Lee who came out of the womb puffing away, a cigarette in place of a rattle. Jackie always looked and smelled like money, even through her cloud of tobacco smoke. Joan had been dying to ask: What scent did Jackie wear?

"I never tell anyone what perfume I wear," Jackie said. "I can't take the competition."

Competition. If there was an overarching theme to life as a Kennedy, this was it.

Joan hadn't come to this lunch in the spirit of rivalry. She wanted Jackie's advice. One of Ted's girlfriends had left a piece of jewelry in Joan and Ted's marital bed. Joan was mortified, devastated, furious. What should she do?

"Forget about it," Jackie said. "You can't take it personally. It's just how Kennedy men are."

Joan knew that Jackie took a European approach to infidelity, but she hadn't expected such radical acceptance. Did Jackie really just sit there and take it?

"Frankly," Jackie said, "their behavior makes me sick."

Maybe that was how Jackie made her peace with it: it wasn't just Jack and it wasn't Jackie's fault, just as it wasn't Joan's. This was a pathology passed down from the father, a kind of negative life force, this treatment of women as accessories, broodmares, chattel. It was in the Kennedy DNA, and there didn't seem to be a cure.

Jackie wasn't going to share her own horror stories with Joan, but she wasn't going to pretend that her marriage was any better. What was the point? Everyone knew.

"Focus on yourself, Joan," Jackie said. "And your kids. Forget Teddy."

In the early days of their marriage, Joan had been happy. She and Ted weren't just sexually compatible; Joan's kindness and decency, her sensitive disposition, brought out a softer side of Ted. The Ted who was teased by his siblings for being overweight was, in Joan's eyes, rugged and athletic, the handsomest Kennedy brother. Only Joan saw in Ted the little boy traumatized by his sister Rosemary's disappearance, terrified that if he failed to please his parents then he might be made to disappear, too.

Joan was among the few who knew that Ted had no memory of his childhood after age seven — that everything was a blank until he hit his teenage years, all that emotional trauma blacked out. He had been bullied mercilessly by his stronger, fitter, smarter older brothers, who liked to call him "fat stuff." Ted had been a very sensitive child, one who intuited that his troubles with reading and writing, his academic shortcomings, were dangerously similar to Rosemary's. There was the four-line letter he'd written at age eight to his father, riddled with errors.

> *Dear Daddy,*
> *We are down in cap-card mother has gone to jacks graduain. Joe is here. The wether is very dad. Would you get me the kings autograph for me I will send you an other letter soon*
>
> *love Teddy*

As Ted matured, his father's critiques remained blistering. In a letter to his thirteen-year-old son at boarding school, written from Palm Beach in January 1946, Joe wrote, in part:

Your letters are coming through all right, but your penmanship hasn't improved much... You really ought to do a little more work on the writing and the spelling. You are getting pretty old now, and it looks rather babyish.

...I am sorry to see that you are starving to death. I can't imagine that ever happening to you if there was anything at all to eat around, but then you can spare a few pounds.

Ted lived in fear of the old man, even now. Maybe that was why he never went deep. Ted was all about a good time, breaking the rules and never admitting regret. It was such an attractive quality then: Ted brought Joan out of her self-seriousness, her self-consciousness. He encouraged her to get in the mix, whether through playing team sports with his ultracompetitive siblings or walking into a state dinner with confidence or speaking publicly or just engaging with people. Ted saw beyond her beauty and she loved him for it.

Soon after their daughter Kara was born in February 1960 — to Joan's great shame, it took her over two years to give birth — she brought up a novel idea: What if they moved to California? There, they could have a life of their own. Joan would be free of Rose's daily phone calls, the check-ins and unsolicited advice and criticisms, and Ted would be, if not free from Old Joe, at least far away enough to grow up a bit. Come into his own.

Ted did not want a life in politics — Joan knew that. She encouraged him to consider other career paths. It was enough that Jack was the star, the favorite son. It was enough that Bobby had dutifully taken second place. Wasn't it enough that Joe Jr. had died attempting to fulfill his father's dream? Surely Old Joe would spare his youngest son — who, Joan knew, did not have the brains or grit or self-discipline to be a serious politician, let alone a future president.

Ted loved the idea of California. He loved that Joan was wary of becoming subsumed by his family, and how wise that was. He loved that she wanted what he wanted, to see him rise or fall on his own merits. He loved that even if he failed she would be okay with that. The idea that Ted could take his young family three thousand miles away and create a life, separate and self-directed, was a revelation. They began house-hunting and planning to move. Even Jack went to bat for them. *Let Teddy live his own life*, Jack told their father. *He doesn't want any of this. He wants a quiet, easier, more private existence. He and Joan should have that.*

Joe was furious. California was out of the question. Ted and Joan weren't to even think about moving out of Massachusetts, because Ted was going to run for one of the state's US Senate seats in 1962 and win. *I bought that seat*, Joe said. *It belongs to the Kennedys.*

No matter that Joe had three daughters, or that Jack thought his sister Eunice was the most naturally gifted politician of them all. The boys were the ones who were bred for power — not just for power, but for world domination. So Ted surrendered, and that decision set the tone for the rest of their marriage. Joan would never come first.

Yet he needed her as he needed no other woman. As Ted's Senate campaign began in the summer of '61, Ted was polling more favorably among women than men, and Joan was a big reason why. Whereas Jackie was cool and aloof, with her strange, airy way of talking, Joan was down-to-earth, riddled with insecurities that any woman could relate to. Reporters loved Joan; part of it was her kindness, but part of it was her candor. Joan hadn't been media-trained. She wasn't fluent in canned sound bites. The very human secrets she let slip — the First Lady wore wigs, the president had an incredibly painful bad back — made headlines.

Joan really beat herself up over that. Jackie told her it wasn't that big a deal, but Ted was apoplectic. Jack and Jackie were stars. Everyone else's job was to prop them up. "What is wrong with you?" Ted raged. "Are you crazy?"

He didn't stand up for her or defend her. Nor was he helping her learn how to be a Kennedy Wife. She got more advice and compassion from Ethel and Jackie, and that wasn't a lot. Ted was happy to show her off at parties in DC or in the pages of women's magazines — right now she was his best asset, the woman who domesticated the fast-and-loose guy once known as "Cadillac Eddie" — but in private he was neglecting her, always off on some fact-finding mission in Southeast Asia or some backroom meeting on the Hill. Unless, of course, he needed her — a last-minute call in the afternoon, telling her he was bringing eight or twelve colleagues home for dinner and she needed to pull off an elegant, multi-course meal. As he would remind her, Jack did the same to Jackie all the time before the White House, and she never complained. "Don't embarrass me, Joansie," he'd say.

Ted was kidding. Or was he? Joan would catch a lot of flak from the DC doyennes over the way she looked, her hair getting blonder and her skirts getting shorter. *Women's Wear Daily* called her tasteless. A female journalist in the *New York Times* made note of her miniskirt and yellow tights, disparagingly calling her "exotic as a butterfly." Even *Cosmopolitan*, a magazine branded on women's liberation and sexual freedom, noted her "cuddly bosom" and "adorable bottom." No one wrote about other Kennedy women like that.

When she was named the most beautiful woman in DC by *The Washingtonian*, Joan felt objectified. Minimized. She wanted people to think she was smart, talented, had something to offer. Her looks were a quirk of genetics, nothing more. She could hardly take credit for them. Jackie was the intellectual, Ethel the politico-slash-supermom—what did that make Joan? The window dressing?

Ted told her to brush it off. He was proud of her. He didn't think she should dim her light. He saw her as his best surrogate, even as she doubted that. Her husband's advisers were putting so much pressure on her—it was up to Joan, they said, to prove to voters that Ted wasn't "some smart-ass kid," but a serious, thoughtful man of substance. Joan became paralyzed by fear of doing or saying the wrong thing. Every time the phone rang, she could feel the sword of Damocles swaying above her head. Who would it be? Rose, with her imperious reprovals? Jackie, pretending none of Joan's mistakes bothered her when Joan knew otherwise? Ethel, with one of her backhanded compliments? Or some staffer of Ted's, some middle-aged guy telling her all the things the Candidate's Wife was doing wrong? Did anybody understand how terrifying it was to be told you had to be perfect all the time? Some days Joan was so depressed that she couldn't get out of bed. She had found herself in a family of ruthless winners. And despite his rising profile, her husband's womanizing had gotten worse. After he won that Senate seat—due, in large part, to Joan—Ted walked into a royal dinner in Belgium with a sex worker on his arm. They were both drunk, just completely hammered, and Ted made a terrible spectacle, making out with this woman on an antique sofa that one of them, in their total inebriation, urinated on. Joan was so mortified that, back home in America, she wrote a note to the party's hosts, apologizing for her husband.

Her health began to suffer. She needed an appendectomy, then a tonsillectomy — operations that most people have as children. She was always fighting some kind of cold or sore throat. She began experiencing such agonizing stomach pains that her doctors ordered exploratory surgery. They found nothing. Maybe she was crazy, like Teddy said.

———

Then came the plane crash. It was only about seven months after Jack's assassination, and Ted had been flying from DC to Springfield, Massachusetts, where he would be named the Democratic nominee for the United States Senate. The plane was an Aero Commander, a small twin-engine that had taken off in terrible weather with poor visibility.

———

Just after midnight on June 20, 1964, Joan Kennedy was resting her eyes and waiting for Ted to arrive when there was a knock on her door. It was Jack Crimmins, one of the Kennedy family's chauffeurs.

"There's been an accident," Crimmins said. Joan didn't cry, didn't collapse, just dressed quickly and had Crimmins drive her to the hospital. On the way, Joan tried to talk herself down. "Sometimes they say a plane has crashed when really it's landed, don't they?" she asked. "Or they say there's been a crash when only something minor has happened, like maybe a tire blew out or it skidded on the runway. Sometimes they say it's bad when it might not even be bad."

It was bad. The plane had crashed into an apple orchard in Massachusetts. Ted had been dragged from the wreckage by a fellow passenger, Senator Birch Bayh, who got Ted out before his own wife. A Good Samaritan came upon the site and took the Bayhs to his house, leaving a gravely injured Ted on the ground, paralyzed from the waist down, close to the plane. The Samaritan, a regular guy named Robert Schauer, called the police and fire departments, grabbed blankets and water and hurried back to the crash site to wait with Ted until the ambulance came. That random act of kindness saved Ted's life. Inside the plane, the pilot and one of Ted's aides were dead.

Ted's back was broken, as were two ribs. He had a collapsed lung. By the time rescue crews got Ted to the hospital he had no pulse. A team from Walter Reed Army Medical Center was flying up.

———————

Once she got to the emergency room in Northampton, Joan realized that her husband might not make it. Her aides helped secure for her a room next to Ted's so she could stay the night. He had been revived in the field, and here she was with him in the emergency room. Ted was under an oxygen tent getting a blood transfusion. It was unclear if he would live through the night.

Joan kept calm. She kept the aides who had taken her to the hospital calm. "I spoke to him and he talked to me," Joan said. "He told me he'll be all right."

She had to believe it. By Sunday, Ted was stable enough for surgery, a six-hour spinal operation that, if successful, would save him from life as a paraplegic. Ted's recovery, his doctors told Joan, would take anywhere from six months to a year.

Joan was stronger than the Kennedys gave her credit for—stronger than maybe even she had known. The Joan Kennedy so devastated by Jack's death that she hadn't been able to get out of bed for days now became a warrior. When Ted's campaign advisers came begging to Joan, asking her to stump for him even though she hated retail politics—Joan, who had enormous public sympathy, the second beautiful young Kennedy wife and mother enduring unthinkable tragedy—she did not think twice. "Of course I will," Joan said. No debate, no self-doubt, no question at all. All of their marital problems were suddenly miniaturized. Ted had lived. He wasn't going to survive for nothing.

A war room was set up in Ted's spacious suite in rehab. Joan—who now had three small children at home, having given birth to Teddy Jr. in 1961—arrived every morning, having risen early for the hour-plus drive, and would meet with Ted as he lay strapped face down in an orthopedic bed. She would sit with him as if nothing had changed, holding her sheaf of papers and speeches, her itineraries and talking points. She brought him newspapers and books and laughed when he joked that he was rotated "like a rotisserie chicken" to prevent fluid from building up in his lungs. She vetted the list of people who wanted to see her husband. Then she would have a quick bite and head out at noon for the first of her day-long campaign stops.

Six days a week, eight hours a day, cities and towns, meet-and-greets and polka dancing and fielding questions from reporters about Ted, lying about how great he was doing, how upbeat his spirits were, how strong their marriage was. It was the only time she felt bad about herself, having to lie like that, knowing that all those reporters knew about Ted's womanizing but were too polite to ever mention it.

Before she had started stumping in earnest, President Johnson called.

"I hear you're goin' out there on the trail," he said. "It's hard work, you know. Sure you can handle it?"

"I must do it," Joan replied. "I know I can. It's my responsibility."

"It is," the president said. "So you go on out there and be a good little girl and do a good job."

Joan didn't just do a good job—she did a great one. She was more popular than her husband, even if she wasn't as naturally garrulous. At heart Joan was an introvert, and as it turned out, these events and exchanges, the sheer number of people who wanted to touch her or talk to her, even for a moment, took something from her. She didn't thrive on it as Teddy did. He really got something from all of it; it fed him. But Joan ended each day feeling depleted. She found herself drinking more frequently. She began focusing on all the little things she got wrong—names or places—and lived in fear of getting up to deliver her stump speech and forgetting it all.

Ted's team told her not to worry; she was doing better than anyone expected. She was going to win this for Teddy. She was a natural, even if she didn't believe it. But nothing could get Joan out of her doom spiral, because the one person who mattered didn't seem to care. Sure, Ted put on a good show when others were around, but even then he found a way to put her down. "You have an opportunity to do something here, Joansie," he said. "So do it. For yourself."

He said this to her in front of a bunch of volunteers — strangers. It was mortifying. She didn't need her husband to direct her, to castigate her for a lack of ambition. She wasn't trying to prove something to herself. This wasn't some "est" course in self-actualization. She was working her ass off trying to win her reckless husband, injured so badly because he decided it was a great idea to *stand up and look at the pilot's controls as the plane was going down*, on the way to accept the nomination to run for a Senate seat his father had bought — a seat that, if Ted had any real work ethic or sense of responsibility, should be his without her help. Without her extremely hard work, which was costing her time with their small children.

God, was he reckless. Years before, flying with Jack in another small plane, Ted had taken the controls and insisted on landing the plane in Vegas. Did Ted have a pilot's license? No. Did Ted have any earthly idea how to fly a plane? Of course not. Were they ferrying precious cargo, the future president of the United States, months from victory? They sure were.

Bobby was the only Kennedy man who didn't seem to have a death wish. He, at least, seemed to think about his children. But Ted was like a big baby, all id: he wanted what he wanted when he wanted it, and everyone else could clean up the mess. Without Joan's day-in, day-out, tireless, unglamorous help he had no shot — but the better she performed for Ted, the higher he polled, the more distant and resentful he became.

And when he did win, he won in a landslide, getting 75 percent of the vote — a record victory in Massachusetts. The Kennedys took note.

"Congratulations," Jackie wrote to Joan, "and a job well done. How wonderful! I hope this shows you how much you can accomplish . . . I am so excited for you."

Ethel called and lavished Joan — whose looks and style she loved taking down a peg — with fulsome praise. "The whole family is proud of you," Ethel said. "What a wonderful job you did. " Joan even heard that

Bobby told Ted that his reelection was due to her. Her mother-in-law sent two bouquets of red roses in congratulations and gratitude.

The only one who never said a thing, not so much as a "thank you," was Ted.

In July of 1969, Joan was on doctor-ordered bed rest, pregnant and at risk of miscarrying for the third time. She heard an influx of staffers downstairs, muffled voices, her husband's among them. He had been away for the weekend, leaving Joan alone on the Cape with their two small children. She wanted to go downstairs and ask all these people, the ever-present sycophants, aides, lawyers, and hangers-on, to leave. But someone had been dispatched to Joan's bedroom and told her to stay where she was. Something was wrong.

Joan reached over to her bedside table and picked up the phone. Her husband was on the line, talking to another woman. Helga, the girlfriend. One of them, anyway. What they were talking about Joan didn't know, but clearly Helga was fluent in Ted's prevarications. He was in a panic, talking about a car accident he had been in on the Vineyard, something about leaving the scene and blacking out and wondering what he should do. Whatever this was, Joan knew it would be her problem, too. She would be called upon to save him yet again. In the eleven years since they had been married, she had become not so much a wife as a professional reputation defender, her warmth and beauty a shield for Ted to hide behind.

After all, the thinking went, if a woman as good as Joan loved and stood by Ted Kennedy, how bad could he be? The answer, as those on the inside knew, was simple: Ted was worse than anyone could imagine.

Weeks after Mary Jo Kopechne's death, Ted had jetted off to Paris, where his sister Eunice and her husband, Sarge, were promoting the Special Olympics. It was an initiative for physically and mentally challenged children, founded by Eunice in tribute to Rosemary. Joan refused to go. She had suffered enough by then and was suffering still. Ted could have used that trip to begin rehabilitating his image, but no. Word got back that Ted had been frequently wandering around the ambassador's residence, where he was staying, drunk and naked.

The American doctor Herbert Kramer was also there. It was Kramer who had written the mission statement for the Special Olympics: "Let me win, but if I cannot win, let me be brave in the attempt." Words a man in Ted's predicament might have taken to heart.

Kramer had gone for a walk with another guest, an insightful economist, and the two spoke of Ted's latest crisis. "What Teddy ought to do," Kramer said, "is to resign from the Senate and take a year, two years to do some good work to redeem himself, to suggest that night at Chappaquiddick had been an aberration."

The economist blanched.

"You've got to be kidding," he replied. Ted would never sacrifice his Senate seat — ever. "This isn't a moral animal. This is a political animal."

It was that same political animal who persuaded Joan to get up out of doctor-ordered bed rest and accompany him to Mary Jo's funeral. And so she was by his side as he wore that stupid neck brace he didn't need, as he insisted on sitting in the front pew and making a show of struggling to kneel.

It was the political animal who decided to announce Joan's pregnancy on July 25, just before addressing the nation that night about Mary Jo's death. And two days after the accident, Ted had pressured Joan into calling Mary Jo's parents. Joan wasn't cynical in the least. She didn't know what to do. A young woman's death had been caused by her husband, yet all these men in suits — and all these Kennedy women, too! — were concerned with one thing: saving Ted's career. They were such sanctimonious Catholics, such hypocrites, Jackie and Ethel and Rose — all of them, impervious to shame. Ruthless. It didn't matter that Joan was really hurting, as much for Mary Jo and for her and Ted's children as for herself. They were all determined to get Ted — lazy, drunk, horny, feckless, remorseless Ted — into the White House.

Joan sat at the dining table downstairs. A rotary phone was placed in front of her.

Ted was being nice to Joan now. Solicitous. He and his aides were talking to her as if she were dumb rather than in shock: *We need you to pull this off,* they said. *If the Kopechnes like you, they'll go easier on Ted. They won't push for criminal charges. They won't sue. They won't bankrupt you and your young family.*

Joan knew better. None of them cared about Mary Jo Kopechne. She was yet another inconvenient woman to be managed and disposed of.

A number was dialed. Mary Jo's mother picked up. Joan had to say something.

Hello, Mrs. Kopechne, Joan said. *This is Joan Kennedy. Ted's wife.*

Mary Jo's mother said hello back. She did not sound angry. This was humbling.

We are so sorry about what happened, Joan said. *The whole Kennedy family. We've had tragedy ourselves and so we empathize with you and I am . . . I mean, we are so, so sorry.*

Mary Jo's mother was weeping softly. Joan looked up. The men in suits were exultant. Ted looked relieved. Happy, almost.

One month later, six days before the inquest into Mary Jo's death, Joan miscarried.

———

This would have been her fourth child, one she badly wanted. Ted had been away, camping with two of their children and John Jr. It was Ethel who had taken Joan to the emergency room. Ted rushed back, but he was the last person she wanted to see.

That was it for her. That was the moment Joan gave up. Chappaquiddick, Mary Jo's funeral, the phone call to Mrs. Kopechne, the inquest — all of it had contributed to her miscarriage. Ted made her lose her baby. That is when she truly became, as she later would say, an alcoholic. That is when she became the object of Ted's utter scorn. At his most vile, after coming home late and gorging on leftovers — that's how Joan knew he had been with other women, because Ted was always ravenously hungry after sex, just a bottomless pit of gluttony — Ted would dismiss Joan as a drunk, a terrible mother who slept all day. Weak. He had a favorite insult.

"Just call McLean," he would say, knowing that her own mother had been institutionalized, "and put Joan in a cab."

Ted, of course, held on to his Senate seat after leaving Mary Jo in that car. How? Well, he leaned heavily on his wife and his three dead brothers and his role as paterfamilias for all the newly fatherless Kennedy children, and all was forgiven. Joan, on the other hand — her life was becoming tabloid fodder now, something for bored housewives to consume as they waited in the grocery store checkout line.

THE JOAN KENNEDY STORY: FROM DREAM TO NIGHTMARE.

Unlike so many other headlines about her, this one, at least, was true.

November would come to hold terrible new memories for Joan, too. It was early that month in 1973 that her youngest son, then-twelve-year-old Teddy Jr. — sweet, shy, obedient Teddy — complained of pain in his right leg, the lower part where a raised bruise had formed. Doctors quickly determined that Teddy had a rare form of cancer called chondrosarcoma. His was an extremely malignant tumor at risk of metastasizing quickly.

The only option, Joan and Ted were told, was to amputate the leg above the knee — immediately.

Early on the morning of November 18, days before the tenth anniversary of Jack's assassination, Teddy Jr. underwent a four-hour surgery at Georgetown University Hospital. When he awoke in his hospital room, Joan was there with Ted, putting on a happy, united front and making sure their boy knew that he was going to be okay.

For Joan, this was yet another crisis that soldered her to her husband's side. Before their son's diagnosis, she and Ted had been on the verge of separation; Joan had spent the summer traveling in Europe with their daughter Kara. Now there was no way they could divorce; she would look like a terrible mother and Ted's eventual run for president would be compromised.

Before the accident that killed Mary Jo, Joan had been seeing two psychiatrists, one on Tuesdays and one on Wednesdays, as a kind of insurance — she always wanted to know what one thought of the other's assessments. She had felt trapped with Ted and was looking for a way out, but as one friend observed, Mary Jo's death further ensnared her in the marriage. "Afterward," her friend said, "she was the only ally Ted Kennedy had. He needed her desperately, and she knew it and rose to the occasion."

The unintended consequence for Joan? She was now a Kennedy for life.

PART SIX
THE MYTHMAKER

JACKIE KENNEDY

J ackie would not recall much of her time at Valleyhead.

It was Jack who put her there, seeking a cure for her depression, the black moods that had plagued her since childhood, and, of course, this new marriage that had left her, as one of their friends put it, walking around in shock, as if she were the lone survivor of a plane crash — that was the analogy. Jack couldn't deal with Jackie's upset, nor did he care to, so off to Valleyhead she went.

This famous Massachusetts institution had treated other very prominent people, so it wasn't as if there was much shame attached. Then again, those same prominent people often kept their stays quiet. Jackie had read *The Bell Jar*; Sylvia Plath had also been to Valleyhead. Here Jackie would undergo three rounds of electroshock therapy in one week. Each time she shook so violently it sounded like her bones were breaking.

Jack never came to see her. He never called. Her days were spent dodging the other patients, forcing down inedible food, and attempting to use the bathroom in private. She was without her two greatest comforts since childhood: her horses and her books. Jacqueline Bouvier Kennedy, dignity her most prized possession, was barefoot and barely dressed in a hospital gown, her husband nowhere to be found.

After that week at Valleyhead, Jack sent an aide to bring Jackie home. His name was Chuck Spalding, and he was a decent guy, not as bootlicking or pathetic as Kenny O'Donnell or Lem Billings or Dave Powers. Jackie liked him. She didn't speak much on the drive back, and Chuck let her be. He was just as gentle when he escorted Jackie into the DC town house, even more so when they found that Jack wasn't there. Her husband hadn't even left a note. Chuck excused himself. Late for an appointment, he said.

Jackie was truly alone. What an embarrassment she was. What a failure. Ethel and Jack's siblings were right: Jackie was as soft as they said. It hadn't seemed possible, but Jackie felt more hopeless now than at the asylum. The parameters of her marriage were extremely clear: Jackie was the political prop, and she needed to accept it. Anger, sadness, needs, wants — Jackie needed to get with the program and pack all those complicated emotions out of sight. Medicate herself, travel, go on shopping sprees — whatever it took to keep herself docile while her husband conquered the world.

And what about that? When Jack ran for president, and the press coverage intensified — someone was bound to find out about Jackie's stay, weren't they? It was only a matter of time before it became national news. None of it would hurt Jack — he was too charming, too self-assured.

Jackie went into the bathroom and opened the medicine cabinet. She reached for Jack's razor blades, the stainless steel Gillettes, and thought about how easy it would be to draw a warm bath and a straight line down each wrist.

Had she ever been truly happy? She thought she had gone into this marriage with eyes wide open, but Jack's cheating was unbearable, the humiliations unrelenting. The babies she lost. Her beloved father's death from liver cancer in 1957, a slow suicide caused by his drinking. Her sister, Lee, so competitive and envious — of what, exactly? Jackie's life was a sham.

Except her love for Jack. That was real. When he came home that night and found Jackie still distraught, not cured by her week in the asylum, he rallied. Jack was the loving, understanding, supportive husband Jackie so badly wanted. He understood that her default emotional settings were labile and prided himself on being the only one Jackie trusted with her weaker self. "He is a rock," she said at that time, "and I lean on him for everything." That night made all the difference. For a while.

On November 27, 1957, Jackie gave birth to their first child, bringing Jack and Jackie closer than ever. They named her Caroline, after Jackie's sister, whose given name was Caroline Lee. Jack was the first person Jackie saw when she came to, and it was he, not a nurse, wheeling the infant into her hospital room. She would often refer to this as the happiest day of her life.

So Jackie *could* carry a baby to term. Her baby was healthy. She was free, for now, of Jack's sexually transmitted diseases. She and Jack were a real family. She could have another child if she wanted, and another. Jack was just as elated and proud.

Now Jackie had power.

The girl who'd wanted to write for the *New Yorker*, who had won *Vogue*'s Prix de Paris award at age twenty, who had hoped her entry-level job as the *Washington Times-Herald*'s Inquiring Photographer would springboard her into serious journalism, who had written a screenplay about former first lady Dolley Madison, had, after all that, bargained that life as Mrs. John F. Kennedy would be a fair trade.

In some ways, it was. Jack loved Jackie's irreverence, her defiant streak, her capacious mind. All the qualities Jackie's mother had sought to contain were admired by the Kennedy men—to a point. What she had learned from a young age she would master as a young wife, both in public and private: Never let anyone know how quickly you see through them.

Never let anyone know how deeply you are hurting.

Dr. Frank Finnerty was young, only thirty-seven, but a distinguished cardiologist and professor when Jackie met him on the Cape in the spring of 1961. He had been called over to the Kennedy compound to treat Jackie for an injured ankle. Finnerty seemed kind and grounded, and something in his manner led Jackie to call him on the phone a week later. She began by telling him how her ankle was doing, then asked a favor. "Would you mind," she said, "if I called you once in a while? Just to talk. To get an outside opinion on things."

Jackie would reach out to him, never the other way around. She didn't need a physician as much as a friend. She was too afraid to see a therapist—if word ever got out, people would think she was crazy. Would Dr. Finnerty help?

"I know what's going on," she told him. "I'm not dumb or naïve, like people around my husband think. His infidelities don't bother me as much as that does." Sometimes Jackie could convince herself of this. It never lasted. "All these reporters—and they're almost always men— think I'm strange, that I must live off in my own world not to see what he's up to. I know exactly what he's up to."

There were so many women that Jackie didn't know all of their names—or so she told the doctor. She was strong and prideful. She suspected that Lee had slept with her husband—just once, she was sure—but never said a thing. She knew about Jack and Pamela Turnure, her own assistant. She knew about Jack's euphemistic "pool parties" held almost daily in the White House—often attended by his brothers Ted and Bobby and by Jack's various lackeys—and the two young White House secretaries who would also join them. Women ran up and down the back stairs whenever Jackie was away, leaving behind blonde hairs and bobby pins, dripping water and passing their half-finished drinks to Secret Service agents as they scurried out the door, no doubt hearing that the First Lady was on her way home.

There was the time Jackie found, in her and Jack's White House bed, a strange pair of underwear. "Would you please shop around and find who these belong to?" she had asked her husband. "They're not my size."

She knew about his penchant for picking up girls while traveling and having three-ways, four-ways, five-ways, swapping hookers with his buddies. She knew about the fifteen-year-old babysitter Jack had gotten pregnant back when he was senator.

The rumors were true—she had cut that deal with Joe then, the one million dollars not to leave the marriage, millions more if Jack ever gave her a sexually transmitted disease again.

Jackie really didn't think Jack loved any of these women. He treated them like the help—they came when he called, left when he told them to, and were led to expect nothing from him. But she was sick of keeping the problems in her marriage secret. "Jack needs to expel some kind of hormonal surge," she told Dr. Finnerty. "I don't think he even has affection for them. It's just this intrinsic part of his life, a vicious trait he inherited from his father."

There was one woman, Jackie said, who did bother her: Marilyn

Monroe. She didn't go into detail, but the doctor intuited that no other paramour made Jackie as insecure. He was right.

Jackie had never talked so freely. In Finnerty she had found a true confidant. His trustworthiness, his lack of judgment or shock, his ability to come at problems practically and clinically gave Jackie the courage to share her most private dilemma: her sex life with her husband.

For a man with such a libido, Jackie said, Jack was terrible in bed. She hadn't had that many experiences before she married, but she wanted more from her husband. Was it her fault?

"He just goes too fast and falls asleep," Jackie said. Little did she know that this was the complaint of every woman who had had sex with Jack Kennedy: no kissing, no buildup, no intensity or sensuality or fun. He just attacked you like a dog humping a leg. He never lasted longer than three minutes and didn't even seem to enjoy sex. It was like a compulsion. There was never anything remotely personal about it for him.

Jackie couldn't abide it. She and Jack were so well-matched, especially intellectually. He relied on her for her emotional radar; no one could see through people like Jackie. He took such pride in her, effusiveness for him otherwise a rarity. When they had visited Paris that spring, Jack credited Jackie's instant rapport with President de Gaulle—the French leader's attention rapt as she spoke to him fluently in his own language about her love of French history, culture, architecture—as the masterstroke of soft diplomacy that it was. Jack went on to proudly refer to himself at a press luncheon not as the president of the United States but "the man who accompanied Jacqueline Kennedy to Paris—and I have enjoyed it." The crowd roared, but Jack meant every word. That trip was a major victory for the Kennedy administration, and Jackie deserved all the credit.

That was Jackie's genius. She knew how to bring people in while keeping herself at bay. She met them at their level but made them want to be like her. As First Lady, with art and culture and beautification projects her self-assigned agenda, Jackie was becoming what she had once jokingly dreamed about: Overall Art Director of the Twentieth Century.

Without making him feel less-than, Jackie had also turned Jack—once so careless when it came to personal presentation—into an exacting clotheshorse. Now he could swiftly spot the smallest stylistic error. "Brown at night?" he would say. "Never!" He had come not just to value aesthetics but to understand the importance of them—that to care about the way things looked wasn't frivolous or feminine but, as Jackie helped him see, another way to nourish the soul while providing an added benefit: he was, with her help, elevating his public image. He was the first president to cultivate real style. His sharply tailored suits and skinny ties were a nod to the mods out of England. He wore the Ray-Ban Wayfarer sunglasses and an Omega Ultra Thin watch, preppy leisure wear, nautical blue polo shorts and white jeans for boating, his windswept chestnut hair making his personal presentation seem effortless. Jack let Jackie take the lead in remaking his image, one never before seen in a US president: Cool.

And then there was her mind. Jackie may have been the most well-read woman Jack had ever known. Their love of books, their compulsive and wide-ranging reading habits, was a shared passion. Every Sunday Jack would read the *New York Times Book Review* and circle the titles that interested him, leaving the paper for Jackie to see. And at each week's end, Jackie would have all those new books piled on his nightstand, ready and waiting. No other woman could compete with her there.

So Jackie wanted their physical connection to be as unique, as unspoken and mutually gratifying as their intellectual one. What could she do to bring her husband around?

Finnerty listened, agog that the most famous woman in the world, the envy of so many who assumed her life and marriage perfect, was so candid. He did not take her trust lightly. He sympathized and told her she was hardly alone. He advised her to proceed gingerly. Jackie, he said, must not risk offending Jack or making him feel like less of a man. Tell him you feel left out, Finnerty advised. Tell him you need more affection, that foreplay would be his gift to you. Have the talk over a meal, in a nonthreatening way, and approach it like any other problem two smart people would tackle together: logically and unemotionally.

Jackie did just that, and Jack's response surprised her. He had no idea that sex was so important to her, he said. Her interest was impressive. How had a nice girl like her become so well versed in all things sexual?

The way I always do, Jackie told him. *Through books.*

Jackie and Jack both thought of themselves as actors. Jack knew he was a product, packaged and sold by his father, but he didn't much mind. He loved Hollywood, movie stars, celebrity, and the rarefied air in VIP rooms, having access to anything and anyone he wanted. Famous people fascinated him. Frank Sinatra, the most famous American singer alive, and his crew known as The Rat Pack became part of Jack's inner circle. He would join them for weekends in Vegas and Palm Beach, where their real-life pleasure-seeking outstripped anything one would see in their movies or nightclub acts or television shows. Image-making was spellbinding to Jack and something of a salvation: he had survived his illnesses, his lonely childhood, and the sudden losses of three young siblings by staying on the move.

Jackie was more complicated. She was introspective and kept her own counsel. Becoming First Lady meant camouflaging the spicier parts of her personality in public: the rapier wit, the rebellious nature, the contempt for pretension and airs—Jackie, behind the scenes, being quite down to earth. The mask she wore was ever placid. Never was a hair out of place, because she seldom wore her real hair. Wigs made for a much more pleasant picture, though she was never more herself than windswept on the beach with her children.

As she emerged in the spotlight, as the American people, women especially, didn't reject her as a snob but expressed admiration for her youth and composure, Jackie came to really enjoy being famous. She learned how to turn off her inner self and transform herself into a character named Jacqueline Kennedy, a woman of destiny, gifted with beauty, style, two beautiful children, and a devoted husband who just happened to be the most powerful man on earth.

Who wouldn't want to be her?

The frustrated actress in her had found the role of a lifetime; Jackie Kennedy would reimagine what it meant to be First Lady of the United States. She was creating a character from the ground up, and if she did it right, with Jack eager to play along, then Jack and Jackie Kennedy would not just be historic but iconic. The White House was her set; her Chanel suits and mink stoles her wardrobe; and her in-laws her supporting players, their toothy, athletic ruggedness the perfect foil to Jackie's graceful reserve.

Jack used to get theatrically exasperated with Jackie's spending. "She's breaking my goddamn ass!" he'd yell, right in front of his staff, and oh did Jackie love that. Didn't she have the right? It wasn't even Jack's own money she was spending. It was the Old Man's, and the Old Man knew Jackie's worth. She was, after all, becoming the global brand ambassador for the House of Kennedy. So what if she wanted Chanel suits in every color, or piles of David Webb jewels, or her hairdresser flown in from New York City? Wasn't that a small price to pay?

It made her feel better. And frankly, it gave her something to do.

Acquiring rare, expensive things filled a hole in Jackie, to be sure. She didn't have to play the faithful wife — that was no act — but she did have to act as a happy one. Like all great stars, she knew when to decline comment, when to play dumb, and when to disappear, as she did the night in May 1962 when Marilyn Monroe, dressed in a shimmering, skintight nude gown in front of a packed Madison Square Garden and the entire world, cooed "Happy Birthday" to her husband as he sat in the audience, all but announcing that she and the married president of the United States were having an affair.

Jackie was a student of art and cinema. She knew the power of silence. She had known her absence that night would be infinitely more powerful than her presence, so she stayed on her rented farm in Virginia with her children and her horses, sending the public a careful, nonverbal message: Your First Lady shares your values, and she is also appalled. The trappings of celebrity and garish shows are not for her. She is happiest taking care of her small children far from the spotlight. A spectacle such as that one is far beneath her.

Those who knew better, the reporters and the friends and the family members, felt sorry for Jackie. But she didn't want their pity. She cared only for her dignity, and Jack had treated that as an afterthought. Jackie didn't think Jack mean, simply careless. And after so many near-death experiences, such heartless neglect in childhood — never once did his mother touch him affectionately, never so much as tousling the hair on his little head — she could understand his impulsivity. Justify it, even.

But this particular mortification was different. It hurt Jackie deeply. Was this revenge for all she had done for him? Was he jealous of her fame? Of the inner strength that allowed her to survive the loss of her babies and his constant infidelities? At times Jackie seemed to need no one, though that wasn't true. As she had shown him after her time at Valleyhead, she really did need her husband. She wanted him and only him, but the more she made that known to him, the more he pushed her away.

This was the second time Jackie really thought she would leave.

She gave him an ultimatum, and she meant it: No more contact with Marilyn Monroe. Otherwise she would divorce him and take the children and cost him reelection, and the American people would finally know why.

Jack complied, immediately. And Jackie, once again, felt her power.

———

After her husband's casket was loaded onto Air Force One in Dallas, Jackie sat alone in the plane in her blood-spattered pink Chanel suit. The men were afraid to talk to her. Everyone was weeping, even the Secret Service. Some were in a panic, convinced that they were sitting targets on the tarmac; one of them, an air force general, was near hysterical.

Jackie had gone into the plane's rear bathroom and cleaned her face and hair of Jack's blood and brains. She was already regretting that. She had been shocked upon boarding Air Force One to find Lyndon Johnson, the sheer physical enormity of him, splayed out on the bed, the bed she and Jack had made love in the day before, giving dictation. Where was the decorum? How could he not assume she would head to the bedroom? That she might need her privacy?

Lyndon had so quickly and easily assumed the mantle of president. Her husband had been dead only two hours. She stood before him in disbelief.

I should have left the blood on my face, Jackie said to herself. *Let them see what they've done.* The rest of her body was still splattered with Jack's blood, one leg slathered in it, her gold bracelet caked with it. She was covered in death.

Lyndon hastily roused himself and left without saying a word, his secretary fast behind him.

Laid out for her on the president's bed was a clean white dress. Who had put it there? No matter—Jackie had no intention of changing into it. She knew what that dress, originally intended for a campaign stop in Austin, would signify: whitewashing the fresh slaughter of her husband for the history books.

Lyndon, like all bullies, was a coward at the core. He was always giving orders while making his staffers watch him sitting on the toilet, or urinating in his sink, or brandishing his penis in front of his female secretaries. But he was different with Jackie, despite the mutual loathing between him and her husband. He was kind to her, gentlemanly, and Jackie liked him. Now, as he came back into the bedroom with his wife, Lady Bird, Lyndon searched for the right words.

"Honey," he said. He put his arm around her but left it to his wife—and Jackie had much in common with her, knowing the pain of your famous husband's philandering—to offer condolences.

"Oh, Jackie," Lady Bird said. "We never even wanted to be vice president, and now it's come to this."

"What if I hadn't been there?" Jackie said. "I was so glad I was there." It had been her first real campaign trip in years.

"I don't know what to say." Lady Bird was crying. "What wounds me most of all is that this should happen in my beloved state of Texas."

Jackie let the *faux pas* go. She could see the instant regret on Lady Bird's face.

"Can we get someone to help you put on fresh things?"

This was no better, but Lady Bird was trying.

"Oh no," Jackie said. "Not right now." The cabin was swelteringly hot, the fuselage absorbing the blazing Texas sun as the plane sat idle, the Kennedy and Johnson men fighting over when to take off.

Jackie was seated on the bed now, squeezed between the new president and First Lady. Trapped.

"Well," Lyndon said. "About the swearing in."

Of course. That was why they were here. They wanted Jackie to stand next to Lyndon as he took the oath of office. It was an image that would go around the world. Without Jackie—instantly the most sympathetic, pitied woman in America—Lyndon could easily lose half the electorate.

No wonder that white dress had been laid out. Jackie was meant to look clean, virginal, cool. Lyndon's bride. America's bride. What a desecration — of Jackie's marriage, her husband's memory, her own shock and trauma. Of what the country was and would be going through. White!

Jackie's inner image-maker guided her now. The Chanel suit, Jack's blood and brains splotched and caked on her pink wool bouclé, would stay on. No matter how hot the cabin was, no matter how stiff the blood or the stench of death. Only like this would she stand next to Lyndon.

———

"You're a brave little lady." This was some congressman from Texas, giving Jackie an unsolicited hug as she entered the main cabin.

Lyndon reached out and took Jackie's hand. "This is the saddest moment of my life," he said, pulling Jackie close. He turned to the White House photographer. "Is this the way you want us?"

Until now, Jackie had been able to keep herself apart from politics, but in this moment she had become the most important political figure in America. Her husband was dead, her small children fatherless, yet the most pressing matters on this plane were: When would Jackie clean herself up? Who could talk her into changing her dress? Would she support the new administration? Or would she join with Bobby and the rest of the Kennedys in undermining Lyndon and making him a one-term president?

Nothing and no one was sacred. Jackie was property now, and there was a battle underway as to who could claim her: the Lyndon Johnsons or the Kennedys. Every moment, every photograph, every note taken by reporters, every detail recorded by all these men who would go on to write biographies of her husband, all of it now had extraordinary weight. She understood instantly: Optics. If she controlled those, she controlled the messaging. She could shape how history viewed her husband.

"It's going to be so long and so lonely," she said, her voice barely above a whisper.

Lyndon took the oath; the plane took off. Then, as if it were any other afternoon, he ordered a second bowl of soup and gobbled it down. The chief of Dallas police — on Air Force One, who knew why? — addressed Jackie loudly enough for everyone to hear.

"God bless you, little lady," he said. "You ought to go back and lie down. You've had a bad day."

Little lady, little lady, do this, do that.

Jackie was tougher than any man on that flight.

She sat herself way back in the plane's tail, next to Jack's casket. It was so cramped, room for only two seats. Jack's men came to her one by one, kneeling down, some in tears, not knowing what to say. Jack's doctor approached her gingerly.

"Another dress?" he asked.

"No," Jackie said. "Let them see what they've done."

She wanted to see the book, she said, the one detailing President Lincoln's funeral. She summoned Mac Kilduff, Jack's acting press secretary. "You make sure, Mac," she said. "You go and tell them that I came back here and sat with Jack."

Kilduff—all of Jack's men—were surprised. The young widow Kennedy was displaying more fortitude than any of them. She was the only one thinking three steps ahead: live television, tragedy, pageantry, history. Jack's aides were focused on more immediate concerns: When they landed in DC, she would want Jack's casket shielded from the press, wouldn't she? They could easily make that happen, take the casket off the starboard side.

"No," Jackie said. "We'll go out the regular way." And because, apparently, she couldn't say it enough: "I want them to see what they have done."

But Jackie would prefer to be shielded from the press, wouldn't she?

No, she said. *Let them get their pictures. Let the news crews film me. Make sure of it.*

Really, why else was she suffering in this blood-stained suit? She wasn't crazy.

Kenny O'Donnell offered her a Scotch.

"I've never had Scotch in my life," Jackie said. "Now is as good a time as any to start." And so began their Irish wake, tears and storytelling and laughter, liquor flowing heavily though none of the mourners, Jackie included, were feeling any effect.

Someone raised the terrible, necessary question: Where should Jack be buried? The men told Jackie they thought Boston, next to Patrick, the

infant Jack and Jackie had lost just three months earlier. She was still grieving her baby, who had been born via cesarean on August 7 and had lived
for two days, struggling to breathe in a hyperbaric chamber in Boston, the
best the doctors could do. She hadn't known the extent of Jack's anguish,
that he kept asking the doctors, "Will he be retarded?," so fearful of what
had happened to Rosemary. He had made sure that Jackie saw the baby
and held his hand before they moved him to another hospital. Jack never
left the baby's side, and after Patrick died, he had never left hers.

"He must be buried in Boston," Kenny told her. "Don't you let them
change it."

No, Jackie thought to herself. *He won't be.*

She had had this conversation with Jack as he neared his first anniversary in the White House. It wasn't morbid to her; it was practical. He had
said they should both be buried in Hyannis, with all the Kennedys, but
Jackie disagreed.

"I think you should be buried in Arlington," she told him. "You just
belong to all the country."

At two minutes before 6:00 p.m., the plane landed at Andrews Air
Force base. Thousands of people were gathered outside, silent. Klieg
lights and TV cameras were in position, broadcasting live as her husband's coffin was visibly lowered to the ground. The sky was dark, a black
backdrop for this terrible tableau.

Bobby had been waiting for Jackie at Andrews Air Force Base. He
boarded Air Force One as soon as it landed and went right to Jackie.
When it was time to lower Jack's coffin they stood together, Jackie's right
hand clutching Bobby's, her black handbag in the other.

It was a detail, a signal, that only other women would notice: *I literally
have my bearings. I am holding all my stuff together.*

An ambulance would take Jack's body to Bethesda for the autopsy.
The driver, Jackie made sure, was Bill Greer, who had driven the black
Cadillac carrying Jackie and Jack in Dallas when he was shot. She wanted
him to know that he was not to blame — that *she* didn't blame him.

She would ride in the ambulance with Bobby, the coffin between
them. She would see the photographs soon, the televised news reports,
and was worried she might not have made her intended effect.

"What is the line," Jackie asked Bobby, "between histrionics and drama?"

She was going for high theater but worried she might verge on camp. She knew that Bobby knew that her question, her intention, was pure. This was all for Jack. From the moment she left Air Force One with Jack's casket until the moment he went into the ground, Jackie was on a self-appointed mission: Statecraft and stagecraft. Legacy.

———————

The three days ahead offered Jackie a kind of respite. She could control what happened next. Woe to anyone who dared deny her.

The funeral would be broadcast live. Three days of ceremonies, all Jackie's brainstorm. The men who'd been so deferential to her on Air Force One were now beginning to push back. She wanted a closed coffin; Bobby Kennedy and Bob McNamara insisted it be open. Traditional with heads of state, they said, as if the First Lady hadn't known.

In that case, Jackie said, *why don't all of you take a look at him and tell me that you think an open casket is the dignified choice.*

One by one, members of the Kennedy inner circle looked and agreed: Jackie was right. Jack, in her words, looked like one of Madame Tussaud's wax dummies.

She was in fighting form, amped up on adrenaline and speed. That was another secret between her and Jack, their confidential appointments with Max Jacobson, the German physician they called Dr. Feelgood. He shot them up with all kinds of drugs: speed, steroids, painkillers, animal hormones, bone marrow, human placenta. Neither Jack nor Jackie knew what, exactly, was in Feelgood's injections. "I don't care if it's horse piss," Jack once said. "It works."

The good doctor flew to DC as soon as he heard, but nothing could knock Jackie out. All that Scotch on Air Force One hadn't made her sleepy. Nor were the sedatives the White House doctors injected her with at night working. She felt as if she were being tossed around in the ocean by giant waves, endlessly fighting to break the surface. Who would take care of her? Her children? Where would she live? What would she do?

What would become of them?

Jackie threw herself into planning Jack's funeral. What she wanted would normally take weeks to execute. She made it happen within hours. Jack's casket would be drawn by a riderless horse out of the White House drive and down Pennsylvania Avenue, on the same caisson that had carried Franklin Delano Roosevelt. Jack would be buried at Arlington, their lost babies disinterred and buried alongside him, an eternal flame lighting their graves. That idea had come to her from visiting the Tomb of the Unknown Soldier at the Arc de Triomphe.

Bill Walton, the abstract expressionist painter and a friend of Jack and Jackie's, advised against it. "Aesthetically unfortunate," he told her.

She ignored him. He was hardly composed enough as it was.

"Bill," she told him, "please. Pull yourself together. You've got to help me get through the funeral. Both of us must be strong."

The flowers, Jackie said, were to be simple. Nothing overwrought. No purples or golds, and for God's sake, no wreaths at the grave. Her great friend, Bunny Mellon, the famed horticulturalist who had helped Jackie design the White House Rose Garden, was put in charge of that.

"When Patrick died," Jackie told her, "you sent such a nice, simple basket. So there's one thing I want at the grave. A straw basket with just the flowers he had in the Rose Garden."

That garden was another aspect of beauty that Jackie had awakened in him; when they returned from that triumphant state visit to France, Jack had looked out the Oval Office windows and wondered why the White House had nothing comparable to the great gardens of Paris, Luxembourg, or the Tuileries.

"Only those flowers," Jackie told Bunny, "and nothing else at the grave."

Jackie would lead the funeral procession, walking the quarter mile from the White House to the church behind Jack's flag-draped casket. The Secret Service was alarmed: Jackie was a target now, too. No one knew if the assassination was part of a larger national threat. The United States could not put foreign heads of state or dignitaries in harm's way.

Fine, Jackie said. She was walking with Jack. She would do it alone if it came to that, but she was pretty sure it wouldn't, because really, how would it look for this young widow to be left walking alone, showing more courage than the most powerful men on Earth?

"They can ride or do whatever they want to," Jackie said.

And no fat black Cadillacs, either, she said. Too ugly. Everything was to be sleek and geometric, clean and purposeful.

Jackie had her eye not just toward history but iconography: The young widow standing with her fatherless children, normally so shielded from the public eye, on the North Portico of the White House. Leading the nation in this funeral march, clutching the folded American flag at her husband's grave, lighting the Eternal Flame. Their two-year-old son, his father's namesake, stepping forward and paying tribute with a salute.

Her husband's death could not be in vain. His funeral would be the first step in consecrating his memory as she saw fit. This wasn't only about history; this was to enshrine their marriage, her love for him and his for her, as sacred and true. She demanded pomp and pageantry. She was going to transform the country's trauma, the violent death of a young president, into something regal and majestic.

Jackie was striking a near-impossible balance of grandeur and minimalism, pathos without mawkishness. America would show the world that this young nation could survive anything, with Jackie leading the way.

Before the funeral cortege was about to begin, Jackie stood among the guests in the State Room and looked around: not another woman to be found.

Jackie's mother, Janet, so often disapproving, wasn't surprised by her daughter's unerring flourishes amid quick decision-making. "Jackie has a great sense of the dramatic," she said. Janet couldn't find a thing to criticize.

Jackie had only one black dress, a Givenchy that she had worn to Eleanor Roosevelt's funeral and for John Jr.'s christening. She would wear it now for Jack. Her maid was told to buy three pairs of sheer black stockings and a black veil—not the mantillas Jackie wore to church, but a full veil that would obscure, but not conceal, her face.

This was the first time Jackie would draw a curtain between herself and the public. There was the Jackie before — the First Lady who favored bright, solid colors, her plumage so people could see her — and the Jackie after.

She didn't know who that was yet. But she knew the mother she would need to become. Caroline and John wouldn't be just the children of a former president, mildly interesting relics of a past administration. They would be living legacies, requiring an upbringing that she would need to invent as she went along.

But first, Jackie needed to get her small children through the next few days. It was a task even more daunting than helping the country through its grief.

She hadn't been able to bear the thought of telling the children. When she heard that the Secret Service had taken them from the White House on the night of the assassination she was enraged. They were so little, she said. They needed to be in their own beds, surrounded by the things and the people they loved. It was left to their nanny, Maud Shaw, to break the news, telling five-year-old Caroline that her daddy had gone to heaven to be with baby Patrick, who had been so lonely. Caroline cried so hard that Shaw feared she would choke. John's third birthday would coincide with the funeral, and Jackie was determined that her son would still have a party. He was too young to understand what was happening; he thought his father had flown away on his special helicopter.

Now Jackie had Caroline and John write a letter to their father. She would do the same, writing five tear-stained pages addressed to "My darling Jack." It was an exorcism of sorts, Jackie expressing herself like the writer she was. To others, she spoke of only two things: what had happened in Dallas, and what she wanted for the funeral. No one, not even Bobby, could draw her out on her emotions.

And so the letter she would leave with Jack, in his coffin, was as much for her as him. She had survived the loss of baby Patrick, she wrote, only because of Jack. She wrote of what she had said to him soon after, that she now knew she could suffer anything except losing Jack. "The blow," she wrote, "I could not bear."

Yet here she was, bearing it.

Within days of the assassination, having also written to Soviet premier Nikita Khrushchev — reassuring him that Lyndon Johnson would seek the peace and nuclear détente that her husband had worked for — Jackie wrote to a newly widowed young mother of three, Marie Tippit. Her husband, a police officer named J. D. Tippit, had been shot to death while trying to arrest Jack's assassin.

Marie had lost her husband to the very same killer on the very same day, yet J.D.'s sacrifice had already been lost to history. Marie, of course, was thinking of Jackie, too, the only other person on earth who could empathize with the sudden, surreal loss of a husband this way. Yet the handwritten condolence letter Marie received on plain white paper, dated November 30, 1963, came as a shock. Jackie wrote that she thought of Marie constantly; that if there was anything Jackie could do for her, ever, Marie had only to ask; and that she knew Marie's sorrow and loss were as deep as her own.

> *You know I lit a flame for Jack at Arlington that will burn forever. I consider that it burns for your husband too — and so will everyone who ever sees it.*

When the funeral was over, Jackie greeted the mourners back at the White House with warmth and stoicism. She spoke at length with French president De Gaulle. Then she went upstairs to her son's birthday party. "I couldn't disappoint little John," she said. She found Britain's Prince Philip playing on the floor with him, and the image was almost too much: no title, no hierarchy or power structure could impede anyone from comforting and distracting a newly fatherless little boy who had just turned three.

With the funeral behind her, Jackie's most urgent task lay ahead. One day before burying her husband, she had told Pierre Salinger, one of Jack's most trusted advisers, of her new life's mission.

"I have only one thing to do now," Jackie said. "I have to take care of these kids. I have to make sure they grow up well. They have to get intelligent. They have to move forward to get good jobs. They have to have a whole, very important life, because if I don't do that for them, they'll spend all their time looking back at their father's death. And that's what they shouldn't be doing."

Jackie was nothing if not a student of history, and she was not about to leave Jack's legacy to strangers or outsiders. No — Jacqueline Kennedy was going to author this particular draft of American consequence. The funeral, Jackie knew, had served its purpose, but it wasn't — could not be — the end of the story. The chronicle of her husband's short administration had yet to be written. What had happened in Dallas, she knew, should not be the end. It had to be a beginning.

No one would expect her to talk so soon. No one, not even their close friend Ben Bradlee, then a journalist with *Newsweek*, had dared ask Jackie for an interview. She didn't want to give him the exclusive anyway. Ben was always covering for Jack's affairs.

Theodore White, though. He had written *The Making of the President 1960*, the definitive account of Jack's campaign. Jack had admired him, and the feeling was mutual. White would cast Jack in the best posthumous light. So one week after the assassination and the day after Thanksgiving, *Life* magazine already on the stands with its JFK memorial issue, Jackie, in retreat at the Kennedy compound, summoned White.

Jackie was going to turn *Life*'s cover story into a palimpsest. She had reached White by phone that morning in New York City, cold-called him as he sat in a dentist's chair. He couldn't get to the Cape fast enough.

———

Jackie greeted White at 8:30 that night, tall and proud in her chic casual wear: camel-colored cigarette pants and black sweater, her hair impeccable, her eyes clear. Her composure was in stark contrast to the rainstorm raging outside, and this played to her sense of theatricality. Jackie thrived in a crisis, grew calm and still. This was something she hadn't known about herself before.

Jackie sat on the sofa. White joined her. She was going to lead but let White feel as if he were in control. She leaned forward, tilted herself toward him, made herself seem vulnerable. Open.

"What shall I say?" Jackie asked him softly. "What can I do for you?" Jackie already knew everything she would and would not say.

"How do you want him remembered?" White asked.

Off she went, talking first about herself. "I'm not going to be the 'Widder' Kennedy in public," Jackie said. "When this is over I'm going to crawl into the deepest retirement." She told White what had happened in the car after Jack was shot. She spoke of the hysterical men, Jack's aides and the priests at the hospital, of her regret at cleaning her bloody face and hair with a Kleenex. Now she was still wearing Jack's wedding band and twisted it around her finger as she chain-smoked. She showed White the emerald ring that Jack had given her to honor baby Patrick.

She knew the kind of color and detail a journalist craved. She would give these things to White in exchange for what she wanted. Her rage at two prominent columnists who had been critical of her husband, hammering at his great failures in foreign policy and race relations, gave way to her fear that he would be remembered poorly, if at all. Jackie could not allow that.

"Every time we got off the plane that day," Jackie told White, "three times they gave me the yellow roses of Texas. But in Dallas they gave me red roses. I thought, 'How funny, red roses' — so all the seat was full of blood and red roses." Jackie knew that people were curious about her, but she spoke only of what she would not do, what she did not want. "I'm not going around accepting plaques," she said. "I don't want medals for Jack. I don't want to go out on a Kennedy driveway to a Kennedy airport to visit a Kennedy school . . . I don't want to be seen by crowds."

Jackie said she was going to focus on raising her children. She did not know where they would live yet, but it would not be in their old Georgetown town house. That night at Bethesda, she said, as Jack's autopsy was being performed, she thought to herself: "How can I go back there, to that bedroom? I said to myself, 'You must never forget Jack, but you mustn't be morbid.'"

White took notes longhand, scribbling furiously, as Jackie spoke uninterrupted. He had barely asked a question; she was so focused, so sure of herself, even as she acted so helpless. "There's this one thing I wanted to say," Jackie said. "I'm so ashamed of myself. Jack . . . Everything he ever quoted was Greek or Roman."

It wasn't. This was the dramatist in Jackie, flowering as she soliloquized.

"No, don't protect me now," Jackie told White. By acting as though what she was about to say was personal, that she was so carried away that she was divulging information she never would otherwise, she knew White would print it.

"One thing kept going through my mind," she said, " — the line from a musical comedy. I kept saying to Bobby, 'I've got to talk to somebody, I've got to see somebody, I want to say this one thing.' It's been almost an obsession with me. This line from the musical comedy's been almost an obsession with me. At night before going to bed... We had an old Victrola. He'd play a couple of records. I'd get out of bed at night and play it for him when it was so cold getting out of bed. It was a song he loved — he loved 'Camelot.' It was the song he loved most at the end... It's the last record, the last side of 'Camelot,' sad 'Camelot': 'Don't let it be forgot that for one brief shining moment there was Camelot.' "

White knew this was patently untrue. Everyone who knew Jack Kennedy did. This was not a man who had been given to poetry or romance or middlebrow Broadway musicals — much less someone who employed such heavy-handed metaphor. Jack Kennedy wasn't the kind of husband who was home with his wife every night, let alone sharing the same bed and cozying up by the Victrola. White looked at the questions he had written, questions concerned with pragmatism and history, none of which Jackie had any interest in answering:

Religion?

Vision for the country?

Did he like the job?

How do we keep him living?

There was one he had written not for Jackie, but for himself: "What does a woman think?"

———

At midnight Jackie showed White to the maid's room, where he set to work on his first draft. *Life* was holding the presses for this Jackie exclusive, literally, at a cost of $30,000 per hour. He had made another note to himself to "write simply," yet he could not resist leading with the imagery of this dark and rainy night, citing the poet Verlaine on the "sobbing of the autumn," rhapsodizing over Jackie's wide brown eyes and thoughtful stillness.

When he was done, White handed Jackie his draft. She began cutting mercilessly, striking out entire passages. This was the deal: *Life* got the exclusive if she got the final edit. So instead of White's confusing and banal original lede — "It was raining the day he returned to Washington; there had been a brief few days of sun and blue on the East Coast" — Jackie insisted that White's third graf, a knockout, become the lede.

"She remembered how hot the sun had been in Dallas" —

Yes. That put the reader right there, in the back of that car with Jackie, just before the first shot. It was compelling, intimate, foreboding.

"And other memories, very private and frightening," White had written. "But mostly how all through the night, they had tried to separate him from her, to sedate her, and take care of her."

Jackie did not like that. She struck out "and take care of her," writing, "she would not let them" sedate her. A lachrymose line about Jackie wearing Jack's wedding ring, "the closest thing she had for memory of him, she said, letting the fingers of the right hand touch the left," was cut, too. She wanted this piece moving at a fast clip until it reached the mythological ending she had crafted for Jack.

Sometime close to 2:00 a.m., White called his editors in New York and dictated the final draft from her kitchen. Jackie stood over him to ensure that her version, word for word, would be the published one. She was right to do so; she listened as White pushed back tensely, his editors calling the Camelot stuff overwrought. Untrue. Laughable.

Jackie looked at White and shook her head back and forth. It was her version or nothing. And so her first draft of history won out, the very last line, the kicker, written in her own back-slanted cursive: "For one brief shining moment there was Camelot."

That fairy tale would captivate America for decades to come — at the cost of many more women.

What, in hindsight, had she wrought?

PART SEVEN
STOLEN YOUTH

PAMELA KELLEY

S ummer of 1973, Cape Cod. Pamela Kelley was one of Hyannis's golden girls, popular and cool, with long blonde hair parted down the middle. She and her siblings had grown up close to the Kennedy compound, going to birthday parties and movie nights at the Robert F. Kennedy house, friends with most of the children. The Kennedy compound, by now, was a storied place in American mythology, but it really wasn't a compound. Rose and Joe Kennedy had a big house on the ocean; that was where they took all those photos of the Kennedys playing touch football or toothily rough-housing. Jackie and JFK had a smaller house around the corner, and other family members wound up buying houses nearby. Summers were the only time that Bobby Kennedy Jr. and his brothers Joe and David were around. All three boys were especially drawn to Pam.

Bobby and Joe were hellions, but David was the sensitive one. That made him weak in the eyes of the other Kennedys, but Pam and her sisters adored David. He was so kind, so genuinely interested in other people.

This would be Pam's last summer on the Cape before graduating high school, and she had begun seeing David. Ethel Kennedy didn't like the Kelley girls, but then Ethel didn't seem to like many people, including, sometimes, her own children. Maybe because Pam was so much like Ethel's boys — wild and impetuous, school not a priority, drinking and taking drugs, no real aim in life. Not yet, at least.

But to Ethel, girls were the problem. It didn't matter that her boys were known as The Hyannis Port Terrors. That they painted their faces black before slipping out into the night to stuff their neighbors' tailpipes with potatoes. Or that they would run into oncoming traffic and fall in the road, pretending to be mortally wounded while their cousins terrorized these random drivers. "You killed a Kennedy!" they would yell. Bobby Jr., as the ringleader, would roam the streets with one of his massive hawks. These birds were a point of pride for him, having taken up falconry after his father's assassination. Everyone else hated those hawks, because Bobby never really learned how to train them, yet he insisted on having his birds and other exotic animals in his room at boarding school. He once threatened a Hyannis police officer with one of his hawks, saying he had trained it to "kill cops." Everything Ethel's kids did on the Cape was to prove a single point: Kennedys could get away with anything.

August 13 on the Cape was gusty and raw, no good for the beach. David and Joe and a bunch of other kids were headed to Nantucket on the ferry. Would Pam and her younger sister Kim like to come? Pam wasn't feeling all that great, but Kim wanted to go—with her sister. Kim was near tears, begging Pam to change her mind. Part of it, Pam knew, was that Kim was trying to cram in as much time together before Pam graduated and headed off to this new life she had planned in San Francisco. Pam and Kim were only one year apart—Irish twins, they were called—and especially close. How could Pam say no?

So they packed their bags, and the next day was as Pam expected: she and Kim among seven kids piled into a Jeep with seating for only four. There was no roof. Joe was at the wheel, tearing through the unpaved roads of Nantucket, kids just spilling out of the Jeep, playing the usual Kennedy game of ducking under low-hanging tree branches as they sped along, a dare that could get you clotheslined by a branch or worse. Joints were passed. Joe drove in circles before crossing into the other lane and into oncoming traffic. He swerved. The Jeep flipped at least twice, its passengers launched into the air like small missiles.

Kim landed on the pavement. Another girl thudded down on top of her. Three others were thrown into the woods.

"Where's Pam?" Kim was frantic. "Where's Pam? Where's Pam?"

Passersby halted. Ambulances came with what small mercies they could offer on such a tiny island, loading Kim and Pam and a girl named Mary into the first ambulance on stretchers.

"Pam," Kim said. "How are you?"

"I can't feel my legs," Pam said.

Mary was screaming her head off.

"I can't feel anything," Pam said.

"You're in shock, Pam," Kim said. "You'll be all right."

———————

Pam had been thrown thirty feet before smashing down onto a tree stump. A priest was called to give her last rites. Then she was carried by stretcher onto a helicopter. Three hours later, Pam was back on the mainland at Cape Cod Hospital in Hyannis, rushed into emergency surgery with a swollen spine. When her surgeons emerged seven hours later—surgeons called in by Ted Kennedy from Boston, among the best there were—they told the Kelleys that it would be two weeks before they would know if Pam would ever walk again.

Her older sister, Karen, was in the tiny Cape Cod waiting room. She had been working her summer job at the CVS pharmacy at the mall when her parents called her manager, asking for Karen to please be sent home. Kim had been checked out of the emergency room hours earlier and was back home in their living room. The sisters sat in silence for a few minutes as they watched a news report about the accident. Kim threw a book at the TV and broke it.

That night, Karen went to the hospital. It seemed like all the Kennedys were there, including others who hadn't been on Nantucket but were summering on the Cape, Joe's cousin Maria Shriver among them. The Kelley kids loved Maria, thought she was a doll. Kim, choking back tears, went outside to smoke a cigarette. Maria followed and did her best to comfort her as Kennedys knew how.

"Don't cry," she told Karen. "Don't cry in front of all these people." Maria herself was maybe eighteen years old, but at least she was trying to help—unlike Joe, who was also at the hospital instead of where he should be, in a police interrogation room. He hadn't been tested for drugs or alcohol after the crash. He hadn't said "I'm sorry," to the Kelleys or to anyone.

Kim would blame herself. "I'm the one who should be hurt," she would say. "I'm stronger than she is."

Why Pam? Sweet, gentle, funny Pam, who loved animals, who would take the blame for any of her siblings, anytime, because her parents knew she was never really the guilty one anyway. Pam, who didn't ask for much in life. Who was happiest sitting under a streetlight on summer nights after family dinners, or stargazing on the beach, breathing in the soft, salty ocean air with her friends—Kim, of course, and Bobby Jr. and Joe and David—promising each other that no matter where life took them, they would always reunite here.

On those evenings, when it was time to go home, Pam and Kim would break off and stay at the beach, gulls smashing shells against craggy rocks, and just sit. The vastness of the ocean against the night sky seemed to embody their future: huge, unknowable, vaguely mystical, touched by this storied American family who shared their largesse along with their danger.

The carnage, as reported, was unbelievable. Mary's pelvis and femur were shattered. Two girls had broken their necks. Six days later Joe Kennedy was in court, standing before Judge George Anastos, a college classmate of his late uncle Joseph Kennedy, who had been killed in the war. There Joe sat, inexpressive and emotionless, as witnesses and drivers testified that Joe had been driving in the wrong lane and speeding while kids were standing up and hanging out of the Jeep. Joe pled not guilty, even though he had told the police that the accident was all his fault.

His mother Ethel was in the small Nantucket courthouse, as was his Uncle Ted. The judge turned to Joe.

"Do you believe that prison sentences deter automobile accidents?" the judge asked.

"I don't think so," Joe said. "I think that someone getting seriously hurt would be more of a deterrent." Four of his seven passengers had been gravely injured.

"You had a great father and you have a great mother," Anastos said. "Use your illustrious name as an asset instead of coming into court like this." He gave Joe a $100 fine and let him go.

It was quick and tidy, both in court and the press. In their coverage of Joe's court hearing, the *New York Times* didn't mention Pam's name, or the extent of her injuries, until the last paragraph.

———

Her mother delivered the news. She told Pam she would never walk again, that the doctors said she would never have children, and that she probably wouldn't live past the age of forty. Pam didn't say a word. Tears spilled down her face. Two weeks earlier, her whole life lay ahead of her. Now she was in a hospital bed, shivering under ice packs meant to relieve her back spasms. She would never go to the bathroom normally again. Her world would be wheelchairs and physical therapy and catheters.

And Kennedys. They kept coming into her room, Caroline and Maria and Joe, bringing flowers and freshly baked cookies and a movie projector—while the older Kennedys, Rose and Ethel and Ted, were talking to Pam's parents about a settlement. No need to involve lawyers or civil lawsuits or the media, they said.

Pam's parents wanted to sue, but Pam wouldn't hear of it. David was her boyfriend, Joe was her friend, and you don't, Pam said, sue your friends. Her parents tried to explain. Pam's condition was going to require a lot more than she could understand now. To begin with, their house would have to be retrofitted for her wheelchair, steps turned into ramps, doorways and at least one shower made wide enough for her wheelchair. She would need a new bed with a bar over it so she could lift herself up in the middle of the night if she had to go to the bathroom, or mornings when no one was home. She would need help cleaning and dressing herself, cooking and going to the bathroom, probably for the rest of her life. She would require constant physical therapy so that her legs wouldn't atrophy. If they sued, her parents explained, Joe would not pay a dime. His insurance company would cover it.

Pam still wouldn't do it. Besides, she said, Joe had promised: Whatever Pam needed, whenever she needed it—he would take care of her. Always.

———

What Pam didn't know was how troubled Joe was—as troubled as Bobby. Joe had entrée to all the best schools but was academically lazy. He wanted special treatment and, when he got it, resented it. To wit: After the accident, a Kennedy family friend had connected Joe with Diane Clemens, a Berkeley professor who had worked on his Uncle Jack's presidential campaign. Out of affection for his uncle, Diane invited Joe to live in her basement apartment while he went to college on the West Coast and waited for the publicity surrounding the crash to blow over. And so it was that Clemens came home one night to find that Joe had scared her eleven-year-old daughter, breaking down a locked door and chasing the girl through the house. "I'll kill you!" he screamed. Not long after that, Joe had two major car accidents: flipping his Toyota pickup into a ravine, and crashing into a car driven by a sixteen-year-old.

David had been in the same hospital as Pam the whole time, in traction with a broken back. He didn't believe it when one of Pam's friends told him that she would be paralyzed for life. He insisted on getting wheeled into Pam's room. "That fucking bitch friend of yours," he said to Pam. "You wouldn't believe the shit she's been telling me."

"It's true," Pam said. It was her first inkling that the Kennedys would try to minimize her agony. To make her go away.

Pam spent three months in Cape Cod Hospital and another nine months in rehab at Mass General. Her mother quit her job to tend to Pam full time. In the end, neither Pam nor the Kelleys sued Joe; they settled instead with the company that had insured the Jeep, and used the $668,000 to buy a large Hyannis house with a swimming pool and a tennis court. It overlooked a big pond and was a permanent reminder of all the things Pam could no longer do.

In public Pam was all cheer, a brave face. She made it a point to travel with Kim, to learn to dance by tipping back her wheelchair, to happily greet strangers and tourists who recognized her as The Girl from the Kennedy Accident. Her pride allowed for nothing else. In private, Pam was shattered. She had to use a catheter to urinate. She had to take suppositories to have bowel movements. Her mother had to roll her over to prevent bed sores. Pam dreaded falling and had to learn how to pick herself up, more than half her body now dead weight. In those first two years Pam would hole up in her room and throw things — at the wall, at her siblings. She cried night after night, loudly enough for the whole family to hear. She would yell at her mother to make everything all right.

She took a lit cigarette and branded her stomach with three letters: *D-I-E.* She would say it out loud: "I want to die."

Meanwhile David, already a drug user, slid deeper into his addiction. After Pam, his next big relationship was with the starlet Rachel Ward, who did not recognize the marks on David's arms for what they were: tracks from shooting heroin five times a day. In and out of rehab, hospitalized twice for endocarditis, David saw himself as the worst things a Kennedy could be: weak. A political liability.

By 1980, two years after Pam's accident, David had broken up with Ward and moved to Sacramento, though he rarely ventured outside. He watched television 24/7 amid drug-induced hallucinations. He came upon a photo of his aunt Rosemary in a magazine, as she was now, and David was stricken: If his grandfather had still been alive, what would have stopped him from doing something similar to David? Was he not as much of an embarrassment? A failure?

Desperate, he called Pam. He begged her to come stay with him for a little while. Pam agreed. He told her that she would need to leave her wheelchair at home.

"I can't leave my wheelchair here, David," Pam said. "It's part of me, and I'm part of it."

That was the end for Pam. The Kennedys were now nothing to her, just as she was to them.

The same stubbornness that had kept Pam from suing Joe was now the very thing that kept her going. She got married. In 1989 she had a baby, a girl she named Paige. Things were good for a couple of years. Then her husband left for work one morning and didn't come home.

Pam began volunteering at CORD, the Cape Organization for the Rights of the Disabled. Within a few years she was running the place and had officially been named director. She fought to make the community college and local courthouse wheelchair-accessible and won. She joined AA after realizing her depression had led to alcohol dependence. She learned how to drive and chauffeured other differently abled people around the Cape, taking them to the supermarket or doctor's appointments.

Pam put herself on the front lines, protesting in a crosswalk that was nonnegotiable for anyone in a wheelchair. CORD gave Pam a sense of purpose she'd never had before, but it didn't pay her bills. It didn't help as her medical needs grew, as she battled recurring back spasms and bladder cancer. It didn't pay for childcare or visiting nurses or a housekeeper. Pam turned to Joe for help several times during such hardships, but each time she was rebuffed. "I'm not made of money," he'd tell her.

In the decades since the accident, Joe married, had twin boys, and moved to a gorgeous 1860s farmhouse. He had founded a nonprofit called Citizens Energy Corp in 1979 and turned it into something of a personal piggy bank, eventually paying himself a six-figure salary.

I'm not made of money.

In 1986, Joe ran for Congress as, he claimed, the candidate of "ordinary, hardworking families." Pam would sometimes be mentioned in articles about Joe, usually not by name. He would call her from time to time and invite her to be his special guest at campaign stops. Neither before his election to Congress nor during his subsequent five terms did Joe ever sit down with Pam, or her siblings or parents, to talk about the accident, or to apologize, or to say what he might do for Pam and people like her.

"Joe doesn't give a shit about me," Pam would say. "He doesn't care."

Her sister Karen knew: Pam was right. Karen had been at a fundraiser for Joe's sister Kathleen, who was running for governor of Maryland, when Joe came in and started working the room, shaking hands and self-deprecatingly introducing himself — "Hi, hi, Joe Kennedy, Joe, hi, hi."

He got to Karen and gave her the same greeting.

"I know who you are," she said.

Joe took a beat.

"Oh, Karen!" he said.

She remembered nothing else except for what he didn't ask: "How's Pam?"

It was a regret for the Kelleys, not having sued Joe Kennedy, or at least not getting an agreement in writing. Over forty-seven years, Joe, who by 2005 had amassed a real estate portfolio worth two million dollars, had given Pam $50,000 in total. She constantly debated whether to go to the press. Her anonymity outside of Hyannis was a blessing and a curse. In every recap of so-called Kennedy tragedies, if Pam was mentioned at all it was never by name. She was just The Girl, one in a long litany. And Pam had been a good girl at that. She had never complained. She had tried not to hold a grudge against the Kennedys.

"What happened to me stinks," she once said, "but I made something good out of it."

She felt that Joe's father, Robert, whom she admired, and his uncle Jack would have been proud of what she'd done for the disabled. It was, after all, his own sister Rosemary who inspired JFK to make advocacy for the physically and mentally disabled part of his administration's agenda. Why couldn't Joe see that?

By 2005, Pam was in terrible shape: sickly and emaciated, she needed a new bed and a new wheelchair. She could no longer drive and was forced to retire from CORD. She was losing her ability to care for herself and required more help than her family could provide.

"I want to stay in my house and I want to be able to leave something to my daughter," Pam said. "When I got hurt in 1973, I really believed [Joe] would do the right thing. That's what I said to my dad: 'You don't have to sue them. They'll do the right thing.' But they haven't done the right thing yet and I'm tired of it."

Her experience in 1999 during the days-long search for JFK Jr.'s plane, reporters on the Cape right in front of her and not knowing who she was, disturbed her greatly. She had no problem going public now. She had no problem offering her unfiltered thoughts about Joe Kennedy.

"I feel like he thinks I'm a piece of trash sitting in a wheelchair," she told a local reporter.

It worked. Joe, who had recently left Congress to return to the energy company that he had founded before entering politics, was shamed into giving Pam help, a little over $2,000 a month. It wasn't nearly enough. In 2019, facing bankruptcy and the loss of her home, she spoke to *People* magazine.

"I don't think anybody still wonders where I am today," Pam said. "I don't think anybody remembers, really."

Pam Kelley Burkley died on November 20, 2020, at the age of sixty-five, of sepsis. The family heard nothing from Joe. The very next month, his checks to Pam stopped.

After the accident, Pam's sister Kim wrote an essay about her sister. It was just for herself and her siblings, no one else. She called it "Wings," a nod to Pam's free spirit and her tenderness, this young girl who sought out injured birds and nursed them until they could fly. A girl whose body began breaking down before its time. A girl who grew into a woman, whose lifelong love of the sea gave her solace, to a point. Kim wrote of taking Pam to the beach after the accident. "I took my sister back to the big breakwater," Kim wrote. "I carried her up, through and over the wet rocks. We sat under the tower with red and green blinking lights and we could hear the gong buoy in the distance. We remembered, and I wiped the tears from her eyes. I turned my head towards the west, so she couldn't see mine.

"I held her tightly and walked her back to where we had played mermaids. We both picked the wild roses, and they smelled as beautiful as ever. We put a few in our hair, which was no longer golden blonde. Some we threw into the ocean, letting the tide take them . . . The petals floated away with many of our dreams.

"When I find red and blue-green sea glass, I think of her. They are the most valuable possession of all mermaids. Her legs no longer work, but underwater she glides swiftly with stamina, grace and dignity, and outdoes any fish in the ocean."

Kim ended with the wish that she could be as strong and self-reliant as Pam. She didn't know if she would ever get there.

"I'm still looking," she wrote, "for a couple pairs of wings."

MARTHA MOXLEY

n one of the diaries that Mary found in her suburban New York home, back when she still shared it with Bobby, he had tucked a newspaper clipping between two blank pages. The headline read:

ETHEL K. NEPHEW CALLED A KILLER

This had become one of Bobby's obsessions, trying to clear his cousin Michael Skakel, who would soon stand trial for murdering a teenage girl.

Why? Why would Bobby risk his reputation doing this?

Everyone knew the Kennedy men could be violent with women. Another cousin, William Kennedy Smith, had been charged but acquitted of raping a woman in Palm Beach back in 1991 — a woman whose reputation the Kennedys had successfully smeared, the *New York Times* outing her by name, implying that she was a party girl, wild, a single mother who, if she wasn't making the whole story up, had kind of gotten what was coming to her.

That trial had been televised on twenty-four-hour cable television. When the woman took the stand, a blue dot had been placed over her face. What was meant to protect this woman had also erased her.

The Kennedys had bullied John Jr. into showing up for Willie. But when it came to Michael Skakel, as the years went by, the most prominent Kennedys would fall away. Except Bobby Jr.

Martha Moxley had been in Connecticut only one year when she was voted best personality in school. It would have been easy to envy her, but among Martha's many gifts was a way of putting people at ease. At fourteen, she was an old soul and a young girl still, with her Snoopy earrings and her braces. Her father still called her by his nickname for her, "Martha Dookie Pie Baby," and she let him.

The Moxleys had just moved from California to Greenwich, her dad a rising star in international accounting. Now they lived in a huge house on three acres with a formal garden, a reflecting pool, a guesthouse, and, for Martha, what her artistic mother called a "garret"—Martha's own little world on the third floor, with a large bedroom and private bathroom. Martha had her own stereo and television set, a faux fur throw on a cot for guests, chairs covered in tapestries, and a wall that she and her friends were collaging with magazine cutouts. She asked her mom to make her a quilt out of gingham checks in pastels.

She lived up there with her beloved cats, Tiger and Junior. She was happy alone—a reader, like her mom, and a diarist. But Martha was also a joiner: swim team, yearbook, gymnastics, ballet. She was co-captain of the basketball team. She was on the pep rally committee and had been voted president of the letterman's club. All within months of a cross-country move.

She knew how to throw a good sleepover. Martha and her new girlfriends would mix Bacardi and coke, drink beer, and try to master the art of looking glamorous while smoking cigarettes. Sometimes Martha fumbled hers; she had burned a hole through a page in her small diary, trying to write and smoke like serious thinkers.

But Martha also had a great sense of humor. *Funzie-wunzies* was her sarcastic way of being enthusiastic; *Yuck-a-Mora* was real-deal disgust. She and her girlfriends would watch *The Wizard of Oz* or *Willy Wonka and the Chocolate Factory*, then call the boys in her class and tell them which girls had crushes on them. Martha liked a boy named Jeff, who called *her* at home and asked who she liked. He was almost all she could think about. Jeff had a girlfriend named Cindy, but he still flirted with Martha all the time.

FEBRUARY 7, 1975

Dear Diary—Guess who was at school today—right, Jeff. And Alan (the little fucker) told him that I like him. Oh, he has had it!

Martha and her friend Christy had this thing where they would take aspirin with a Coke and wait to see what happened. Rumor had it you would either get really high or you would die from the combination, but every single time they felt nothing. One of the boys at school called Martha and made her promise him she'd stop doing that. It was dangerous, he said, and he didn't want anything to happen to her. If only that boy had been Jeff.

Belle Haven was nothing like the Bay Area. Her new neighbors had last names like Versailles and Shakespeare. Her new friends' fathers were people like Charles Schwab or the head of Chevron. Her friend Helen's dad was heir to the Schweppes fortune.

Then there was the Skakel house. Everyone knew that the Skakels were related to the Kennedys: Rush Skakel, the dad, was Ethel Kennedy's brother — brother-in-law to the late RFK, which made the Skakel kids the cousins of Bobby Jr., Joe, and David. Rush was raising all seven children on his own; their mother had recently died of brain cancer, and Rush was having a midlife crisis, never really home.

It was too much for any one parent to handle. And two of his sons, seventeen-year-old Tommy and fifteen-year-old Michael, were definitely too much to handle.

School on the East Coast had an edge, and to Martha's surprise, she liked it. She was a sunny California girl with sass and never granted authority figures unearned respect. She reserved her true thoughts about her teachers for her diary:

"Sit on it and twirl, Mr. Stein!"

"I can't stand Mrs. McGregor...If I ask her a question, it's 'come after school.' Listen lady, I'm in your class too!" For Christmas, Martha and her friends gave their teacher Miss Rogers a jock strap, its lace cover sewed on by Martha herself.

"Mr. Zerega is so nice, he told me a joke but I didn't get it — How do you keep a Jewish girl from screwing? — Marry her. Huh?"

This was a fancy school, but there weren't many protections for girls. Boys were always pushing Martha into darkrooms or locker rooms and holding her arms, trying to kiss her or shove their hands down her pants. A boy named Kenny took Martha into the bathroom one day and turned off all the lights.

"Why is it always me?" Martha wrote in her diary. "What can you do when they have your hands and arms? Nothing."

Everyone knew that lots of boys had crushes on Martha—Ray, Peter, Bill. She tried to avoid the boys who she didn't like back; she didn't want to hurt their feelings. Besides, Peter was getting close to asking for a date; she could tell.

JANUARY 22: Peter was supposed to ask me out today, but I hid from him at lunch. I guess I'm afraid of him asking me 'cause I don't know what to say. I don't want to but I don't know how to say no. At lunch I got pushed into the bathroom by about ten guys. After I got out, about three or four guys picked me up and almost carried me in, but they didn't get that far.

Jeff wasn't like these other guys. He circled around Martha, asking her friends whom she liked, or if she would go for a guy like him. One day at lunch, when Jeff and Martha were sitting at the same table, one of Jeff's friends turned to him and said, "How long has Martha liked you?"

Martha felt her face burn right up.

———

She tried to distract herself. There were pizza parties, house parties, movie nights, shopping with friends, or with her mom in New York City, at Saks and Bergdorf's. Martha loved Lacoste and was growing into her East Coast preppy-dom. Her mom gave her a fifty-dollar clothing allowance and a credit card to Ann Taylor, so she could buy what she liked when she liked.

Oh, how Martha wanted to be a grown-up. She would greet her parents' party guests at the front door and take their coats, once borrowing a glamorous guest's fur wrap and entering the party with one of her dad's unlit cigars between her teeth. Everyone loved that.

DECEMBER 31, 1974

> *Dear Diary,*
> *Today is the last day of 1974. Boo hoo. '74 has been one of the best years of my life... Well, hope '75 is as good.*

———

That next year was a big one for Martha: She turned fifteen. She rode in a Ferrari. She had her eye on a new bicycle, a yellow ten-speed Atala, and was fairly sure her parents would get it for her. She smoked pot for the first time and went to the US Open, where she got Jimmy Connors's autograph and watched Björn Borg play. On a waterskiing trip to Tahoe she met a boy named Mark, a few years older than her—*El Foxo*, she called him.

One night Mark asked her if she wanted to go all the way and she said no. Not at fourteen years old. For someone so young, Martha had a sense of herself. It wasn't based on how pretty and well dressed she was, or her liveliness or her smarts or popularity. It was a quieter thing, innate. She was a magnet for other kids who lacked that stillness, that grounding.

Kids like Michael Skakel.

Martha wanted nothing to do with Michael. He was obnoxious and creepy and mean, always hovering around Martha with his dark energy, as if he could force her into liking him back.

> *SEPTEMBER 17: Michael was so totally out of it that he was being a real asshole in his actions & words. He kept telling me that I was leading Tom on when I don't like him (except as a friend) & I said, Well, how about you and Jackie? You keep telling me that you don't like her & you're all over her. He doesn't understand that he can be nice to her without hanging all over her. Michael jumps to conclusions... He kept calling {two other boys} fags... I really have to stop going over there.*

———

Just over one month later, Martha found herself grounded on Mischief Night — Halloween eve, when all the kids in Belle Haven were running around, no school the next day. She was dying to join them. John, her older brother, was out with friends. Her dad was on a business trip in Atlanta. Her mom was busy painting mullions in the master bedroom and freshening the windows for the new draperies she had ordered. It was cold outside, already very dark.

Martha begged her mom: *Please, everyone else is out tonight, don't make me be the only one to stay home.*

And Martha really was such a good kid. It would only be a few hours.

She never made it home that night. Dorothy was frantic, even though the idea of a child being abducted in Belle Haven — one of the wealthiest, safest, most secure neighborhoods on the East Coast — was unthinkable. But so was the notion that Martha wouldn't come home by curfew. Dorothy called the police at 3:45 a.m., and when four officers arrived at the house, they found nothing. They put out an APB for Martha and left.

Martha had been nearby the whole time, in her yard, in the grass, under a pine tree. Parts of her scalp had been shorn off. One of her earlobes was torn in half. Her little nose was bashed in. Her face had been punctured with small holes that looked like craters. A broken bottle had been jammed inside her. One of her blue eyes was still open. She looked like a baby, pure and helpless.

Martha had bruises on the back of her upper thighs. A narrow metal shard was jammed through her neck, inches to the right of her chin. Her pants and underwear had been yanked down to her ankles.

Her friend Sheila was the one to find Martha that next morning. She ran to the Moxley house and told Dorothy that she couldn't tell if Martha had been attacked by dogs or raped but they better call an ambulance immediately, and Mrs. Moxley should not go out there no matter what.

Over at the Skakel house, a number of strange cars with out-of-state license plates began parking in the driveway.

The murder weapon, police quickly determined, was a golf club—specifically a No. 6 Toney Penna golf club. Three pieces had been found near Martha's body. She had been hit with such brute force, over and over, that the club had shattered. Part of the shaft had been used as the dagger through Martha's jaw. She was covered in so much blood that the responding officers thought Martha, a long-haired white blonde, was a redhead.

Drag marks showed that Martha's body had been moved from the place where she was killed to the tree, about sixty or eighty feet. She had tried to run from whoever attacked her and made it about forty feet before she was tackled. Martha was slight, only five-foot-five and 115 pounds, but to move a dead body that far would require significant strength, and her manner of death was classic overkill. The murderer was likely someone Martha had known.

Who among Belle Haven's elite would have done this?

It turned out Belle Haven's elite had little interest in the answer. The detectives questioned every neighbor, every friend and family that knew the Moxleys, and they all seemed as concerned as if a cat had gone missing.

Dorothy, meanwhile, could barely function. Why had she let Martha go out that night? She prayed that Martha never saw the first blow coming, that she had been knocked unconscious and never felt a thing. She prayed that Martha had died immediately. It took her years to accept what the autopsy found, that Martha had lived through most of the attack. Only the stab wound under her chin was inflicted postmortem.

Everyone in Belle Haven was whispering about the Skakels, about Tommy and Michael most pointedly. The rumor was that one or both had killed Martha Moxley, but at the same time the community seemed in denial—even though the golf club used to kill Martha, police determined eighteen months later, had come from the Skakel house and in fact had belonged to the late Anne Skakel, Michael and Tommy's mother. Some of the other mothers, individually and often, began confronting Dorothy Moxley:

Why can't you drop this? Why can't you just let it go?

David Moxley stopped working for a while. He never spoke of Martha. He couldn't bring himself to talk about her, the daddy's girl who loved picking out his clothes for work, laying them out each night so he didn't have to think about it.

One year became two. Martha's brother John felt as if time had stopped. He had gone to a high school football game shortly after her murder, and when the announcement came over that Martha had died John had felt all eyes on him and knew, in that moment, that his life would never be the same again.

David Moxley died suddenly in 1988. The official cause was a heart attack, but Dorothy knew: the stalled investigation, his heartbreak over Martha, and the failure to arrest her attacker had killed him. This brilliant, driven, accomplished, extremely successful man, only fifty-seven years old, had been destroyed.

Martha went unmentioned at David's funeral service and in his obituary, a testament to David's devastation in that last decade of his life. He was laid to rest in Greenwich, next to his beloved daughter.

John couldn't bear talking about Martha, either. It was Dorothy who became her avenger, talking to the few reporters who maintained an interest in the case: Len Levitt at *New York Newsday*, Dominick Dunne at *Vanity Fair*. Dunne had reached out to Dorothy in 1991 while he was covering William Kennedy Smith's rape trial in Palm Beach; the Kennedy strategies at play reminded him of that cold case in Connecticut, long forgotten, involving a teenage girl's murder and a suspected Kennedy cousin.

Dunne was initially saddened, but not surprised, to learn that nothing had happened with Martha's case. But it remained on his radar, and five years after William Kennedy Smith was acquitted of rape Dunne caught a big break, slipped a copy of a "speculative document" that came to be known as "The Sutton Report." The same year as the Smith trial, 1991, Rushton Skakel decided to secretly hire Sutton Associates, a private detective concern in New York, to investigate and psychologically evaluate Tommy and Michael—to figure out if one or both had killed Martha.

The investigation took three years. Every detective and analyst was made to sign a nondisclosure agreement. Even if Tommy or Michael confessed, that confession would remain secret. This deep dive into Tommy and Michael's psyches was meant to help prepare the brothers for further interrogations with law enforcement. The investigators behind the Sutton Report hired The Academy Group, a private company that employed former police investigators and at least one FBI agent, to work up a profile of Martha's killer.

On some level, Rush must have suspected that one or both of his sons could have been responsible.

According to the final report that wound up in Dunne's possession, Tommy and Michael were both deeply disturbed young men with extreme emotional swings, and immature by every measure.

> "...Both boys are impulsive personalities," the report read in part. This passage quoted from an assessment of Michael done at Elan, the controversial reform school he was sent to after another encounter with the police. "Both have very poor ego development and a bad self-image. Both are sexually immature and blocked emotionally. Both have an alcohol and possibly drug problems. Both are very likable and outstanding athletes. Both are lost, personally disorganized and have no life plan. Their only point of departure is in the fact that Tommy feels loved by his family and Michael does not." The Elan assessment also quoted Rush Skakel saying that their sister, "is frightened to death of Michael."
>
> Tommy had suffered a grave head injury at age four, one that knocked him "allegedly unconscious for ten hours." Afterward, he was prone to violent rages—once punching his fist through a door, another time reportedly ripping a telephone off a wall. Tommy had no respect for parental authority. He was seemingly unafraid of the police or of being the subject of a homicide investigation. He was possessed, the report said, of a "formidable" ability to lie.

Among many falsehoods Tommy told the police, the most glaring was about liking Martha. Multiple witnesses, Michael Skakel among them, reported seeing Martha and Tommy engaging in sexually charged horse-play in the Skakel driveway. Tommy later claimed that he and Martha had met up later and, he said, engaged in mutual masturbation.

The report quoted Tommy's lies directly. In a passage addressed to Tommy, but to be read also by his father Rush, the Sutton investigators concluded that Tommy's explanation of what he told the police was too rehearsed and proper to be believed:

> "We know that you lied to the police. 'They questioned me about whether I had any sexual feelings or sexual desires or any sexual activity with Martha or whether I approached her sexually. I didn't like that because that's not like me and my family. They questioned me in pretty hard terms, terms we don't commonly use. They questioned me many times with regard to the details of what had taken place and what I had done.' And you didn't tell them the truth. Why? It must have taken a lot of guts to keep lying to the police like that?"

The Academy Group's profile of the probable offender shares many obvious characteristics with Tommy Skakel (as well as with other leading suspects). Most notably, The Academy Group believed the offender was between 14 and 18 years of age, resided within easy walking distance of the victim's residence, was in the same socioeconomic status as the victim, had regular interaction with the victim, would have exhibited strong sibling rivalry tendencies, would have experienced behavioral problems both at school and at home, and was under the influence of drugs and/or alcohol at the time of this crime. Some pertinent excerpts:

> **Offender Resorted to Violence:** His immaturity and/or intoxicated state left him inadequately equipped to effectively deal with the victim on an emotional or intellectual level equivalent to the victim.

Choice of Weapon: The weapon utilized to commit the murder is not one normally associated with violence. Its use is strongly indicative of impulsiveness, immaturity, and/or lack of experience in violent crimes on the part of the offender.

Overkill: Overkill is defined as using much more violence than necessary to kill a person. In this case there were 14 to 15 blows to the victim's head. Any one of several of the blows would have resulted in death. Again, this is strongly indicative of anger and rage directed in a very personal way to the victim.

Body Disposal Site: The area selected to dispose of the body is not one that would be selected by a person unfamiliar with the area. It is a considerable distance from the major attack site and subjected the killer to much greater possibility of being observed while moving the body. The killer had to know of the location of the tree and the cover it provided.

The Academy Group went on to cite certain characteristics for the probable offender which, to our knowledge, were not consistent with Tommy Skakel. Michael, however, is a different story. It is uncanny, in fact, how closely these other characteristics match with Michael's personality, behavior, and the diagnosis of his psychological evaluations.

Most notably, The Academy Group believe the offender was sexually inexperienced, had not killed before, was a habitual window-peeper and consumer of pornography, and an "emotional 'loner.'"

The report concluded that these behaviors were not consistent with Tommy at the time in question.

But they were consistent with Michael.

The magnitude of certain psychological and emotional problems from which Michael has suffered is considerable. Dr. Sue Wallington Quinlan, who examined him on 3/3/77, has written: Projective testing suggested a severe agitated depression, a sense of being overwhelmed by a sense of evil and the futility of life. The depression is possibly of psychotic proportions but the protocol was too guarded to be certain. Mental functioning is clearly fragile. Extent of pathology is evident in borderline features: 1) intrusions of personal concerns into intellectual functioning, 2) primitive fantasy content, e.g. mutilated bodies, masked, distorted figures, concerns about bodily integrity and deformity, 3) inadequate capacity for attatchment [sic] to other people.

Borderline feature number two is, obviously, of special concern to us. Such preoccupations are alarming, and suggest an unusual capacity for violent thought. Later in the report, Dr. Quinlan states: **Impulse control is marginally adequate.**

The report determined that Michael, at some point, had been romantically involved with Martha, a conclusion her friends and family rejected. Martha, they were sure, had no feelings at all for Michael—in fact, according to her diary entries, she was actively trying to avoid him. But in this theory of the case, the Sutton Report suggested that Michael committed the murder in an act of rage over being sexually rejected by the same girl who had just engaged physically with his brother.

Martha had been a fifteen-year-old virgin. Her description in this report was perhaps a reflection of its time, but is shocking nonetheless. There was a suggestion that Martha had brought this all on herself by playing with the affections of two teenage boys. That if Martha had only been a bit more selective—well, that night might have ended differently.

"Tommy had no great love for Martha," read one passage. "To him, unfortunately, she was a piece of ass."

Under a list called **PRESSING QUESTIONS:**

"Would Tommy and Michael try to have sex with Martha together?"

By this point, police and reporters, through nearly twenty years of speaking with Martha's mother, her best friends, and in reading her diary, had all concluded that Martha was a confident girl with a healthy sense of her own sexual boundaries—boundaries presumably known to both brothers. Even the Sutton Report said as much: "No one considered [Martha] to be promiscuous, or inappropriately preoccupied with sexuality. Rather, her flirtatiousness seems to have been of the 'nice girl' variety, and was indicative of a self-confident and cheerful disposition."

That question really should have been: "Would Tommy and Michael attempt to rape Martha together?"

And really, it was Michael, not Tommy, who would emerge as the prime suspect.

The report found that Michael suffered from a serious addiction to alcohol and cocaine and harbored great rage toward his father. He was a self-admitted neighborhood Peeping Tom, and there was one woman in Belle Haven he stalked. As Dunne reported in *Vanity Fair*, two of Michael's best friends had shunned him ever since Michael told them that on the night of the murder, "he had been masturbating in a tree next to Martha's house."

And Michael's story kept changing. At the reform school he had been sent to after catastrophically crashing a car, he was reported to have confessed to the murder, then recanted. He tried to kill himself not long after Martha's death, jumping out of a car in heavy traffic on New York City's Triborough Bridge — later the Robert F. Kennedy Bridge — and attempting to climb over the guardrail. Michael told his chauffeur that he "had done something very bad, and that he needed to get out of the country, and that he had to kill himself."

A memo cited in the Sutton Report quotes Tommy and Michael's aunt, Sue Reynolds, as saying she thought Michael "is capable of murder." The report also notes that Michael once went after his aunt Ethel with a kitchen knife after he tried to steal some liquor.

The morning after Martha's murder, Michael was, according to the report, "going nuts" over the police presence at the Moxley house.

Three years later, Michael, driving while drunk, totaled his car. "He showed little or no remorse," the report said, "for having nearly killed the companion in his car," another young woman. The cops arrested him, and soon after Michael was sent to a school for troubled youth, the now-infamous Elan, in Maine.

Prevailing wisdom in Greenwich, and for many following the case, was that Rush Skakel wanted Michael far from renewed police interest.

As memorialized in the Sutton Report, when it came to Martha's murder, "Even his own father has conceded that Michael could be capable of this."

———————

In 1998, almost a quarter-century after Martha's murder, Michael, out of desperation or hubris or both, hired a ghostwriter to work on a book proposal called *Dead Man Talking: A Kennedy Cousin Comes Clean*. It was explosive, but not for the reasons one might expect. In this memoir, Michael Skakel was a hero.

Here he was, spilling all kinds of Kennedy scandal. He promised to tell the real story about his cousin Michael Kennedy, Bobby Jr.'s brother, who was married with children and sleeping with his fourteen-year-old babysitter. Most male Kennedys, Michael wrote, didn't consider this rape or child abuse. But Michael Skakel, in his telling, did. "I don't care who you fuck, okay?" he wrote of confronting Michael Kennedy. "But this is wrong. This is a kid. You have to stop."

He wrote about Bobby Kennedy taking offense — not to Michael Kennedy's behavior, but to Skakel's. "I don't see how that's any of your business," he quotes Bobby saying to him. Michael Kennedy's brother Joe — who had paralyzed Pam Kelley — also told Skakel to back off. "My brother," Joe says in this proposal, "can fuck anybody he wants."

Skakel writes that Michael Kennedy "had instructed me to tell the press" that the babysitter was a "promiscuous little slut who had come on to him, been rebuffed, and was angry," and had instructed "a well-placed henchman . . . to dig up dirt on the babysitter's father . . . 'Maybe he beats his wife or something.'" He writes that once the babysitter's parents got her away from Michael Kennedy, he began stalking the teenager and 'she'd become afraid of him.'"

After he broke into her parents' garage and left a dildo on the windshield of the babysitter's car — a crime caught on surveillance video — Michael writes, Bobby Jr. allegedly said to Skakel, "Oh my God, he's just like Willie!"

He then claims that Bobby Jr. admitted that "William Kennedy Smith was guilty of rape, that his acquittal was the result of Kennedy power."

"He did it," Michael writes. But the Kennedys always banded together: "Circling the wagons to protect the cesspool."

The heart of the proposal, though, is a sample chapter titled "Murder Most Foul." This is Michael's account of the night Martha was murdered, and of his feelings toward her. "I thought Martha was really pretty," he writes. "I really liked her. I wanted to kiss her. I wanted her to be my girlfriend, but I was going slow, being careful . . . I thought that maybe . . . something romantic might develop between us."

There it is. Martha, despite the Skakel camp's claim otherwise, had not been involved with both Tommy and Michael. She was not playing sophisticated sexual head games or leading these boys on—and even if she had, so what? Does that mean she deserved to die? For all of the Kennedy machine's attempts to portray Martha as a vixen, she was a sweet, happy, well-brought-up young girl who, Skakel writes, politely rejected him that night.

After they parted ways, he writes that he kept thinking about Martha, even after going home and getting into bed. "I couldn't settle down," he writes. "A part of me really wanted to go to sleep but I was keyed up, nervous and horny. After a little while longer, still unable to fall asleep, I kicked off the covers and decided, 'Fuck it. I'm going out.'"

And that is how Michael Skakel ended this most consequential passage.

In 2002, Michael Skakel would be convicted of killing Martha Moxley. Entered into evidence was the murder weapon, that golf club belonging to Michael's late mother. During the trial, Michael had gotten in Dorothy Moxley's face. "You've got the wrong guy," he said. His aunt Ethel wrote a letter to the judge, pleading for mercy upon Michael's sentencing. It read:

> Dear Judge Kavanewsky,
>
> With a heavy heart, yet with hope born of the morning sun, I write to ask that your compassion will tip the scales in your decision regarding my nephew, Michael Skakel.
>
> I beg you to take into account the qualities in him that appeal to those of us who love him and end this nightmare.

To understand the man you are considering, please remember that he was born to a mother who is the epitome of the virtuous woman, whose lingering death to cancer left a bereft and shaken father of seven unable to cope. Instead of discovering joy in his children, he found solace in alcohol, rendering him unavailable to them, leaving his family virtually abandoned.

A more sober father might not have dismissed Michael's troubles in school as laziness, stupidity and rebellion, but seen the dysfunction for what it was: a severe learning disability.

A bright child was gradually becoming the victim of alienation, infuriation and permissiveness. Financially privileged, Michael was growing emotionally destitute.

That twenty years later he would graduate from college and become a world class athlete demonstrate his mental toughness, fortitude, courage and tenacity.

It pains me that others miss his sweetness, kindness, good cheer and love of life; his perceptiveness, exuberance and extraordinary generosity. His exquisite manners are a mark of his consideration of others, as his remarkable gift of story telling with an ear for the idiom and accent of multiple languages demonstrate a desire to please and give joy. Even provoked, I have never heard him cuss or use bad language. Above all, that the depth of his spirituality from which all else flows, like a daystar shines unnoticed, is heartrending.

Your Honor, when you are deciding the length of Michael's incarceration, I hope you will weigh these things I know to be true:

- by sheer character he overcame a difficult childhood.
- he put behind him adolescent institutional abuse.
- his sobriety has been a productive example to the many he has reached out to, transforming, and in some cases, saving their lives, with his vigilance, forbearance, compassion, persuasive reasoning, steady helping hand and, perhaps most importantly, his kindness and caring.
- he is a loving father to his own adorable three year old son

who, like those of us who know Michael, holds him in great affection.

In short, Your Honor, Michael has soul. I pray that you will season justice with that twice blessed attribute of God, mercy, and let him continue to enrich our lives.

Out of the depths, but with hope,

Ethel Kennedy

She never said he didn't do it.

On June 7, 2002, Michael Skakel was sentenced to twenty years to life, in large part due to Dorothy Moxley's unfaltering demands for justice. She was in court every day with John and Martha's best friends. She said yes to almost every interview, no matter the emotional cost. In her victim impact statement, she was candid about that toll.

"I have spent almost twenty-seven years of hell and anguish," she said, "trying to live what some think of as a normal life, but stressed to the limit trying to find truth and justice . . . I am a victim. My son, John, is also a victim."

Martha's brother, John, in his victim impact statement, spoke of his life as being forever altered. "Please understand that I am incapable of expressing in words the full scope of the impact Martha's murder had and will continue to have on my life," John said. "My mother and I, we will continue to endure a life sentence wondering about what might have been."

Whatever solace the conviction brought Dorothy and John would not last. After serving eleven years in prison, Michael Skakel's conviction was vacated by the Connecticut Supreme Court in 2018, after his lawyers successfully argued that his former defense lawyer had, from the beginning, failed to pursue someone who turned out to be an impartial alibi witness. At one point in the appeals, Michael had argued that his trial lawyer should have tried to accuse Tommy in order to create reasonable doubt as to his own guilt.

The decision to vacate
unanimous. Justice Carme
that Skakel's station in life a
and convicted felons of lesser m
nately for them," she wrote, "the va
er's financial resources, social standi
political dynasty."

PART EIGHT

FALLING STARS

MARILYN MONROE

M arilyn filed for divorce from the playwright Arthur Miller on January 20, 1961, the day Jack Kennedy was inaugurated. It was a victory for Marilyn, a liberation from a man who had made her feel dumb and a repatriation of sorts.

So what if Jack had disappeared during the campaign? Marilyn had problems; she knew that. Maybe Jack had felt as desperate; after all, their affair threatened his chances of becoming president. Beyond all that, she remained in love with Jack. He was more than the leader of the free world; to Marilyn, he was her cult leader, her guru, her ruler. She was the submissive and he was the dominant. She had recently told Dr. Ralph Greenson, her longtime psychoanalyst, as much.

"Marilyn Monroe is a soldier," she said. "Her commander-in-chief is the greatest and most powerful man in the world . . . He says this, you do it. He says that, you do it. This man is going to change our country . . . I tell you, doctor, when he has finished his achievements he will take his place with Washington, Jefferson, Lincoln, and Franklin Roosevelt as one of our greatest presidents . . . I will never embarrass him. As long as I have memory, I have John Fitzgerald Kennedy."

Marilyn had believed Jack when he said he would leave Jackie and marry her, that she would be First Lady for his second term. It wasn't so crazy: Marilyn had had Jack on the hook for years. She was like a photo negative of Jackie: white-hot blonde, pure sex, a global supernova. The men who married her sought to possess Marilyn, to annex and control her. She was meant to redound to their stardom, to ratify them as alpha males, the rarest of the rare who could satisfy the world's most desired woman. But that was all image. Fantasy. In truth, these men were insecure and jealous. Their only means of trying to keep Marilyn to themselves was to shame her.

Jack Kennedy did not have that problem — not at all. He relished Marilyn's sex appeal. He admired it. In Marilyn, he saw a feminine version of himself: greedy for sex yet taking no pleasure in it. Yearning for the approval and love of the opposite sex while only ever distrusting that love and fearing its loss.

Jackie didn't know all of this, of course. But she knew enough to understand that Marilyn was dangerous.

The dress.

This was going to be the biggest night of Marilyn's life, performing for Jack at Madison Square Garden, a fundraiser under the guise of his forty-fifth birthday party. This seemed proof of Jack's intentions. He was edging closer to making their romance public. Without saying a word, she could out them to America, and what a headline: Marilyn Monroe, the biggest movie star ever, and the president of the United States. She wanted to look like Marlene Dietrich in one of her sparkly soufflé gowns, but sexier, edgier, more risqué. And so Dietrich, the one-time lover of Old Joe and Jack himself, sent Marilyn to her designer, the great French costumer Jean Louis. For Marilyn, he conceived a gossamer flesh-toned dress glittering with thousands of hand-sewn rhinestones, so figure-hugging that it had to be sewn onto her body, so tight that she couldn't wear undergarments.

When the Garden lights hit her, alone on that stage, Marilyn was ablaze with carnality yet somehow purified by all those tiny fake diamonds.

Half an hour earlier, she had been in her dressing room, alone with Bobby Kennedy for fifteen minutes. Both Kennedy brothers wanted her, and she both of them. Jack, of course, had power, but Bobby had a seriousness that eluded Jack. She wanted some of that gravitas for herself. And Bobby could be kind. The first time they had met, at a private dinner party in LA, Marilyn had stashed crib notes into her handbag, facts about world events that otherwise eluded her. Bobby noticed but said nothing; Marilyn's lack of cynicism, her eagerness to please, was poignant.

———

Late to the stage, drunk and flush with fresh, transgressive sex, her dress so tight she could hardly walk, Marilyn approached the podium swathed in a white mink stole. She handed her mink off to her escort, flicked the hot microphone with her finger and moved to the side, revealing herself. Forty thousand people reacted like a single organism, including the president and everyone seated in his box—from which Jackie, presciently, was absent. "You could just smell lust," was his friend Hugh Sidey's description. The president, he said, had gone limp with desire.

Marilyn cooed "Happy Birthday" as if it were the greatest come-on ever written. The president was left slack-jawed but regained his wit, taking the stage with one intent: acknowledge but minimize. "I can now retire from politics," he told the crowd, "having had 'Happy Birthday' sung to me in such a sweet, wholesome way." He laughed. The crowd roared. Later that night, at the private afterparty in a clubby Manhattan room filled with mahogany bookshelves and important men, the only known photo of Bobby, Marilyn, and Jack was taken. Marilyn stood between them, in profile, looking serious. Bobby and Jack turned themselves away from the camera.

———

After that night, Jack faded from Marilyn's life. She didn't know about the ultimatum Jackie had given him, but she also didn't like being frozen out. It triggered her worst fear: abandonment. She would try the White House but was never able to reach Jack. Instead, another Kennedy was suddenly making himself available to Marilyn: Bobby. When he came to LA to visit his sister Pat and her husband, Peter Lawford, Marilyn was often there. Of dancing with Bobby, she wrote to her friend, the screenwriter Norman Rosen:

"He was very nice, sort of boyish and likable. Of course he kept looking down my dress, but I'm used to that. I thought he was going to compliment me, but instead he asked me while dancing who I thought was the handsomest man in the room. I mean, how was I going to answer that? I said he was. Well, in a way, he was!"

Bobby and Jack had overlapped in Marilyn's bed, as had Jack's friend Frank Sinatra. Her psychiatrist was worried that Marilyn was way in over her head but felt it was equally dangerous to discourage her. Marilyn had never felt so seen, so wanted, so gratified. Extracting her from these entanglements would be like a military operation. Despite her enormous success, she still primarily defined herself through men. In January 1962, when Marilyn bought her dream house at Fifth Helena Drive, a cozy hacienda with her longed-for swimming pool, she cried. These were not tears of joy.

"I felt badly," she said later, "because I was buying a home all alone."

That was not technically true. Her ex-husband Joe DiMaggio had loaned her money for the down payment. But for Marilyn, gestures like these could never fill the void.

She and Bobby had their own relationship, and she thought he was a better version of Jack: his sense of purpose, his deep belief in the civil rights movement, his righteousness, his intellect. She had been so humiliated when, at a dinner party with a famous heiress, one guest called Marilyn out for her improper grammar. She had left that table in tears. Now she studied even harder to improve her vocabulary; for Bobby, she wanted to use big words to express big thoughts.

His sister Jean gave Marilyn the Kennedys' enthusiastic endorsement in a handwritten letter. "Understand that you and Bobby are the new item!" she wrote. "We all think you should come with him when he comes back East!"

Marilyn still had feelings for Jack. She would still see him from time to time at the Lawfords' or with Sinatra. But Bobby could make Marilyn a great woman, and none of her friends could talk her out of this next delusion, that Bobby would leave Ethel, mother to his seven children—and counting. What Marilyn could not see was that Bobby, like Jack before her, was less interested in strengthening her than annealing her: heating her up like white gold, then leaving her alone to cool down, making her more pliable, bendable, easier to manipulate. Wearing down her strength.

Marilyn's psychoanalyst consulted with colleagues. "Above all," he wrote, "I try to help her not be so lonely, and therefore escape into the drugs or get involved with very destructive people, who will engage in some sort of sadomasochistic relationship with her." Almost everyone in the Monroe-Kennedy social circle knew of her entanglements with Jack and Bobby. The men were titillated — all but DiMaggio. He thought the Kennedys were using Marilyn. So did the women in Marilyn's circle, especially the famous singer Phyllis McGuire and Jeanne Martin, married to Frank Sinatra's great friend and fellow Rat Packer Dean Martin.

Jeanne in particular was none too impressed with the way Jack and Bobby conducted themselves at Hollywood parties; she found the brothers juvenile, boorish, and way too aggressive with women. One of her female friends had found herself alone with Bobby at one party and, next thing she knew, he had locked the door and pushed her down on a couch.

But that wasn't Marilyn's Bobby. "The General," she said, always took her calls at the Justice Department, no matter how busy he was. He would sneak off on trips to LA and pull up in his white 1956 Thunderbird and spirit her away for evening strolls on the beach, just the two of them. She taught him how to do the Twist. He asked her to call his father, because few things would impress the Old Man more than a call from America's number one sex symbol.

Oh, the influence she felt. If only it had a way of sticking.

When Bobby went back to his life in DC, or to his wife and children at Hickory Hill, Marilyn — ever insecure, ever lonely at heart — began floundering. She would drink champagne from morning till night, pop pills, and stop showering. Neither Kennedy was ever far from her mind. In written answers to interview questions in 1962, Marilyn listed the people she most admired:

"Eleanor Roosevelt — her devotion to mankind

"Carl Sandburg — his poems are songs of the people by the people and for the people

"Pres. and Robert Kennedy — they symbolize the youth of America — in its vigor its brilliance and its compassion."

In March of 1962, fourteen months after she had filed for divorce from Arthur Miller, he remarried the set photographer from *The Misfits,* the movie he had written for *her*! Arthur had replaced the most famous woman in the world with a mere crew member. So much for beauty as the ultimate currency. Marilyn took to calling herself "a negated sex symbol."

A few weeks later, the president came around again. Had he sensed her despair? Her vulnerability? Her shifting affections? She was falling in love with Bobby but she still loved Jack Kennedy, too. When he flew into Palm Springs in March of 1962, she spent a secret weekend with him in a cottage on an A-list star's estate. A certain young White House intern was along on that excursion, coming down from an involuntary drug trip inside the main house. Neither the intern nor Marilyn knew of the other's presence, not that it would have mattered.

There was no therapy session or drug or starring role that gave Marilyn Monroe the high of knowing the president still wanted her. During that liaison she made sure that one of her best friends spoke to Jack on the phone; proof that it was real, that it happened, a witness, if he ever tried to deny it. If he ever called her crazy.

Then Jack was off and Bobby returned, and Marilyn's sense of potency started giving way to suspicion: Was she being used? Were Jack and Bobby Kennedy having some kind of proxy war with Marilyn, some incestuous sexual competition? Underneath all the stealth and glamour, did they both really think she was just another disposable blonde? Was this a game to them? Was she a pawn?

Now her psychoanalyst was trying to coax her into breaking off both relationships. What was fun for Jack and Bobby was treacherous for Marilyn. But she said it was impossible. She had these two extremely powerful men, brothers at that, vying for her — the lonely baby, the abandoned girl, the abused preteen who had only gotten one message from the men in her life: You are worthless. Yes, sometimes Jack and Bobby could make her feel that way. But when she was with them, she felt quite the opposite, worth very much indeed.

Her psychoanalyst warned her: *Conduct these relationships with the Kennedy brothers because you want to, because in each of them you find something valuable, but be careful. Don't have sex with one or both of these men because of their power. Don't have sex with them because you think you should.*

Dr. Greenson underestimated how little control Marilyn actually felt when it came to the Kennedy brothers. Her emotional disruption extended to her career. She was about to be named Female World Film Favorite at the Golden Globes yet was despondent, in part because she could not celebrate with Jack or Bobby on her arm. She had become a liability on set, holding up production of her latest film, *Something's Got to Give*, with her persistent inability to get out of bed. Calling in sick and showing up instead at Jack's Madison Square Garden birthday fundraiser had not endeared her to the studio or her director, George Cukor. She was on the verge of getting fired. Marilyn showed up drunk to the Golden Globes Awards ceremony, baby-stepping her way to her table in a liquid emerald backless sequined gown, yet another dress that amplified her sex appeal while constraining her. It was the ultimate metaphor for being Marilyn Monroe.

She wanted out.

Her unraveling alarmed both Kennedy brothers. From time to time Jack would call Marilyn and try to soothe her, but his crisis management wasn't working. Bobby began distancing himself as well.

Over two weeks in June and July 1962, Marilyn made eight calls to Bobby at the Department of Justice, and anytime he refused the call was reason for her to panic. When Bobby came to LA with Ethel for a party at the Lawfords', Marilyn sent her regrets. It wasn't as if Ethel's presence would have stopped her. In a telegram dated June 13, 1962, Marilyn explained her absence:

ASK NOT

UNFORTUNATELY I AM INVOLVED IN A FREEDOM RIDE
PROTESTING THE LOSS OF THE MINORITY RIGHTS BELONGING TO
THE FEW REMAINING EARTHBOUND STARS. AFTER ALL, ALL WE
DEMANDED WAS OUR RIGHT TO TWINKLE.

Marilyn's star was dying.

———————

Desperate to find out what Jack and Bobby were thinking, Marilyn turned to one of her best sources: Mickey Song, the hairdresser she shared with the Kennedys. Hairdressers heard and saw it all. But Song was a veteran, and he had already been tested by Bobby and Jack, given false pieces of information to see if these items turned up in the press.

It didn't matter how much he liked her: Song was very resistant to Marilyn's questions about whether Jack and Bobby were seeing other women.

"Don't you want to help me?"

"Marilyn," Song said, "I don't want to get involved."

"They're using you," she said to him. "Just like they're using me."

"I'm not being used," Song said. "They're treating me great."

Marilyn went to Peter Lawford's wife, Pat, sister to Jack and Bobby. She had no illusions about her brothers. "Forget it," Pat told her. It was the advice Jackie would give Joan, advice all the Kennedy wives and sisters-in-law passed to each other. "Bobby's still just a little boy."

But Marilyn could not forget it. She was inconsolable, and Pat and Peter were increasingly afraid to leave her alone; her consumption of alcohol and pills was staggering. They let her stay with them for a bit, took her on vacation, and one morning, Peter woke up to find Marilyn on their balcony, looking down as if she might jump, her face streaked with tears.

I'm ugly, she told Peter. *I'm worthless. I'm a thing that Jack and Bobby used up.*

When the studio inevitably fired her from *Something's Got to Give*, a public humiliation, Marilyn took it as a challenge. She was going to prove to Hollywood—and to all the Kennedys, Jackie included—that Marilyn Monroe was irreplaceable. That underneath that soft, white-blonde cotton-candy hair whirred one sharp mind. She had been here before, at the beginning of her career.

"When you're a failure in Hollywood," Marilyn wrote of that time, "that's like starving to death outside a banquet hall with the smells of filet mignon driving you crazy. I lay in bed again day after day, not eating, not combing my hair ... I felt like an idiot. There was going to be no luck in my life. The dark star I was born under was going to get darker and darker." These thoughts were coming like waves now. Marilyn had spent her whole life fighting them. She had to give survival one more try.

Marilyn summoned reporters from three major national magazines. She was thirty-six years old, at the height of her beauty. The famous photographer Bert Stern was sent to shoot her for *Vogue* and found himself awestruck. He shot Marilyn at night at the Hotel Bel-Air, champagne bottles strewn out of frame, his subject a Rorschach of American postwar sexuality. Wearing Dior's New Look, Marilyn was elegant and evasive, her head turned in one shot, hand over her mouth as if to stop herself from what she wanted to say.

In other shots she was nude behind a pink veil; covered in diamonds; bridal in a hat and veil of white fishnet; lounging nude in bed; covering her breasts with swaths of pink tulle shaped like rose petals, the eye drawn to a long, deep scar below, the result of gallbladder surgery six weeks before. Here was a physical manifestation of how Marilyn felt: gutted, vandalized, a part of her deepest self removed, taken, tossed like the medical waste it was.

But that wasn't the Monroe Bert Stern saw. "Marilyn had the power," he wrote of that photo shoot. "She was the wind, that comet shape that Blake draws blowing around a sacred figure. She was the light and the goddess and the moon. The space and the dream, the mystery and the danger. But everything else all together, too, including Hollywood, and the girl next door that every guy wants to marry."

Why couldn't Jack and Bobby see that?

———

Six weeks later, on August 4, Bobby Kennedy was in California with his wife and children. He went straight to Marilyn's house.

"Where is it?" he yelled at her. "Where the fuck is it?"

He wanted her wiretap. He wanted her recordings of conversations with him and Jack. The FBI and the CIA, Bobby and Jack discovered, had bugged Marilyn's house and her phone line. It was a coordinated attempt to bring down both Kennedys—didn't she get that? Marilyn had no idea what Bobby was talking about.

Peter Lawford arrived and Bobby tried to play good cop. "We have to know," Bobby said. He was still yelling, but trying now to bargain rather than bully. "It's important to the family. We can make any arrangements you want, but we must find it."

"Calm down," Lawford told Bobby. *"Calm down."*

Something or someone got pushed into the wall or down to the floor. Then Bobby and Peter left. Hours later, at 7:30 that evening, Marilyn called Peter at home. He and Pat were throwing a party; Bobby would probably come, and they were all still expecting Marilyn, too. But she would not be coming, now or ever. She had no last words for Bobby.

"Say goodbye to Pat," Marilyn said to Peter, "say goodbye to the President, and say goodbye to yourself, because you're a nice guy."

Her body was found early the next morning, in the predawn dark, by her housekeeper. She was face down on her bed, nude, with her phone still in her hand. She had been dead for hours.

Marilyn Monroe's death was officially ruled a massive barbiturate overdose. She was thirty-six years old. Whether it was accidental or purposeful or subconscious suicide will never be known, but those who knew and loved Marilyn best, Lawford included, blamed Jack and Bobby Kennedy. Both, along with the Lawfords, were banned from Marilyn's funeral by Joe DiMaggio. Nor did Arthur Miller attend. As he wrote in a personal essay: "Instead of jetting [from New York] to the funeral to get my picture taken I decided to stay home and let the public mourners finish their mockery. Not that everyone there will be false, but enough. Most of them there destroyed her."

For Miller, that may have meant Hollywood. For DiMaggio, it meant the Kennedys. "If it weren't for her so-called friends," DiMaggio said,

"Marilyn would still be alive today." He took charge of all the arrangements, and her funeral service was that of an innocent: Marilyn was laid out in her favorite green Pucci dress with its modest neckline and a miniature bouquet of pink roses in her hands. Judy Garland's rendition of "Over the Rainbow" from *The Wizard of Oz* played during her service, lyrics that poignantly epitomized Marilyn's desperation for love and happiness.

If happy little bluebirds fly
Beyond the rainbow
Why, then oh why can't I?

JACKIE KENNEDY ONASSIS

A ri Onassis was a Greek shipping magnate, a billionaire, an antisemite, a vulgarian, and a bisexual with a string of bought-and-paid-for young men that he savagely beat after sex. On October 17, 1968, he and Jackie Kennedy, thirty-nine years old to his sixty-two, announced they would marry in three days' time.

Their engagement made the front page of the *New York Times*, above the fold: "The Reaction Here Is Anger, Shock and Dismay," read the headline. Jackie was not called by her first name. She was still "Mrs. John F. Kennedy."

Germany's *Bild*, the second-most-read paper in Europe: "All the World Is Indignant."

A Fleet Street tabloid: "Jackie Weds Blank Cheque."

Stockholm's *Expressen*: "Jackie! How Could You?"

The *Atlanta Constitution*: "Jackie Fell for Onassis' Plush Yacht."

Rome's *Il Messaggero*: "JFK Dies a Second Time."

The Vatican denounced her.

Jackie Kennedy, the faultless widow and America's most admired woman, was no more.

———

Jackie Kennedy was talked and written about as a prostitute who sold herself on the global marketplace, an unscrupulous viper who had stolen her sister's lover. This part was true: Lee, still married to the Polish prince Stanislaw Radziwill, had been involved with Ari and was hoping to marry him — till Jackie became the world's most famous widow. This was something Jackie and Lee had in common with the Kennedy men, an incestuous tendency to compete for lovers and sometimes share them.

Jackie felt certain that she and Lee would get past this. Less so as to whether America would forgive her.

Jackie's psyche was not part of the national conversation. Nor was her trauma after Bobby Kennedy's assassination four months prior, which she had predicted. Bobby had not died instantly, as Jack had. He was conscious after he was shot. Later, in the hospital, the doctors broke the news that Bobby was brain dead. It had been Jackie who persuaded Ethel to turn off the machines. She had been the strong one that day, too.

But in the weeks to follow, Jackie was experiencing episodes of psychosis. She would be in her apartment at 1040 Fifth Avenue in New York, and suddenly Jack and Bobby were alive. But Jack was Bobby, Bobby was Jack, and both were her husbands. Then she would be in the back seat of that Lincoln Continental with Jack, holding his head and his brain matter before finding herself in that Los Angeles hospital, right beside Bobby and the respirator. She was having nightmares, vivid and unceasing. Most days she couldn't get out of bed. She was as inconsolable as ever, reminiscent of the months after Jack's death when little Caroline told her schoolteacher, "My mommy cries all the time."

Bobby had been more than a brother-in-law to Jackie; before his assassination, in the wake of Jack's death, the two of them destroyed and disconsolate, they became romantically involved. It began not long after Jackie and the children relocated to a Georgetown town house at 3017 N Street; unable to afford the mortgage, Bobby negotiated the price down from $215,000 to $195,000 and had $100,000 paid out from Kennedy family funds.

But the help he gave her wasn't just practical. It was Bobby alone who could rouse Jackie from her grief, from sleeping her days away, from drinking and weeping and fearing ever going outside. She told Franklin D. Roosevelt Jr. that she couldn't find slumber at night despite all the sleeping pills she took, that her medications did nothing to stop her mind from obsessively replaying the assassination. She told Roosevelt that Bobby Kennedy was the only person keeping her from killing herself.

For Bobby, the same was true of Jackie. He had been the sibling closest to Jack and the one who, as attorney general, had done whatever it took to protect his brother. He was the only other family member grieving as deeply as Jackie—the only blood Kennedy who could not adhere to the family's mantra: *Move forward, get on with it, stop feeling sorry for yourself, life is for the living.* Bobby, already wiry, began dropping an alarming amount of weight. He, too, cried all the time. He couldn't sleep, either, and now began spending more time at Jackie's, more time with her children than his own. Like Jackie, he bristled when well-meaning people, including his wife, Ethel, tried to explain Jack's murder as "God's plan," or suggest that he was now in a better place.

Faith, for Bobby and Jackie, had its limits. Jackie was offended when her friend Susan Alsop—one of the rare guests Jackie hosted during this time—came for tea and offered the consolation that "at least Jack is resting peacefully with God."

"That's the silliest thing I've ever heard, Susan," Jackie said. Alsop never had a social engagement with Jackie again.

Bobby found Ethel's religiosity equally unbearable. When one guest at Hickory Hill brought up a governmental conundrum, Ethel said, "Well, Jack will take care of that. He's up in heaven, and he's looking down on us, and he will show us what to do."

"The voice you just heard," Bobby replied, "belongs to the wife of the attorney general of the United States. Let's hear no more out of her."

Through late 1963 and early 1964, Bobby was on the verge of quitting public life and never running for elected office. Jackie talked him out of it. When one was in the depths of despair, it was the other who pulled them out.

"Now that Jack's gone," Jackie wrote to him, "Caroline and John need you more than ever . . . Jack would want us both to carry on what he stood for, and died for."

After Jack had been interred at Arlington, the two of them restless at the White House that same night, Bobby turned to Jackie and asked, "Shall we go visit our friend?" It was an explicit acknowledgment of this new, terrible, special bond, Jackie and Bobby the most important people, aside from the children, in Jack's life. There was no room for Ethel here.

Jackie and Bobby's affair, which was on-and-off from 1964 to 1968, was whispered about in their social circles and well known among the press corps. Jackie and Bobby would be seen dining out in New York

City, openly kissing and cuddling, but because it was the Kennedys — because of what happened to Jack, and because of Jackie's strength
in the days to follow — the secret had been kept.

No more. Jackie had left the proverbial compound.

———————

"If they're killing Kennedys," Jackie said, "my children are the number
one targets. I want to get out of this country." Aristotle Onassis had a
private island, a private army, and a yacht the size of a navy destroyer. It
was the spring of 1968, and Jackie was done, as she had told Theodore
White all those years before, being "The Widder Kennedy."

As Bobby's presidential campaign heated up around that same time,
he tried to talk her out of the marriage. He had known Onassis for years
and hated him. The feeling was mutual, for both personal reasons and
business. Onassis worried that if Bobby became president, he would keep
Onassis's oil tankers from ever docking in American ports. And Bobby,
to Onassis's mind, had had the temerity to call him years prior and tell
him to stop sleeping with Jackie's sister Lee — the Princess Radziwill by
her marriage to Stas.

Onassis could not bear the hypocrisy. He knew that Bobby and Jack
Kennedy were both having affairs with Marilyn Monroe. "Bobby," Onassis told him, "you and Jack fuck your movie queen and I'll fuck my princess." Before Jack was assassinated, Bobby had suspected Jackie of having
slept with Onassis despite, or because of, Lee's involvement with him. He
was wild with rage. "Tell your Greek boyfriend," Bobby told Jackie, "he
won't be coming back here until Jack's reelected . . . a fucking long time
after. Like maybe never."

Now Onassis was offering Jackie the one thing Bobby could
not — marriage — and the possibility that he was endangering Bobby's
presidential chances was something that surely gave the shipping magnate great pleasure. A Jackie–Ari union would be a public relations disaster. It would make Jackie a Kennedy apostate. It would cast the entire
Kennedy family out of Jack's revered legacy and into the realm of gossip
and tabloids. "For God's sake, Jackie," Bobby said. "This could cost me
five states."

She agreed to wait until after the election. If Bobby won, Ethel would become the next First Lady, which would make Jackie, in America, something of a dowager empress—useless, ornamental, second in the family hierarchy. All the more reason to marry Ari.

Jackie's next hurdle was her mother-in-law, Rose. Jackie broke the news strategically, calling her sister-in-law Jean Kennedy Smith, who Jackie knew would tell the family. It was smart, because Rose was shocked—stunned, she would later say. She, too, knew Onassis, but only slightly, and the idea of Jackie choosing Ari after Jack... Ari, this much older man, this garden gnome, a divorced Greek who would now become Caroline and John's stepfather. What was Jackie thinking?

And then Rose realized: Jackie would never do anything that would hurt the children. She had endured a lot while married to Jack, and now she had the chance at a second chapter, one in which she and her children would be provided for. Rose herself had once wanted a different life, one without her husband, but she had been refused. She did not want that for Jackie—a life frozen in amber. That Jackie wanted Rose's approval meant something—quite a lot, actually. It signaled Jackie's desire to remain a family member. It meant that Rose, in being supportive, could continue to have relationships with Caroline and John Jr. So when Jackie finally called her, Rose, without hesitation, gave her blessing.

Jackie was blown away.

"She of all people was the one who encouraged me—who said, 'He's a good man,' and 'Don't worry,'" Jackie said. "Here I was—I was married to her son and I had his children, but she was the one who was saying, 'If you think this is best, go ahead.'"

Jackie called Rose "Belle Mère," French for mother-in-law. It was her way of telling Rose that she would always be Jackie's second mother, even as Onassis was Jackie's way out—out of the Kennedy crucible, out of being a living American saint high on a pedestal. She wanted to smash that image to bits: break it, destroy it, pulverize it. Marrying Ari would do that. And she could do something for him, too.

As she wrote one former lover, Ari "is lonely and wants to protect me from being lonely...Only I can decide if he can, and I decided. I know it comes as a surprise to so many people. But they see things for me that I never wanted for myself."

———————

Ari had been in Jackie's life for a long time. They had first met in the late 1950s, when she and Jack accepted his invitation for drinks on his yacht, the *Christina O*. The Kennedys moved in the same circles as the Winston Churchills, whom Ari also knew, and the infamous Greek wanted to meet this young man who everyone said would become an American president someday. It was Jackie, however, who impressed him. Years after that initial meeting, he claimed to remember exactly what she was wearing — "a white, very simple, very expensive suit" — and her movie-star demeanor. "She had a withdrawn sort of quality," Ari said. "It wasn't shyness. It wasn't boredom, either. She wasn't conspicuously friendly, but she had a way of making you look at her."

Ari invited Jackie for an extended stay on his yacht after the death of baby Patrick — a stay she accepted, much to Jack's chagrin. It turned out to be quite healing for her and was a kindness she never forgot. When Jack was killed, Ari was among the chosen few to stay at the White House in the immediate aftermath.

Ari had always seen beneath Jackie's prim veneer to what he called her "carnal soul." He wasn't conventionally attractive like Jack, but he was highly sexual. Among his favorite possessions was a set of barstools that he'd had covered in whale scrotum. But mere objects could not compare to acquiring famous women.

"There's something damned willful about her," Ari said of Jackie. "Something provocative."

He knew that the *beau monde* thought him crude. "Fortunately, people with class are usually willing to overlook this flaw," he said, "because I am very rich." Upon her engagement to Onassis, that was what the world now thought of Jackie: *crude*. Ari was her sugar daddy, "Daddy O." Jackie and Ari could claim a second shot at love all they wanted, but this marriage was also transactional, the merger of two global brands, and no woman could compete with The Widow Kennedy, who had a commensurate number in mind. Her financial adviser, André Meyer, proposed that Ari pay $20 million to make the marriage happen.

"Your client," Onassis told Meyer, "could price herself right out of the market."

Jackie wound up getting $3 million up front from Ari, $1 million for each of her children, $600,000 a year for travel, millions more in the event of divorce or Ari's death, and stipulations as to how many times a year she would be required to have sex with Ari. She also insisted on separate bedrooms at shared residences, though theirs would be a marriage in every sense, save children. On that they agreed.

On October 20, 1968, Jackie wed Ari on his private island of Skorpios, wearing a high-necked, knee-length, white Valentino dress, her hair pulled back in a half-ponytail and tied off with a white ribbon. It was a rebuke to the church that had denounced her, dressing like a young girl taking her First Communion, and to everyone who thought she was greedy or gone mad. No—Jacqueline Kennedy was quite in her right mind. She was a middle-aged icon who had rewritten her first husband's problematic history and had just negotiated a marriage contract containing 170 clauses. Most importantly, she had successfully killed off her former incarnation. Jackie Onassis would be a different person entirely. Let the world recoil in disgust—all the better. All the more freedom for her.

"Jackie needs a small scandal to bring her alive," Ari said at the time. "The world loves fallen grandeur." He was right: Jackie was reanimated, as was the public's fascination with her.

Gone were the prim lady jackets and bouffants—the bras, too. Jackie O was dressing for a new era, the dawning 1970s. She was shedding her old skin while casting back to the ambitions of her youth, her dreams of becoming a great writer someday, known not for whom she married but what she did, how she worked.

"Why do people always try to see me through the different names I have had at different times?" she asked in 1972. "People often forget that I was Jacqueline Bouvier before being Mrs. Kennedy or Mrs. Onassis." She was modern now in her tight white capris and tissue-thin black tees, her nipples poking through. She strolled the streets of Greece and Italy barefoot. She wore her hair long and loose or parted down the middle, wrapped in a chic low ballet bun. She adopted two accessories that would be named after her: a slouchy Gucci horsebit handbag and enormous black sunglasses that obscured half her face. The effect was pure Garbo: Look-at-me-don't-look-at-me-I-can't-*bear*-it-if-you-don't-look-at-me.

New York City Jackie O was a variation on the theme, a long, black, belted leather trench coat her armor. This Jackie O was a dominatrix. She was entering the most openly sexual chapter of her life. She was no longer the woman Jack Kennedy had humiliated. In marrying Ari, she had publicly triumphed.

If only she felt that way in private.

Nearly one month to the day after her second wedding, Jackie, in Greece with Ari's sister Artemis, broke down. It was November 22, 1968, the fifth anniversary of Jack's assassination. In all that time she hadn't been able to stop talking about that day in graphic detail. It was like a compulsion and an attempted exorcism, as if enough people knew and could understand, then Jackie wouldn't be so alone, so fundamentally apart from everyone else.

It was hopeless.

"I'm a freak," she would say. "I'll always be a freak. Sometimes I think I will never be able to be truly happy again." She had aged rapidly. One woman who met Jackie in this era was shocked: Jackie, as ever, photographed beautifully, but those big black sunglasses were obscuring tiny lines and cracks, her face a spiderweb of anguish. She suffered excruciating, pulsating pain in her neck, which she believed was permanent nerve damage from clutching Jack's shattered head in her lap. The horrors of that day lived in her body, on her face, and in her nightmares.

Ari spoiled Jackie. Expensive jewels were nestled on her breakfast tray. She lunched. She sunbathed. She did yoga by the pool and shopped extravagantly. As in the White House, she demanded that her bed linens (she had twelve pairs of hand-embroidered pink sheets, Italian, which she always traveled with) be cleaned and ironed every morning and every afternoon, after her daily nap. She was fascinated by Greece and Greek culture yet often found herself touring ruins and antiquities alone, her new husband, she suspected, already bored with his latest acquisition and secretly romancing his old flame, the famous opera singer Maria Callas.

Callas, who had been photographed with Marilyn Monroe the night of the Madison Square Garden disgrace.

There were still days when Jackie couldn't get out of bed. Oh, how the tabloids loved this detail — Jackie O, spoiled and lolling her days away. Wasting them, killing time, nothing else going on in that head but where to fly next or what to buy next or what she was doing to the Kennedy legacy. No one saw it for what it was: deep depression and post-traumatic stress disorder.

No one on Earth, not even the woman whose husband was killed while trying to arrest Jack's assassin, could relate to what Jackie had been through — not the scale or scope of it, the enormous burden that came with carrying Jack's legacy. The shrinks, the pills, the vodka and cigarettes took the edges off sometimes, but then she'd suddenly find herself back in Texas, her husband's brains exploded all over her lap, she herself exposed to another gunshot. So what if she shopped? *So what?*

Part of it was her natural acquisitiveness, sure: Jackie liked nice things. But there was also the fear of poverty drilled into her from early childhood by her mother, whose own second marriage was driven by the need for financial security. Deep down, Jackie held the irrational fear that no matter how much money she had, it would never be enough. The existential dread that no one would ever really know or understand her could be quelled, for a little while, with things. So could her anxiety that, at any moment, Ari might tire of her, the latest *objet* in his empire. She exacted her revenge by running up his credit cards at the world's most expensive department stores and design houses, buying doubles and triples and secretly reselling half her purchases at a profit.

No matter the conventional wisdom about the gold-digging Jackie O, every woman still wanted to look like her — to be her. She became an icon even in the punk scene, where the Boston band Human Sexual Response paid tribute to her in a song called "Jackie Onassis":

I want to be Jackie Onassis
I want to wear a pair of dark sunglasses

Her face was her credit card. She could walk up to any airport ticket counter and board any Olympus flight—her husband, after all, owned the airline. Did that make her a prostitute? There were times when Ari treated her like one. He would summon Jackie from her New York apartment at a moment's notice and send her away just as swiftly, to remind her, he said, of "what she really was." He loved to have sex with Jackie in spaces where people could see them—behind a first-class curtain, in a tender tethered to his yacht, in his bedroom with the door cracked open. He got off on defiling this American icon of dignity, showing he owned her and could humiliate her. For Jackie, there was something novel in Ari's open lust. Jack had never been so covetous of her, so passionate. Ari unlocked something in Jackie and loosened her up sexually. His vulgarity, unlike Jack's, was out in the open. One could think the worst about Ari Onassis, but at least he wasn't a hypocrite.

The idea that Jackie would become the inspiration for a sex doll was once unthinkable; now, in fact, she was. Her maids began selling her bras and underwear on the black market. Ari commissioned Halston to replace Jackie's dowdy lingerie with custom-made bras and panties. She was photographed exiting a showing of a pornographic movie in New York. Coco Chanel, whose image Jackie embodied in the pink bouclé suit and pillbox hat on the day of the assassination, said the world had never met the real Jacqueline Kennedy.

"Everyone knew," Chanel said, that Jackie "was not cut out for dignity. You mustn't ask a woman with a touch of vulgarity to spend the rest of her life over a corpse." On and on it went. "No courtesan," said one famous male American columnist, "ever sold herself for more."

No one criticized the buyer. Nor did anyone accuse Ari of behaving badly when he began cheating on Jackie, two weeks after their wedding, with Maria Callas. No one reported Ari's betrayal when he gave paparazzi the day, date, and time that Jackie regularly sunbathed on his private island, nude, and allowed them to shoot her with their long lenses.

No one stood up for her when *Hustler* magazine published pictures of Jackie exercising topless. Or when they called her "THE BILLION DOLLAR BUSH." No one asked who could have been behind a second intrusion, paparazzi getting unobstructed shots of Jackie and Ari having sex on the beach. No one at the time reported Ari's sinister machinations, the rumors that he had his enemies, including Bobby Kennedy, killed. Jackie wouldn't have heard that rumor, but she knew that Onassis and Bobby shared a vengeful streak. Onassis had been among those who knew about Marilyn Monroe's house having been bugged shortly before her death. He was among those who suspected—as did his friend Rupert Allan, Monroe's personal publicist—that her death had not been an accidental overdose nor a suicide. He thought the Kennedy brothers had something to do with it, and his hatred for Bobby was not tempered by Jack's assassination. Years after Ari and Jackie died, an esteemed biographer who had worked with Ari reported that Onassis had paid a member of the Palestinian Liberation Organization—which regularly extorted Onassis and other airlines in exchange for not hijacking their planes—to kill Bobby.

Some historians believe it; others do not. But its existence as a theory speaks to the monster that was Aristotle Onassis, experienced by his lovers, children, business partners, rivals, plus politicians and royals the world over.

But, the tabloids speculated, it would soon be this thirty-nine-year-old widow, with her black cloud and Kennedy Curse, to do him in.

———

When she agreed to marry Ari, Jackie felt as though he were casting her in a movie: Ari as Odysseus, Jackie the woman in need of saving. She had buried an essential part of herself, her burgeoning independence, to play that role for him. She was a kept woman on Skorpios, but she didn't love it. Her mind was too sharp, her creativity too suppressed. After their wedding, Jackie made a book for Ari, huge and bound in leather, in which she copied the *Odyssey,* in both Greek and in English. She had drawn one hundred pages of Ari as a Greek God.

First Camelot, now the *Odyssey.* Jack had been no King Arthur, nor would Ari prove as devoted to his wife as Odysseus. But Jackie did love her mythology.

She used these heroes as a framing device, a way of distancing herself from the ugliness of her life so far. Two years into the marriage, Ari, like any insatiable Greek satyr, had become openly contemptuous of her; as she feared, she had become a purchase that had lost its novelty. He began to insult Jackie in front of their guests. One night on Ari's yacht, as Jackie greeted their dinner guests Loel and Gloria Guinness—he the famed British parliamentarian and explorer, she the mysterious socialite of dubious origin, known as the world's best-dressed woman—she remained bare-faced and wore a simple, unflattering cotton dress, a scarf tied awkwardly around her large head. This was not the seafaring style icon of Hyannis, billowing Hermès scarf at her nape, cocktail and cigarette in hand, bending just so and looking ever graceful. This was the private Jackie, the real one, barely keeping it together.

"Look at you!" Onassis exclaimed. "How can you be seen looking like that? You don't see Gloria in that kind of getup. What is your problem?" For a brief moment, Jackie looked hurt and embarrassed. Then she rearranged herself: The wife who would not be beaten down. The little girl, slapped by her mother, who refused to cry. Jackie smiled. "Yes," she said to Ari. "Don't they look great?"

There had been another dinner party on the yacht, Jackie reading her book on Socrates as the men talked, raising her head to interject and ask whether they thought Socrates was real or fictional. "What is the matter with you?" Ari raged. "Why do you have to talk about such stupid things? Don't you ever stop to think before you open your mouth?" Jackie fled in tears. A few days later, by way of apology, he gave Jackie a gold bracelet.

The jewels were wearing thin.

———

Jackie increasingly sought refuge in New York City and in Montauk, where Lee had fallen in with Andy Warhol's crowd. It was through Warhol that she met Dr. Marianne Kris, a psychiatrist in private practice, in 1971. As an experiment, she reached out to Dr. Kris for advice: President

Nixon had invited her and her children to the White House for a private visit, but she hadn't been back since the assassination and was afraid of the emotions it might unearth. Dr. Kris suggested that Jackie's upset could be due to another trauma: Jack's constant infidelities, his assignations in the White House pool and their marital bed. The truth of what their lives had been like there, and how often Jackie simply left, fleeing to Glen Ora or her mother's house in Rhode Island or Europe or, in one crucial example, to Ari Onassis's yacht.

Maybe facing her fears would be helpful, Dr. Kris said. And it could be good for her children, so little when their father was killed, to experience the White House through the generosity of another First Family. Jackie took that advice and was glad she did. She began seeing Dr. Kris regularly and found it liberating. Here she could speak freely about her private torments — like the recurring dream she had in which she drowned, a dream that was disturbing not so much for her death as for how much, in the dream, she welcomed the calm that came over her as she decided to let go, give in, stop trying to keep her head above water.

There could hardly have been a more literal message from Jackie's subconscious. She no longer considered herself suicidal, certainly not in the way she was after the assassination, but her depression and sadness still threatened to take her down. Dr. Kris diagnosed Jackie with PTSD and explained that her trauma had as much to do with November 22, 1963, as it did with her marriage to Jack, and that made sense to Jackie. She still had so much rage toward Jack for everything he put her through. For not coming home when she delivered a stillborn Arabella. For all the other women, so many of them. The lies and the selfishness and hiding behind her skirt as a happy family man when often he would rather be anywhere else. For being such a terrible husband and such a distracted, unaccomplished president that she had to create an entire fiction, which had only served to trap her.

She was furious about the way he died and was finally able to say it out loud: *It wasn't fair to her.*

"His death really robbed me of my chance to be angry with him," Jackie told Dr. Kris. "He really went out in a blaze of glory."

How could there ever have been room for her rage? How could she allow herself to feel what she felt — that a part of her hated him? America would never accept that. The Kennedys never would, either, no matter how much of Jack's bad behavior ever became public. So Jackie, as she had done since childhood, turned all that fury inward, and it was killing her. Even her therapy offered no escape from Jack's other women: Jackie's stepbrother, Yusha Auchincloss, upon meeting Dr. Kris, recognized her name and did some digging. As it turned out, Dr. Kris had also treated another iconic, troubled woman: Marilyn Monroe. It was Dr. Kris who had forcibly institutionalized Marilyn in 1961, and once Marilyn's ex-husband Joe DiMaggio secured her release, Marilyn moved on to Dr. Greenson.

Jackie had no idea. When Yusha told her about Dr. Kris and Marilyn, she could not comprehend why Kris hadn't disclosed what, to Jackie, was a clear conflict of interest. Jack's other women, after all, were the animating force behind her complicated grief. That was why she was in therapy with Kris! *How could you not tell me?* Jackie asked.

"How is this relevant?" Kris responded.

Jackie was bewildered. "How is it *not?*"

American and European tabloids were all over the rumors that Jackie and Ari were separating, that Ari had had enough. Jackie — callow, selfish, vainglorious Jackie — was getting what she deserved.

> ONASSIS DID NOT SPEND CHRISTMAS WITH JACKIE
>
> JACKIE-ARI SHOWDOWN OVER MARIA CALLAS
>
> "FLAMING ROW" BETWEEN JACKIE AND ARI AT LONDON AIRPORT
>
> CALLAS ATTEMPTED SUICIDE AFTER ONASSIS LEFT PARIS WITH JACKIE

Most embarrassing was a photo of Jackie on the cover of the *National Enquirer*, her belly distended: "Is she or isn't she expecting?" Always fanatical about her weight — really, always in the throes of disordered eating, attempting to control the one thing she could — Jackie went on a

crash starvation diet. Each day she allowed herself half a grapefruit, a little yogurt, 2½ ounces of meat, one apple, 3½ ounces of green vegetables,
and a salad without dressing.

Jackie began having panic attacks and outbursts and was still taking
drugs: tranquilizers to sleep, possibly amphetamines to kill her hunger.
She lost twenty-four pounds in nine days and could barely stand up. She
wound up in the hospital, and the European press reported that Jackie
Kennedy Onassis might be on her deathbed. Not so, said one of her
friends. In a piece aptly headlined "Jackie's Illness Is Onassis," the Italian
magazine *Gente* reported: "It is false that Jacqueline Kennedy has cancer,
said one of her intimate friends, but she is in a disastrous spiritual condition and is not well."

Her marriage had become comparable to cancer.

As Ari was making his affair with Callas exceedingly public, Jackie
was reliving Jack's humiliation of her on a global scale. Ari had always
loved flaunting Callas to denigrate Jackie. "Everybody knows three
things about Aristotle Onassis," he would say. "I'm fucking Maria Callas,
I'm fucking Jacqueline Kennedy, and I'm fucking rich." But now he was
about to lose Jacqueline. Dr. Kris may have been problematic, but she
had helped Jackie to realize: She had a right to be angry. She had a right
to refuse such abuse.

"I will help and protect you," Ari had once told Jackie. "Always." How
quickly he had changed. Now Ari had nothing but contempt for Jackie.
He couldn't understand why she hadn't held up her end of the bargain by
making him palatable to politicians and CEOs. By making him a part of
her world. He had no tolerance for her depressions, her increasingly
lengthy absences, rumors of her own affairs. He would sit across the table
from her and mock her: "I'm so afraid. Death all around me. Only Aristo
can save me."

Hadn't he wanted that role? Hadn't he wanted to save the legendary
Jacqueline Kennedy?

Rose Kennedy saw what was going on and was outraged—for Jackie.
She flew to Greece in March 1970 and made a public show of support for

her daughter-in-law. Rose was sure to be photographed with Ari — boxing him in, as it were, to his new life, despite carrying on with Callas.

When Jackie greeted Rose on Skorpios, she was near tears. Rose, who had lost three sons and two daughters, still thought Jackie's sadness was important — something Rose hoped to fix, or at least lighten. But Rose also reminded Jackie of her importance: not just as a member of the dynastic Kennedys, but of her singular power as an American icon. It was everything untraditional about Jackie that had drawn Ari to her, wasn't it? Rose encouraged Jackie to lean into her strengths. Ari may have thought he was getting a young, broken widow, but Jackie had another side, a side she had so far hidden from him. The side her mother Janet described as terrifying: "Once my daughter sticks a knife in someone," Janet once said, "she never pulls it out."

Jackie couldn't unsheathe that dagger yet. Part of her pitied him. Ari may have fetishized her pain as something that made her more feminine and him more masculine, but he had miscalculated. In truth, Jackie was the dauntless one. It would be Jackie more than anyone who, three years later, would help Ari grieve the death of his twenty-four-year-old son Alexander, who would die in January 1973, one day after his private plane crashed fifteen seconds into takeoff. Jackie had lost one pregnancy and two babies; she knew Ari's pain and she held him and let him cry. To distract him, she took him home to the States for a week to her mother and stepfather's Hammersmith Farm estate on Rhode Island, and the kindness shown by her mother and stepfather moved him.

That softening didn't last long. Within that same year — 1973, their fourth anniversary — Ari, bitter and drinking heavily, began to blame Jackie for Alexander's death. She was the Black Widow, the living embodiment of the Kennedy Curse. He hit Jackie in the face and gave her a black eye.

That year was also the tenth anniversary of Jack's assassination. November had, ever since, been Jackie's most dreaded month. But this November 22 was different. Worse. Magazines and books and television coverage made reliving her nightmare inescapable. All of the coverage asked the same questions: What would Jack Kennedy have become? How would America be different — the implication being better, stronger, more prosperous — had he lived? Could the country ever move past this trauma? All of it was predicated on lies — that Jack had been a good man, that Jack and Jackie were a happy couple, that he would have been one of our greatest presidents.

She was not about to disabuse the nation. She was, once again, here to comfort and sustain the myth that she had created.

"One must not let oneself be numbed by sadness," she wrote for the JFK Library. "He would not have wished that. I don't know how he would have coped with the problems that lay there like sleeping beasts, but I know how he would have approached them . . . He would be older now and wiser, and he would still maintain his deep belief that problems can be solved by men."

The Jackie of a few years later would have ended that last sentence with: "and women."

Jackie was on the verge of many things: Leaving Onassis and figuring out who she wanted to be — without a man. She saw what was going on in America. She saw the way women were fighting for reproductive rights and equal pay and the ability to open bank accounts without a man cosigning for them. Burning their bras. Motherhood was becoming optional. So was marriage. Women were entering the workforce as never before.

Could Jackie ever work?

First things first: she was going to get herself free and get what Ari owed her for suffering through this marriage. The Onassises had yet to meet the steely Jackie, the negotiator who got Old Joe to pay her a million dollars for keeping up appearances, who promised to come back for even more money if Jack continued to torment her. Now that she was in touch with her rage, she was looking for people and places to target and unleash it.

But Jackie wasn't all vengeance. She also leaned, to a degree that continued to surprise her, on Rose Kennedy, her Belle Mère. Rose had never once said that the marriage to Ari had been a disaster, or that Jackie had sullied the Kennedy name. She never said that a divorced Jackie would be a Kennedy liability. Jackie was now taking inspiration from Rose's strength and the ways that Old Joe, no matter how much Jackie had loved him, had continued to underestimate Rose.

"If I ever feel sorry for myself, which is a most fatal thing," Jackie said, "I think of her. I've seen her cry just twice, a little bit. Once was at Hyannis Port, when I came into her room. Her husband was ill, and Jack was gone, and Bobby had been killed...and the other time was on [a] ship after her husband died, and we were standing on the deck at the rail together, and we were talking about something—just something that reminded her. And her voice began to sort of break and she had to stop. Then she took my hand and squeezed it and said, 'Nobody's ever going to have to feel sorry for me. Nobody's ever going to feel sorry for me,' and she put her chin up.

"And I thought, 'God. What a thoroughbred.'"

PART NINE

HOMES FOR WAYWARD GIRLS

ROSE FITZGERALD KENNEDY

The only Catholic more devout than Rose Fitzgerald Kennedy may have been the pope. Rose's mother worshipped at the altar of the Virgin Mary, having built a permanent shrine in their home. Rose went to parochial school, where she was taught by nuns who believed that a woman's greatest accomplishment was to suffer well—also a literal teaching. The sisters wore hardware around their necks and wrists meant to inflict pain at the slightest movement.

It was masochism enshrined as virtue, a lesson Rose also absorbed at home. Women suffered; men sought pleasure. Her mother spent her nights at home, on her knees in prayer, while Rose's father, John Fitzgerald, the mayor of Boston, ran around town with a parade of women.

This was Rose's preordained future: to be a supplicant, not the fierce intellect she was at her core, the political animal who thrived under her father's tutelage—her father being one of the few American politicians to court the support of women, even though they couldn't yet vote. He recognized that one day they would, and until that day it was still women who ran their families and made most of the decisions about where to live, what to buy, how best to educate their children. Yet they were nonetheless creatures of domestication, as Rose would become: a woman who would marry, have many children, be faithful to her husband, and never question what he did or with whom.

After convent school in the Netherlands, Rose graduated from Dorchester High in Boston in 1906. She was eager for college and badly wanted to go to Wellesley, the private women's liberal arts school. Instead, her parents forced her to enroll at Sacred Heart Catholic College in Boston. Missing out on a Wellesley education would be the greatest regret of Rose's life.

None of this stopped her from marrying the man her parents disapproved of: Joe Kennedy, whom she had fallen in love with at age sixteen and with whom, as she said, she never fell out of love. He, too, was the product of a political Boston family, two years older than Rose and already well on his way: after Harvard, Joe was amassing an incredible fortune as a banker and stock market investor. Joe's father, P.J., and Rose's father, known as Honey Fitz, were both major figures in the Democratic Party and sometime rivals. Rose came to the marriage with a whiff of controversy — her father, after serving two terms as Boston's mayor, was forced aside due to what came to be called the "Toodles scandal" — rumor was Honey Fitz had been carrying on an affair with a cigarette girl known as Toodles Ryan. It was 1913; Rose was twenty-four years old and needed to be married soon. Honey Fitz's decision not to run again was ascribed in Boston's press to "the petticoat element": the women in his life, his daughters mainly, who needed the chance to marry well. His scandal would not help that.

And so, in 1914, Joe and Rose were married in a modest Catholic ceremony in Boston, united not just by their faith and politics but also a mutual grudge against Protestants, WASPs, and any other group that routinely ostracized Irish Catholics. Their exclusion from Boston's polite society would fuel Joe's determination that he or one of his sons would become the first Irish Catholic American president.

When it came to sex, however, Rose and Joe were at odds. Rose subscribed to the Church's teachings that sex was permissible only for making babies, not for intimacy and certainly not for pleasure. After having Teddy, her ninth and last child in February 1932, Rose told Joe she would never have sex with him again. "This idea of yours that there is no romance outside procreation is simply wrong," Joe said. "It was not part of our contract at the altar. The priest never said that, and the books don't argue that."

Did Rose have it coming? Did she leave her husband no other option than to sleep with other women? And if so, did she deserve this degree of suffering? Joe stayed out night after night and constantly traveled on so-called business, even as she had baby after baby in those first years of marriage: Joe, Jack, Rosemary.

Rosemary.

Oh, the trauma of that birth. It was September 13, 1918, a Friday, and the influenza pandemic was tearing through Boston. Rose's obstetrician was running late, attending to Boston's sick and dying, and the nurse who arrived wasn't permitted to give anesthesia. It was Rose and the nurse alone in her bedroom.

As Rose's labor progressed, her pain intensifying, the baby making her way through the birth canal, Rose desperately tried not to push but was physically unable to—despite the nurse yelling at her to *stop, stop, stop!* She clamped Rose's legs together and pushed the baby back inside. All this pain, Rose kept telling herself, was God's cost. First suffering, then joy.

The nurse, trained in obstetrics, could have delivered this baby. But this was yet another thing women weren't allowed to do, because that meant earning money that otherwise would have gone to the doctor. If Rose's nurse were to deliver Rose's baby, then Frederick Good, the otherwise-occupied obstetrician, would not be able to bill Joe Kennedy his standard $125 fee.

And so this capable nurse, upon seeing the baby crown, felt no other option but to put her palm on that tiny head and shove the baby back inside, holding her there for two hours.

———

When Rosemary didn't make her milestones—when her little sister Kick, eighteen months younger, began outpacing her—Rose and Joe knew that something was very wrong. The perfectionists in them were loath to admit it, raising their ever-growing family with militaristic fervor. The children were weighed every day and kept trim and athletic; quizzed on economics, geopolitics, world religions; taught to ski, sail, and swim, each child's progress detailed on index cards, with only one outcome acceptable.

"We only have winners in this family," Joe and Rose would say. "We don't allow losers."

Rosemary was slow, but Kick especially doted on her. In some ways it assuaged her guilt; Kick was really the second-oldest daughter, but because Rosemary was — what? Defective? Was Rosemary, to her parents, a loser? — Kick had been elevated, treated as the true oldest daughter, afforded the respect of her father and brothers.

Jack and Joe Jr. especially treated Kick not just as a peer but as the star she was. She had heard the admiring whispers about the three of them, that of all the Kennedy siblings they were The Ones, a closed VIP circle glowing within an already shining constellation. And Kick had been dutiful, hadn't she? Not only that, but Kick was the only child who had stood up for her mother, defending her against Joe Jr. and Jack. It was Kick alone who told them they were callous, that they ought to sympathize with their mother and the brutalities she endured. Oh, how her brothers would laugh and make fun, mocking their mother behind her back for the way their father cheated on her, flaunting his infidelity. Joe would bring his lovers home, parade them around the front porch, take them sailing — Jack, at twelve, had actually plunged off the side of a boat once he realized that Dad and his movie star girlfriend were having sex on board. Joe had his paramours over to family dinners, seated at the table like any other guest.

It was Kick who exploded the last time he did that, bringing yet another woman to the Cape. None of her siblings had the guts; they were all afraid of Old Joe. But Kick was fed up with his flagrant disrespect of their mother and, really, every one of his daughters. His temerity was an insult to every Kennedy woman who sat at that table.

Coincidentally, it was Kick whom her mother had been pregnant with the first and only time she left Joe, so fed up with his women, his lies, his utter disregard for their marriage. Rose had packed up her things, left her three children behind, and gone back to her childhood home on Welles Avenue in Boston, where she slept in her old bed, took solace in the company of her siblings and her beloved father, and tried to make sense of what had happened to her young, once-glittering future. She had been "the belle of Boston Irish society." Now she was relegated to the metaphorical back room.

Rose had gifts, not least her smarts, her high organizational skills, and her energy, but these had been dimmed by the men in her life. First, her father, whose insistence on a Catholic college over Wellesley was not about Rose's best interests at all but, as she would later learn, political expediency: the great feminist mayor of Boston had sold out his daughter after he was warned by the archbishop, no less, that he would lose the Catholic vote if he allowed Rose a secular, liberal education.

As for that Catholic education? Well, Rose had been taught that a woman's highest and truest calling was motherhood. She was promised total fulfillment in that role, assured that all of one's creativity and intellectualism would, if channeled properly into her husband and children, be satisfied. "The most beautiful station" of her life, Rose was told.

It wasn't. Not even close.

Her husband, whom she loved deeply, whose nimble, capacious mind she adored and wanted access to, shut her out. He wouldn't tell her where he was or what he was doing. He kept a suite at the Ritz in Boston and another at the Waldorf in Manhattan, while she was shut up in the suburbs. She, every bit as urbane and sophisticated as Joe, had been left to atrophy. It was as if she were an object he had thoughtlessly left behind, the way one would realize while traveling that they must have left their hat somewhere and — oh, well. Rose needed something other than babies and paid bills to feel fulfilled. She wanted to be around interesting people and things, the theater and corporate boardrooms and political campaigns. She had so much to offer, but Joe wouldn't share anything of his political maneuverings with Rose: not his strategies or his enemies, his fears or his goals.

Did he really think so little of her? Of the children he left her with?

It wasn't just Rosemary who concerned her; little Jack was a very sick toddler. He had been ill with scarlet fever when she left Joe — that's how desperate she was. She left poor Jack with the nannies to save herself.

It was the winter of 1920. Women had just won the right to vote. Rose Fitzgerald Kennedy, wife and daughter to two political geniuses, had never felt so powerless.

Her childhood home would prove no haven. Rose's twenty-year-old sister Eunice, her favorite sibling, was dying of tuberculosis. Their father was consumed with Eunice's care. There was no room for Rose's pain in this house.

There was no room for Rose.

Her father came to her childhood bedroom one night, snow falling outside, and told her to deal with her problems alone. He had never liked Joe Kennedy anyway. He had tried to talk her out of marrying him, but Rose just had to defy her father. Wayward girls got their comeuppance.

"You've made your commitment, Rosie," he told her. "You must honor it now. What is past is past. The old days are gone. Your children need you and your husband needs you."

What about Rose's needs?

"You can make things work," her father said. "I know you can. If you need more help in the household, then get it. If you need a bigger house, ask for it. If you need more private time for yourself, take it. There isn't anything you can't do once you set your mind to it.

"So go now, Rosie. Go back to where you belong."

———————

Did her father know what — who — was waiting for her back home?

Rose's husband wasn't just promiscuous. He wasn't just an adulterer. He was also, according to Gloria Swanson, a Hollywood star and Joe's longtime mistress, a rapist.

Of their initial encounter in 1927, Swanson said that Joe Kennedy came to her hotel suite in Palm Beach, entered with total force and, she said, "moved so quickly that his mouth was on mine before either of us could speak. With one hand he held the back of my head, with the other he stroked my body and pulled at my kimono . . . He kept insisting in a drawn-out main, 'No longer, no longer. Now.' He was like a roped horse, rough, arduous, racing to be free. After a hasty climax he lay beside me, stroking my hair. Apart from his guilty, passionate mutterings, he still had said nothing cogent, I had said nothing at all . . . And I knew, as we lay there, that it would go on."

Rose never knew about this attack. But she knew this side of Joe — the violent side, the predatory side — and it was one she chose to ignore.

ROSEMARY KENNEDY

S he no longer had the word for it, but she knew the feeling: lonely. She had her nuns and her nurses, and they were lovely, but this wasn't her real home and they weren't her siblings. She only ever saw her brothers on TV. She saw the news footage of Jack that terrible day and knew something bad had happened to him, but she couldn't understand what. Sometimes she got a glimpse of her sisters or her mother and daddy, but none of them ever came to visit.

What had Rosemary done? She had been such a good girl.

They all called her Rosie, which had been her mother's nickname, too, and it suited her: she was a beauty, prettiest of all the Kennedy girls, always happy and, most of all, pleasing to her father. She adored him. She wanted to be his favorite and had reason to think she was. After all, it wasn't Kick or Eunice or Pat or Jean whom Joe had chosen to stay with him in London. It wasn't one of her brothers, even though it was no secret that the boys were treated far better than the girls—as if they *were* better. No. Joe had chosen her.

It was September 1939. England had declared war on Germany. Joe had sent all the other Kennedy sons and daughters back to the States with Rose. Only Rosie had been allowed to remain with Joe, who was still serving as the US ambassador to the United Kingdom despite his well-known affinity for Hitler. It was a strategic ploy by Roosevelt, who loathed Kennedy's antisemitism but worried that cutting him loose too fast would spur Kennedy to start a rival isolationist movement. As it was, Kennedy had given an interview in which he blamed Eleanor Roosevelt for "always sending me a note to have some little Susie Glitz for tea at the

Embassy." It was yet another example of Joe's hypocrisy — the man whose vaulting ambition was fueled by prejudice against Irish Catholics was every bit as hateful of another persecuted group facing eradication. Of that he cared nothing.

"The war would drain us," he said. "It would turn our government into national socialism . . . What would we be fighting for? . . . Democracy is finished in England."

But he was happy to leave Rosemary there. Rosemary, who with her limitations would never have survived the horrors of Hitler's eugenics. Was he aware of having a death wish for his daughter? Joe was on record as supporting Hitler's forced sterilization plan, its number one targets those with "congenital mental deficiency." Joe called it "a great thing. I don't know how the Church feels about it, but it will do away with many of the disgusting specimens . . . which inhabit this earth."

———————

Rosie didn't feel left behind or less cared for. In fact, Joe had told her the opposite: he had chosen her to stay in England because she was special. "You are going to be the one to keep me company," he told Rosie. She was twenty then, fresh off her triumphant debut at Buckingham Palace. Everyone had been so worried about how she would do. Would Rosie embarrass the Kennedys?

Well, yes, a little. It was the smallest, most frustrating thing, Rosie tripping in front of the king and queen. Everyone else shook it off, including Rosemary, but not her mother. This was a test, and Rosemary had failed it, even after her mother had arranged those weeks-long etiquette lessons: how to curtsy, how to dance, how to behave with men.

The men. They liked Rosemary a lot, and she liked them. Her brother Jack was the kindest of all her siblings in helping Rosie to socialize; he would bring her with him to nightclubs and parties, and their sister Eunice took note. "He would dance with her and kid with her and make sure a few of his close pals cut in so she felt popular," Eunice said. "He'd bring her home at midnight, then he'd go back [out]."

There were whispers at the palace party that Rosie had propositioned not one but two waiters — a family scandal, a Kennedy girl being so forward. It didn't matter that Old Joe snuck into guest rooms whenever Kick or her sisters had teenage friends sleep over. It didn't matter that these young girls didn't want Old Joe in their beds. It didn't matter that sometimes he had his way with them, whether they wanted to or not. No one talked about it. Joe took whom he wanted when he wanted, and Rose Kennedy couldn't do a thing about it. That her boys were turning out the same way didn't seem to be a problem.

Rosie, though: she was a problem. Rose had so little tolerance for Rosie as it was—how slow she was at school, how earnest and childlike, how needy. Rose hated neediness. Even Jack, with all his serious illnesses, had learned to suffer silently. But Rosie wasn't quiet about it.

Besides, Jack was smart. He kept his nose in a book, was quick with a quip, a sharp rebuke that could set even their mother back. He was reading Winston Churchill's *The World Crisis* at age thirteen. He mocked his ever-growing family, once telling two friends who had picked him up from boarding school, "I want to stop by the house for a minute and check the nursery and see if there's anybody new in the family." Gallows humor was his preferred coping mechanism during his multiple hospital stays: "Took a peek at my chart yesterday," he wrote a college friend in 1935, "and could see that they were mentally measuring me for a coffin. Eat drink and make love as tomorrow or next week we attend my funeral."

Rosie wasn't glib like that, not remotely. Things came much harder for her, reading and writing especially. She was the only Kennedy sibling who wasn't athletic. She struggled with her weight, always up or down five or ten pounds. All the others knew to stay thin and tanned. Even disheveled, they all looked so athletic and stylish. Not Rosie. She would never be that carefree girl on a Kennedy sail, windswept hair and white sweaters, weightlessly bobbing on ocean swells while the men sipped bourbon and smoked cigars. She couldn't even row a dinghy—a basic expectation for a Kennedy. Rosie's beauty, even to her vain parents, didn't compensate for any of this. Nor did her essential sweetness. Theirs was a family of winners—and Rosie, well, she was beginning to look like a loser. She was self-aware enough to know something was wrong with her. She just still didn't know what.

Neither did her parents. Joe had enrolled Rosie at a special school called Assumption at the Belmont House in Kent, thirty miles outside London. Here she was placed under the tutelage of a Mother Isabel, who favored the Montessori method. It was a revelation. Rosemary was as much a teacher as a student, working with younger students as an aide. Her self-esteem rose, and Assumption's bucolic setting settled Rosemary. Everything was calmer, slower, cleaner. There were no high stakes. All Rosie had to do was concentrate on reading and writing, which remained big challenges, as well as smaller tasks. Joe Kennedy was relieved.

As he wrote to Rose in October 1939, Rosemary "is contented completely to be teaching with Mother Isabel. She is happy, looks better than she ever did in her life, is not the slightest bit lonesome, and loves to get letters from [her siblings] telling her how lucky she is to be over here (tell them to keep writing that way). She loves being the boss here and is no bother or strain at all."

Her progress pleased Joe, to a point. He still considered Rosemary a liability to Brand Kennedy and had no intention of welcoming her back into the fold. "She must never be at home," he wrote Rose, "for her sake as well as everyone else's."

———

Joe was raising future US presidents. As the war raged and America's involvement became more likely, Joe Kennedy, with his antisemitism and isolationism, was political poison. His long-harbored dream to become the first Irish Catholic president of the United States was dead. If it couldn't be him, it would be Joe Jr., whether he wanted it or not.

So better, too, he wrote to Rose, that Rosemary stay in England that Christmas, even though Joe wouldn't be back there until the following March or April. Mother Isabel concurred, writing to Rose that December of Rosemary's personal growth. All who were working with Rosemary, Mother Isabel wrote, "are very satisfied with the result of this term. Rosemary is very well, obviously happy, [and] she has made much progress in many ways . . . She has some supervision of the children in the garden, she also has a stated time for reading to them; she prepares [and] gives them their lunch in the middle of the morning; has many other occupations of a domestic kind which she can do *alone*—not the least of which is putting away the dining room things [china, silver] in the cupboard."

Rosie was also quite self-aware, Mother Isabel wrote, and was working hard on managing her emotions. She wasn't proud of the fits she threw. "She asked me one day to tell her what faults she had, as faults spoil people. This struck me, showing me how much she thinks things out. We have had more talks, [and] she has been trying hard to 'think of what pleases others *before* what pleases herself,' and 'to be nice to people even when *she* thinks they are not nice to her.' She comes to me whenever anything upsets her, [and] we 'have it out'—along those lines."

———

Rosie was working so hard to impress her father. With the new decade approaching, her father still Roosevelt's ambassador to the United Kingdom, he would visit her from time to time. Sometimes he would even take her out of school and bring her to London for special weekends together. She had never felt so capable; her father, the very important ambassador preparing for war, chose to rely upon Rosie more than anyone. Not Joe Jr., who was going to be president. Not the brilliant Jack. Not even his own wife. Rosie took such pride in pleasing him, and they would often socialize with Joe's great friends Eddie and Mary Moore. Rosie had become the ambassador's companion in England, something of a surrogate wife. The combination of her father's intense attention, his longed-for approval, and a new realization—that what made Rosie different also made her special—was gratifying. When Joe left, whether for the city or America, he was never far from her mind, as she expressed so poignantly in a March 1940 letter to him:

> *Darling Daddy,*
> *Mother {Isabel} says I am such a comfort to you, never to leave you. Daddy, I feel honour because you chose me to stay. And the others I suppose are wild…P.S. I am so fond of you. And love you very much.*

In the countryside, alone with the children and the nuns, Rosie thought only of Joe. She took every criticism to heart.

"You are getting altogether too fat," Old Joe had told her. Her other progress paled. He said the same thing to Rosie's teachers after an in-person visit: "She is getting altogether too fat and I told her in no uncertain words. So I wish, if you could, you would try to build up the idea that she should lose weight. I told her that her mother would be very disappointed and also that I could not have her picture taken for America if she remains as stout as she is."

Rosie was mortified.

"I would do anything to make you so happy." Rosie would say this to her father over and over. She went on a strict diet. She took the red pills her father gave her and the three-times-per-week injections that Joe said were their secret. Rosie didn't know what was in any of these medications or why she needed them; the same doctor had given Rosie her physical and declared her to be "in perfect condition." It seemed like they were really for her father, who was ecstatic she was taking this stuff.

In May 1940, Rosie was awarded her diploma. Germany was advancing through Europe, and Joe felt there was no other option but to get her out, if only briefly. As he wrote to Rose, "When things settle down here under any regime" — meaning the Nazis — "they will be delighted to have her back and I'm sure she'll come back hopping." In the meantime, Rosemary would return to the Kennedy home in Bronxville, flown from London to Lisbon to New York by family friends and private Kennedy secretaries Eddie and Mary Moore.

No one was prepared for Rosie's reentry into Kennedy family life nor for what she needed. She had spent a year at the Belmont House, and now she was without everything that had helped her to flourish there: Mother Isabel, the children, the one-on-one talks and lessons, the structure and the quiet. The Kennedy house was a cauldron of competition, of strictly enforced exercise and feeding, a chaotic environment that all too often lacked the presence of either parent. Rosemary may have been home but she was also, at the same time, completely lost. Unable to keep up with her siblings, to participate in the dinner-table discussions of foreign policy or their athletic excursions, Rosemary was the odd girl out. Rose herself conceded as much: "In our family," she said, "if you're not doing anything you're left in the corner."

Rosie was excluded from parties and family vacations. Her mother had tried putting Rosemary in sleepaway camp in western Massachusetts that summer, but the staff—uninformed by Rose of her daughter's special needs—were horrified by Rosemary's condition. Her shoes were so small that her feet were bleeding. She tended to wander out late at night and wound up sleeping in the same room as the camp's director. Rosemary began acting out, missing her father especially, but was heartbroken when she was asked to leave the camp after only three weeks.

"I am going to work so hard for my daddy," she said before leaving, "and he deserves it. Pray for me. God bless you."

Rose refused to get her daughter; instead, she remained ensconced at a luxury spa and retreat in Maine. Joe was traveling. Once again, Eddie Moore was called upon to fetch Rosemary and find some other place to put her.

Saint Gertrude's, a private boarding school in Washington, DC, for low-IQ middle-school girls, was next. Rosemary was twenty-two years old, and whatever happened during her brief time here was enough to escalate her tantrums. She snuck out most every night; whether she was looking for someone or trying to find her way home or was trying to escape abuse, sexual or otherwise, is unknown. But Rosemary, serially abandoned by her father and mother, made to feel that she was the defective product in a line that otherwise produced Outstanding Kennedy Offspring, had understandably become a tearful young woman with lots of rage.

Or, as Rose Kennedy put it, "disquieting symptoms began to develop." Rosemary would remain at Saint Gertrude's for the next thirteen months, until November 1941. That's when Joe came upon his own final solution to the Rosemary problem.

Joe Kennedy had heard of an experimental new procedure for the hardest cases—women, mostly, who were moody or sad or sexually promiscuous—and asked Kick to look into it.

Kick was now working as a reporter at the *Times-Herald* in DC, killing time while waiting to return to Billy. She confided in her quasi-romantic interest, her colleague John White, about her older sister. It took a while for Kick to work up the courage to tell White just what was wrong with Rosemary. White felt Kick's hesitation. "It was as though she was confessing something quite embarrassing, almost shameful," he said. "I got the feeling that her family viewed Rosemary as a beloved failure. Perhaps a disgrace." But Kick got the information she had been tasked with finding, and came back to her mother with an informed opinion.

"Oh, Mother, no," she said. "It's nothing we want done for Rosie."

Rose was relieved. The idea hadn't sat well with her from the beginning.

"I'm glad to hear that," she said. But Rosie couldn't live with the family — that was for sure.

We don't tolerate losers.

One day in November of 1941, Joe told Rosie he wanted her to meet someone new, a Dr. Freeman over at George Washington Hospital. It would be their secret, not even for Rose to know.

Freeman was famous and brilliant, and he was working on a revolutionary treatment for people like Rosie. Joe didn't tell her what he had discussed with the great doctor — that would be a surprise. Rosie complied.

I would do anything to make you so happy.

Everyone in and around the Kennedy family knew that Rosemary would never say no to her father, no matter what. One of Jack's friends found something sinister in Joe's dynamic with Rosemary. She wondered, and she wasn't alone, if Joe had been sexually abusing his daughter. Leaving her alone in England, using her as his "companion," shuffling her among all these institutions and keeping her away and quiet and apart from her siblings — it made sense, she thought.

The day after Thanksgiving, November 28, 1941, Rosie walked into the appointment Joe had set for her. The doctors had strange questions, and they wanted to shave her head. Would that be all right? If Rosie wanted to be like her siblings, brilliant and athletic and always doing and saying the right things, if she wanted to be a real Kennedy — well, this was the first step in fixing her.

Rosie's hair. Her beautiful, thick, dark, wavy hair, the perfect contrast to her blue eyes and ivory skin. Why would they take that from her? Her beauty?

Oh, this was only temporary, she was told. Hair grows back. The nurses wouldn't even need to shave all of it — just half, from, say, her forehead to the crown.

Rosie was given a hospital gown. Her hair fell to the floor in soft clumps. A sedative, a stretcher, an operating room, a stainless steel table. Restraints. Her head strapped down. White towels and sheets swathed around her. Bright white lights. She couldn't see what was happening. There was a whirr, powerful and loud, followed by the scent of metal upon bone, sharp and smoky.

The doctors told Rosie not to worry. She didn't even need anesthesia — that's how simple and painless this was. Everything that was happening to her, she would be awake and aware. Not many operations you could say that about.

Pressure above her eye now. Rosie's head was vibrating, the side of her head pulsating. The doctor talking to her seemed pleased. The way they once did this was so much less pleasant. Those other patients he had had to knock out — not with anesthesia but with electroshock through the brain, even though it could take five or six tries and the patients convulsed and howled and cried. Sometimes they would beg to die.

Rosie didn't have to suffer that. Nor did she have to endure Dr. Freeman's earlier method, ice picks from his kitchen drawer positioned right above his patient's eye, a white cloth draped diagonally over the face as he hammered through the eye socket straight to the brain, moving the pick back and forth like a metronome till he heard the *pop pop pop!* of nerves being sliced apart, like the sound of a soda can opening and decompressing. Then he knew his work was done.

All those patients would emerge with two black eyes, really bruised up, and have to wear dark sunglasses for weeks. Rosie wouldn't have to worry about that. Her looks would be untouched.

The doctor moved to her other side now. What was he doing? Was he doing it again? Why did one of the nurses look terrified? The drill against Rosie's other temple was grinding against bone. Granules as smooth and sharp as a shark's tooth were splattering against Rosie's head and onto the table. Why was she awake? What was this torture? Where was her daddy?

The drill went quiet. The heavy tool went down. Clattering on a tray, like silverware. Something slim slid into one of the holes in her skull. Dr. Freeman stood above her. He was still talking to her, asking her questions.

What was her name? Who was the president? Could she sing a song? Could she count backward from the number ten? Rosie could do all these things with holes in her head and a man using what felt like a dull butter knife to root around her brain. But the deeper the tool went the harder it was to understand the doctor, to understand what was happening to her. When it was finally over, Rosie wasn't Rosie anymore. She would never be able to do anything again: talk, walk, swim, dance, flirt with boys, smoke cigarettes, meet future queens, accompany her father to dinner. Go to the movies. Take a shower, comb her hair, feed herself, use the toilet. She would never again go home or be one of the Kennedys. Her brain's circuitry, like a string of Christmas lights crushed one by one, had gone dark.

Rosie was left, functionally, as a two-year-old. Whenever reporters asked what happened to Rosemary, Joe had a ready explanation: she was following her life's calling in another state, teaching children who were, as they were called back then, mentally retarded. Rosie's own siblings would never even know exactly where she was. Her mother's round-robin letters to the children would forevermore include each of them by name — except Rosemary. She had been stashed away in another state, left without any contact from her siblings or her parents, erased.

PART TEN

REBELS

JOAN KENNEDY

"How swinging should a First Lady be?"

In the run-up to Ted's inevitable announcement, this was what the media focused on: Joan's looks. In the style sections and women's magazines, other women disparaged Joan's appearance and affect, taking her apart surgically in ways Ted never had to endure.

They criticized her miniskirts, her knee-high boots, how she wore her hair and makeup. They pilloried her for wearing skirts without slips and gowns with side slits. Even the doctor treating Joan for alcoholism called her assistant, Marcia, and asked if she might persuade Joan to tone down her makeup and wardrobe — to look like less of a showstopper and more, well, ladylike.

Ted had put him up to that. Joan knew it. No one was telling Ted to go on a diet or do something about his ruddy alcoholic complexion or quit drinking altogether, which he really needed to do. No — Joan and her hemlines were the problem.

No one understood that Joan was trying to get the attention of the only man who mattered, her husband, while also sticking it to him. Her clothes were acts of rebellion. She was a gorgeous woman in her mid-thirties, coming into her own alongside American feminism. She was asserting her independence as the wife of the country's leading Democrat, a man who fought for the country's downtrodden — for civil rights and universal health care.

But when it came to women, forget it. Ted refused to support the Equal Rights Amendment. At least it was in keeping with his terrible treatment of women in private. Few aside from Kennedy wives knew the indignities as Joan did, of slinking away from a party thrown in your own home, having watched your husband flirt with every other woman in the room, only to hear the whispers later that he'd had sex in the library with one of your guests after you went to bed. Or to have lunch with a friend at the Ritz, seen by all of Boston's high society, only to learn that that friend, too, had slept with Ted, and that Joan was the last to know. Or to have your husband picking up women and bringing them, along with his supplicant aide, back to the house to do lines of cocaine and have sex while the children were upstairs, presumably asleep. Those encounters usually took place in the Jacuzzi that Ted had installed in the backyard for threesomes.

There was nothing he wouldn't lie about, no corner he wouldn't cut. He was a supremely unserious man who the media kept propping up as Camelot's next hope, even as they knew better. Everyone on the Hill knew about the drug box Ted kept in his desk in the Senate. They'd all heard the story about the fourteen-year-old girl he'd tried to rape and whose parents he had paid off. Or the high school girl he had hired as an intern and begun having sex with; she was only seventeen. The waitresses he'd sexually assaulted. The cruises around DC in the back of his limo, rolling down his window, trying to pick up young women.

Who could forget the time he caught two of their children using cocaine and, during his subsequent antidrug talk — telling them they had to be careful, their mother suffered from addiction, and it was her bad genes that put them at risk — deciding to do a few lines with them? Or the two abortions at least one of his mistresses had?

How about the doctor who would show up to Ted's office and treat him for gonorrhea? Did Joan ever wonder if, like Jackie, her miscarriages, the enormous amount of hormones she needed to take to get pregnant with their youngest, Patrick, all may have been caused by Ted's constant sexually transmitted infections?

Probably not. Joan, after all, was a virgin when they married.

There was the dinner party Ted threw in their home, making their nanny dress in Joan's clothes, playing hostess while Joan was asleep. It was as if Ted was saying that his wife was on par with the hired help — that she was there to cook and host parties and dress up and be sexually available, nothing more, and if his actual wife couldn't fulfill these very basic duties (really, what did a Kennedy man have to do around here for a little respect?), any woman would do. Joan Kennedy, he seemed to be saying, was interchangeable. Inconsequential. Unnecessary.

The only other humiliation that came close was Ted walking a reporter out to their parked car, where Joan had passed out. "Do you see what I have to deal with?" he asked.

Ted was a drunk, too, but no one criticized him the way they did Joan. His pain was valorized, his drinking, drugging, and womanizing excused. He had three dead brothers, an alcoholic wife, and now, in Teddy Jr., a very sick child, so hey, he was entitled — that was the thinking.

So it was Ted on the cover of *People* magazine with Teddy Jr., teaching the twelve-year-old to ski four months after losing part of his leg to cancer. It was Ted and his team who told the media that he had been the one to break the news to their son that he was going to need an amputation. Ted's team told *People* that Joan wasn't on this momentous ski trip because she "was not feeling well."

Joan had kept it together through the worst of Teddy Jr.'s illness and treatment, and only then, when he was home and safe and recovering, did she let herself fall apart. The month after that story ran, Joan found herself on the cover of the same magazine.

"JOAN KENNEDY," the headline read. "It wasn't a nervous breakdown, she only needed a rest."

The story inside, by well-known journalist Liz Smith, explained why Joan had just spent three weeks at Silver Hill in Connecticut, which Smith described as "a private sanitarium." Joan's alcoholism was minimized; indeed, Silver Hill was, and remains, known as a rehabilitation facility for the rich and famous. Smith instead cited the pressures of being a Kennedy wife.

"She has accepted the realities of her married life," Smith wrote, " — the senator's frequent neglect ('Ted only pays attention to Joan when he needs her,' says one jaundiced Washington source), his eye for a pretty girl, his early-to-late political habits."

She also noted Ted's desire that Joan not seek outside help. "Senator Kennedy," Smith reported, "didn't want his wife to see a psychiatrist in the first place and had to be convinced some years back that it was vital."

Among Joan's many torments was her fear that Ted, despite all he put her through, would meet the same fate as Jack and Bobby. A part of her was still deeply in love with Ted, who could turn his attentions to her at any given moment and make her feel like the only woman he had ever loved. "Nobody wants him to run," her father, Harry, said. "Nobody in the family on either side. They're all scared to death. Over and over, Joan keeps saying that she hopes he does not run. Can you blame her? But what they know, and Joan knows it too and this is what terrifies her, is that he's got to do what he feels he must. But they all pray he doesn't."

In the end, he did. Months before Ted announced in 1980 — mounting an intraparty challenge against President Jimmy Carter, whose personal character was unassailable — meetings were called, strategies debated. The main worry wasn't Chappaquiddick or Ted's alcoholism or his rampant womanizing. The real problem was: How to handle Joan?

Sometimes she was apprised of Ted's prep meetings, sometimes not. Sometimes she was invited to participate, sometimes not. She could tell herself that it was the nature of the beast, or that their unconventional marriage explained his campaign's unorthodox approach. That was fine; they could handle Ted as they saw fit. But they weren't going to handle Joan.

Joan was reinventing herself on her own terms, and had been for some time. In 1972, she had sat down with *Good Housekeeping* for a cover story and spoken candidly of things few women did: Joan was in analysis, seeing a psychiatrist three times a week. She was working hard on her sobriety. She was still struggling with her self-worth. "It's very easy to feel insecure when you marry into a very famous, intelligent, exciting family," Joan said. "It's been very difficult. You start comparing yourself to the other Kennedy women and somehow your confidence in yourself begins to evaporate."

Jackie remained the lone sister-in-law Joan truly enjoyed. As Liz Smith wrote in a separate column, "Joan admires Jackie's bright culture, taste,

FRIDAY, MAY 18, 2012 / Sunny, 76 / Weather: P. 18 ★ ★   **LATE CITY FINAL**   www.nypost.com   • • • •   75¢

The tragic despair of a Kennedy wife

BROKE, LONELY AND AFRAID

Grant Leslie/Corbis Outline

Mary Kennedy, deep in debt and going through a painful divorce from RFK Jr. when she killed herself, was "all alone in this house that she built," a pal said. **PAGES 4-5**

Mary Richardson Kennedy was revealed to have suffered profoundly in her marriage to Robert F. Kennedy Jr. After her suicide in 2012, RFK Jr. had her coffin secretly and illegally exhumed from the Kennedy family plot, burying her far away and alone. *(Grant Devlin/Use of the* New York Post *courtesy of NYP Holdings, Inc.)*

Mary Kennedy, her dark beauty reminiscent of Jackie, with husband Bobby Jr. at a charity ball at New York City's Plaza Hotel in November 2000. The diaries Bobby kept and discovered by Mary, containing his multiple sexual conquests listed by name and rankings, destroyed her. *(Ron Galella, Ltd./Getty Images)*

Curb Your Enthusiasm actress Cheryl Hines with husband Bobby Kennedy Jr. Reports that Bobby was cheating on Cheryl weeks before their 2014 marriage did not deter her from becoming the third Mrs. RFK Jr. *(Axelle/Bauer-Griffin/Getty Images)*

Bobby Jr. with his and Mary's children at her casket. In his eulogy, Bobby took no responsibility for the agony his repeated adulteries caused her. "I know I did everything I could to help her," he said. *(Michael Dwyer/Associated Press)*

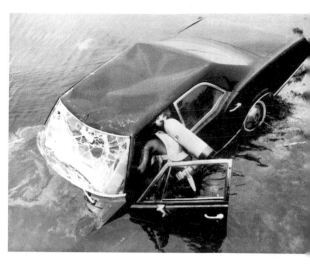

A diver inspects the car in which young campaign aide Mary Jo Kopechne died, left alone by Ted Kennedy, who had been driving. Upon fleeing the scene, he passed pay phones, lit houses, and the fire department, not reporting the accident until the next morning—after he shaved, showered, and had a hearty breakfast. She could have been saved. *(Popperfoto/Getty Images)*

A craven Ted Kennedy wears a neck brace he didn't need to Mary Jo's funeral. He conscripted his pregnant wife, Joan, to accompany him, despite doctor's orders that she stay on bed rest. One month later, she miscarried. *(Bettman/Getty Images)*

The headline said it all. Mary Jo's name was dwarfed in reports of her own wholly avoidable death. Ted Kennedy was never criminally charged and took the events of that night to his grave. *(@ Daily News, L.P. (New York). Used with permission. Photo of Mary Jo courtesy of the Kopechne family. Crash scene, Associated Press.)*

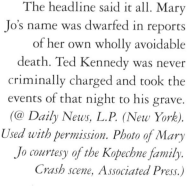

FINAL ★★★★ **SUNDAY NEWS**
NEW YORK'S PICTURE NEWSPAPER ® **20¢**
Vol. 49. No. 12   Copr. 1969 News Syndicate Co. Inc.   New York, N.Y. 10017, Sunday, July 20, 1969*   WEATHER: Mostly cloudy, warm, humid.

TEDDY ESCAPES, BLONDE DROWNS
Kennedy Car Runs Off Bridge

Jersey Girl Crash Victim

Mary Jo Kopechne—dies in Teddy's car.

Spectators watch as officials examine Sen. Edward Kennedy's car after it was pulled from water at Chappaquiddick Island off Martha's Vineyard, yesterday. The auto, driven by Kennedy, plunged from the bridge and landed on its top. Kennedy escaped without injury. A passenger in the car, Mary Jo Kopechne, 28, who once worked in office of the late Sen. Robert F. Kennedy, drowned in the automobile. Later in the day, Kennedy told police he had tried to save her but was not successful.—*Stories on page 2*

Eagle Lands in Moon Dust Today

Stories on Page 3

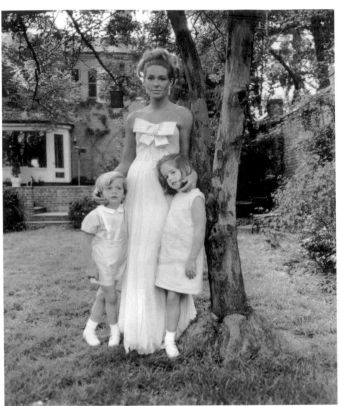

Joan Kennedy poses with two of her children. Her youth, beauty, and maternal warmth were recognized by patriarch Joe Kennedy as enormous gifts that would redound to Ted's benefit, but these qualities only evoked a seething resentment in her husband. (*Bruce Davidson/Magnum Photos*)

Joan Kennedy campaigns with Ted during his 1980 presidential run. To their mutual surprise, Joan — liberated, confident, a vocal supporter of women's rights — became the star of the show, but even she couldn't save Ted's campaign. After withdrawing from the race, Ted dropped her immediately. (Boston Globe/*Getty Images*)

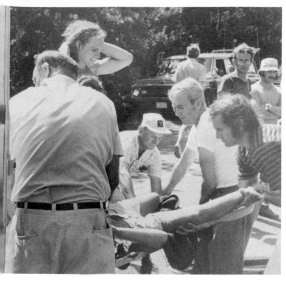

Joseph P. Kennedy III watches as the teenagers injured in a Jeep he recklessly drove are loaded into an ambulance on Nantucket, August 13, 1973. Several were grievously injured, but the *New York Times* would call this Joe's "mishap." *(Bettman/Getty Images)*

Joe Kennedy III leaves a Nantucket hearing, released with a $100 fine and no jail time. "David and two girl passengers were injured," the *Times* reported. One of those girls, eighteen-year-old Pamela Kelley, was paralyzed for life, but her name wasn't mentioned until the last paragraph. *(Bettman/Getty Images)*

Pam with her adoring golden retriever, Chloe, who suffered hip problems as a puppy. On her veterinarian's recommendation, Pam decided Chloe should have her leg amputated to avoid problems later in life. For Pam, who had wanted to die after the accident, Chloe was perhaps her greatest therapy. *(Courtesy of Karen Kelley)*

Martha Moxley was fourteen and new to the wealthy suburb of Greenwich, Connecticut, where she thrived. Her savage murder in 1975 shocked the community, which soon closed ranks around the suspects — Kennedy cousins Tommy and Michael Skakel, who lived nearby. *(Erik Freeland/Getty Images.)*

Martha Moxley's mother, Dorothy, stands before her daughter's portrait in 1998. When Michael Skakel was put on trial for Martha's assault and murder, he confronted Dorothy in court. "You've got the wrong guy," he told her. *(MediaNews Group/ Boston Herald via Getty Images)*

Kathleen "Kick" Kennedy bicycling to work at the Red Cross in WWII London, 1944. For the crime of marrying a Protestant, becoming a wartime widow, then falling in love with a married man, Kick would be disowned by her mother. When Kick died in a plane crash in May 1948, her mother refused to fly over for her funeral. Kick's gravestone does not bear the Kennedy name. (*Keystone/Getty Images*)

Rosemary Kennedy was considered the beauty of the Kennedy girls, but her learning disabilities and unstable moods brought shame to her parents. Her father, Joe, a Nazi sympathizer, left her alone in London during the war—which he thought Hitler, who exterminated the cognitively impaired, would win. (*Kennedy Family Collection, John F. Kennedy Presidential Library and Museum, Boston*)

Jack with Rosemary, whose unexplained disappearance would haunt her siblings. They were never told that their father forced her to undergo a lobotomy. Rosemary lived out her days hidden in a facility, left with the mental and physical capacities of a two-year-old. (*Kennedy Family Collection, John F. Kennedy Presidential Library and Museum, Boston*)

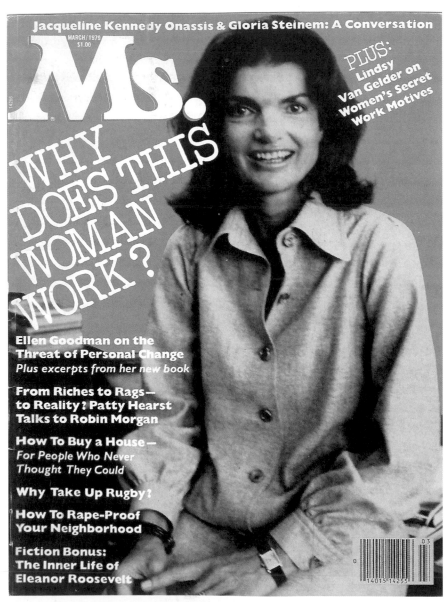

Jacqueline Kennedy Onassis & Gloria Steinem: A Conversation

MARCH/1979
$1.00

Ms.

PLUS:
Lindsy Van Gelder on Women's Secret Work Motives

WHY DOES THIS WOMAN WORK?

Ellen Goodman on the Threat of Personal Change
Plus excerpts from her new book

From Riches to Rags— to Reality? Patty Hearst Talks to Robin Morgan

How To Buy a House— *For People Who Never Thought They Could*

Why Take Up Rugby?

How To Rape-Proof Your Neighborhood

Fiction Bonus: The Inner Life of Eleanor Roosevelt

Jackie Onassis, in an image otherwise lost to history, beaming as the face of the American working woman. She never seemed more herself than here. *(Image used by permission of* Ms. *magazine © 1979)* and most of all witty bitchery." Jackie herself loved poking fun at Joan's naïveté. "Joan," she would say, "you're hopeless. We'll never corrupt you."

Joan didn't want to be corrupted. She did, however, long to be considered as stylish as Jackie. That same year, sick of criticism from top fashion magazines and supermarket tabloids, Joan traded in her more overtly sexy evening wear for more sophisticated, well-tailored clothes meant to reflect a new Joan. A more mature Joan. A woman embracing her natural beauty.

Still, she refused to apologize for the way she had previously dressed. If other people were scandalized, that was on them. To *Good Housekeeping*, she dismissed reports of Ted's womanizing and said she believed everything he had told her about Chappaquiddick. The last thing she wanted was pity or sympathy.

When that cover story hit newsstands, Joan thought Ted would be proud, but she had violated the number one rule of being a Kennedy: Do not air your problems in public. Drinking, adultery, rehabs, Kennedy family squabbles — that was all bad enough, but *psychiatry*? It was enough of a concession on his part that she even got treatment. Why did she have to be so public about it? Did she want people to think she was crazy? Was she trying to torpedo Ted's chances?

His coldness and criticism sent Joan back to the bottle, which only made Ted more contemptuous. "Here she goes again," he'd say, right in front of the children. "Oh my God . . . I can't believe it."

But he wouldn't divorce her. It was a kind of excruciating punishment, being needed by her Catholic husband as a political prop but feeling only his disgust. Being so public about her struggles was revenge, to be sure, but using her platform for good was gratifying. She was helping people — namely, other unhappy women who, like her, had been inspired by Gloria Steinem and Betty Friedan.

The culture was waking up. In October 1974 Joan found herself, along with Betty Ford and Pat Nixon, on the cover of *Time* magazine. "The Ordeal of Political Wives," was the headline, and inside were multiple pieces on the demands specific to these women who were expected to be domestic goddesses, paragons of femininity, perfect mothers, tireless campaign surrogates, and stoics nonpareil. Joan was covered with extreme sensitivity.

In writing of her struggles, *Time* noted: "Ted has not been much help, with his frequent absences and his magnetic attraction for women. 'She is almost never alone with him,' notes a family friend, 'although she is always hopeful. There are always ten advisers around the house, 84 people on the boat, and sisters-in-law and kids everywhere.' Ted does not deliberately ignore her, but he scarcely treats her as his equal. Though he did take her to Russia last spring and let her meet Party Leader Leonid Brezhnev, he wanted her to listen without asking questions."

Such intense pressures, *Time* concluded, understandably resulted in Joan's substance abuse and subsequent need for help. *Of course* she needed treatment at Silver Hill. *Of course* she was seeing a psychiatrist. *Of course* she deserved to "recover her health and develop a greater sense of her own self."

There, in the august pages of the nation's foremost weekly news publication, Joan Kennedy had been vindicated. She wasn't mentally ill. She wasn't crazy, as Ted would have her believe. Her yearning for accomplishments on her own terms was a human desire, not specific to gender, and she was learning that she was not alone in feeling dissatisfied as a wife and mother. That being depressed did not make her ungrateful or weak. She was not only allowed to find her bliss — she owed that to herself.

The bicentennial, 1976, was a consequential year for Joan. She found herself still grappling with alcohol and checked into a New York City facility. One of her fellow patients in group therapy sold Joan's confessions to the *National Enquirer*, among them her criticisms of Ethel ("you don't dare discuss sex in front of [her] . . . and there's no sex education for the kids"), Rose Kennedy (a "harridan" who "has a fit when she thinks I don't behave properly"), and the family itself.

"I'm not as bright as they are," Joan said, "and I'm so tired of being the dumb blonde of the Kennedy family . . . I've never been able to compete, so I've always been on the perimeter instead of inside the family circle."

While under in-patient care, Joan often used her maiden name. "I'm not a Kennedy by birth," she said. "I want to be recognized as an individual. I'm the wife of a Kennedy, but I'm not one of the Kennedy girls. I live and think differently."

Even Jackie, whom Joan claimed to have the most in common with, wasn't spared. Joan's complicated feelings toward the sister-in-law she admired and envied—and who kept Joan at a certain remove, despite Joan's wish for a closer relationship—were unleashed in one of these sessions. "Jackie has always been the queen," Joan said. "She can't stand competition from anybody. And considering how the other Kennedy girls look, I guess Jackie felt I was the only Kennedy who could be competition for her. Jackie and I were never very close."

She spoke of hitting her limit and exploding during a Kennedy family gathering. "I ran through every one of the damn Kennedys like a machine gun. I'd just had enough. I'd had it up to here. I blasted them all to their face . . . I let them know exactly how I feel about them. That was the only time you could hear a pin drop in a room full of Kennedys . . . It was something I'd wanted to do for a long time but I hadn't had the courage. I decided I wasn't going to be a mouse anymore."

The mouse, indeed, had roared. Ever self-protective, the Kennedys backed Joan, calling that report, which gained national traction, "unadulterated gossip." But the chasm caused by that exposé was permanent, and perhaps Joan wanted it that way. By the fall of 1977, Joan had quietly left Ted and moved into her own place, a gorgeous condominium in Boston's Back Bay. Publicly, they were still a married couple, but Joan was breaking away. She was immersing herself in movies and books that depicted the modern woman's struggle; Marilyn French's feminist novel *The Women's Room* and Anne Bancroft's performance in *The Turning Point* particularly resonated. She began attending AA meetings and found the candor and solidarity there more therapeutic than any of the fancy rehabs she had been to, or any of the mental hospitals where Joan had been diagnosed with numerous nervous and psychiatric disorders.

As Joan was learning, she was just depressed. And much of her depression wasn't congenital or chemical—it was situational. It was her marriage and what she had been expected to tolerate.

As for her vaunted rival: Jackie was in psychoanalysis, too, and had gotten a job as a book editor in New York, working at Viking for $200 a week. If the most famous woman in the world could earn her own money, derive self-esteem from using her brain, and carve out a post-Kennedy identity for herself while confronting her demons — well, why couldn't Joan?

She went back to school to get her master's in education, even though she doubted she would ever really teach. "I want the credibility that little piece of paper will give me," she said. "Once I have that, I won't just be Joan Kennedy. That's important for a lot of women my age." She was only forty-one. No woman in political life besides Betty Ford had ever been so open about her struggles with addiction and mental health.

"I couldn't believe how hard it was to stop," Joan told *People* magazine for a cover story that Ted had set up to ease his path to the 1980 nomination. "Alcoholism is a baffler. I was a periodic drinker, not a daily one, but God knows, toward the end of my drinking — talk about being enslaved!" Her sobriety had set her free, in many ways. It had given her a sense of who she was, what she wanted, and how to stand up for herself. "It was hard for Ted at first," she said, "because I used to say, 'Yes, dear,' to everything. And now I can say, 'No.'"

The tenth anniversary of Mary Jo's death was approaching. As with every reelection cycle, his staff encouraged him to call Mary Jo's parents and feel them out.

"Oooooh, brother," Ted said.

As ever, when he did make the call, he did not take responsibility or offer Gwen and Joe Kopechne any of the details he kept promising to share. He just apologized that this *thing*, the anniversary, was going to generate renewed headlines, and for that Ted was sorry. He took their temperature about his presidential run by obliquely referencing the media speculation surrounding it. The Kopechnes, who had heard so much of this before, let him speak and got off the phone. Ted took that to mean they would keep quiet.

"Thank God that's over with," Ted said. Going forward, he and his staff would call Chappaquiddick "a manageable problem." Joan, however—Joan was not.

But he needed her. He needed her as Jack had needed Jackie: domesticity, above all, was what Ted needed to sell. But he wasn't moving with the times. He didn't realize that American women were questioning sexual mores and politics, rejecting the idea that men somehow knew better. Wondering why they could get fired for being pregnant—or if they weren't fired, why there was no paid maternity leave. Why the wage gap was something they were just supposed to accept. Why, if their husbands made them have sex when they said no, that wasn't considered rape. The American woman was changing. Ted didn't spend enough time with Joan to realize that she was changing, too.

So when Joan sat for yet another profile, this one for the women's monthly *McCall's*, Joan on the cover in a white dress, Ted was at her side, holding her arm as if to keep her in line. This new Joan, the one Ted had spent no time getting acquainted with, went rogue. She validated the whispers about Ted's womanizing.

The rumors and stories, Joan said, "hurt my feelings. Of course they hurt my feelings. They went to the core of my self-esteem. When one grows up, feeling that one is sort of special and hoping that one's husband thinks so, and then suddenly thinking maybe he doesn't . . . Well, I didn't lose my self-esteem altogether, but it was difficult to hear all the rumors. And I began thinking, 'Well, maybe I'm just not attractive enough or attractive anymore.' . . . And so rather than get mad, or ask questions concerning the rumors about Ted and his girlfriends, or really stand up for myself at all, it was easier for me to just go and have a few drinks and calm myself down as if I weren't hurt or angry."

Joan had gone off script. Her husband's advisers, including his sister Eunice, had given Joan in-depth media training, telling her how to answer every question sure to come her way. She was supposed to dismiss all those stories about Ted and other women as gossip and lies, give boilerplate answers, pretend theirs was a happy marriage. Pretend that she, Joan Kennedy, was happy.

When one reporter asked her point-blank if her husband still loved her, she answered honestly. "I don't know," she said. "I really don't know."

But Joan still loved him. His need for her on the campaign trail was real, and she was flourishing. Once an introvert who could barely get through a weekend with the extended Kennedy clan without stealing away for hours to read a book or take a nap, Joan was now feeding off the reception that other women gave her, who saw in Joan a woman done wrong, a woman stronger than Ted or any of the Kennedys gave her credit for.

When Ted had decided to run for president, Joan not only supported him but agreed to campaign wholeheartedly, despite her fears for his safety. She was beginning to understand what an asset she was. It helped that there were more women in the press pool now. It helped that there was a winnowing of Kennedy worship.

Ted's run made people look more closely at him, more critically, and the public didn't like what it was seeing. Throughout a key hour-long primetime interview Ted did for CBS News, Joan was notably absent. Ted was unable to give a coherent answer about what had happened at Chappaquiddick or why he wanted to be president. Ted's drinking never came up, but he made sure to bring up Joan's struggles with alcohol.

"I don't know whether there's a single word that should...have a description for it," he said. "Joan's involved in a continuing program to deal with the problems of... of alcoholism, and... and she's going magnificently well, and I'm immensely proud of the fact that she's faced up to it and made the progress that she's made. And I'm—but that progress continues, and that... it's the type of disease that one has to... to work."

Ted's usual deflections were no longer acceptable. As far back as 1972, *National Lampoon* ran a parody of a Volkswagen ad, written by the future star humorist Anne Beatts, with the car floating upright in a pond: "If Ted Kennedy drove a Volkswagen," the copy read, "he'd be president today." In 1979, *Saturday Night Live* aired a brutal sketch of Bill Murray as Ted, soaked with seaweed hanging off his shoulder, arriving late and breathless to a campaign stop: "I think that Joan might still be in the car."

Women especially were no longer buying Ted's excuses. They were no longer willing to look the other way as voters, to minimize what was openly known as Ted's relentless womanizing. They were no longer going to allow all his problems to be blamed on Joan.

Suzannah Lessard wrote a groundbreaking, six-page piece that ran in the *Washington Monthly*, which picked it up after the *New Republic*, original commissioners of the piece, had killed it. Charlie Peters, the *Monthly's* editor-in-chief, said that he thought Lessard's piece had "important and wise things to say about women and their relationship" to Ted Kennedy.

Headlined "Kennedy's Woman Problem, Women's Kennedy Problem," Lessard's piece argued that female voters had been hoodwinked by "the boys in the press" who kept Ted's philandering secret. Despite the male-led apologia that such talk was sleazy or betrayed a lesser mind—that of course women, their small world defined by domestic concerns, would be more preoccupied with a male politician's sex life than his policies—Lessard argued that Ted's chronic cheating was legitimate cause for concern.

"It suggests an old-fashioned, male chauvinist, exploitative view of women as primarily objects of pleasure," Lessard wrote. "It gives me the creeps; the constant pursuit (although the image is almost passive, in a way) of semi-covert, just barely personal and ultimately discardable encounters is a creepy way to act.

"What it suggests," she continued, "is a severe case of arrested development, a kind of narcissistic intemperance, a huge, babyish ego that must constantly be fed. It suggests: if he is immature in this area, mightn't he be in others? It bothers me because I associate this type of behavior with misogyny. I don't believe men who really like women carry on in this way."

Jackie wrote Joan a letter, making the same argument: *Save yourself. Get a divorce.*

"You're no prude or fool," Jackie wrote. "But having your own little black phone"—as Ted did—"so that you can talk to Mootsie or Pootsie every night—right in the house with his wife & children—and bringing them there when you're away. What kind of woman, but a sap or a slave, can stand that & still be a loving wife—& care about him & work like a dog for him campaigning."

Jackie could have been talking to a younger version of herself. This was the Jackie who would tell her grown children that if Jack had somehow returned to her now, she very well might turn him away.

But Joan couldn't leave Ted while he was running for president. The Kennedys would not allow it. Besides, what Jackie didn't understand was the salutary effect campaigning was having on Joan. People were coming out to see *her*. They wanted to talk to her and, more incredibly, *they wanted to hear what she had to say*. And what do you know: the more favorable her press coverage became, the worse Ted's got. Soon his aides were begging Joan to make extra stops and be seen with Ted as much as possible, and when she did, Ted could barely look at her. He never touched her. And once again, he never said thank you.

Joan's sobriety had given her a gift: the ability to embrace her rage. Instead of dulling it with alcohol she was feeling it now, and it felt good. Justified. Appropriate. She was too well-mannered to ever show it in public, but in private she let loose, one day retreating from her window as Ted drove up to her condo. "Oh Christ, here he comes," Joan said. "I'm getting out of here." And she left.

America was getting a second look at Joan Kennedy, and they were rooting for her. The unspoken consensus was that marriage to Ted Kennedy was a burden no woman should have to endure.

"JOAN'S JOURNEY: Back on Board with Steady Eyes and New Strength," said Myra McPherson in the *Washington Post*.

Time magazine explored "THE VULNERABLE SIDE OF JOANSIE," writing of her alcoholism as a disease, not a moral failing, and the toll Ted's womanizing had taken.

The *Boston Globe*: "JOAN STRIDES OUT OF HER DARK AGE."

The *New York Times* ran a glowing piece on Joan's advocacy. She was fighting for passage of the Equal Rights Amendment, saying things that, at the time, were still controversial: That all women should have access to higher education, to employment, to the same pay as men. That motherhood was devalued in American society and too often left women financially dependent on their husbands. On the surface, Joan appeared to be campaigning for her husband—but whom was she fighting for, really? "I know that if Ted is elected president of the United States," Joan said, "I will commit myself to the ongoing struggle for women's equality with everything I have and everything I am."

It was an outgrowth of all the inner work she had done on herself, admitting that the Joan Kennedy of the 1960s didn't get it—feminism, the ERA, the fight for reproductive rights and equality within marriage itself. "I really thought it was for other women," Joan said. "Now I know it's for me, too."

She could have stayed. Even after he dropped out of the race for president on August 11, 1980, Ted, for the sake of his career, would have done anything to keep the marriage intact.

But Joan, it turned out, had been campaigning for herself all along.

CAROLYN BESSETTE KENNEDY

C umberland Island was like no place Carolyn had ever seen. Remote, untouched by industry or technology, maybe forty people total lived on this strip of land situated between Florida and Georgia. Its pristine beaches were the domain of wild horses and enormous sea turtles and resembled a land before time, before humans existed. The only place to stay was a mansion-turned-inn, run by descendants of Andrew Carnegie. On the other end of the island was a tiny white chapel built in 1893.

John wanted them to be married here. No one would know. They could keep the guest list small and be off on their honeymoon before the press ever got wind of anything. Already Carolyn was torn. John wanted her wedding party to be all Kennedys: his sister, Caroline, the maid of honor, his nieces the flower girls, his nephew the ring bearer, his cousin the best man. Didn't that say it all? This wasn't a joining of families. There was no room for Carolyn's twin sisters, Lisa and Lauren, or for any of her relatives in the bridal party. Carolyn, like so many women before her, would be subsumed into the Kennedys.

Was this what she wanted? When John proposed, a part of her thought: *This is it. As big as it gets.* But she had her doubts. John expected her to cook, clean, and throw dinner parties — things she had had no interest in. She asked her friends what she was supposed to do as Mrs. JFK Jr: "Do I start my own foundation?" she would ask.

After quitting Calvin Klein, she refused to entertain getting another job; she had already cut out one high-profile fashion friend who had been dropping her name all over New York. She didn't know what profession was suitable for the future Mrs. John F. Kennedy Jr., but surely he or another senior Kennedy would help her figure it out.

Carolyn's mother was against the marriage. Her sister Lauren, who was currently working as a banker in Hong Kong, was not going to fly in. Her biological father, who hadn't really been in her life since she was eight years old, would not be invited. Carolyn hated him yet was haunted by him. She remained very much a Bessette. On her forefinger she wore her mother's wedding ring from that first marriage. She and her mother had dipped it first in holy water, as if to purify it. "Isn't that fucked up?" she'd say. Yet she wore it constantly.

It wasn't her birth family that she was looking to for validation now, anyway. Carolyn had spent her young adult life trying to land handsome, prominent men, as if to prove she wasn't just worthy of love but worthy of *important* love. She had known, from a very young age, that she was destined for big things, but she didn't know that for all her cool self-possession, her friends were deeply worried about this marriage. They saw the real Carolyn beneath that veneer, desperate to become Mrs. JFK Jr. "She's so fucked up," one of them said.

Carolyn had a reckless streak, just like John. As a teenage girl, raised by her mother and stepfather, an orthopedic surgeon, she had wanted for nothing, had every advantage, was the product of a great Catholic high school education, yet had undergone more than one abortion. She talked about those terminated pregnancies with her close friends all the time, as if she still needed forgiveness. The miscarriage she had suffered — was it a miscarriage? — shortly before she and John got engaged was another concern. As was the huge fight she'd had with John in Washington Square Park, the two of them shoving and hitting each other, Carolyn's blonde hair flying and whipping around as she confronted him about Sharon Stone or Cindy Crawford or Julia Roberts or whatever famous women he was currently rumored to be seeing on the side. That very public, very physical argument put John's family and friends on edge. Carolyn, to them, looked like a liability, a shrew. Underneath that classy veneer was a feral girl, low-rent and trashy, sure to bring him down.

No matter that paparazzi had photographed John taking his palm to Carolyn's face and shoving her back by her head. Or that he tried to rip her engagement ring off her finger with such force that the stone broke off, or that he tried to pull their dog's leash out of her hand so many times that she almost fell. They were a combustible match, toxic, and when Carolyn's friends saw those pictures in the tabloids they almost felt sorry for John. "That's the real Carolyn," they would say.

No wonder Carolyn's mother didn't approve. Another of Carolyn's friends was vocally unimpressed, too. He would meet John and Carolyn for drinks and come away perplexed; he found John weird, often disrespectful — in his words, "totally disengaged, so weird. Kind of a dick."

Yet another formerly close friend was surprised to see Carolyn at the fashion-forward uptown department store Barneys — he hadn't seen her since she had become serious with John. He went over to where she was sitting, in the shoe department. "Carolyn," he said. She lowered her eyes. "Yes?" she asked. Her affect struck him as deferential and a little bit frightened. "What are you doing?" he asked, and she said, "Shoes," before turning away from him and back toward the salesperson helping her.

Her friend was hurt. He had known Carolyn since they were both new to the fashion industry. He had kept so many of her secrets, and now she brushed him off like some overeager fan. He came away from that encounter less angry than worried — for her. Carolyn looked, to him, like a woman who had been ground down until she had molded herself into a Kennedy woman. Her light, her spark, had disappeared; she just seemed lost. He thought about Carolyn's former best friend, her hairdresser Brad Johns, who had transformed Carolyn into a white-blonde reminiscent of John's famous ex-fiancée Daryl Hannah. Brad had been one of Carolyn's closest confidants, among her best friends, but John had put an end to that relationship, threatening to sue Brad over anodyne quotes to the press about how he lightened Carolyn's hair.

"John wanted certain people out of her life," her friend said. "Anybody from her past he wanted gone. They were grooming Carolyn to be John Kennedy's wife, and John Kennedy was being groomed to go into politics. I think the problem is that Carolyn created this Stepford political wife to please John. That's when she started to die."

Carolyn's obvious depression came as no surprise to people who knew her before John. Her fashion-world friends may have had an image of Carolyn as a man-eater, but in high school and college she had a habit of choosing boyfriends who treated her terribly: rude, mean, sometimes abusive. The world at large would never see John as less than perfect, but he could be terrible in his way, too. His arrogance was perhaps the trait that most reminded Carolyn of her father: John was stunningly attractive, tall, charismatic, smug, and most of all, he didn't care what anyone else — at least anyone besides Jackie — thought. About that: why hadn't John ever introduced Carolyn to his mother? Why had he waited until she died before he began seeing Carolyn again?

His mother — really, she was the key to understanding John, but not in the way one might think. Everyone assumed that John, thanks to his mother's influence and his devotion to her, was a different kind of Kennedy man. But the truth was that John had a blind spot when it came to women. Only women who got close enough could see it — like his ex-girlfriend Christina. It wasn't about his own womanizing, either. It was something deeper, an anger at his mother that manifested in strange and public ways. How else to explain asking Drew Barrymore to dress up as Marilyn Monroe for a *George* cover, re-creating the iconic image of Marilyn Monroe singing "Happy Birthday" to his father? That had been the greatest public indignity Jackie had suffered in that marriage, and John was using it to save his failing magazine. Or why he had invited Larry Flynt, the *Hustler* pornographer who had published nude photos of Jackie sunbathing, to sit with him at the White House Correspondents' Dinner? His friend Christiane Amanpour, the esteemed journalist, was horrified. "If it's me," she said later, "I'm saying, 'John, what are you doing talking to that guy who's spent his whole life debasing the idea of what it is to be female and a woman?'"

There were other troubling uses of his fame. John championed Mike Tyson even though the boxer had served a six-year prison sentence for raping an eighteen-year-old girl, a contestant in the Miss Black America Pageant. As John wrote to Tyson in 1997, "Most folks think you have considerable talents balanced by some faults. Just like the rest of us."

John's support was more astonishing, considering that Tyson's victim's testimony had been well publicized during his rape trial in 1992. She recalled that the famous boxer had brought her to his hotel suite, saying he needed to make a phone call. She waited in the suite's foyer before, she testified, he asked her to join him in another room. "I was terrified," she testified. "I said, 'It's time to leave.' He said, 'Come here.' He grabbed my arm and stuck his tongue in my mouth. He pulled me fast toward him. I pulled back. He said, 'Don't frighten. Don't frighten. Relax.' I tried to punch him, but it was like hitting a wall.'

At the time, Tyson was five-foot-eleven, weighed over 200 pounds, and was the most fearsome heavyweight boxer in the world. His teenage victim was five-foot-three and 108 pounds.

"The next thing I knew he slammed me on the bed," she testified. "He put his hand in my vagina. He jammed his fingers in me really hard. I said, 'Ow, please stop. You're hurting me.' My eyes were filling up with tears. Then he started laughing like it was a game."

Tyson forcibly performed oral sex on her and then, she said, he raped her. "It felt like someone was ripping me apart," she testified, and when he was done he called her "a baby, a crybaby."

Tyson's prison sentence at the end of the 1992 trial was followed by another in 1998 for assaulting two men. John made a show of visiting Tyson at the Rockville detention center in Maryland and compared Tyson's troubled reputation to that of his own father, the former president, whose legacy was becoming sullied by multiple reports of his own womanizing. In that letter to Tyson, John said that his father's moral failings only showed how "human" he was: "That's why, 35 years after his death, my father still sells books, miniseries, magazines, etc."

"He sympathized with me in some way," Tyson later recalled.

Defending someone accused of rape wasn't new for John. In 1991, his cousin William Kennedy Smith stood trial in Palm Beach for raping a twenty-nine-year-old single mother named Patricia Bowman. John showed up to court in a public display of support, even though Jackie refused to do the same. John told his friend James Ridgway de Szigethy that the Kennedy family "should have done something about Willie years ago when he first started doing this"—meaning, raping women. Bowman's story was entirely credible. After meeting Smith at a high-end bar in Palm Beach, Florida, she testified that she went back to the Kennedy estate with Smith because there could be no safer place, because "there was a senator there"—Smith's uncle, Ted Kennedy—and "I didn't feel I was in any danger whatsoever." Smith then walked her down to the beach, where she said he raped her so savagely that, Bowman testified, "I thought he was going to kill me."

A jury of six swiftly acquitted Smith, who had been surrounded by Kennedys in court since the trial began. Everyone involved in the rape investigation—the police, the prosecutors, Bowman's doctors and rape counselors—believed she was telling the truth, despite the Kennedy machine painting her as a promiscuous drug addict who, as mother of a two-year-old, had no business being out at 3:00 a.m. with Kennedy men.

Of course, no one asked the question: If they really thought such a woman should be at home, then what were Kennedy men doing out with a single mother at 3:00 a.m.?

During the trial, Bowman had been accused by Roy Black, Smith's defense attorney, of being mentally ill. When the "not guilty" verdict came in, she collapsed. It was still a shock, even knowing how ruthless the Kennedys could be toward inconvenient women. "Each and every day...in each and every newspaper, I had to see the face of the man who raped me," Bowman said. "That's hard. Then I had to see the face of the man who raped me change into a man with a puppy, a man kissing schoolchildren." Bowman later told the journalist Dominick Dunne that Smith's was "the acquittal [that] money can buy," and that after the rape—after she told Smith he had just raped her—"he looked at me, the calmest, smuggest, most arrogant man, and he said, 'No one will believe you.' And the jury came in and said, 'Not guilty,' and I was right back in that room with that man telling me no one would believe me." Three other women who had accused Smith of sexual assault in the 1980s were not allowed to testify. Bowman, whose face and identity were obscured during the televised trial, went public after the verdict because, she said, she was "terrified that victims everywhere who have seen my case . . . will not report because of what's happened to me . . . I'm a human being. I have nothing to be ashamed of."

"How does it feel to be a character assassin, John?" de Szigethy asked him after the verdict. "How does it feel to be [this woman's] Oswald?" John hung his head. He always hung his head when confronted with something he didn't like. It was a signal to his interlocutor to back off. In his own defense, John muttered an explanation. "You just don't understand the pressure I'm under," he said.

It was a pattern with John, dismissing the credible claims of vulnerable women who were otherwise crushed by political power. When Monica Lewinsky, then a twenty-two-year-old former White House intern, was thrust into the national spotlight for having had a sexual relationship with then-president Bill Clinton, she became suicidal. Clinton publicly denied ever having sex with Lewinsky, a claim that even his most ardent supporters didn't believe — but one that John did. After reading a particularly embarrassing detail — that Lewinsky had performed oral sex on the forty-nine-year-old Clinton while kneeling under JFK's old desk — John sent Clinton a handwritten note. "Dear Mr. President," John wrote. "I have been under that desk. There's barely room for a three-year-old, much less a twenty-two-year-old intern. Cheers, John Kennedy." Oh, how Clinton and his male aides laughed at that. John said the same thing to his friend Billy Noonan, except this time with more vulgarity: Lewinsky, he said, was too much of a "fat ass" to fit.

And of course, there was his uncle Ted Kennedy, perhaps the most dangerous Kennedy man of all. As a new millennium approached, Ted still had not been held to account for the death of Mary Jo Kopechne. He suffered not a single consequence for being the ringleader the night Bowman was raped, drinking with Smith and his son Patrick at Au Bar, later roaming around the Kennedys' Palm Beach mansion so drunk that he appeared in the doorway of Patrick's bedroom, wearing only boxers, and stared at his son and the woman he was having sex with.

John would always circle those Kennedy wagons to protect the cesspool. He admitted as much during an interview with NBC's Tom Brokaw, plugging *George*.

Brokaw: "Can we expect some tough stories about Uncle Ted?"

John: "Never."

Five years earlier, Ted had been the subject of an infamous *GQ* profile. "Senator Bedfellow," as writer Michael Kelly called him, was known for extreme licentiousness, infamously hitting on two sixteen-year-old girls, pages on the Hill, trying to lure them into his limo. Reported here again was the senior aide who had really been a pimp; Ted driving drunk on sidewalks at the Cape; all the underage girls. But there was a new account here: the sexual assault of a waitress in DC, "Uncle Ted" attacking her with his equally disgusting friend, the senator Chris Dodd. As *GQ* reported:

> As she enters the room, the six-foot-two, 225-plus-pound Kennedy grabs the five-foot-three, 103-pound waitress and throws her on the table. She lands on her back, scattering crystal, plates, and cutlery and the lit candles. Several glasses and a crystal candlestick are broken. Kennedy then picks her up from the table and throws her on Dodd, who is sprawled in a chair. With [the waitress] on Dodd's lap, Kennedy jumps on top and begins rubbing his genital area against hers, supporting his weight on the arms of the chair. As he is doing this, [another waitress] enters the room...[They] both scream, drawing one or two dishwashers. Startled, Kennedy leaps up. He laughs. Bruised, shaken, and angry over what she considered a sexual assault, [the waitress] runs from the room. Kennedy, Dodd, and their dates leave shortly thereafter, following a friendly argument between the senators over the check.

But his nephew didn't want to take on Ted Kennedy, the last lion of the Kennedy dynasty. Instead, John took shots at lesser Kennedys: his cousin Joe Kennedy, who used Kennedy privilege to get an annulment against the wishes of his ex-wife, followed by thirty-nine-year-old Michael Kennedy, the married father of three who had been having what John called "an affair" with a fourteen-year-old babysitter. It was flowery language for what prosecutors were looking into as its legal definition: statutory rape.

John piously denigrated Joe and Michael in his editor's letter for *George*, running it alongside an artsy black-and-white beefcake photo of John, shirtless and seated, looking up at a dangling apple. Hey — the fall of Eden was all Eve's fault, right? The letter opened a special issue of *George*, one devoted to "the 20 most fascinating women in politics," with Barrymore as Monroe on the cover.

John wrote, in part:

"Two members of my family chased an idealized alternative to their life. One left behind an embittered wife, and another, in what looked to be a hedge against mortality, fell in love with youth and surrendered his judgement in the process. Both became poster boys for bad behavior.

"Perhaps they deserved it. Perhaps they should have known better. To whom much is given, much is expected, right? The interesting thing was the ferocious condemnation of their excursions beyond the bounds of acceptable behavior. Since when does someone need to apologize on television for getting divorced?"

John's cousins were less upset about their own respective scandals than John's disloyalty to fellow Kennedy men. His first reaction, Joe told the Associated Press, was: "Ask not what you can do for your cousin, but what you can do for his magazine."

There was something ominous about Cumberland: the thousand-year-old oak trees, their thick branches twenty feet in circumference, knots the size of jagged boulders, curling and bending down toward the grass, hovering inches above in suspended animation. Witness trees, they call them, so old that they had lived through history, great and terrible. Ancient Spanish moss one hundred feet high, draping either side of the pathway to Greyfield Inn, two weblike, gothic green curtains daring visitors to pass through. The island's wild animals — the hogs and armadillos, the tiny chiggers latching onto human skin for days and feasting, sucking blood and leaving huge red pustules. Spectral and eerie, at night especially, Cumberland still possessed its pre–Civil War colonialism; populated by anonymous titans of industry, Cumberland's residents still talk about the slaves who had toiled on the island and farmed it as "lucky." Well treated. *Whipped only when they really deserved it.*

Cumberland did not augur well for this marriage.

The night before, at the candlelit rehearsal dinner on the porch of the old Carnegie mansion, Carolyn wore a custom slinky pale-pink number handmade by one of her best friends at Calvin, Narciso Rodriguez, who had also designed her wedding dress. After this weekend, Narciso's life would change: he would instantly become a major designer, known to the entire world, catapulted into a realm few inhabited. The power she suddenly had to star-make was intoxicating. The excitement, the daring in marrying America's prince in a sexy slip dress—a dress as formfitting and soon-to-be-iconic as Marilyn Monroe's—turned to shame, however, when she caught the eye of John's friend Billy Noonan. He clearly disapproved. Sheepishly, Carolyn asked for Billy's blazer. It was a sweltering summer night, but she could see the relief on Billy's face. Later she heard he had been criticizing her, telling other guests that Carolyn didn't look like a proper Kennedy wife.

"That dress," he said, "is too revealing for anyone but her gynecologist."

No one told Billy to shut up. In fact, they laughed. John still allowed Billy to be the wedding's informal videographer, and Billy would zoom in, more than once, on Carolyn's backside in her wedding dress—a dress he called "scandalous," the bride "angelic-looking, with a body that . . ."

Billy didn't finish the thought. John's other great friend, John Perry Barlow, made a vulgar comment at the rehearsal dinner about Carolyn's beautiful twin sisters. Carolyn was appalled; John said nothing. Kennedy family and friends gave toasts: What an important night. How privileged they all were to be among the chosen few, now and forever. How momentous for John to have finally chosen a wife. How lucky for Carolyn to be The One. John got up. "It still sticks in my craw that, come Sunday, Carolyn will be called 'Mrs.,'" he said.

Was that meant to be a joke? *It still sticks in my craw?* The Kennedy contingent didn't pick up on that. They noticed John's other *faux pas*—the wedding was tomorrow, Saturday. They were all leaving on Sunday.

Carolyn's mother rose and made a toast of her own. *I don't know if this marriage is good for my daughter*, she said. *I don't know if John is right for her.*

John was stunned. In all his life he had never heard nor expected such a sentiment, let alone one voiced in public on the eve of his wedding — a wedding that was the most coveted invite on the planet, that would make headlines all over the world.

Ann sat down, and the night went on. But no one ever forgot what she'd said — heresy to them, fact to her.

Ann wasn't reacting only to that evening. She had known that the past three years had not been easy for her daughter. Carolyn had been met with suspicion by John's family and their inner circle. John's brother-in-law, Ed Schlossberg, was especially cold to Carolyn. His aunt Ethel, during Carolyn's first visit to the Cape, brusquely suggested that Carolyn familiarize herself with geopolitics and policy if she wanted to be invited back. Worse were the rumors that John's so-called friends spread about Carolyn's devotion to his terminally ill cousin Anthony, implying that the care she showed for him — taking Anthony to his doctor's appointments, sitting with him for hours as he underwent chemotherapy, visiting him constantly while he was in the hospital — was all a cynical ploy to get to John.

Carolyn had tried with the Kennedys and their sycophants — she really had. But with some of them, nothing was good enough. And now she was here, on the night before her wedding, about to make the biggest mistake of her life. Even the friends whom Carolyn had cast aside knew that John wasn't for Carolyn. It was evident in the months before the wedding: Carolyn had gone into hiding, refusing to leave the Tribeca loft, avoiding the paparazzi. This once-vibrant girl, electrified by her life and the city, had instead become withdrawn, isolated, and paranoid. She was underweight and anxious all the time, using antidepressants and cocaine. Carolyn confessed to her mother that she still thought about her ex-boyfriend, the underwear model. She said that he understood her as no one else had — which would not have surprised her friends, the ones she had either abandoned or allowed John to push aside. One in particular thought that John was never going to be the love of Carolyn's life.

"She was sold a bag of goods," recalled this friend, "and what she signed up for is not what she got."

But Carolyn was still going through with the wedding. How could she not? There was no way she wasn't going to be Mrs. JFK Jr., an instant addition to America's living history. And John, she told her mother, promised that all the attention would die down once they were married. There was no interest, he said, in an off-the-market JFK Jr.

How wrong he had been. How stupid of her to have believed it.

———————

September 21, 1996, the day of the wedding. John's friends took antique Chippendale chairs from the inn and put them in pickup trucks, bouncing along Cumberland's unpaved roads and white-sand beaches. If those chairs broke, they broke. John, meanwhile, was running late. He couldn't find his tie and was yelling at his friends, his maid, and the inn's staff to find it.

Carolyn was even later — by hours. She had struggled in pulling Narciso's silk bias-cut gown over her head. How much of her anxiety was the dress, and how much of it was the marriage? Their guests, Kennedys mostly, were waiting outside the chapel, their fancy clothes soaked through with sweat, women pulling up their styled hair into messy ponytails, drinking beer and water and waiting for hours in ninety-degree heat, oppressive humidity, no shade, no cool place to sit and rest. This was already a disaster.

By the time Carolyn arrived, struggling to walk in her heels, it was just before 8:00 p.m. The evening wasn't any cooler than the daytime had been, however, and it was readily apparent that John had not thought this through: the tiny chapel hadn't been modernized at all. There was no air-conditioning, no electricity, no ventilation. He hadn't even had it opened and unshuttered before the guests arrived. The windows were painted shut!

Packed tight with forty people, it was hard to breathe, let alone stand. It was so dark inside that the guests strained to see. The vows were said quickly, and the ceremony was over as soon as it began.

The lone wedding picture released to the press — Carolyn and John exiting the chapel, not a hair out of place or a bead of sweat anywhere, John kissing Carolyn's tulle-gloved hand — was a metaphor for the weekend and the marriage to come: a pre-Instagrammable image that looked perfect and effortless but was really a lie. That quaint little chapel, built by Cumberland's enslaved workers, had an ugly history. John had not seen the problem with that. Nor had he seen the problem with including Willie, the cousin who had stood trial for rape in the early 1990s, even though the guest list was so small that other family members and friends were excluded.

John's ex-girlfriend Christina learned of the wedding when she passed a newsstand in New York City and saw that photograph on the cover of the *New York Post* and the *New York Daily News*: Camelot's prince finally finding his perfect bride. It was a gut-punch. Christina was the one who had first taken John to Cumberland Island. She had made it their special place. John would never have known it existed if not for Christina, and now, for his wedding to another woman, he had chosen *their* spot, despite knowing how badly she had wanted to marry him. He hadn't so much as given her advance warning.

Everywhere Christina looked, there was Carolyn on some fancy magazine cover, her coronation as America's princess complete. Carolyn's friends raved to the press about how perfect she was for John, how fully prepared she was for this shiny new role. Weeks after the wedding, Carolyn was on the cover of *New York* magazine, John whispering in her ear, his profile cut off by the editors. "MEET THE MRS.," ran the headline. Inside, a dissection of what made Carolyn The One. Titled "Instant Princess," it contained quotes from John's friends, who had clearly been granted permission to talk.

"She is a very strong person," said John's longtime friend Richard Wise. "He always found her provocative; she always drew something out of him that other women hadn't." Another compared her to the late Jackie O, with her charm and inscrutability. "She is certainly a challenge," a former colleague said. "It would be hard for any woman to stay mysterious to this guy, who basically can order it up. If there is anything she is up to, it is that task: Never seeming easy." Barlow, a longtime friend and mentor to John, called the wedding weekend "a good, warm, intimate familial gathering — a bunch of people that, if I had to start the human race from scratch, I'm not sure I could imagine a better forty people than were there."

But many of Carolyn's old friends were less optimistic. One thought Carolyn was in way over her head, a girl from the wrong side of the tracks now on board a high-speed train. He thought John, Carolyn's Ultimate Trophy Husband, her knight in shining armor, was a loser wrapped in tinfoil.

He thought, deep down, that Carolyn knew it, too.

She had definitely harbored misgivings. In 1992, when Carolyn and John had first started dating, she went along with how loose John kept their relationship, how he would never take her out but instead come visit at her small West Village apartment building, just three units, Kate Moss living upstairs. It grated on Carolyn: Was John trying to hide her? Was he ashamed of her? He had once described her to Barlow as "nobody, really...a functionary of Calvin Klein's." But who was he, really? John Kennedy was a middle-aged man with no real accomplishments. Carolyn had worked her way up from a sales associate in a Boston mall to Calvin Klein's most trusted adviser and something of an informal brand ambassador within the span of a few years. Not that John would understand that or find it all that important. Carolyn wasn't working in the halls of Congress, after all.

And then it finally occurred to Carolyn that in all the months they'd been dating, they had never once been photographed. The most eligible bachelor on Earth with a new woman — how was that not newsworthy? She was a new Mystery Blonde — that recurring character in tabloids, cast and recast in perpetuity — except no one knew that yet. When was Carolyn going to be John's new Mystery Blonde?

A few weeks later, Carolyn had her answer. Or so she thought.

John — at the last minute, of course — had invited Carolyn to spend Memorial Day weekend at the modest Hamptons house he had rented with Anthony. Carolyn had happily gone, certain that this was a mean-ingful step. But in the days to follow, Carolyn heard nothing. Next week-end came, and the next, and there were no more invitations to the Hamptons, no calls, nothing. Then she saw the picture in the paper — John with his ex-girlfriend Daryl, the Hollywood actress, at a movie premiere. She looked like Carolyn, too: tall, rangy, angular fea-tures. The long blonde hair and blue eyes. Oh, the humiliation. The tears. All that work to seem so carefree. Maybe too carefree.

Carolyn's mother saw that photo, too. She clipped it out of the paper and mailed it to her daughter, and over this glamour shot, like graffiti defacing a wall, she had written: "Carolyn, please get on with your life. Love, Mom." Underneath she had drawn a sad face.

That was Warning One.

_____

In August of 1994, a few months after his mother had died and two years before the wedding, John came back around. It was over with the actress for good, he said.

That November, John escorted Carolyn to his sister Caroline's thirty-seventh birthday at her New York City apartment. It was a test of sorts to see if Carolyn could fit into his world — a world where he was always the most sought-after person in the room. If he took her on, Carolyn would become famous, too. John needed to see if she could handle it. If she could bask in his light.

That night she performed ably. Carolyn entered the uptown lobby dressed in black, holding John's hand, relaxed and regal. Inside the party she hobnobbed and made small talk and bent down to eye level with John's nieces and nephew, charming them with her beauty and warmth. Carolyn was great with children, and this was one of the things John found most appealing about her. He wanted a big family of his own, sooner rather than later.

As the weeks and months went by, as Carolyn and John got more seri-ous, so too did the paparazzi. First it was one, two, then dozens. It was like being exposed to an alien species, this swarm of photographers whose own faces were obscured by gigantic lenses, running backwards and knocking over old ladies and mothers with strollers. The more Carolyn begged to be left alone — the more she hid her face and curled into herself — the more they took her picture.

Soon enough, Calvin made his thoughts known: *You look like the Hunchback of Notre Dame*, he said. *You're a beautiful girl. Just give them a good picture and they'll leave you alone.* Unspoken but understood was the subtext: *Like it or not, you are now my number one brand ambassador. Comport yourself accordingly.*

That was pretty much what John said, too. But he had never known anything different. A shock, to him, would be stepping outside and *not* finding a horde of press. She wondered if he ever thought about how much he needed the attention. And there was no point in complaining, because everyone around them said the same thing: *What did she think would happen when she started dating JFK Jr.?* Let alone when she agreed to marry him?

John asked her, too. Really, what was the problem? He didn't like confrontation, mainly because he had lived his whole life without it — until Carolyn came along. Here was a nearly forty-year-old man who never heard *no*, who had everything so easy that he never really developed a personality or an edge. John was conditioned — enabled, really — to see himself not just as a good guy but a great guy, the complete package. "People often tell me I could be a great man," he would say. "I'd rather be a good one." It was so inauthentic, the kind of thing for future biographers to lap up, to use as the thesis of their books, not at all the way anyone really talks. But every time John said it, people marveled.

It wasn't until after the wedding that Carolyn realized that her mother was right, and that her skeptical friends weren't jealous but concerned. John Kennedy, as he preferred to be called, wasn't that complex or interesting. He wasn't bright or all that curious. When they married she thought she had won The Prize. Everyone had. But now she saw how foolish she had been.

How had Ann seen it? How had she known that if anyone was going to be the problem in this marriage, it was only ever going to be Carolyn? Not John, never John.

Over lunch one day, the newest Mrs. Kennedy tried to explain her dilemma to Billy Noonan. It didn't go over well. "Carolyn," he said. "You're beautiful, you're the envy of every woman in New York, and you're the dream girl for all men. Why not enjoy this? Part of the deal with John is that everyone indulges him."

Billy didn't get that she was sick of indulging John. That it was hard when your husband, who had been famous his whole life, couldn't understand your anxieties and didn't have much interest in them anyway. When your husband's sister wouldn't offer advice and barely tolerated you because you hadn't been born into their world. Carolyn wasn't a member of Camelot, not even a courtier. She was nothing. John had said it himself, more than once: Those who married into the Kennedy family weren't really Kennedys. Having children didn't change that. John said it so often about his brother-in-law, Ed Schlossberg, that Carolyn got the message. Was it any wonder that Carolyn was struggling? Whenever she flailed, John just watched it happen. He wasn't helping her. But she wasn't helping herself, either, and her fury began poisoning the marriage, their reputations, and John's easygoing nature. Carolyn got so angry with one female photographer that she spat in the woman's face. John, who had always liked the press, had physically gone after another female photographer parked outside their building. A little more than one year into their marriage, rumors circulated about John's wrist injury, a severed nerve that everyone suspected was Carolyn's fault, that she had attacked him.

It wasn't outside the realm of possibility. Carolyn had real rage, and she could come at you with no warning. As her closest friends often said: Carolyn isn't easy. But neither was John. This marriage wasn't bringing out the best in either of them.

So as Carolyn and her mother walked out of her apartment building one afternoon, the photographers following, today at least being polite—not the taunts she normally heard, *whore, slut, bitch, ugly,* anything to get a reaction—Carolyn kept her head down and her mouth shut.

"I don't know how you put up with this," her mother said.

"I love him," Carolyn replied.

"It's not worth it."
Warning Two.

———————

July 16, 1999. As much as Carolyn's gut was telling her not to fly with John that night, she was pushing through. She and John hadn't even hit their third wedding anniversary, and already their marriage was in shambles. Multiple tabloid stories, many of them well sourced, were reporting that John was having affairs, that his ex-girlfriend Daryl was back in the picture, that John was disappointed that Carolyn couldn't rise to the level of a Kennedy wife. One of his relatives had told Carolyn that she'd better "get her act together." Meanwhile, John was demanding that Carolyn be a stay-at-home wife but had no sympathy for her boredom and frustration. He had written in his editor's letter for *George*—the same letter he had used to simultaneously attack and defend his cousins—that he was tempted to cheat on Carolyn. "I've learned a lot about temptation recently," he wrote. "But that doesn't make me desire any less." There were reports he was getting ready to file for divorce.

That last one was easy enough to believe. They had fights about it, one on a commercial flight to the Vineyard, loud enough for fellow passengers to hear. "Maybe we should get divorced," John said to her. "We fucking talk about it enough."

"Oh no," Carolyn shot back. "We waited for your mother to die to get married. We're waiting for my mother to die to get a divorce."

I'll be living in a trailer park going: I used to be married to JFK Jr.

So that afternoon Carolyn went to Saks and shopped for a dress for his cousin's wedding. It was a way of telling herself she was really doing this, but she was so skittish that she divulged her anxieties to a shopgirl, a total stranger. John had only gotten the cast off his leg the day before. He had logged only fifty-five hours of night flight and wasn't instrument-rated—he didn't know how to read and rely on his controls, which often contradicted what a pilot could actually see.

"I don't know if he's ready yet to fly again," Carolyn told the salesgirl. "I'm really not looking forward to it." That night, John got to Essex County airport in New Jersey later than planned, around 8:10 p.m. It was a Friday, the traffic heavy with New Yorkers driving to their summer homes. With him was Lauren; Carolyn herself was coming on her own from the city. John was still on crutches and taking Vicodin for bone pain, along with his regular Ritalin and thyroid medication. He carried a half-empty bottle of white wine.

His doctor had warned him not to fly. His flight instructor had offered to come along; he had had to assist John, with his compromised ankle, in a landing three weeks before. John declined. "I want to do it alone," he said.

Roy Stoppard, another small-plane pilot, had run into John earlier that evening. Stoppard himself had just flown into New Jersey from the Cape and was alarmed by the worsening visibility. "I ran into thick haze on the way down," Stoppard told John. "You might want to wait awhile."

"No chance," John said. "I'm already late." The wedding wasn't till Saturday; there really was no rush. Carolyn, in her black sleeveless top and cigarette pants, arrived ten minutes later.

Before John's scheduled takeoff, four other pilots hadn't been able to land at the Essex County airport that evening without using their instruments. The haze was getting so thick that one pilot decided not to take off that night; visibility was only about four miles, and none of that pilot's friends were willing to get in his plane.

John, hobbling on his crutches around his six-seat Piper Saratoga, was given clearance to take off at 8:38 p.m., despite defying one of aviation's most basic rules: Filing a flight plan. Once in the air, he defied another and cut off all communication with air traffic control.

It was the pilot of American Airlines flight 1484, with 128 passengers and six crew members aboard, who averted one disaster that night: a small Piper Saratoga had climbed above its designated airspace. This was John, in the air less than twenty minutes, now on a collision course with a commercial airliner.

John was oblivious. Ground control alerted the American Airlines pilots.

8:52:22 p.m., ground control: American 1484...Unverified, appears to be climbing.

8:52:29 p.m., pilots: American 1484. We're looking.

8:53:02 p.m., ground control: Um yes...I think we have him here, American 1484.

8:53:10 p.m., pilots: I understand he's not in contact with you or anybody else.

8:53:14 p.m., ground control: Uh nope, doesn't — not talking to anybody.

Without knowing which way the clueless pilot of a small prop plane was going, the American Airlines pilots had to divert from their flight path to avoid a midair collision.

John kept on climbing. At 5,500 feet, despite warnings of extreme haze, John didn't turn on his autopilot. He didn't hug the lit-up coastline. Instead, he turned right and went out over the Atlantic, and before he knew it the sea and sky had turned into one seamless black mass and he couldn't tell up from down.

Now would have been the time to start using his instruments — but John couldn't. Now would have been the time to radio ground control — but John, who loved to get himself into near-death situations, did not. Was he that sure he could get himself and Carolyn and Lauren out of it? Or was there a part of him, subconscious or not, that didn't care if he died, taking his wife and sister-in-law with him? His magazine was on the verge of collapse. His marriage was failing. His sister, upset that John was trying to stop her from auctioning off their mother's possessions — Jackie's deathbed suggestion — was now barely talking to him. His life was coming apart on all fronts, and John did not have great internal resources to draw upon, the kind of inner strength forged only from being humbled, humiliated, pushed down and then forcing oneself to get up again.

The plane went into a graveyard spiral, falling 900 feet per minute.

Carolyn and Lauren would have known they were going to die. The sheer force of gravity and speed would have been terrifying as they spun at 200 miles per hour, nose first, into the ocean.

———

When the shattered plane was recovered five days later, its cabin was upside down. The debris field spanned 120 feet. Only five of the six passenger seats were found. John's body was bent backwards at the waist, his head touching his feet. It was rumored on the Cape that the force of impact caused Carolyn's seat belt to sever her body. Reports were that Lauren may have been in the missing seat.

———

Ted Kennedy rushed in to do damage control. He had the remains hastily autopsied, the medical examiner's report and photos sealed, then arranged for cremation. The Kennedys had little compassion for Carolyn and Lauren's family. John's sister, Caroline, and her husband, Ed, showed not the slightest remorse or kindness to Ann Freeman. She had lost two of her three daughters; Lauren's twin sister, Lisa, was now her sole surviving child.

Ann was terrified that the Kennedys would use their power to bury what remained of Carolyn and Lauren at the family plot in Brookline, Massachusetts. Ann wanted her girls close to her in Connecticut, and she needn't have worried: the Kennedys told Ann that they did not care. John's remains, however, belonged to them, and he would be buried separately in Brookline.

Even Robert F. Kennedy Jr. was horrified. As he wrote in a diary entry dated July 19, 1999:

> The agenda for the day was to get Caroline and Ann together without intermediaries so there wouldn't be too many cooks in the kitchen.
>
> When Ann came down to NYC, however, Caroline didn't show. Instead she sent [her husband] Ed and Vickie Reggie [Ted's second

wife]. All the Bessette family knows that Ed hated Carolyn and did everything he could to make her life miserable. He bullied, bullied, bullied the shattered, grieving mother. They told her that John would be buried in Brookline and that they could do with Carolyn as they pleased.

In death, as in life, they never considered Carolyn Bessette a real Kennedy. And as per Kennedy tradition, burying troublesome women alone was nothing new to them.

PART ELEVEN
SURVIVORS

MIMI BEARDSLEY ALFORD AND DIANA DE VEGH

M imi had always planned to keep her relationship with the president secret. Only her first husband, Tony, had known about it. Not her best friends, not a single trusted family member. She had built a life, had two daughters, divorced Tony and remarried, found rewarding work as an administrator at the Fifth Avenue Presbyterian Church in Manhattan.

Then, decades later, the eminent historian Robert Dallek, while working on a JFK biography, unsealed an oral history that named Mimi as the president's in-house teenage mistress. Another biographer had reached out to Mimi one year before. It was only a matter of time before the front-page headline in the *New York Daily News*, which ran in May 2003.

"Fun and Games with Mimi in the White House," it read. The headline inside: "JFK had a Monica." The headline denigrated both Monica and Mimi as bimbo interns—not young women overwhelmed by the sexual attentions of a United States president.

After the *Daily News* outed her, she decided: the only person to tell her story would be Mimi Alford. It took no time for her to find a literary agent and to sell her book to a major publishing house. Mimi wasn't going to be anyone's victim. She had been with JFK during the Cuban Missile Crisis, for God's sake! She was a consequential part of his life! The historical record had Jackie with him the entire time, but in truth the president had persuaded Jackie and the children to go to her beloved Glen Ora in Virginia. And as soon as the First Lady was gone, Dave Powers had called for Mimi, who arrived at once. She had spent the next two days in the White House watching the president go downstairs for lengthy meetings, hiding from a disapproving Bobby Kennedy and feeling safe, swaddled like a baby in the finest bedsheets, as the president set about saving America's eastern seaboard from nuclear oblivion—a catastrophe, really, of his own making.

Mimi knew she was witnessing history. She also knew she had no business being there. She didn't know that so many of JFK's staffers felt the same way. In 2004, Mimi was shocked to find herself described in Sally Bedell Smith's Kennedy biography, *Grace and Power*, observed crouching in a car as she was ferried to the president. Here was a scene in which JFK's top press aide, Pierre Salinger, and his assistant, Chris Camp, were seeing "the top of a little head over the door" and thinking "there was a little child sitting in the front seat of the car."

So more people had known about the affair than Mimi had believed, or had wanted to believe. It was the beginning of this relationship—of the specialness with which she had always regarded it—getting away from her. "I realize now that I suffered two humiliations that day," she would later write of that moment. "The first was in having to hide in the car. The second was that the people in the press office knew about me, were talking about me behind my back, and were laughing at me."

Mimi discovered another bombshell while reading *Grace and Power*: She hadn't been the only mistress of JFK's who was still in school. Here she learned of Diana de Vegh, the beautiful, high-class Radcliffe girl whom JFK also brought to the White House when Jackie wasn't there. Diana and the president had dinners in the residence with Mimi's great pal—or so she thought—Dave Powers. JFK had sex with Diana in the Lincoln Bedroom multiple times, another desecration. Not enough that the president took Mimi's virginity on Jackie's bed; he had to defile his wife's favorite room in the White House, a room she compared to a church.

What had Jack Kennedy really thought of women?

The adult Mimi learned that the president said that "the chase is more fun than the kill," that he called his paramours "kiddo" or "sweetie" because there were so many that he couldn't remember their names. That aside from Jackie, whose intelligence was a political asset, JFK couldn't abide women who were as smart as or smarter than he was. In choosing Mimi and Diana, two well-bred girls from the right schools and social class, JFK had gifted them with extraordinary access to power while treating them like sexual marionettes.

Upon graduating from Radcliffe, Diana had moved to DC to be closer to Jack, then still a senator but now on the verge of becoming president. He still had never kissed her. He never told her he loved her. He preferred to imply, to let his young girlfriends fill in the blanks. "You know how I feel about you," he would say. And that was okay. Diana could rationalize this, because he showed her in other ways, He led her on so smoothly. "I'm so attracted to you," Jack would say. "You're smart. You have a spark."

None of his displays of affection were more significant than his invitation to his and Jackie's Georgetown home, celebrating his inauguration as the thirty-fifth president of the United States. Of course Diana went. How could she miss this? It was history and glamour and power, but it was also the illicit thrill of knowing that the most powerful man in the world wanted her there.

When she arrived, he was cold. "So," he said to Diana, "are you any relation to the Swiss banker I met this summer?" Diana's father wasn't a banker. He was an economist. Jack Kennedy hadn't ever asked what her father did. It hadn't occurred to him that someone with such an unusual last name, who moved in these same circles, was probably related.

"Of course," Diana said. "He's my father." Jack blanched. This was something. Imrie de Vegh was a Harvard overseer, a member of the Council on Foreign Relations and someone whom Jack had consulted. It took a lot to rattle Jack Kennedy. Diana was no longer an exciting secret: she was a liability now, and she knew it. She felt rivulets of sweat pouring beneath her dress. Her bones went liquid.

"We'll meet when all of this is over," he said. "You're tired. We all are. We should get you home."

Was this really how it ended? Diana proceeded to go home, get drunk, throw up, and wake the next day — and the next, and the next — waiting for Jack Kennedy to call. Now she was left with no illusion that theirs had ever been a relationship of equals. He was the president, she was just out of her teens, and she had been so, so naïve. "In that displeasure," she wrote much later, "I realized that I was generic. Mine is a distinctive surname, yet it had taken him six months to put it together."

Diana's greatest fear now was her father finding out what she had done. Like Mimi, she had no one to turn to, no one to ask: Is what's happening here normal? Even though he's the married president of the United States, should I be treated this way? Weeks went by, then months. And just as Diana gave up all hope, the president's secretary called. How was Diana doing? Could she come to the White House? The president wanted to see her.

Diana felt no anger, no bitterness, only relief. But if she held out hope that she and the president might rekindle their romance, he appeared to have other things in mind. He arranged a job for her as a research assistant at the National Security Council, a job she later learned was payback to his national security adviser, McGeorge Bundy, who had wanted the pretty but inexperienced Radcliffe girl gone — but who would now have to see more of her than ever. Diana felt, as never before, that her relationship with the president had an expiration date, and that date was nearing.

"Was he thinking," she wrote later, "about his own daughter, small then, but future prey for men just as charming as he was?"

Had Diana known about Mimi, she might have felt jealous. But Mimi's physical proximity to the president hadn't made her any more emotionally secure. Quite the opposite, in fact. Things were moving fast now that JFK was in the swing of things at the White House, and Mimi was struggling to make sense of it all. There were the invitations to travel when the president did, increasingly with a degree of separateness. Mimi was finding herself on a downward trajectory, stashed in cheap motel rooms and told never to leave, not for anything, until she was summoned to the president's five-star hotel or family estate. She called it "The Waiting Game." Mimi could feel the disdain among the president's closest aides but she didn't care; she was more worried about pleasing the most powerful man in the world and keeping her friends and family, and the American public, from learning about their relationship. It never occurred to her to ask herself: Why was *she* the target of other staffers' contempt? Why didn't they blame the president, whose newborn son, Patrick, had lived less than two days? Why didn't they give him hell for traveling around with a teenage intern when he should have been at home, comforting Jackie?

It was all too confusing for Mimi, who felt that the president had come to rely on her emotionally. After Patrick died—while Jackie was still in the hospital, recovering from her emergency C-section and double-unit blood transfusion and the trauma of never having held her baby—he invited Mimi up to the private residence and onto the portico, where he read condolence letters aloud and cried.

This may have been the most profound violation of his marriage to Jackie, but Mimi couldn't see it as anything but confirmation of her importance to the president. It was she to whom he had turned for comfort, she whom he trusted with his tears. What was this, if not intimacy?

The president never even used protection with Mimi. Was this part of his recklessness? Or was this his way of tempting fate? He was the most famous Catholic in the world. If Mimi got pregnant with their child—well, he must have considered that possibility, right? He would have to take care of them. Maybe he would leave Jackie someday, maybe not, but whatever happened with his marriage, getting Mimi pregnant would mean that she would always be in his life.

Was that what he wanted?

There were more trips, and his cruelty grew exponentially. The president now seemed to get off on degrading Mimi in front of other men. At a druggy party in Palm Springs at the famous entertainer Bing Crosby's house, the president asked Mimi if she would like to try amyl nitrate, a medication sometimes used recreationally to enhance sex. She said no; she didn't even smoke cigarettes. He took the capsule, popped it, and put it under Mimi's nose anyway. Her heart began pounding so fast she thought she was having a heart attack. She fled in tears.

The president did not go after her. He did not check on her. He spent the night in a private room on the other side of the estate with a guest Mimi did not know was there: Marilyn Monroe.

It was Dave Powers who sat with Mimi for an hour, calming her down, assuring her that she would be fine. And she was. Mimi still felt great affection for Dave. He had become something of a father figure to Mimi, stuck in a scene so fast that she was losing herself. In order to survive she had to deny the worst of it, just compartmentalize and move on. It was a coping mechanism required of anyone close to Jack Kennedy, from his own wife to his most trusted staff to his other women. That had never been clearer than that afternoon in the White House pool in late summer, Mimi and the president splashing around, all very childlike and fun, until the president's mood suddenly darkened.

"Mr. Powers looks a little tense," the president whispered to Mimi. "Would you take care of it?" Mimi was shocked. But what if she didn't do as JFK had asked? Would the president think her a prude? He could have any woman he wanted. She needed to keep him. And Dave, seated poolside in his suit with his feet in the water, laughed as Mimi made her way to him, stood up, and performed oral sex on him. The president watched avidly, never saying a word.

When it was over, Mimi was ashamed. "It was a pathetic, sordid scene," she wrote much later. Dave Powers had two teenage daughters of his own. "Much as I try," she wrote, "I cannot bring back anything — any emotion or thought — from that episode that would begin to explain why, without hesitation, I obeyed the president's command...I was deeply embarrassed afterward."

She had no idea that this wasn't personal or unique to her. She had no idea how utterly lacking in boundaries the Kennedys were, that the president frequently enjoyed group sex, that he and his brothers and father considered it normal to sleep with the same women and pass them around. And even if she had, she still wouldn't have been able to leave his orbit. It was too intoxicating, too rarefied.

There was the weekend trip to Boston, Mimi flying on an Air Force support plane to join the president in his suite at the Sheraton Plaza — proof that she remained important! — only to find his brother Teddy, then a brand-new senator, sitting there looking far less stylish and cool than the president and absorbing all of Jack's insults. "Mimi," the president said, by way of introduction, "why don't you take care of my baby brother? He could stand a little relaxation."

Mimi, surprising herself, said no. But she still couldn't bring herself to leave the room. She couldn't bring herself to leave the president. She didn't yet realize that Dave Powers wasn't so much her friend or ally as her handler, that JFK always used others to dispense with unpleasant things or inconvenient people — and "people" most often meant women.

And so it was that Mimi, during one of the president's phone calls to her dorm, told him she was late and might be pregnant. She didn't know what to do. She knew nothing about birth control or when her most fertile time of the month was. There was no such thing as an at-home pregnancy test yet.

The president responded as if Mimi told him it might rain later. As soon as they got off the phone, Dave Powers called. He gave Mimi the number of a woman who knew an abortion provider in Newark, New Jersey — one of the poorest cities in the United States — and that's where Mimi was to go and get this problem solved. It didn't occur to Mimi that Dave had probably done this many times before.

Mimi was panicking. She didn't even know if she wanted an abortion! And here was yet another secret. There was no one she could go to for consolation or counsel, and when she got her period a few days later, she resolved never to mention it to the president or Dave Powers again.

On May 13, 2003, when Mimi's relationship with JFK was revealed, she reached out to Diana, whose relationship with JFK had ended much as Mimi's had — the president pulling away without either young woman fully grasping what was going on. Starstruck at such tender ages, both had done their best to move on: Mimi with a young Army reservist, Diana by relocating to Paris, alone.

"When John Kennedy lost interest in me," Diana wrote years later, now a renowned New York City psychotherapist in her eighties, "I also lost interest in me. Inexperienced in adult relationships, it didn't occur to me that women could be angry with men, so instead I turned on myself. Paralysis, confusion, and ever more waiting ensued."

She was, she wrote, "mired in shame."

Mimi got engaged to her Army reservist after a few months of dating.

She realized, years later, that she had been trying to pull a ripcord, to parachute her way out of DC and the president's realm without getting hurt any worse than she already had been. She had done her best to ignore the president's *other* other women.

Diana was savvier. As he had become less and less available to her, she heard that JFK was also sleeping with Helen Chavchavadze, a member of Jackie Kennedy's circle, and Mary Meyer, sister-in-law of JFK's close friend Ben Bradlee, now editor-in-chief of the *Washington Post*. She believed it all.

Jack Kennedy, she realized, wasn't in love with Diana de Vegh. He probably never had been. She was a convenience, a source of narcissistic supply. "By overwhelming majority, John Kennedy sails to victory!"

When Diana's father died after a serious illness in February 1962, the president called. It wasn't Diana he asked to speak to, but her stepmother, and in that moment she knew: she had to get out. She was helped by her boss, Marc Raskin, who approached Diana one day as she sat at her desk, drowning in paperwork and reports. "Why are you doing this shit?" he asked her.

Did he know? He must have. "You don't like this," he told her. "You're bored. Do something else."

JFK's national security adviser, Bundy, had come to feel protective of Diana since she'd moved to the National Security Council, and now summoned her to his office. He thought it was the healthy thing for her to leave, too, but his approach was gentler. "Now, Diana," he said, "what are you going to do?"

The word flew out of her mouth: "Paris." And off she went to find herself. Soon she was living in a tiny flat on Rue de l'Université, still, sometimes, waiting for the president to call.

Mimi wasn't as strong. She had agreed to another secret trip with the president, this one to Dallas in November 1963. But then Mimi was informed that her presence on this campaign stop would no longer be necessary. Weeks before, the president had begun easing Mimi out of his life, though at the time she hadn't realized that. He had given her several gifts, including two diamond and gold pins and an autographed photo of himself captaining his boat. "To Mimi," he inscribed, "with warmest regards and deep appreciation."

"Only you and I," he told her, "know what that really means."

———————

Diana de Vegh was alone on November 22, 1963, having dinner in a Paris bistro, when the TV over the bar switched to breaking news. It took her a moment to grasp what was happening. There was no one for her in Paris. This may have been the loneliest moment of her life.

"You ask me now what I felt and I wonder, still," she wrote later. "To say I had no feelings at all was not because I'd hardened my heart. But because I could not comprehend. I'd grown up in a world where bad things did not happen to important people. I lingered for some time, then walked through the city alone until I found my apartment, where I remained all night, numb, alone."

It certainly was the most traumatic event of Mimi's young life. That night, while watching the wall-to-wall news coverage and seeing Dave Powers deplane with the president's casket, she burst into tears.

———————

Decades later, when Mimi told her story in her best-selling memoir, her goal wasn't to sully the president but rather to reclaim a significant, historic part of her life.

"It hung around like unfinished business," Mimi said in 2012. "I tried to be honest and faithful to that nineteen-year-old as I remember her ... Now, looking back, I can see it's not a good place for a nineteen-year-old to be, in a relationship that's so imbalanced and with such a powerful person, and with an older man and at the beck and call. I see how sad it was."

Nine years after Mimi's book, Diana published her own account, a personal essay that went viral. Her relationship with the president in no way resembled a love affair, she realized now. She was but one of so many young women, "a conveyor belt of young women," who were there to sexually service John F. Kennedy, aided and abetted by other powerful men who kept a cone of silence. Her secret, Diana said, had always been a heavy weight. She called it the "pocket of dead energy" she had forever carried. She was ready, finally, to drop it.

"What happens when the star strides on?" Diana wrote. "Useless, futile, ridiculous rage aimed at his disappearing back? A rapid ride down the escalator of self-hatred? All of the above... Back then, I thought my job was to become pleasing, an enabling acolyte to a master of the universe. I know now that my job was to become myself."

PART TWELVE
PHOENIX

JACKIE BOUVIER ONASSIS

While still married to Ari Onassis, Jackie had almost taken on a project with NBC. The network had offered her $500,000 to host a special about endangered relics in Angor Wat and Venice — subject matter perfectly aligned with her interests in history, travel, culture, and preservation — but Ari forbade it. "No Greek wife works," he said. It was 1973.

Jackie may have wanted for nothing, but intellectually she was wasting away. Watching Ari cavorting with other women was one thing, but being told to ignore her ambitions was increasingly untenable.

Jackie began spending more time in New York City and traveling to points elsewhere, her restlessness evident to all who knew her. She was becoming a seeker: aside from her psychiatrists and analysts, she had a chiropractor and a massage therapist and an acupuncturist — a doctor for everything, she often joked. Really, she was trying to exorcise her stubborn demons. Her newfound fascination with India, which she had initially visited as First Lady, was rooted in a similar hope: that someone somewhere, a guru or healer or sage, could free her of her PTSD, of the nightmares she still had, of the anxiety and depression she had lived with since the assassination. That the month of November, after all these years, would finally cease being her most difficult. Her most dreaded.

As she did this work, Jackie came to three realizations. First, that the best thing she could do for herself was to make peace with never being at peace with what had happened that day in Dallas. The way Jack died, the way that she nearly died, and the assassination's constant existence in the media were not "things" one got over. She just had to accept it, integrate it as best she could, and learn to live with it. Second, Jackie concluded, an idle mind would only exacerbate her perseverations. She needed to work.

Third: the only way to become who she wanted was to divorce Ari. This marriage had long ago stopped serving her.

In late 1974, Jackie approached William Shawn, the legendary editor of the *New Yorker*, about possibly writing a piece. She had wanted to write for the magazine since she was a young woman, and now, at age forty-five, she summoned the courage. Her pitch: She wanted to cover the imminent opening of the International Center of Photography in New York City. Jackie, who had been an "Inquiring Photographer" as a young, single woman working for the *Washington Times-Herald*, was particularly interested in ICP's mission to preserve and promote the work of photo-journalists. Here was the most photographed woman in the world, an icon immortalized in the Zapruder film and by Andy Warhol and by the paparazzo Ron Gallela—whom she had sued for invasion of privacy— recognizing the importance of uncomfortable imagery. It was a brilliant idea, one that was *New Yorker*–worthy on every level.

Wallace accepted, with the caveat that her piece would run without a byline. And that freed her up; the article would live or die, be accepted by readers or not, on its own merits.

Jackie's finished story ran up front, in the weekly's "Talk of the Town" section, on January 13, 1975. Her attention to detail was impressive: from the look and body language of her subjects to the thought behind the center's interior and layout to the current debate over the medium in France, where Henri Cartier-Bresson had sparked controversy by saying that he considered his paintings far more legitimate, as art, than any of his photography.

Jackie ended her piece by quoting Cartier-Bresson on his philosophy, in which she no doubt saw herself: "I'm . . . a bunch of nerves, but I take advantage of it . . . You have to be yourself and you have to forget your-self . . . The world is being created every minute and the world is falling to pieces every minute . . . It is these tensions I am always moved by . . . I love life, I love human beings, I hate people also . . . I enjoy shooting a picture, being present. It's a way of saying 'Yes! Yes! Yes!' . . . And there's no maybe."

The same month that her first and only *New Yorker* piece ran, Jackie joined the famed architect Philip Johnson in a last-minute bid to save Grand Central Terminal, a crown jewel of New York City's architecture, from being demolished and replaced with a grim fifty-story office tower. Their press conference, held at the Oyster Bar on January 30, made the front page of the *New York Times*. Her presence had ensured that. "Jackie Onassis will save us," Johnson said at the event. "Europe has its cathedrals, and we have Grand Central."

Her activism was powerful because it was rare. "I think this is so terribly important," she said. This was the first time America had heard Jackie speak directly to them, on television, since she was a broken young widow in 1964, thanking the nation for its outpouring of sympathy, nearly 800,000 letters of condolence in all. Bobby had been by her side then. Today, however, Jackie was speaking to the country as a soon-to-be-divorcée leveraging her power unabashedly. In doing so, she was signaling her intent to remain a public figure — on her own terms.

"We've all heard that it's too late, or that it has to happen, or that it's inevitable," she said of Grand Central's impending demolition. She was at the height of her beauty, her dark hair falling in loose waves past her shoulders, large gold hoop earrings dangling to her jawline, looking like a modern woman in every way. "I don't think that's true," she continued, "because I think that if there's a great effort, even if it's the eleventh hour, then you can succeed and I know that's what we'll do . . . If we don't care about our past, we cannot hope for our future." A few weeks later, in a handwritten letter to New York's mayor, Abe Beame, Jackie made a similar plea.

"Is it not cruel," she wrote, "to let our city die by degrees, stripped of all her proud moments, until there is nothing left of all her history and beauty to inspire our children? If they are not inspired by the past of our city, where will they find the strength to fight for her future? Americans care about their past, but for short term gain they ignore it and tear down everything that matters." Within weeks of reading Jackie's letter, Beame announced that he would do everything in his power to preserve Grand Central, which he called "a symbol of life in the City of New York."

And he did. It was Jackie's second big win of the new year, proof that she had something to offer other than wifedom.

Ari and Jackie had been living largely separate lives when he died in March 1975 in Paris, following months of ill health. She didn't pretend that theirs had been some grand love story. "Aristotle Onassis rescued me at a time when my life was engulfed in shadows," she said. "He meant a lot to me. He brought me into a world where one could find happiness and love."

And with that, Jackie Onassis began searching for a purpose. A few who knew her — her former social secretary Letitia Baldridge and *New York Daily News* columnist Jimmy Breslin, among them — suggested that Jackie consider working in book publishing as an editor. "What do you think you're going to do?" Breslin asked her. "Attend openings for the rest of your life?"

It did make sense. Books were among Jackie's great loves; she was a voracious consumer and reader of them, and aside from her children, books were her solace, her emotional sustenance. And editing would fit with her baseline personality: Jackie was social and loved meeting new and fascinating people, but she was also, at her core, a loner. Becoming an editor would mean lunches and book launches and office work, but it would also allow her hours away on her own, reading and thinking and refueling.

On the other hand, entering the workforce would be a risk. She would be opening herself up to a world she knew nothing about, to colleagues who might sell her out. The press, she knew, would laugh at her — Jackie Onassis, out of nowhere, a book editor! Then again, they treated her far worse when she married Ari. Why not give it a go? She called Jason Epstein, an executive at Random House, and asked him to lunch at Lutèce. Epstein couldn't refuse. "My friend Pete Hamill, who had once taken Jackie out, said it was like 'taking King Kong to the beach,'" Epstein wrote. It was, in fact, like that.

"Might there be a job for me?" Jackie asked.

Epstein was taken aback. Jackie had no practical experience as a book editor. She hadn't worked in a professional setting, period, since 1953. The learning curve was steep, there were very few entry-level positions — which she wouldn't want, surely — and he would have to knock someone else out of the way, someone qualified, to make room for her. Jackie didn't debate. She knew that if Epstein really wanted Jackie Onassis, he would have found a way.

"I understand," Jackie said. "I don't want to impose."

She turned to family friend Tom Guinzburg, publisher at Viking. He had concerns, too, but he saw Jackie as an asset. Her celebrity could lure the kind of high-profile authors that Viking wanted: A-list stars, bestselling novelists, presidents and potentates. Who would refuse her phone call? She wasn't qualified to be a hands-on editor in terms of conceptualizing a book or building narrative structure or line editing, but she would nonetheless be an enormous draw. He offered Jackie a position as an acquisitions editor, with a chance to learn how to edit books if she buckled down. "You're not really equipped to be an editor [yet]," he told her. "It's not that you don't have the talent for it, the ability for it, but you don't have the background and the training." Her salary would be $200 a week, $10,000 a year. She would have a junior office with no window. There would be no special treatment.

She was dying for the job and she took it, negotiating work-from-home one day a week. The launch party for the first book she acquired, *In the Russian Style*, was held at the Carlyle Hotel — where Jack had kept a residential suite — and the event was covered by the *New York Times*. "Mrs. Onassis displayed considerable knowledge of Russian history as she spoke," the paper noted. It was another coming-out party for Jackie of sorts, showing her bona fides to a media horde skeptical of this new incarnation: Jackie Onassis, Working Woman. But this 184-page book, a lavishly illustrated and photographed history of wealthy bygone aristocrats, was the real deal. As was its editor, who had spent two weeks in the then-Soviet Union researching and visiting museum archives and working as the book's art researcher, editor, and caption writer. Jackie O was going to prove herself the real deal.

"Wearing little makeup and no jewelry," the *Times* reported, "the 47-year-old Mrs. Onassis said she felt no longing for the opulent clothes and lifestyle of the Russian nobility. 'You love to see it, the way you love to see "Gone With the Wind,"' she mused, leaning back in her chair, chewing a shortbread cookie. 'But wouldn't you rather wear your blue jeans than wander around in a hoop skirt?'"

Jackie had shed that proverbial hoop skirt, and the world would just have to accept it.

———

Her attitude toward sex and marriage was undergoing a profound shift, too. When her teenagers had their significant others to any of her homes — at 1040 Fifth Avenue or her retreat in New Jersey or the house she had shared with Jack on the Cape — Jackie allowed them to sleep in the same bedroom; she thought it was silly at best, damaging at worst, to pretend that they weren't having sex. She had told both John and Caroline that she didn't want them to grow up with the same twisted ideas or hang-ups about sex as most Kennedys had. Jackie told an adult John one November that she had been rethinking her first marriage and didn't think it would have survived today. She would have left Jack Kennedy. The most interesting men to her now were the smart ones, writers and artists. Among her suitors was a TV producer she had asked to lunch, then back to her place for sex. He never heard from Jackie again and told a mutual friend that the encounter had left him shocked that women now treated sex the way men did — fun, casual, meaningless. She dated the married cartoonist Charles Addams and, more seriously, the famed New York City columnist Pete Hamill. Jackie's attraction to Hamill could have had something to do with his closeness to Bobby; he had urged Bobby to run for president and had been by his side when Bobby was shot. Jackie was seen in public with Hamill so frequently that in 1977, mere months into their relationship, rumors of engagement swirled.

But then Page Six began running a series of Jackie-centric items, one for nearly every day of the week, under the headline, "Who Wrote This?" They were timed to her marriage to Ari and were lacerating, if unoriginal, in excoriating Jackie as, yes, that whore who sold herself shamelessly. The final item, on Friday, read: "no courtesan...ever sold herself for more."

Above that was a photo of Pete and Jackie, looking at each other and beaming.

Hamill was the author. He had written that column in 1971 and spiked it, but it was fished out of the archives in a spectacular bit of revenge by *Post* editor Rupert Murdoch. Pete Hamill, progressive New York liberal, Kennedy loyalist, and champion of the little guy — well, it turned out he was just another male media figure who thought Jackie was a high-end hooker.

He never heard from her again.

———

Jackie kept trying to forge her own identity, but it was only getting harder. Her first year at Viking, meant to be slow and instructive, proved a challenge. *Shall We Tell the President?* was a buzzy novel being shopped to all the major publishing houses, a surefire bestseller by Jeffrey Archer. The story centered around Ted Kennedy, whom Archer imagined as president of the United States, and a plot to assassinate him. Random House had already made a strong offer for $200,000, but Guinzburg badly wanted it for Viking. Before going to Archer's agent, he talked to Jackie face to face.

"I've got a problem with a manuscript," Guinzburg said.

"How?" Jackie asked.

"It's a caper thriller novel . . . Like many of these things, this has a gimmick. An assassination plot."

"What are you getting at, Tom?"

"In this case it's Ted Kennedy, and the year's 1983."

Jackie blanched. She took a moment to gather herself.

"Is it really a pretty good book?" she asked. "Is this pretty commercial?"

It is, Guinzburg said. She told him that she appreciated his coming to her and that he should buy the book. He did.

Guinzburg would be proven right; the book was commercial, one of the most talked-about of the year — just not in the way he foresaw. A review by the prominent critic John Leonard in the *New York Times* closed with these three lines: "There is a word for such a book. The word is trash. Anybody associated with its publication should be ashamed of herself."

Herself. He meant Jackie.

Within five days, her job was no more. On October 15, 1977, the *Times* ran a front-page story headlined "Mrs. Onassis Resigns Editing Post." It quoted Jackie, who issued a statement through her longtime assistant, Nancy Tuckerman. "Last spring, when told of the book, I tried to separate my lives as a Viking employee and a Kennedy relative. But this fall, when it was suggested that I had had something to do with acquiring the book and that I was not distressed by its publication, I felt I had to resign."

It was a heartbreak. Jackie had been in the job for ten months and had begun finding her rhythm. Her colleagues were no longer showing up to work in their finest clothes; they had stopped addressing her with stiff formality. At Viking she was just another beginning editor with a crappy office who got her own coffee, made her own photocopies, and placed her own phone calls. With *Shall We Tell the President?* she had taken one for the team. She had wanted Guinzburg to have a win, to publish a novel that looked like a blockbuster. And not that the media cared, but her brother-in-law Steve Smith, Ted's presumptive campaign manager for the 1980 presidential election, had been given an advance copy of the book. As had Ted himself.

It was clear that Jackie's unique fame cut both ways: it had gotten her the job at Viking, and it had cost her the job. Would anyone take her seriously again? Consider her anything but a liability? *Time* magazine's coverage, right after her resignation: "Situation Wanted, References Available." And to Jackie's delight, Doubleday came calling: they offered her $20,000 a year, twice her Viking salary, with a three-day in-office workweek.

On February 13, 1978, Jackie began her new job as associate editor, reporting to two women, Lisa Drew and Betty Prashker. This was a revelation — especially at Doubleday, where even the top female editors were called "brides." Jackie had a similar awakening when her daughter

Caroline told her to see the feminist workplace comedy *9 to 5*. "I've never known professional women," Jackie told one of her colleagues. "I've never worked for women before."

As at Viking, Jackie kept her head down and her door open. She worked Tuesdays through Thursdays, bringing her own lunch and eating at her desk, usually a tuna fish sandwich with celery and carrots for snacks. She never pretended that her celebrity hadn't gotten her catapulted above entry level; in fact, she used her status when asked. In the mid-1980s, even though she had preferred not to, Jackie flew to London and approached Princess Diana about writing her memoirs. (That was a no.) It was the same when she was asked to persuade Michael Jackson to write his autobiography, swallowing her distaste and flying to his Neverland Ranch, this time succeeding.

But Jackie also had her passion projects: she acquired Joseph Campbell's *The Power of Myth* and Bill Moyers's *Healing and the Mind*—two books quite personal to her, given her obsession with mythology and her lifelong attempts to heal herself—and both became bestsellers. Her lifelong love of ballet helped Jackie to persuade prima ballerina Gelsey Kirkland to write her autobiography, also a critical and commercial success. And Jackie worked closely with the African American author Dorothy West on her novel *The Wedding*, which would come to be regarded as a modern-day classic.

"She, this elegant and gracious woman, and [I], this writer of considerably more years, would bond in a miraculous way," West wrote of Jackie. "I think I was as unique to her as she was unique to me... She came to see me every Monday to assess my progress, driving herself... Though there was never such a mismatched pair in appearance, we were perfect partners."

Jackie was also proud of editing *Remember the Ladies*, a nonfiction account of eighteenth-century women in America. During her work on that book, she encouraged more inclusion of Indigenous, working-class, and Black women, as well as guidance from a contemporaneous sex manual about an edible root that could induce abortion.

Jackie had found her groove. She was done with being the story, and while she was with Ari she had been evolving, whether she was aware of it or not, into something of a literary midwife, coaxing stories out of others. It was a pattern of interest that predated her career: years before, on Skorpios, Jackie had encouraged her friend Barbara Chase-Riboud to write her groundbreaking book about Sally Hemings, Thomas Jefferson's slave and the mother of at least six of Jefferson's children—a disturbing part of American history that, at the time, remained little known.

Jackie and Barbara first met in 1974 through mutual friends in Greece. "The Onassises had greeted us at the helicopter pad, this mythic couple both dressed in white pants and black T-shirts, framed by the *Christina*," Chase-Riboud later wrote. "After lunch, sitting on the beach while boats filled with paparazzi circled the island with telephoto lenses that resembled bazookas, I told Jacqueline the story of Sally Hemings, my desire that the world know who she was, and my own frustration at perhaps not having the skills or the stamina. 'I'm a poet, a sprinter—not a long-distance runner,' I said, 'and no one seems to be interested in the life of an American Revolution–era enslaved Black woman.'" Random House, including her editor there, the legendary Toni Morrison, had passed on the book.

"It took three years," Chase-Riboud wrote, "from the time a concerned Jacqueline Onassis had turned to me and said, 'You must write this story,' to the time it was published at Viking Press with her as my acquiring editor...I realized that sitting beside me in a black one-piece swimsuit was one of the few women in the world who could explain political power and ambition, American sex and American autocracy, the back stairs at the White House and the intolerable glare and flame of living history. Who else?"

Who else, indeed?

———

Now fifty years old, Jackie was in her prime. She was building her dream house on Martha's Vineyard, had raised two children in uniquely difficult circumstances, had earned the respect of her peers in publishing, and had fallen in love with Maurice Tempelsman, a man she had known since her years with Jack. She had no desire to marry again, ever, and that was just fine with him; he remained married to his first wife and had no desire to divorce. Jackie had always had a penchant for married men and the emotional distance baked into those arrangements, but Maurice was different; he was devoted to her. Jackie Onassis, in short, had found her bliss. She was now the architect of her own life.

Watching from afar was an unusual admirer: Gloria Steinem, editor-in-chief of *Ms.* magazine and, at the time, the face of American feminism. Steinem asked Jackie, who hadn't given a proper interview since her days in the White House, if she would do so for *Ms.* To Steinem's surprise, Jackie agreed. She appeared on the March 1979 cover, perched on her desk in her wide-collared shirtdress, books piled on either side, her Cartier Tank wristwatch the only nod to her extraordinary wealth, beaming next to the question: "WHY DOES THIS WOMAN WORK?"

It was a double entendre of sorts: Why did Jackie have a job, yes, but also: Why did Jackie O, of all people, work as an idea and example for the average woman? Why did they relate to her—why was she inspiring them—at this very moment?

"What has been sad for many women of my generation," Jackie told Steinem, "is that they weren't supposed to work if they had families. There they were, with the highest education, and what were they to do when the children were grown—watch the raindrops coming down the windowpane? Leave their fine minds unexercised? . . . You have to be doing something you enjoy. That is a definition of happiness: 'Complete use of one's faculties along lines leading to excellence in a life affording them scope.' It applies to women as well as to men. We can't all reach it, but we can try to reach it to some degree."

In an accompanying stand-alone article, Steinem gently chided Jackie for refusing to publicly support the Equal Rights Amendment—though privately she backed it—and for declining to use her power politically. "That's the unique individual she is," Steinem wrote. "Neither Kennedy nor Onassis nor even her own glamorous public image, but a woman who remains sensitive, funny, slightly outrageous (the sort of person to whom you find yourself saying things you had previously only thought); creative, intelligent, loyal to her friends, very demanding of loyalty, consistent in her interests over the years, and the very private center of a very public storm."

Steinem concluded that Jackie Bouvier Onassis, as she now preferred to be known, was a net plus for modern feminism. For any married or divorced or single woman wondering if she, too, could have a career and be independent, look no further than this most unexpected role model. "Given the real options of using Kennedy power or of living an Onassis-style life," Steinem wrote, "how many of us would have the strength to return to our own careers — to choose personal work over derived influence? In the long run, her definition of work may be more helpful to women than the kind of conventional power she has declined."

Ever the storyteller, Jackie knew how to deliver a kicker. "I think that people who work for themselves have the respect of others," Jackie told Steinem. "I remember a taxi driver who took me to the office. He said, 'Lady, you work and you don't *have* to?' I said yes. He turned around and said, 'I think that's great!'"

Left unsaid was Jackie's other personal triumph: she never thought twice now about grabbing a pair of big bold sunglasses from the basket near her door, belting her black leather trench, swinging her namesake Gucci bag over her shoulder, and heading out of 1040 Fifth Avenue, off to work. Right across the street, in the Metropolitan Museum of Art, was the ancient Egyptian Temple of Dendur, which Jackie had officially received as a gift to the United States back in 1965. Another time, another life.

Then Jackie would look south, turn left, and disappear into the crowd, just another New York woman on the go.

EPILOGUE

J ackie Onassis once told Gloria Steinem, "What I like about being an editor is that it expands your knowledge and heightens your discrimination. Each book takes you down another path. Some of them move people and some of them do some good."

Such is the guiding philosophy of this book. The most famous of these women have too often been recast as architects of their own demise, or as women who were asking for it, or as imminent threats to the Kennedy dynasty. Those who were less well known, or merely teenage girls, have become footnotes to history — if they are remembered at all.

There are more than a few women and families who, quite understandably, find solace in that. They have survived and built new lives for themselves, among them the brave Patricia Bowman, who came forward to tell her story after William Kennedy Smith was acquitted of raping her. Bowman gave her exclusive interview to Diane Sawyer of ABC News. It aired on December 19, 1991.

Sawyer asked Bowman why, after her "aggressive effort to protect your privacy," she was going public with her name and face. "I'm not a blue blob," Bowman said. "I'm a person."

The verdict, she explained, was why she had come forward. "I know that the reporting of rapes has gone down," she said. (They had, by 40 percent.) "I'm terrified that victims everywhere who have seen my case, and potential victims who have seen my case, will not report because of what happened to me. And that is one of the strongest motivations to quote, 'come out,' because you can survive." Bowman was also eager to disprove the unfounded accusation that Kennedy Smith's defense lawyer, Roy Black, made on CNN and elsewhere that she had "obvious mental problems," was "disturbed," that she had been a sex worker, and that her overall instability and sexual promiscuity were the basis of her accusation.

"It's well known about [the Kennedys'] PR campaign," Bowman said.

"Tell me about it," Sawyer replied. "What do you mean?"

Sawyer—who had been a member of President Nixon's staff, worked on his memoirs, and was well versed in political warfare—went on to counter that Kennedy Smith, not Bowman, was the victim here: "He can't get his name back," Sawyer said. She mentioned in a voice-over that Bowman was "living off a trust fund from her rich Republican stepfather," as if her accusation had been a partisan smear campaign. Sawyer also said that Bowman, as reported in the tabloids, "had lived in the 'fast lane' [with] hints of drug use," mentioned "her abortions," said that "she was sexually abused as a child" and that "she decided to have a child while unmarried." She mentioned that Bowman had once had "a one-night stand," and, the night she met Kennedy Smith, had clearly been dressed for male attention. Why had she been out at three in the morning? "So was he," said Bowman. "Because I was out at three o'clock in the morning, does that mean he has the right to rape me?"

Sawyer pressed on, telling Bowman that even the *New York Times* reported that she was "a little wild."

One can only imagine what must have been going through Patricia Bowman's mind during this interview, sitting across from a famous female journalist who, one would imagine, might have promised a sisterly, feminist approach to helping Bowman tell her story. Instead, Sawyer was as savage as any of Smith's misogynistic attorneys. The idea that Sawyer had no idea what the Kennedy machine did (and still does) to troublesome women beggars belief.

I reached out to Bowman for this book several times but never got a reply. And so I took the nonanswer for what it seemed: All of this was in her past. Reliving it, in a book that may remain relevant for far too many years, was not in her best interests. What else is there to do but respect that silence? The treatment of Bowman by the media, however, remains relevant.

This also holds true for the babysitter whom the late Michael Kennedy statutorily raped. Those interested enough can find her name on Google; I won't repeat it here. She was fourteen years old when this abuse began, successfully reframed by the Kennedys and repeated, to this day, as a "love affair" resulting from the seductions of this teenage temptress. Her parents were prominent in Massachusetts business and political circles, and, as this so-called affair made headlines, her mother attempted suicide. The story faded from public view in 1998, after Michael Kennedy was busy breaking more rules on Aspen, Colorado's, Copper Mountain, endangering the lives of others as he and fellow Kennedys tossed a football while skiing downhill. Michael, who wasn't wearing a helmet, crashed into a tree and died on impact. This was covered not as an entirely avoidable reckless act but yet more proof of the so-called Kennedy Curse. That Michael was guilty of statutory rape, of abusing and stalking this teenage girl over at least three years, was forgotten if not forgiven.

Maria Shriver, daughter of Jack's sister Eunice, seemed one of the few third-generation Kennedy women to have forged a successful career and marriage. But when her movie-star husband, Arnold Schwarzenegger—himself an admitted serial sexual harasser and groper of women—became governor of California in 2003, Shriver was forced to retire from journalism. Her career, went the thinking, would have been a conflict of interest. For this sacrifice, Shriver was rewarded with the public revelation, in 2011, that her husband had been involved with the family's longtime housekeeper, who had secretly given birth to his then-thirteen-year-old son. Schwarzenegger, rumored to have had political ambitions well before marrying Shriver, enjoys great popularity still, his Kennedy-level immorality a bug rather than a feature of his otherwise charming persona.

These are but a few of the many examples, more than we probably know, of girls and women brutalized by Kennedy men. It's a legacy that is very much alive: it's infiltrated our water supply, the air we breathe. Every time a woman accuses a famous, powerful, wealthy man of sexual harassment, abuse, or rape—and when one survivor comes forward, more usually follow—tactics from the well-worn Kennedy playbook are weaponized. Such women are still routinely called liars or mentally unstable or women scorned or any number of characterizations that are often treated as legitimate rather than suspect.

False reports of rape are vanishingly rare. In fact, more rapes go unreported than reported in America still, and it's not hard to see why. Any woman who comes forward, especially against a machine that rivals the Kennedys—think Clinton, Cosby, Weinstein, Trump—is likely to have her reputation shredded and her entire sexual history plastered in the public square.

We are making progress, especially in understanding that there is no perfect female victim, but we have many miles to go. When a life-size bronze statue of JFK was unveiled in DC in 2021, not one bit of news coverage addressed his treatment of women. Not one journalist, essayist, political writer, or cultural critic asked whether this was a man deserving, in our new era, of such a memorial. Not one asked what kind of message his continued celebration sends to women and girls, now and in the future. *Ask not*, indeed.

As of this writing, Robert F. Kennedy Jr. is running for president as an independent. Again, he is taken to task for his anti-vax stance, his trafficking in conspiracy theories, his antisemitism—but not for his lifelong mistreatment of women. Not for helping to free his cousin Michael Skakel, once convicted in the brutal sexual assault and murder of fifteen-year-old Martha Moxley. All the evidence used to convict Skakel, including the murder weapon, is now sealed in perpetuity. This is a catastrophic outcome for future journalists and historians. Nor has RFK Jr. been confronted about falsely accusing two boys from the Bronx, one Black and the other of mixed race, of traveling all the way to a wealthy Connecticut suburb to, in effect, go "wilding" on a young blonde girl. Nor for the way he continues to vivisect his late wife Mary's character in the national media after she committed suicide, then dug up her remains and secretly reburied her alone.

Why isn't RFK Jr. being held to account? Which journalist, male or female, will find the courage to confront him? Shouldn't we, as voters, demand better? Donald Trump's infamous comment to *Access Hollywood*'s Billy Bush, "Grab 'em by the pussy," horrifies. So, too, should this ugly, shameful, very-much-with-us Kennedy legacy.

Rosemary Kennedy, her unspeakable lobotomy Joe Kennedy's personal original sin, was twenty-three years old when her father rendered her mute and helpless in 1941. It wasn't until his death in 1969 that Rose Kennedy felt she could tell her sons and daughters where Rosemary was, and that they felt it was safe to visit her. Rosemary had lived for nearly thirty years without any contact from her parents or siblings. Can you imagine a lonelier life?

Rosemary last saw her brother Jack on television, in replays of the assassination. Did she know it was him? Probably. The nurses who cared for her said that whenever Rose secretly visited, Rosemary shrank and turned away. She became visibly upset and wanted nothing to do with her mother. Rosemary's nurses became her surrogate family, and they came to believe that somewhere in Rosemary's mangled brain lived the memory of weakness—her mother's, not hers. Where had her mother been to defend her from that monster? To save her?

Rosemary's true end belies the Kennedy version, that Rosemary went off to live a private life teaching mentally impaired children. The rest of the women in this book suffered similar false codas, written by the Kennedys or their enablers, in ways that invariably blame them. These are false endings full of slander, misogyny, and character assassination, and they have wrought untold collateral damage, not just for the victims and their families but for all of us.

These women's real endings are not always happy. But they are true. And therein lies their power.

CAROLYN BESSETTE KENNEDY

Carolyn Bessette Kennedy was thirty-three when she died. Her sister Lauren Bessette, a rising star at Morgan Stanley, was thirty-four. John F. Kennedy Jr. was wholly responsible for this entirely avoidable tragedy, yet it's Carolyn who has been blamed as the cause ever since. It was her vanity, her superficiality, her drug use, her all-around-shrewish behavior that led an inexperienced, hubristic pilot—a man who, in taking to the air that night, broke just about every rule of flying—to crash his plane into the ocean.

Biographer Ed Klein wrote that Carolyn was "downright bitchy," and that even though John and Lauren reached the airport that night a little after 8:00 p.m. — the sun soon going down — Carolyn's lateness was to blame. And why was she late? Klein quoted a hairdresser named Colin Lively, who claimed he had been sitting next to Carolyn as she was getting a pedicure that very afternoon.

"She made the pedicurist redo her toenails...three times," Klein quoted Lively. "She wasn't overtly bitchy" — there's that word again — "but she was so self-involved. If this was a key to her personality, then I would say she was obsessive about a lot of things."

Another blame-shifting version has Carolyn waiting for her tardy drug dealer. In the twenty-five years since the crash, she has been depicted — in countless articles, biographies, memoirs, documentaries, and TV specials — as the drug-addled harridan who made the last days of America's prince so miserable. And, so goes the implication: if John Jr. hadn't been so miserable he wouldn't have been so distracted, and if he hadn't been so distracted he wouldn't have crashed the plane.

This has become conventional wisdom, accepted as fact, and it's left Carolyn's sister Lauren a footnote — still more collateral damage.

In truth, the resulting investigation by the National Transportation Safety Board found John alone responsible for the crash. The report is online, and to read it is to endure a litany of John's errors, rule-breaking, and refusal to adhere to fundamental safety measures, such as filing a flight plan and remaining in contact with air traffic control. It all begs the question: Was John, who had a reckless streak bordering on — and perhaps crossing over into — a death wish, flirting with murder-suicide that night? He was expressly told by far more experienced pilots, more than once, not to pilot the plane that night. He waved off a willing flight instructor who offered to co-pilot that night. He nearly crashed into a commercial airliner that was on its approach to New York's Kennedy International Airport. John F. Kennedy Jr. took the lives of two innocent, beautiful, successful, vibrant young women with bright futures, yet one of them has been vilified while John remains lionized. Beloved. Free of fault.

Nearly two years to the day of the crash, in July 2001, Carolyn and Lauren's mother Ann Freeman reportedly received millions in a wrongful-death settlement against John's estate. Ann has never spoken publicly about her lost daughters or the accident. As of this writing, her only surviving daughter, Lauren's twin, Lisa, lives quietly in the American Midwest. Every July, Lisa reportedly leaves the country to escape anniversary coverage of the crash.

MIMI AND DIANA

Mimi Beardsley Alford's memoir, *Once Upon a Secret: My Affair with President John F. Kennedy and Its Aftermath*, was published in 2012. Despite a critical pillorying in the media, with journalists such as the late Barbara Walters and the *New York Times Book Review*'s Janet Maslin denouncing Mimi as a sad woman defaming JFK and his legacy, the book became a number one *New York Times* bestseller. Robert Dallek, the esteemed historian and JFK biographer, called Mimi "entirely credible" and her book a key part of our historical reckoning with President Kennedy. "You're not going to put the genie back in the bottle anymore," Dallek told the *Washington Post*. "This has become part of the public discourse." Mimi has retreated from public life.

Diana de Vegh published her own account in *Air Mail* in 2021, having reevaluated her relationship with JFK thanks to the #MeToo movement. "I began eventually to question the culture, because the culture was about enabling a Great Man," de Vegh said. "John Kennedy did not have his womanizing life all by himself. He had it thanks to many, many, many other men." She practices as a psychotherapist in New York City.

MARILYN MONROE

Marilyn died on August 4, 1962, at her home in Brentwood, California. The official cause was "probable suicide," but suspicion has forever hung over John F. Kennedy and Robert F. Kennedy. Earlier that day, Marilyn had told her friend Jeanne Carmen that she'd gotten harassing phone calls the night before, a familiar woman's voice telling her to "leave Bobby alone." The FBI was dispatched to Marilyn's home immediately after her death; former senior FBI agent James Doyle later went public, saying the

Bureau had been ordered to eliminate certain phone records. Monroe biographer Anthony Summers uncovered some of them; one record showed that Monroe had called the Justice Department in Washington, DC — Bobby's workplace — eight times from June 25 to July 30, 1962. Her final call got through and lasted eight minutes. She had reportedly had an abortion at Cedars of Lebanon Hospital in LA on July 20, 1962, and in recent years it's been theorized that this was Bobby's baby. That would explain why Marilyn was so desperate to reach him in that time frame.

Audiotapes from Marilyn's surveillance system also went missing, as did her diary, which Bobby Kennedy had reportedly told her to "get rid of" in the months before her death. Former LA County deputy district attorney John Miner, who officially observed Monroe's autopsy, later reconstructed the 1962 memorandum he gave police for Summers. He wrote that her psychiatrist, Dr. Ralph Greenson, had spoken to him at length and had let Miner listen to a forty-minute tape of Monroe sharing plans for the immediate future. "As a result of what Dr. Greenson told me," Miner wrote in part, "and from what I heard on tape recordings, I believe I can say definitely that it was not suicide."

In the 1980s, ABC News planned to air a special regarding the Kennedy brothers' involvement in Marilyn's death. But at 6:00 p.m. on the day the broadcast was to air, with mere hours to go, ABC pulled the plug. "A dead president belongs to history," host Hugh Downs said by way of explanation, "and he belongs to accurate history." ABC News president Roone Arledge, who canceled the documentary, was a longtime friend of Ethel Kennedy. He denied any conflict of interest.

Joe DiMaggio told his biographer Dr. Rock Positano more than once that the Kennedys were responsible for Marilyn's death. "I always knew who killed her, but I didn't want to start a revolution in this country," DiMaggio said. "She told me someone would do her in, but I kept quiet. The whole lot of Kennedys were lady-killers, and they always got away with it. They'll be getting away with it a hundred years from now."

MARY RICHARDSON KENNEDY

Those who knew and loved Mary acknowledge how difficult she could be, but insist that nothing she had ever said or done justified her husband's treatment of her. They described a woman who had been psychologically and financially beaten down by Bobby Kennedy Jr., a man held in low esteem to this day by many of Mary's loved ones. So far, he has had the last word: in the immediate aftermath of Mary's death, Bobby Jr. gave an interview to the *New York Times* about the marriage being difficult for him, and the ensuing media coverage hewed to that narrative: Bobby was the victim, Mary the problem, and wasn't it incredible that Bobby survived? Kerry Kennedy told the *Times* that Mary had been in Alcoholics Anonymous, sober for the past five months. "She fought with every ounce of her mission to overcome that horrible disease," Kerry said. Another source said that Mary was a depressive with a history of suicidal ideations. Mary's siblings refused to address any of these accusations and said, in a statement, "We deeply regret the death of our beloved sister Mary, whose radiant and creative spirit will be sorely missed by those who loved her. Our heart goes out to her children, who she loved without reservation."

The exhumation of Mary's body and her secret reburial have, as of this writing, been forgotten.

KICK KENNEDY

Kick, full name Kathleen Cavendish, Marchioness of Hartington, had been lost to history until the publication of two recent books: Barbara Leaming's *Kick Kennedy: The Charmed Life and Tragic Death of the Favorite Kennedy Daughter*, and Paula Byrne's *Kick: The True Story of JFK's Sister and the Heir to Chatsworth*. Her brief life was a torment thanks to a double standard that allowed her fathers and brothers sexual freedom to the point of depravity, while Kick was punished for falling in love with a Protestant and, later, a married man. Her father was the lone Kennedy to attend her funeral. Kick's friend, the famous socialite Debo Mitford, was left to write the inscription on Kick's headstone: "Joy she gave—Joy she has found."

MARY JO KOPECHNE

Mary Jo's parents, Gwen and Jo Kopechne, never recovered from their only child's death or the pervasive falsehood that Mary Jo was a Kennedy groupie who had gone off that night to have sex with Ted. They found support in no less a figure than Muhammad Ali, who sent Gwen and Joe a handwritten letter days after Ted's televised address to the nation, which he gave shortly after the official inquest—the ill-advised speech in which Ted had offered vague excuses for his actions, acknowledged that they "make no sense to me at all," and speculated about "whether some awful curse did actually hang over all the Kennedys." In his letter, dated July 31, 1969, Ali urged the Kopechnes to sue Ted Kennedy—"that no-good son of a bitch," in Ali's estimation—for everything he had. Ali also wrote that he believed Ted had intended to force himself sexually on Mary Jo that night, that Ted should be criminally tried for her death, and that nothing Ted said in his speech to the nation, written by Kennedy yes-men, excused what he had done or was remotely credible. In short, Ali's assessment was withering and correct:

> There were no mitigating circumstances. His TV speech was written
> for him by a dozen lawyers and speechmakers and was not his own, the
> cheap two-bit hypocrite!

Joe and Gwen didn't have the strength or financial resources to sue. It was a struggle enough for them to survive day to day after their Mary Jo's death.

Ted Kennedy served as the senior US senator from Massachusetts, uninterrupted, until the end of his life. In his 2009 memoir, *True Compass*, published one month before his death, Ted gave four of 507 pages to explaining that night.

"My car," he wrote, "slipped off the side of the narrow bridge." Note the passive voice. He goes on to write: "I was afraid. I was overwhelmed. I made terrible decisions. Even though I was dazed from my concussion, exhaustion, shock, and panic, I was rational enough to understand that the accident would be devastating to my family. They had suffered so much, and now they would be forced to suffer again because of me. And I knew it would be damaging to my political career as well."

Despite promising to one day tell Mary Jo's parents, his own children, and the world what really happened the night he left Mary Jo to her certain death, Ted took it to his grave.

JOAN KENNEDY

In 1982, Joan divorced Ted; Jackie referred her to the same divorce attorney she'd consulted when planning to leave Onassis. Joan has never remarried. In the years since her divorce, she has published a book about classical music and survived breast cancer, kidney damage, multiple arrests for DUIs — the first in 1974, one year after Teddy Jr.'s leg was amputated — dire struggles with sobriety, and the death of her daughter Kara, from cancer, in 2011. Joan's openness about addiction changed the public discourse, especially for women, though her struggles have indeed been lifelong. In 2006, after her children tried to take control of her care and finances, she was placed under court-mandated supervision to stop drinking. Now eighty-seven, she lives in Boston and Squaw Island, Massachusetts.

PAMELA KELLEY BURKLEY

Pam died on November 20, 2020, at age sixty-five. Before her death, she worked as an activist for the differently abled. She spent her last months in a Cape Cod nursing home during the COVID pandemic, suffering from loneliness and depression. She developed a bedsore so painful that she couldn't use her wheelchair — a result, her family believes, of shoddy care. Pam's sister Karen told me that Joe Kennedy, and the Kennedy family, could have done far more to make Pam's life easier, and that her death was wholly preventable. Pam left behind a thirty-one-year-old daughter, Paige, and two grandsons. She worried that, in death as in life, she would be forgotten. "I don't think anybody still wonders where I am today," Pam said in 2019. "I don't think anybody remembers, really."

MARTHA MOXLEY

Martha Moxley was buried on November 4, 1975, in Greenwich, Connecticut. Five hundred people turned out for her funeral, but despite the attention her case attracted, it would take decades before Michael Skakel was arrested for her murder. He was convicted in 2002 and sentenced to twenty years to life. In 2013, after years of agitating, his cousin Robert F. Kennedy Jr. helped push for a retrial; Skakel was released on $1.2 million bond. His conviction was vacated in 2018. The prosecutor ultimately decided to drop all charges against him. In November 2021, I became the last person to see the state's evidence in Martha's case, which contained everything from her personal diary to the murder weapon. Under state law, the evidence was about to be sealed away forever. The prosecutor in the case, Susann Gill, told me she hopes the court will someday reverse that decision, given the historical importance of the case. Her greatest fear is that the evidence will be destroyed.

ROSE KENNEDY

Rose Kennedy, most historians believe, had no knowledge of her husband's plan to lobotomize their daughter. Yet it was only after Joe's death on November 18, 1969, that Rose visited Rosemary, who had been hidden away at a facility in Wisconsin. Rose Fitzgerald Kennedy outlived three of her nine children and died from pneumonia on January 22, 1995, aged 104.

ROSEMARY KENNEDY

Rosemary Kennedy spent the rest of her life post-lobotomy at St. Coletta's, a private Catholic facility in Jefferson, Wisconsin. She lived in a small, one-story cottage and was attended to by nuns and lay nurses. After Joe's death, Ted Kennedy, Eunice Kennedy, and Rosie's nephew Tim Shriver became the closest to Rosie, flying her to Kennedy homes and playing with her in their pools.

On what would be her final birthday, the nuns threw Rosemary a party; on her cake was a drawing of her as a winged angel, a child, held in two female hands. The curlicued icing above read, "God Bless Rosie on Her Happy 86th Birthday!" When she was admitted to the hospital for the last time in January 2005, all of her surviving siblings dropped everything to fly to her bedside; against all odds, Rosie stayed alive until the last one got there.

Rosemary Kennedy was buried near to her mother and father in Brookline, Massachusetts. Seventeen years after her death, the cottage in Wisconsin was closed, with no plaque or memorial to Rosemary Kennedy or her life there. The indoor pool that Rose and Joe Kennedy installed so that Rosie could stay fit and do her laps—even though she could no longer swim—remains the only sign of her existence.

JACQUELINE BOUVIER KENNEDY ONASSIS

Jacqueline Bouvier Kennedy Onassis died on May 19, 1994, after a brief yet brutal battle with lymphoma. She was sixty-four years old. As per her wishes, her wake was held in her beloved apartment at 1040 Fifth Avenue, her body in a closed coffin. This was her last masterstroke of image control, preventing anyone from getting a shot of the dignified Jackie O taken out in a body bag: Overall Art Director of the Twentieth Century. A relief of her face in profile greets travelers in Grand Central Terminal's Jacqueline Kennedy Onassis Foyer, where footage of her press conference, urging its preservation, plays on a loop. Central Park's main reservoir, where she jogged often, is also named in her honor.

Despite her enormous wealth, fame, and privilege, Jackie Onassis was mourned by the nation, but most especially by New Yorkers, who saw her as one of them. Thousands lined the streets as her coffin made its way along Park Avenue to the Church of St. Ignatius of Loyola, where her funeral mass was held. Among the 1,000 mourners were Lady Bird Johnson, who had succeeded her in the White House, and then-First Lady Hillary Rodham Clinton. Jackie's longtime companion Maurice

Tempelsman read from one of her favorite poems, Constantine P. Cavafy's "Ithaka," based on Odysseus's years-long journey to make his way back home. Jackie no doubt related to the poem's philosophy of mortality, Ithaka the final destination for us all:

> Keep Ithaka always in your mind.
> Arriving there is what you are destined for.
> But do not hurry the journey at all.

After the hour-long funeral service, Jackie's casket was flown to DC, where thousands more, rich and poor, lined the route to Arlington National Cemetery. Three days before, on May 20, then-president Clinton eulogized her from the White House Rose Garden—the garden she designed with her great friend Bunny Mellon. "More than any other woman of her time," Clinton said, "she captivated our nation and the world with her intelligence, her elegance, and her grace. Even in the face of impossible tragedy, she carried the grief of her family and our entire nation with a calm power that reassured the rest of us." Church bells tolled sixty-four times, marking the age at which she died. Then she was buried next to Jack and her babies, the Eternal Flame she lit now burning, too, for her—Jackie belonging, as each of the girls and women of this book, to all the world.

ACKNOWLEDGMENTS

S o many people contributed to this book — and as with the best stories, more than a few asked not to be named. You know who you are, and each of you have my enduring respect and gratitude.

Thanks to the brilliant Vanessa Mobley, who acquired this book and understood its importance as both reconsidered history and a reflection of women circa now.

Alexander Littlefield, my incredible editor, brought incisiveness, wit, sophistication, and a mutual love of Keith Richards, whose framed portrait looked back at me in more than one meeting. I'd like to think there's a little rock 'n' roll spirit in a book like this, and there's no better twentieth-century godfather than that.

Thanks to Morgan Wu, who not only addressed every aspect of editing and production but brought a younger generational eye to these pages. Her input was invaluable.

And huge appreciation to Katharine Myers, Michael Noon, Danielle Finnegan, Marieska Luzada, Lucy Kim, and everyone at Little, Brown.

Deep thanks to Joel Simons, my acquiring editor at HarperCollins UK, for seeing the reach of these women beyond American shores.

To my longtime agent Nicole Tourtelot, who never doubts that the next idea is a good one. She is wise, fun, strategic, and exactly the person you want on your side of the table. Deep thanks as well to Chris Parris-Lamb, who gracefully stepped in while Nicole was on maternity leave, and to everyone at The Gernert Company.

To Steve Lynch, editor in chief at the *New York Post,* who emailed me long ago with two words: "Kennedy book!" And to Isabel Vincent and

ACKNOWLEDGMENTS

Melissa Klein, the fearsome investigative team who broke the story of RFK Jr.'s sex diaries and Mary Richardson Kennedy's torment way back in 2013.

Melanie Locay eased my way into the Center for Research in the Humanities at the New York Public Library, where so much of my research was conducted and where I found that rare image of Jackie on the cover of *Ms.* magazine. To have a study room at the majestic main branch of the NYPL, during a pandemic no less, was to feel all the romance and excitement of history, books, and ideas.

Profound thanks to my researcher Julia Kott, who found articles and periodicals I thought impossible to find, took some of her own vacation time to plumb the Library of Congress, then edited photos for this book with speed and a rare attention to detail. I doubt I would have made my deadlines without her.

Thanks to Andy Young for fact-checking with verve and bonhomie, and to Jamie Johnson for transcribing countless interviews briskly and with discretion.

Thanks to Dr. Sheenah Hankin, Peter Bienstock, Colleen Breeckner, Karen Kelley, Georgetta Nelson Potoski, William Nelson, William C. Kashatus, Timothy Dumas, Donna Potter at the now-closed Rosemary Kennedy residence at St. Coletta's, Dorothy Moxley, Susann Gill, Jennifer Allen, Bob Drake, John Manchester, and Heyden White.

To my phenomenal editors at the *Daily Mail,* who have been incredibly supportive of this project: editor in chief Gerard Greaves, the ne plus ultra of electrifying journalism, Matt London, and Henry Jones.

Susannah Cahalan, as was the case with my last book, gave inspired, meticulous, and challenging edits while pregnant and writing her own nonfiction book—except this time with four-year-old twins. She really needs to stop showing off. And thanks to her incredible husband, Stephen Grywalski, for loaning her out and for offering support amid unforeseen roadblocks.

Abbott Kahler and Ada Calhoun were also first readers. Their generosity is matched only by their formidable talents and intellect. Both also gave edits while writing their own books and making their general overachieving look easy.

ACKNOWLEDGMENTS

My sister-in-law Laura DeMattia, who I'm lucky to rely on as my universal reader, generously looked at an early draft. She sees the worst of humanity in her own work but never stops believing in the best of it, too. Her initial reaction told me I was on the right track.

Thanks as well to Sophie Knight, who has helped this book in innumerable ways. It's rare to work with someone who makes you look, sound, and be better and not resent them an iota for it, but such is Sophie's gift.

To Bill Callahan, a rock.

A little origin story: My dad loved the Kennedys, JFK and his modernism especially, and imparted that fascination to me. My mother was much more cynical about the Kennedys and loathed their hypocrisies. This book is, in many ways, an inevitable reckoning with both points of view, though—as with many adolescent girls—I never foresaw siding with my mom.

I've written critically about the Kennedys for years; following one typically scathing column, an aunt said to me, "I can't believe your father still talks to you after what you write about the Kennedys." It was funny and true. But he loved my contrarianism, and before he died told me that he couldn't wait to read this book.

My mother was, I think, something of a Joan Kennedy: Beautiful, charismatic, born a little too early, and not quite sure what the women's movement had to offer her. She poured her creative energy into her children, never quite sure she should, or could, go back to her working world of Wall Street. I think of Jackie's words to Gloria Steinem about what women should be expected to do with themselves after raising children—and how generations of women were never encouraged to ask themselves that question, promised total fulfillment in wifedom and motherhood.

The idea that women should work is, if you think about it, still relatively new. Women have come a long way, but we still have a long way to go. While reporting and writing this book, I thought often of the world my beloved goddaughters, Daniela and Genevieve, will walk into—a better and safer one, I hope, that allows them every freedom.

My last and equally heartfelt thanks to my readers, who I never take for granted and who allow me to do what I love: Carry on the tradition of pugnacious Irish people fighting it out in print. Long may we writers and readers cause trouble.

The Kennedy Family Tree

Joseph Patrick Kennedy, Sr. (1888–1969) and **Rose Elizabeth Fitzgerald (1890–1995)**

Children:

- **Joseph Patrick Kennedy, Jr. (1915–1944)**

- **John Fitzgerald Kennedy (1917–1963)** [MARRIED] **Jacqueline Lee Bouvier (1929–1994)**
  - Marilyn Monroe (1926–1962)
  - Diana de Vegh (1938–)
  - Mimi Beardsley (1943–)
  - [CHILDREN]
    - Caroline Bouvier Kennedy (1957–)
    - John Fitzgerald Kennedy, Jr. (1960–1999) [MARRIED] **Carolyn Bessette-Kennedy (1966–1999)**
    - Patrick Bouvier Kennedy (1963)

- **Rosemary Kennedy (1918–2005)**

- **Kathleen Agnes Kennedy (1920–1948)** [MARRIED] William Cavendish, Marquess of Hartington (1917–1944)

- Eunice Mary Kennedy (1921–2009) [MARRIED] Robert Sargent Shriver, Jr. (1915–2011)
  - [CHILDREN]
    - Robert Sargent Shriver III (1954–)
    - Maria Owings Shriver (1955–)
    - Timothy Perry Shriver (1959–)
    - Mark Kennedy Shriver (1964–)
    - Anthony Paul Kennedy Shriver (1965–)

- Patricia Helen Kennedy (1924–2006) [MARRIED] Peter Lawford (1923–1984)
  - [CHILDREN]
    - Christopher Kennedy Lawford (1955–2018)
    - Sydney Maleia Lawford (1956–)
    - Victoria Francis Lawford (1958–)
    - Robin Elizabeth Lawford (1961–)

- Robert Francis Kennedy (1925–1968) [MARRIED] Ethel Skakel (1928–) — [Also Connected To Marilyn Monroe and Jackie Kennedy]
  - [CHILDREN]
    - Kathleen Hartington Kennedy (1951–)
    - Joseph Patrick Kennedy II (1952–)
    - Robert Francis Kennedy, Jr (1954–) [MARRIED] **Mary Kathleen Richardson (1959–2012)**; **Martha Elizabeth Moxley (1960–1975)**; **Pamela Kelley Burkley (1955–2020)**
    - David Anthony Kennedy (1955–1984)
    - Mary Courtney Kennedy (1956–)
    - Michael LeMoyne Kennedy (1958–1997) — **The Babysitter (1978–)**
    - Mary Kerry Kennedy (1959–)
    - Christopher George Kennedy (1963–)
    - Matthew Maxwell Taylor Kennedy (1965–)
    - Douglas Harriman Kennedy (1967–)
    - Rory Elizabeth Katherine Kennedy (1968–)

- Jean Ann Kennedy (1928–2020) [MARRIED] Stephen Edward Smith (1927–1990)
  - [CHILDREN]
    - Stephen Edward Smith, Jr. (1957–)
    - William Kennedy Smith (1960–) — **Patricia Bowman (1961–)**
    - Amanda Mary Smith (1967–)
    - Kym Maria Smith (1972–)

- Edward Moore "Ted" Kennedy (1932–2009) [MARRIED] **Virginia Joan Bennett (1936–)**; Victoria Reggie (1954–); **Mary Jo Kopechne (1940–1969)**
  - [CHILDREN]
    - Kara Anne Kennedy (1960–2011)
    - Edward Moore Kennedy, Jr. (1961–)
    - Patrick Joseph Kennedy II (1967–)

BIBLIOGRAPHY

SPECIAL COLLECTIONS

The Browne Popular Culture Library at Bowling Green State University

The Dominick Dunne Papers at the Briscoe Center for American History at the University of Texas at Austin:

   The Sutton Report

The Edward M. Kennedy Oral History Center at the University of Virginia's Miller Center:

   Oral history of Nance Lyons

J. Edgar Hoover's FBI files:

   Senator Edward "Ted" Kennedy, July 20, 1961

   Robert F. Kennedy, July 7, 1961

   Marilyn Monroe, Main File, August 16, 1955

   Marilyn Monroe, "Cross References," February 13, 1956

John F. Kennedy Presidential Library and Museum:

   Oral history of JFK's personal physician, Dr. Janet Travell

   Oral history of Jackie's mother, Janet Lee Auchincloss

   Oral history of White House reporter Laura Berquist Knebel

   Personal papers of Theodore H. White

The Women's Magazine Archive at the Center for Research in the Humanities at the New York Public Library

DRAFTS

Theodore White's original handwritten notes of November 29, 1963, interview with Jacqueline Kennedy, taken in her presence and including the question, "What does a woman think?"

Jacqueline Kennedy's line edits of what she titled, in her own handwriting, the "First Draft of 'Camelot.'"

Original copy of White's typed transcript of his interview with JBK, "delivered to Mrs. Kennedy," dated December 19 and sent with a typewritten letter from White addressed to "Dearest Jacquie," dated April 27, 1964.

Michael Skakel with Richard Hoffman. "Dead Man Talking: A Kennedy Cousin Comes Clean."

TESTIMONY

Mrs. John F. Kennedy to the Warren Commission, June 5, 1964.

COURT DOCUMENTS

State v. Michael Skakel Sentencing Hearing, August 28 and 29, 2002.

PERIODICALS AND NEWSPAPERS

Anonymous. "The Agony, Ecstasy & Nudity of Jacqueline Kennedy Onassis." Hustler, *August 1975.*

Anonymous. "Jackie's Marriage: From Camelot to Elysium (Via Olympic Airways)." Time, *October 25, 1968.*

Anonymous. "Princess Carolyn: Bessette Is Shaping Up to Be the Perfect Bride for America's Would-Be Royal Family." W, *August 1996.*

Anonymous. "As JFK Jr.'s Magazine Stumbles... What Will He Think of Next?" Spy, *March 1998.*

Applebome, Peter. "Rancor Flaring as Funeral for a Kennedy Approaches." New York Times, *May 18, 2012.*

Barnard, Anne. "Robert F. Kennedy Jr. Says Wife Struggled with Depression." New York Times, *May 17, 2012.*

Barringer, Felicity, with Michael Wines. "The Accused in the Palm Beach Case: Quiet, Different, and Somewhat Aloof." New York Times, *May 11, 1991.*

Batelle, Phyllis; David, Lester; Wechsler, Joan. "Joan Kennedy: Life Without Ted." Ladies' Home Journal, *April 1981.*

Beamish, Rita. "Unsolved but Not Forgotten." Washington Post, *August 2, 1998.*

Bennetts, Leslie. "Two Wives Finding Rewards on the Campaign Trail: Joan Kennedy Uses Theme of Feminism to Win Supporters." New York Times, *February 24, 1980.*

Brower, Brock. "The Fateful Turn for Ted Kennedy: Grave Questions about His Midnight Car Accident." Life, *August 1, 1969.*

Burleigh, Nina. "RFK Jr. Was a Compulsive Womanizer and Yes, We Should Care." New Republic, *August 1, 2023.*

Butterfield, Fox, with Mary B. W. Tabor. "Woman in Florida Rape Inquiry Fought Adversity and Sought Acceptance." New York Times, *April 17, 1991.*

Callaway, Libby. "Carolyn's Terrible Premonition—She Told Saks Girl She Dreaded Flying That Night." New York Post, July 22, 1999.

Cawley, Janet. "Women Tell Similar Tales of Attacks." Chicago Tribune, July 24, 1991.

Collins, Nancy. "New Questions Arise about Mary Richardson Kennedy's Suicide." Daily Beast, July 17, 2017.

CONFIDENTIAL Report: Jackie Onassis special edition, 1975.

Daily Mail Reporter: "Pictured: Mary Kennedy's New Grave after Husband RFK Jr. Moved Her Body 700 Feet 'So It Would Be Less Crowded.'" Daily Mail, July 15, 2012.

De Vegh, Diana. "JFK and the Radcliffe Girl: For the First Time Ever, One of the Former President's Lovers Tells Her Story." Air Mail, August 28, 2021.

Diliberto, Gioia. "On the Job with Jackie: The World's Most Famous Working Woman Gets Her Own Coffee and Stands in Line at the Copier, but—Believe It—When She Speaks, Authors Listen." People, June 18, 1984.

Dunne, Dominick. "Triumph by Jury." Vanity Fair, August 2002.

Edgington, Harry J. "Scuba Diver Will Tell Kennedy Inquest: 'If I Had Been Called Soon after the Accident, She Could Have Been Saved.'" National Enquirer, October 12, 1969.

Flanagan, Caitlin. "Jackie and the Girls: Mrs. Kennedy's JFK Problem—and Ours." The Atlantic, July 2012.

Henry, Diane. "Jackie Onassis Fights for Cause: She Joins in Forming Group to Rescue the Grand Central." New York Times, January 31, 1975.

Hoffman, Betty Hannah. "Joan Kennedy's Story: What She Wants for Herself—and Ted." Ladies' Home Journal, July 1970.

Hoy, Michael J., and Ken Potter. "Joan Kennedy Admits: I've Been an Alcoholic for Years." National Enquirer, April 13, 1976.

Jennes, Gail. "Joan Kennedy: She's Proud of Drying Out and Living Alone, but if Ted Ran for President She'd Be at His Side." People, August 7, 1978.

"Joseph Kennedy Is Found Guilty of Negligence in Road Mishap." New York Times, August 21, 1973.

Kelly, Michael. "Ted Kennedy on the Rocks." GQ, February 1, 1990.

Kennedy, Robert F. Jr. "A Miscarriage of Justice." Atlantic Monthly, January/February 2003.

Klemesrud, Judy. "The Reaction Here Is Anger, Shock, and Dismay: Few View Mrs. Kennedy's Plans as Just Her Own Business." New York Times, October 19, 1968.

Kopechne, Gwen, as told to Suzanne James. "The Truth about Mary Jo." McCall's, September 1970.

Kurtz, Howard. *"Fury at N.Y. Times Over Rape Policy."* Washington Post, *April 20, 1991.*

Kwitny, Jonathan. *"Public Interest, Public Naming: The Palm Beach Case Goes Beyond Privacy."* New York Times, *May 8, 1991.*

Lawrenson, Helen. *"Jackie at 50."* Washington Post Weekend Magazine, *July 28, 1979.*

Leamer, Laurence. *"The Last Days of Mary Kennedy."* Newsweek, *June 11, 2012.*

Lessard, Suzannah. *"Kennedy's Woman Problem, Women's Kennedy Problem: The Intelligent Woman's Guide to the Touchiest Issue of the 1980 Campaign."* Washington Monthly, *December 1979.*

Levine, Jon. *"RFK Jr. Says COVID May Have Been 'Ethnically Targeted' to Spare Jews."* New York Post, *July 15, 2023.*

MacPherson, Myra. *"Joan Kennedy: No Cracks in Family Image."* Washington Post, Times Herald, *November 1, 1970.*

Marchant, Robert. *"Mary Kennedy's Death Still Puzzles Friends."* Westchester County Journal News, *May 13, 2013.*

Maslin, Janet. *"Sure, Mr. President, if You Really Want Me To."* New York Times, *February 8, 2012.*

McCrindell, David. *"How Jackie Went From . . . Mourner to Swinger."* National Enquirer, *May 14, 1967.*

McLendon, Winzola. *"Sen. Kennedy on Mediterranean Trip Unaware His Wife Has Lost Baby."* Washington Post and Times Herald, *August 25, 1956.*

Mead, Rebecca. *"Meet the Mrs.: What Does John Kennedy Jr. See in Carolyn Bessette?"* New York, *October 7, 1996.*

O'Brien, Edna. *"Jacqueline Kennedy Onassis: A Mystery Even to Herself."* UK Independent, *May 21, 1994.*

Onassis, Jacqueline Kennedy. *"Being Present."* New Yorker, *January 13, 1975.*

Oppenheimer, Jerry. *"How Serial Cheater Bobby Kennedy Jr. 'Exposed Himself Around the House, Demanded a Ménage à Trois with Tragic Wife Mary — and Told Her Things Would Be Easier if She Killed Herself after He Went Public with Cheryl Hines.'"* Daily Mail, *September 15, 2015.*

Roshan, Maer, ed. *"Prince of the City: The New York Life of John Kennedy Jr. in the Words of Some Who Knew Him."* New York, *August 2, 1999.*

Shaw, David. *"New York Times' Coverage of Florida Rape Case Debated: Ethics: First, the Paper Printed an Inflammatory Profile of the Alleged Victim — Including Her Name. Then It Ran a More Flattering Story about the Accused Rapist, William Kennedy Smith."* Los Angeles Times, *August 18, 1991.*

Sheehan, Susan. *"The Happy Jackie, The Sad Jackie, The Bad Jackie, The Good Jackie."* New York Times Magazine, *May 31, 1970.*

Smith, Liz. *"Jackie Onassis: Her Life with an Ailing Ari."* People, *October 14, 1974.*

———. *"Joan Kennedy: It Wasn't a Nervous Breakdown; She Only Needed a Rest."* People, *June 24, 1974.*

Steinem, Gloria. *"Jacqueline Kennedy Onassis Talks about Working."* Ms. *magazine,* March 1979.

———. *"RFK's Diary: Stars, Yachts and Falcons."* New York Post, *September 15, 2013.*

Vincent, Isabel, and Melissa Klein. *"RFK's Sex Diary: His Secret Journal of Affairs."* New York Post, *September 8, 2013.*

BROADCASTS

CBS Reports: Teddy with CBS News Correspondent Roger Mudd. November 4, 1979, CBS.

I Am JFK Jr., *documentary, 2017.*

JFK Jr. and Carolyn's Wedding: The Lost Tapes, *documentary, 2019.*

Jacqueline Kennedy Thanks the Nation. January 14, 1964. www.NBCUniversalArchives .com.

JFK's Intern: Always Mr. President. Interview with Meredith Vieira, NBC News, January 3, 2013.

"The Lobotomist." American Experience, Season 20. *PBS, January 21, 2008.*

A Tour of the White House with Mrs. John F. Kennedy, February 14, 1962, CBS and NBC.

PrimeTime Live: *Diane Sawyer Interviews Patricia Bowman. ABC, December 19, 1991.*

SPECIAL REPORTS

The Warren Commission Report: President's Commission on the Assassination of President Kennedy. September 24, 1964.

The National Transportation and Safety Board Accident Report NYC99MA178, on John F. Kennedy Jr.'s fatal plane crash, released to Congress and the public on July 6, 2000.

BOOKS

Alford, Mimi. Once Upon a Secret: My Affair with John F. Kennedy and Its Aftermath. *New York: Random House, 2012.*

———. The Good Son: JFK Jr. and the Mother He Loved. *New York: Gallery Books, 2014.*

Anderson, Christopher. Jackie after Jack: Portrait of the Lady. *New York: William Morrow & Co., 1998.*

Banner, Lois. Marilyn: The Passion and the Paradox. *New York: Bloomsbury USA, 2012.*

Barlow, John Perry, with Robert Greenfield. Mother American Night: My Life in Crazy Times. *New York: Crown Archetype, 2018.*

Bergin, Michael. The Other Man, A Love Story: John F. Kennedy Jr., Carolyn Bessette, & Me. *New York: William Morrow, 2004.*

Berman, Matt. JFK Jr., George, & Me: A Memoir. *New York: Gallery Books, 2014.*

Bradford, Sarah. America's Queen: The Life of Jacqueline Kennedy Onassis. *New York: Viking, 2000.*

Bryant, Traphes, with Frances Spatz Leighton. Dog Days at the White House: The Outrageous Memoirs of the Presidential Kennel Keeper. *New York: Macmillan, 1975.*

Burke, Richard E., with William and Marilyn Hoffer. The Senator: My Ten Years with Ted Kennedy. *New York: St. Martin's Press, 1992.*

Byrne, Paula. Kick: The True Story of JFK's Sister and the Heir to Chatsworth. *New York: Harper, 2016.*

Capote, Truman. Answered Prayers. *London: Hamish Hamilton, 1986.*

Casillo, Charles. Marilyn Monroe: The Private Life of a Public Icon. *New York: St. Martin's Press, 2018.*

Chellis, Marcia. Living with the Kennedys: The Joan Kennedy Story. *New York: Simon & Schuster, 1985.*

Clarke, Gerald. Capote: A Biography. *Fresno, CA: Linden Publishing, 1988.*

Collier, Peter, and David Horowitz. The Kennedys: An American Drama. *New York: Encounter, 1984.*

Dallek, Robert. An Unfinished Life: John F. Kennedy, 1917–1963. *New York: Little, Brown and Company, 2003.*

Damore, Leo. Senatorial Privilege: The Chappaquiddick Cover-Up. *New York: Regnery Gateway, 1988.*

David, Lester. Joan: The Reluctant Kennedy. *New York: Funk & Wagnalls, 1974.*

DuBois, Diana. In Her Sister's Shadow: An Intimate Biography of Lee Radziwill. *New York: Little, Brown and Company, 1995.*

Dumas, Timothy. Greentown: Murder and Mystery in Greenwich, America's Wealthiest Community. *New York: Arcade, 1998.*

Evans, Peter. Nemesis: Aristotle Onassis, Jackie O, and the Love Triangle that Brought Down the Kennedys. *New York: William Morrow, 2004.*

Farrell, John A. Ted Kennedy: A Life. *New York: Penguin Press, 2022.*

Gallagher, Mary Barelli. My Life with Jacqueline Kennedy. *New York: David McKay Company, 1969.*

Gibson, Barbara, and Ted Schwarz. Rose Kennedy and Her Family: The Best and Worst of Their Life and Times. *New York: Birch Lane Press, 1995.*

Gillon, Steven M. America's Reluctant Prince: The Life of John F. Kennedy Jr. *New York: Dutton, 2019.*

Goodwin, Doris Kearns. The Fitzgeralds and the Kennedys: An American Saga. *New York: Simon & Schuster, 1987.*

Haag, Christina. Come to the Edge. *New York: Random House, 2012.*

Hamilton, Nigel. JFK: Reckless Youth. *New York: Random House, 1992.*

Hersh, Seymour. The Dark Side of Camelot. *New York: Little, Brown and Company, 1997.*

Heymann, David C. A Woman Named Jackie: An Intimate Biography of Jacqueline Bouvier Kennedy Onassis. *Englewood, NJ: Lyle Stuart, 1989.*

———. American Legacy: The Story of John and Caroline Kennedy. *New York: Atria, 2007.*

———. Bobby and Jackie: A Love Story. *New York: Atria Books, 2009.*

Hill, Clint, with Lisa McCubbin. Mrs. Kennedy and Me. *New York: Gallery Books, 2012.*

Hogan, Michael J. The Afterlife of John Fitzgerald Kennedy: A Biography. *Cambridge, UK: Cambridge University Press, 2017.*

Jacobs, George, and William Stadiem. Mr. S: My Life with Frank Sinatra. *New York: It Books/HarperCollins, 2003.*

Kashatus, William C. Before Chappaquiddick: The Untold Story of Mary Jo Kopechne & the Kennedy Brothers. *Virginia: Potomac Books, 2020.*

Kashner, Sam, and Nancy Schoenberger. The Fabulous Bouvier Sisters: The Tragic and Glamorous Lives of Jackie and Lee. *New York: Harper, 2018.*

Kelley, Kitty. Jackie Oh! *New York: Ballantine, 1979.*

Kennedy, Edward M. True Compass: A Memoir. *New York: Twelve, 2009.*

Kennedy, Patrick J., and Stephen Fried. A Common Struggle: A Personal Journey through the Past and Future of Mental Illness and Addiction. *New York: Blue Rider Press, 2015.*

Kennedy, Rose Fitzgerald. Times to Remember. *New York: Doubleday, 1974.*

Kennedy, Sheila Rauch. Shattered Faith: A Woman's Struggle to Stop the Catholic Church from Annulling Her Marriage. *New York: Pantheon, 1997.*

Kessler, Ronald. The Sins of the Father: Joseph P. Kennedy and the Dynasty He Founded. *New York: Warner Books, 1996.*

Klein, Edward. Farewell, Jackie: A Portrait of Her Final Days. *New York: Viking, 2004.*

———. Just Jackie: The Private Years. *New York: Ballantine, 1998.*

———. The Kennedy Curse: Why Tragedy Has Haunted America's First Family for 150 Years. *New York: St. Martin's Press, 2003.*

Koehler-Pentacoff, Elizabeth. The Missing Kennedy: Rosemary Kennedy and the Secret Bonds of Four Women. *Baltimore, MD: Bancroft Press, 2016.*

Kuhn, William. Reading Jackie: Her Autobiography in Books. *New York: Nan A. Talese, 2010.*

Larson, Kate Clifford. Rosemary: The Hidden Kennedy Daughter. *New York: Houghton Mifflin Harcourt, 2015.*

Lawford, Christopher Kennedy. Symptoms of Withdrawal: A Memoir of Snapshots and Redemption. *New York: William Morrow, 2005.*

Lawrence, Greg. Jackie as Editor: The Literary Life of Jacqueline Kennedy Onassis. *New York: Thomas Dunne, 2011.*

Leamer, Laurence. The Kennedy Women: The Saga of an American Family. *New York: Ballantine, 1994.*

Leaming, Barbara. Jacqueline Bouvier Kennedy Onassis: The Untold Story. *New York: Thomas Dunne Books, 2014.*

————. Kick Kennedy: The Charmed Life and Tragic Death of the Favorite Kennedy Daughter. *New York: Thomas Dunne Books, 2016.*

Leland, Leslie H., and J. B Shaffer. Left to Die. *New York: Strategic Book Publishing, 2009.*

Levitt, Leonard. Conviction: Solving the Moxley Murder: A Reporter and a Detective's Twenty-Year Search for Justice. *New York: Regan Books, 2004.*

Littell, Robert T. The Men We Became: My Friendship with John F. Kennedy Jr. *New York: St. Martin's Press, 2004.*

Maier, Thomas. The Kennedys: America's Emerald Kings. *New York: Basic Books, 2003.*

Manchester, William. Controversy: And Other Essays in Journalism, 1950–1975. *New York: Little, Brown and Company, 1976.*

————. The Death of a President, November 1963. *New York: Harper & Row, 1967.*

McTaggart, Lynne. Kathleen Kennedy: Her Life and Times. *New York: Doubleday, 1983.*

Miller, Arthur. After the Fall. *New York: Bloomsbury, 1964.*

Monroe, Marilyn, with Ben Hecht. My Story. *Lanham, MD: Taylor Trade Publishing, September 29, 2006.*

Monroe, Marilyn, and Bernard Comment. Fragments: Poems, Intimate Notes, Letters. *New York: Farrar, Straus and Giroux, 2012.*

Noonan, William Sylvester, with Robert Huber. Forever Young: My Friendship with John F. Kennedy Jr. *New York: Viking, 2006.*

Oppenheimer, Jerry. RFK Jr.: Robert F. Kennedy Jr. and the Dark Side of the Dream. *New York: St. Martin's Press, 2015.*

BIBLIOGRAPHY

Potoski, Georgetta, and William Nelson. Our Mary Jo. *Self-published, Kindle edition,* 2017.

Radziwill, Carole. What Remains: A Memoir of Fate, Friendship, & Love. *New York: Scribner, 2007.*

Reeves, Thomas C. A Question of Character: A Life of John F. Kennedy. *New York: Free Press, 1992.*

Simon, Carly. Touched by the Sun: My Friendship with Jackie. *New York: Farrar, Straus and Giroux, 2019.*

Smith, Amanda. Hostage to Fortune: The Letters of Joseph P. Kennedy. *New York: Viking, 2001.*

Smith, Sally Bedell. Grace and Power: The Private World of the Kennedy White House. *New York: Random House, 2004.*

Spada, James. Peter Lawford: The Man Who Kept the Secrets. *New York: Bantam, 1991.*

Stern, Bert, and Marilyn Monroe. The Last Sitting. *New York: William Morrow, 1982.*

Summers, Anthony. Goddess: The Secret Lives of Marilyn Monroe. *London and New York: Macmillan, 1985.*

Taraborrelli, J. Randy. Jackie, Ethel, Joan: The Women of Camelot. *New York: Warner Books, 2000.*

————. Jackie, Janet & Lee: The Secret Lives of Janet Auchincloss and Her Daughters Jacqueline Kennedy Onassis and Lee Radziwill. *New York: St. Martin's Press, 2018.*

————. Jackie: Public, Private, Secret. *New York: St. Martin's Press, 2023.*

————. Madonna: An Intimate Biography. *New York: Simon & Schuster, 2001.*

Tedrow, Richard L., and Thomas L. Death at Chappaquiddick. *Ottawa, IL: Green Hill, 1976.*

Terenzio, Rosemarie. Fairytale Interrupted: A Memoir of Life, Love, and Loss. *New York: Gallery Books, January 24, 2012.*

Thayer, Mary Van Rensselaer. Jacqueline Kennedy: The White House Years. *New York: Little, Brown and Company, 1967.*

Wolfe, Donald H. The Last Days of Marilyn Monroe. *New York: William Morrow, 1998.*

NOTES

This book is the product of years of reporting on the Kennedy dynasty and the women who had the misfortune of entering its orbit. In the course of that investigative journey, the Vartan Gregorian Center for Research in the Humanities at the New York Public Library was an invaluable resource for me. The Library of Congress in Washington, DC, and the Browne Popular Culture Library at Bowling Green State University were also great resources for mass-media news coverage. As, of course, were broadcasts made by Jacqueline Kennedy and Ted Kennedy, most especially, plus news coverage of various Kennedy trials.

In addition to these overarching sources, I used a trove of books, print and broadcast news reports, social media posts, and original interviews to substantiate the stories of these thirteen women. What follows are the key sources for each chapter that are not already cited in the body text of the book. A complete bibliography can be found online at: maureencallahan.net.

PART ONE: ICONS

CAROLYN BESSETTE

Much of Carolyn Bessette's life before meeting John F. Kennedy Jr. and her career at Calvin Klein has never been reported; after her death, her close friends almost unanimously erected a cone of silence. As I began working on this book in early 2021, a few of those friends told me that they felt enough time had passed and that it was worth setting the record straight. Most prefer to remain anonymous. Rhona Nack, who worked with JFK Jr. during his time at the Manhattan DA's Office from 1989 to 1993, provided information as to his work there. Other sources close to Carolyn spoke on the condition of anonymity.

America's Reluctant Prince, by JFK Jr. friend and colleague Steven Gillon, was a font of information about JFK Jr.'s approach to his magazine and the ever-evolving state of his marriage. The death of his then-girlfriend Daryl Hannah's dog while in John's care is reported in Gillon's book and was also confirmed to me by someone close to John, who prefers to remain anonymous. The story of John's dog Sam being put down after biting people, including John's employee Susanna Howe, was relayed by Howe in an oral history for *New York* magazine's August 2, 1999, edition.

Details about Carolyn's reinvention and John's attitudes about Kennedy lawlessness in Massachusetts come from C. David Heymann's *American Legacy: The Story of John and Caroline Kennedy.* Carolyn's sphinxlike nature, her self-invention, and one instance in which she violently attacked her on-off boyfriend Michael Bergin is detailed in the latter's memoir, *The Other Man: A Love Story: John F. Kennedy Jr., Carolyn Bessette, and Me.*

The documentaries *I Am JFK Jr.* and *JFK Jr. and Carolyn's Wedding: The Lost Tapes* informed this chapter, as did Christina Haag's memoir, *Come to the Edge,* in which she recounts her yearslong relationship with John, the multiple times he put their lives in danger, his reckless streak that bordered on a death wish, and his mother's attempts to get John to control his worst impulses.

JACKIE BOUVIER KENNEDY

Jackie Kennedy spoke to close relatives and friends about JFK's assassination and gave two five-hour-long interviews to journalist William Manchester for his book *The Death of a President,* commissioned by her. Jackie subsequently suffered source remorse and roped Bobby Kennedy into her public fight to cancel the book, which drove Manchester to a nervous breakdown and damaged her popularity. After a yearslong battle and an out-of-court settlement, the book was published in 1967, with several cuts made to mollify Jackie—in particular, Manchester's son John told me, Jackie's disclosure that she and the president had made love the night before he was killed. That detail was removed from the final book, and the audio of her interviews with Manchester—replete with the ambient sounds of cigarettes being lit and ice cubes clinking in constant cocktails—remains sealed until 2067.

Theodore White's handwritten notes from his interview with Jackie, which she commissioned one week after Jack's assassination, are archived at the John F. Kennedy Presidential Library and Museum, as are White's interview questions and his first draft of the *Life* magazine cover story, which includes Jackie's handwritten edits, strikethroughs, and additions, most notably her "Camelot" fabrication. Other aspects of the assassination and its aftermath come from *Mrs. Kennedy and Me,* the 2012 memoir written by Clint Hill, the Secret Service agent who pushed Jackie back into the car that day and remained a favorite among her detail.

Her courtship with Jack Kennedy, her insecurities about her own looks and about Jack's obsession with Marilyn Monroe were drawn from several books, notably Kitty Kelley's *Jackie Oh!,* Edward Klein's *Just Jackie: Her Private Years,* Barbara Leaming's *Jacqueline Bouvier Kennedy Onassis: The Untold Story,* and Sally Bedell Smith's *Grace and Power: The Private World of the Kennedy White House.*

PART TWO: THE GIRLS, & PART ELEVEN: SURVIVORS

MIMI BEARDSLEY ALFORD AND DIANA DE VEGH

Mimi Alford documented her relationship with JFK in her memoir, *Once Upon a Secret*, and in numerous print and television interviews; that material forms the basis for her portions of these two chapters. She also appears, though not by name, in Robert Dallek's biography *An Unfinished Life: John F. Kennedy, 1917–1963*. She is also mentioned by former JFK staffer Barbara Gamarekian in her oral history for the John F. Kennedy Presidential Library and Museum dated June 10, 1964.

Diana de Vegh's first-person account for *Air Mail*, titled "JFK and the Radcliffe Girl," also informed much of her parts of these chapters, as did an interview I conducted with her for this book. De Vegh said recent events, notably the Harvey Weinstein verdict and our subsequent reexamination of what constitutes abuse, had caused her to revisit this most consequential relationship through an entirely new lens.

PART THREE: THE BOMBSHELL

MARILYN MONROE

Jack Kennedy's self-described "hunting expeditions" for women, Marilyn's first marriage, and Kennedy in-law Peter Lawford's role in arranging Jack's extramarital sexual encounters were sourced from *Peter Lawford: The Man Who Kept the Secrets* by James Spada.

Threats made to Marilyn Monroe, excerpts from conversations she had with her psychiatrist, Dr. Ralph Greenson, and her hospitalization during Jack's 1960 campaign for president were reported in *The Dark Side of Camelot* by Seymour Hersh. The love letter that Arthur Miller wrote to Monroe was sold through Heritage Auctions on September 29, 2015, and can be read on their website.

Monroe herself often kept a journal of her thoughts, dreams, and anxieties. Many of these entries, along with various correspondence with friends and confidantes, are contained in the book *Fragments: Poems, Intimate Notes, Letters* by Marilyn Monroe.

PART FOUR: THE LONELY GRAVES

MARY RICHARDSON KENNEDY

Mary's mindset during the most difficult parts of her marriage to, and separation from, Robert F. Kennedy Jr. was shared with me for this book by three key people in her life: her divorce lawyer, Peter Bienstock; her therapist, Sheenah Hankin; and her yoga instructor, Colleen Breeckner, who provided details of Mary running over the family dog and killing her, and Mary's estrangement from her children in the aftermath. Mary's stated fear that the Kennedys "could destroy me" was repeated to me by Bienstock.

Previously published portions of RFK Jr.'s sex diaries also informed this chapter. Specific conflicts involving his sexual demands of Mary, his romance with his current wife, Cheryl Hines, and Mary's claim that RFK Jr. told her she would be "better off dead" came from Jerry Oppenheimer's *RFK Jr.: Robert F. Kennedy Jr. and the Dark Side of the Dream*. Details of Mary's last months and RFK Jr.'s attempts to starve her out, with Mary begging other mothers for $20 at the school run to buy gas or food, were reported by Melissa Klein in the *New York Post* on July 1, 2012: "RFK Jr. cut off late wife's credit and stiffed lawyers: court papers."

Nancy Collins wrote a column for the *Daily Beast* in 2013 about Mary's suicide, asking the question: "Was Richardson mentally ill or tormented by her husband?" This followed interviews that RFK Jr. and his sister Kerry Kennedy gave to the *New York Times* claiming that Mary's alcoholism and "demons" drove her to kill herself, cited in the article "Robert F. Kennedy Says Wife Struggled with Depression," alternately headlined, "A Kennedy Is Remembered for Struggles, and Warmth," May 17, 2012. Included was the salient detail that RFK Jr. was living with his new girlfriend Hines in a house a few hundred yards from the one he had shared with Mary and their children.

In 2012, shortly after Mary's suicide, I was contacted by Patricia Lawford Stewart, Peter Lawford's fourth (and final) wife. In an interview published in the *New York Post*, she told me of her first meeting with RFK Jr. in 1976, when he would have been about twenty-two years old. He showed up at their house, having been kicked out by his mother, Ethel, and was wearing his late father's suit. Peter Lawford was in another room. As she recalled of her encounter with RFK Jr., "He said, 'I wish you weren't married to my uncle—I'd like to fuck you right here on the couch.'" Stewart was nineteen then, and says that when she told Peter, he said, "Nothing's changed."

RFK Jr.'s sealed divorce affidavit, all sixty pages, made its way into the hands of Kennedy historian Laurence Leamer, who wrote a cover story on Mary for *Newsweek* after her death. "Exclusive: The Last Days of Mary Kennedy," published on June 11, 2012, also included an interview with a Kennedy housekeeper who claimed to have found a drunken Mary passed out, face down in a plate of food. Leamer further reported that RFK Jr. had been granted temporary custody of his and Mary's children; that she had been stealing and hoarding items belonging to Bobby's daughter Kick; that Mary had been diagnosed with borderline personality disorder—a detail confirmed to me by Hankin—and that Mary's siblings had refuted the *Newsweek* article in its entirety, claiming it was full of "vindictive lies."

Mary's funeral was covered nationally, but the secret exhumation of her remains seven weeks later, and the illegal reburying of her casket alone and far away from the Kennedy family plot in Centerville, Massachusetts, was reported by Boston's ABC affiliate WCVB: "No permits issued when Mary Richardson Kennedy's body moved." According to that report, "An attorney for Richardson Kennedy's family told *Newsday* that they were not asked about the move and were completely blindsided by it."

NOTES

KATHLEEN "KICK" KENNEDY

One of the two "forgotten" Kennedy daughters, Kick has been the subject of the recent biographies *Kick Kennedy: The Charmed Life and Tragic Death of the Favorite Kennedy Daughter* by Barbara Leaming and *Kick: The True Story of JFK's Forgotten Sister and the Heir to Chatsworth* by Paula Byrne.

Letters from Kick to her parents and siblings, and patriarch Joe's letters to her, are found in *Hostage to Fortune: The Letters of Joseph P. Kennedy*, edited by his granddaughter Amanda Smith.

John White's recollections of Kick and his shock at what he called her uncritical mind and naïve attitudes toward sex come from his oral history for the John F. Kennedy Presidential Library and Museum. The emotionally incestuous bond among many of the Kennedy siblings, specifically Kick's covetous nature toward Jack and her jealousy of his then-girlfriend Inga Arvad, a rumored spy for Germany, is quoted in *JFK: Reckless Youth* by Nigel Hamilton.

Kick's letter describing how underwhelmed she was by the future Queen Elizabeth II comes from *Hostage to Fortune*. Parts of her life in England, her excommunication by her mother, Rose, and what Kick wore on the last day of her life were found in *The Fitzgeralds and the Kennedys* by Doris Kearns Goodwin.

The circumstances leading up to the avoidable plane crash that took Kick's life, and the lives of all aboard, as well as the condition of the bodies, comes from *Kathleen Kennedy: Her Life and Times* by Lynne McTaggart.

PART FIVE: TED'S BLONDES

MARY JO KOPECHNE

Mary Jo Kopechne's cousin Georgetta Potoski and Potoski's son William Nelson had me to their home in Pennsylvania, where they spoke for hours about Mary Jo. They are the co-authors of the self-published e-book *Our Mary Jo*, which was invaluable for me as I sought to understand her early life. Georgetta and Bill are the keepers of Mary Jo's flame, and their most fervent hope is that Mary Jo is never lost to history. They shared their time, memories, and a small box of Mary Jo's modest possessions: her handwritten notes from her college classes in Greek and Roman philosophy, etched in perfect blue penmanship; her coursework on ethics, demarcated by her as "1. Politics 2. Economics 3. Social sciences"; costume jewelry; a lacquered compact decorated with beads, pearls, and seashells.

Carol Teague Condon, who went to high school with Mary Jo and was in the same Catholic Youth Organization (CYO) group, shared her memories with me as well, as did fellow high school classmate Til Pleva. I also interviewed Owen Lopez, Mary Jo's boyfriend for two summers, as well as Mary Jo's biographer William C. Kashatus, author of *Before Chappaquiddick: The Untold Story of Mary Jo Kopechne and the Kennedy Brothers*.

An interview given by Mary Jo's mother, Gwen, to *McCall's* magazine for their September 1970 issue contradicts the Kennedy line that Mary Jo was obsessed with Bobby and Ted: "I am also tired of hearing the stories about Mary Jo's heading for a nervous breakdown after Robert Kennedy's death, and about her needing to feel that she was still part of the Kennedy family . . . [At twenty-eight years old,] Mary Jo was so self-assured and so happy."

Mary Jo's father, Joe Kopechne, spoke to the Women's News Service in July 1979, ten years after Mary Jo died, as Ted Kennedy was on the verge of announcing a run for president. "I'll never forgive him," Joe said of Ted. "I don't believe the truth has been told. I don't know the truth. None of us knows the truth."

Joe feared that younger voters had no idea who Mary Jo was or what Ted had done — and not done — at Chappaquiddick. "The younger people, yes, perhaps they've forgotten, but you know, it's the older people who go out and vote," he said. "There was just too much deception, too much double-talk and cover-up." Ten years on, their agony remained raw and fresh. "I sometimes dream about her," Joe said of his daughter, "and when I wake up in the morning, just for a minute or two, I forget she's dead. Then it hits you and the pain is as bad as it ever was."

Joe didn't seem to think Ted Kennedy had a chance of winning. "If Kennedy does run and he loses, it won't bother us very much," he said. "We lost our whole life."

The plot to blackmail the Boiler Room Girls into silence after Mary Jo's death was reported by Bob Woodward and Carl Bernstein in the *Washington Post* on August 1, 1973. There is no greater investigation of what happened the night Ted Kennedy crashed and left Mary Jo to die, as well as the coordinated effort by the Kennedy machine to conceal Ted's craven, criminal behavior, than the book *Senatorial Privilege: The Chappaquiddick Cover-Up* by Leo Damore — a copy of which sat prominently in Potoski and Nelson's dining room when I spoke with them.

Kennedy loyalist, JFK speechwriter, and JFK biographer Arthur Schlesinger Jr. is quoted as saying that the death of Mary Jo Kopechne, an event so often referred to simply as "Chappaquiddick," had made Ted more of a man and leader: "Iron had gone into Edward Kennedy's soul." This comes from the book *The Kennedys: An American Drama* by Peter Collier and David Horowitz.

The book *Left to Die* by Chappaquiddick grand jury foreman Leslie H. Leland and J. B. Shaffer was also a source, as was the oral history given by Boiler Room Girl Nance Lyons on May 9, 2008, at the John F. Kennedy Presidential Library and Museum. It is archived at the Edward M. Kennedy Institute at UVA's Miller Center of Public Affairs, and Lyons is particularly straightforward when describing what it was like to work for Ted Kennedy, both before and after Mary Jo's death: "I know he was not willing, pretty much, to communicate directly with me for a long time, not just because it was me, but with me, I felt, because I was a girl."

In an addendum to her oral history, Lyons wrote:

"I have never discussed the tragedy at Chappaquiddick. The events of that weekend were tragic. Mary Jo was my roommate. I knew her parents. Chappaquiddick changed my life. First, the women who had had significant responsibility in the national campaign for Bobby Kennedy were portrayed as 'girls' of no significance—even as 'party' girls. It was humiliating—but no one bothered to set the record straight. Then, for the next ten to twelve years on each anniversary, we were pursued by the press, subjected to hate mail and demeaning descriptions of our work and those veiled accusations about our moral rectitude.

"Even though I returned to work within ten feet of his office, [Ted Kennedy] never, never, never asked how I was doing; or said how sorry he was that I and the other women were subjected to such scrutiny. And I certainly didn't feel welcomed back by this staff. Still, he never mentioned Mary Jo to me. No call during each year's anniversary scrutiny. No thank-you for supporting him during these 'trying' times. To me this was unbelievable, and I have not forgiven him for that insensitivity. The women from Chappaquiddick suffered greatly both personally and professionally. Some lost jobs, some didn't get jobs, no judgeships in Massachusetts for [my sister and fellow Boiler Room Girl] Maryellen or me, etc. Frankly, I believe he set my departure up. He knew I wanted to leave. I was offered a job in New York through one of his associates. It took me a while to understand the ploy, but I did move on to New York.

"Many years later, Joey Gargan is quoted in a book accusing me of being the one who suggested that we come up with a story that someone else was driving the car. In fact, it was the women who derailed that brilliant idea."

JOAN BENNETT KENNEDY

Key sources for this chapter include the biographies *Joan—The Reluctant Kennedy* by Lester David; *Living with the Kennedys: The Joan Kennedy Story* by Marcia Chellis; *The Kennedy Women: The Saga of an American Family* by Laurence Leamer; and *Jackie, Ethel, Joan: The Women of Camelot* by J. Randy Taraborrelli. The latter contains the story of Ted dressing a female household staffer as Joan:

"'I remember the time that Ted had a dinner party while Joan was knocked out in the bedroom,'" recalled Barbara Gibson. "Ted dressed the children's nanny in Joan's chic clothing and had her act as hostess. The implication was obvious, especially given Ted's reputation. Ethel was outraged when she showed up, demanding to know, 'What the heck is that woman doing in Joan's clothes?' She wanted to see Joan."

Taraborrelli also reports that it wasn't just Joan's alcoholism affecting the marriage:

"Joan," he writes, "was becoming a lonely, desperate woman. The one thing she and Ted had always enjoyed together was a satisfying sex life... The more Ted drank, the less he was able to function. 'Joan once told me she missed more than just physical passion,'" he quotes a longtime friend. "'She longed for simple physical intimacy. She so wanted a man to be close to, to hold, to make her feel that she wasn't alone.'"

Joan was also the subject of numerous magazine and newspaper articles, profiles, and essays. Her abandonment by Ted early in their honeymoon was reported in the November 1970 issue of *Motion Picture* magazine. Also vital for this chapter were the articles "Ted and Joan Kennedy: Why this marriage couldn't be saved," published in *Ladies' Home Journal*, March 1983, and "The Tragic Life of a Kennedy Wife," published in the Irish *Independent*, April 23, 2005.

PART SIX: THE MYTHMAKER

JACKIE KENNEDY

Jackie's time at Valleyhead and the electroshock therapies she underwent there were first reported by Kitty Kelley in *Jackie Oh!*, which was published during Jackie's lifetime. Insights about Jackie's determination never to show her emotions in public were recorded by Carly Simon in her memoir *Touched by the Sun: My Friendship with Jackie*, in which Simon writes, "She told me never to let anyone know how much things hurt." Kennedy family friend and *Washington Post* editor-in-chief Ben Bradlee observed firsthand Jackie's ability to disconnect as early as 1959, as recounted in *America's Queen: The Life of Jacqueline Kennedy Onassis* by Sarah Bradford:

"I remember most watching Jackie," Bradford quotes Bradlee as saying, "and the almost physical discomfort she showed, as she walked slowly into this crowded hall to get stared at — not talked to, just simply stared at. Her reaction, later to become so familiar, was simply to pull some invisible shade across her face and cut out spiritually. She was physically present, but intellectually long gone."

Bradford also noted Jackie's innate ability to read people, and, according to JFK adviser John Kenneth Galbraith, how "absolutely indispensable" this was to Jack: "He tended to take people at their face value; she looked at them much more scrupulously to see what they were up to, to distinguish between those who had something from those who were promoting themselves . . . For all the people that I have known, she had the shrewdest eye for a phony or somebody who was engaged in self-advancement, and she didn't conceal it."

The pool parties and orgies thrown at the White House while Jackie was away have been well documented, but a firsthand account comes from the memoir *Dog Days at the White House* by longtime presidential kennel keeper Traphes Bryant. So does the oft-told story of Jackie finding another woman's panties in her bed; Bryant also was among the first to report the rumor around Jack's White House that he had impregnated a fifteen-year-old babysitter.

"Even though [Jack's] wife was brunette," Bryant wrote, "his girls all seemed to be blonde — and one a near redhead. The backstairs help used to mutter, 'Why can't he make it easier for us? Why do we always have to be searching for blonde hairs and blonde bobby pins?' . . .

"The story around the White House was that the blow [Jackie] finally could not forgive had come when a fifteen-year-old babysitter accused the [then-] senator of making her pregnant. That . . . was also, supposedly, what the ambassador was trying to soothe her for" with the reported $1 million in what could most honestly be considered hazard pay.

What happened on Air Force One after the assassination was documented in detail in Manchester's *Death of a President*. The panicked air force general who demanded immediate take off comes from *A Woman Named Jackie* by C. David Heymann. Jackie's question to Bobby about her public presentation in the blood-splattered Chanel suit — "What's the line between histrionics and drama?" — was part of her interview with Theodore White. Her diktats regarding Jack's funeral and its aesthetics, with Jackie's unforgettable order — "no fat black Cadillacs" — comes from Bedell Smith's *Grace and Power.*

Jackie's reliance on heavy drugs and her relationship with the physician known as "Dr. Feelgood" has been reported in many places, and here *Jackie after Jack* by Christopher Anderson was a good source, as was Bradford's *America's Queen.*

The chief of Dallas police addressing the newly widowed Jackie Kennedy as "little lady" on Air Force One comes from Leaming's *Jacqueline Bouvier Kennedy Onassis*. In 2014, Leaming was the first to theorize that Jackie suffered from post-traumatic stress disorder — an assuredly accurate assessment and a lifelong battle for Jackie.

PART SEVEN: STOLEN YOUTH

PAMELA KELLEY

Karen Kelley, Pam's sister, gave me hours of her time in interviews on Cape Cod. Karen recounted Pam's accident, her difficulties coping in the immediate aftermath, her wish to die, and what the Kelleys saw as a dereliction by Joe Kennedy to pay for Pam's increasing medical costs.

Coverage of Joe Kennedy's brief trial for the accident that paralyzed Pam permanently, for which he was fined $100 and given no jail time, comes from the *New York Times*. That article, blithely headlined "Joseph Kennedy Is Found Guilty of Negligence in Road Mishap," ran on August 21, 1973. Much as Ted's car "left the bridge" that night at Chappaquiddick, the Jeep that Joe drove recklessly was said to have "overturned a week ago," leaving Joe's brother David "and two girl passengers" hurt — a mere blunder, the *Times* would have it, for the young Joe. Pam wasn't mentioned by name until the last paragraph.

She described her recollection of the accident to Peter Collier and David Horowitz for their book, *The Kennedys: An American Drama*. "We were all sort of standing up in the jeep," Pam said. "Joe was cutting through the woods, spinning the jeep in circles. We were yelling and laughing and acting crazy. There was a rest area on the other side of the highway and Joe started to cross over to it. He didn't see this station wagon heading toward us until the last minute. Joe swerved and we hit a ditch with our tires on the right side, breaking the jeep's axle and flipping us. We held on to the roll bar for a couple of flips and then had to let go. Me and David were right together... in the air. I remember tumbling and seeing David's face. I hit the ground. When I tried to get up, nothing happened."

The marauding by "the Hyannis Port Terrors," as RFK Jr. and his brothers called themselves, as well as their brother David's heroin addiction, are documented here as well: "shoot[ing] water balloons at passing cars from the summit of a hill, aiming especially at police cars," and stuffing objects into tailpipes of parked vehicles. The book also describes Bobby approaching a police officer who had caught them, "his hand inside his coat. 'I have a hawk, and he's trained to kill cops,'" Bobby said.

Pam's belief that Joe Kennedy regarded her as little more than a persistent nuisance comes from an interview she gave to the *Boston Herald*, published on August 31, 2005: "I feel like he thinks I'm a piece of trash sitting in a wheelchair."

Liz McNeil of *People* magazine interviewed Pam and her family several times, and her obituary for Pam, dated December 3, 2020, paid tribute to a life well lived despite enormous hardship. Pam spent her last months in a Cape Cod nursing home at the height of the COVID-19 pandemic, and Karen wonders if loneliness was as much the cause of Pam's death as the shortage of available nurses.

The personal essay that Pam and Karen's sister Kim wrote, "Wings," was provided by Karen.

MARTHA MOXLEY

On Wednesday, November 24, 2021, the day before Thanksgiving, I drove to Connecticut's state supreme court to go through evidence submitted in Martha's trial. Susann Gill, the prosecutor in that case, had arranged it, and when I arrived three large boxes were wheeled into a small, windowless conference room. "Oh," the clerk said, "you'll probably want to see the murder weapon." She left and returned with the golf club used to bludgeon Martha's head and face—there it was, the Toney Penna, in a plain brown cardboard box. I removed it and placed it across the table, just above Martha's little diary, cheerfully emblazoned with red and yellow flowers. Another folder contained the crime scene photos, and it was clear to see why responding investigators thought the white-blonde Martha had been a redhead: she was practically scalped.

Martha's mother, Dorothy (she prefers her name spelled this way), invited me to her apartment in New Jersey, filled with light and two large portraits, one of Martha and one of Martha and her brother, John, sitting with their dog. She spoke lovingly of her daughter, shared family photos, and expressed no bitterness at the vacated verdict for Michael Skakel—only gratitude for the journalists who kept Martha's story alive, the late Len Levitt and Dominick Dunne especially, and for the investigators and prosecutors. She said that she believed Martha's murder was to blame for her husband's premature death.

Dorothy put me in touch with Robert Drake, who has become something of a historian and archivist for this case. He shared his institutional knowledge and his organized version of Martha's diary, and he reached out to those who might help me, Martha's friend Jennifer Allen especially. Now well into middle age, Jennifer's emotions remain raw; despite Martha's diary entries about the boys she liked, Jennifer was reluctant to speak about any of that. "I hesitate a little," she told me, "because at the trial, they really tried to paint Martha as this—to use a dated word here—a little hussy kind of thing. I don't want to say 'slut,' because that's not [it]. It was more that she was somewhere between a hussy and a slut...You know how it is. They always paint the victim that way."

Dead Man Talking, Michael Skakel's proposal for a tell-all Kennedy book, was another source for this chapter, as was Dunne's courthouse reporting for *Vanity Fair*. Levitt's book *Conviction* provided detail and context. Author and reporter Timothy Dumas, a Greenwich native, spoke with me at length; his book about the case, *Greentown: Murder and Mystery in Greenwich, America's Wealthiest Community*, also helped inform Martha's chapter.

Included in the evidence boxes were transcripts of phone calls made by Robert F. Kennedy Jr. to Tony Bryant, cousin of the late Kobe Bryant, attempting to build a case that two young boys, one Black and one of mixed race — not Michael Skakel, even though the murder weapon came from his own house — sexually assaulted and murdered Martha.

Ethel Kennedy's letter to the judge in this case, pleading mercy for Michael, was published in multiple newspapers, as she surely intended.

The Sutton Report, as quoted here, comes from Dominick Dunne's archived papers at the Briscoe Center for American History at the University of Texas at Austin.

Susann Gill also facilitated my access to court transcripts, the aforementioned crime scene photos, Martha's autopsy report, police interviews with the teenage boys and girls who had been out with Martha, Tommy, and Michael that night, victim impact statements given by Dorothy Moxley and her son John, and the transcript of Michael Skakel's sentencing. In that hearing, Superior Court Judge John F. Kavanewsky Jr. said, in part:

"The nature of this murder was not only violent, it was especially vicious. We can recall, and I won't recount here, the number and nature of the wounds the defendant inflicted on Martha Moxley. And Dorothy Moxley and others have spoken powerfully about how this tragedy has affected them through today.

"I don't claim to know for certain what prompted or caused the defendant to kill Martha Moxley, but by the verdict delivered I do know that for the last twenty-five years or more, a period well into his adult life, the defendant has been living a lie about his guilt...Most important, this defendant has accepted no personal responsibility. He has expressed no personal remorse to this present day. All of this persuades me to impose a sentence which, on balance, is more substantial."

Michael Skakel was sentenced to twenty years to life. On October 30, 2020, thanks in large part to Robert F. Kennedy Jr.'s efforts, Skakel's conviction was vacated.

That day I spent with the evidence right before Thanksgiving 2021 was timed better than I'd known. It wasn't until I began going through those boxes that the court officer told me they would be sealed, forever, the Monday after Thanksgiving weekend. Martha's evidence could never again be examined by anyone — not future journalists, biographers, or historians. As of this writing, Michael Skakel has filed a lawsuit to reclaim audiotapes used against him at trial. He maintains his innocence in this case.

PART EIGHT: FALLING STARS

MARILYN MONROE

Marilyn's admission that she got no pleasure from sex, as well as the story of the incestuous relationship between Marilyn and Jack and Bobby Kennedy, is in *Goddess: The Secret Lives of Marilyn Monroe* by Anthony Summers. The author quotes Marilyn's friend and neighbor Jeanne Carmen, who saw Jack and Bobby pick Marilyn up from her Doheny Drive apartment one night, and who recalled another evening that Marilyn spent drinking wine with Bobby Kennedy — Jack having visited Marilyn "sometime earlier." Her ex-husband Joe DiMaggio's anger at Bobby Kennedy for his affair with Marilyn is also documented here, as is the report of her overnight stays with the Lawfords as her depression intensified.

Marilyn's use of crib notes so that she could talk of current events with Bobby comes from *Marilyn Monroe: The Private Life of a Public Icon* by Charles Casillo, as does her drunken appearance at the 1962 Golden Globes. Casillo also quotes Jeanne Martin, wife of Frank Sinatra's friend Dean Martin, about the "sophomoric" behavior of Jack and Bobby at parties and about a friend of hers who found herself alone in a room with Bobby, who locked the door and threw her on the couch. No other details about this incident were reported.

The reference to Peter Lawford's LA party house as "High-Anus-Port" is recounted in *Mr. S: My Life with Frank Sinatra* by George Jacobs and William Stadiem. Marilyn's insecurity about her vocabulary comes from Spada's *Peter Lawford: The Man Who Kept the Secrets*, as does a report from an FBI file on Monroe in which she is described as despondent over ex-husband Arthur Miller's remarriage: "The subject was much disturbed...and feels like a negated sex symbol." The wiretapping of Monroe's house, her conversations about Jack and Bobby with her hairdresser Mickey Song, and Song's assessment of her involvement with the Kennedy brothers are also covered in Spada's book: "I think she was abused," he quotes Song as saying. "They played with her and they got tired of her and I think they found her a lot of trouble to get off their hands. She wasn't going to go that easily." Bobby's final visit to Marilyn shortly before she died, and his recorded demands to know where her wiretap was hidden — "Where is it? Where the fuck is it?" — with door slamming and the sounds of bumps and thumps also reported by Spada, along with her final phone call to Peter Lawford and Joe DiMaggio's belief that Lawford, Sinatra, and the Kennedys were to blame for her death.

The letter that Jack and Bobby's sister Jean Kennedy Smith wrote to Marilyn, on letterhead from the Kennedy family home in Palm Beach, Florida — "Understand that you and Bobby are the new item! We all think you should come with him when he comes back East!" — was reprinted in *Goddess*, the Summers biography, as were parts of a letter that Marilyn's psychiatrist, Ralph Greenson, wrote to a colleague in May 1961: "I try to help [Marilyn] not to be so lonely, and therefore to escape into the drugs or get involved with very destructive people who will engage in some sort of sado-masochistic relationship with her..."

Summers also spoke with Dr. Robert Litman, cofounder and chief psychiatrist of the Los Angeles Suicide Prevention Center, who had spoken to Greenson after Marilyn's death. Per one of Litman's reports, quoted here: "Around [early 1962], Marilyn started to date some 'very important men.' Greenson had very considerable concern that she was being used in these relationships..." Summers reprints parts of Marilyn's phone records that show eight calls being made to Bobby Kennedy's DC office in the days before her death. Bert Stern's quotes about Marilyn's "power" at her final photo shoot are also contained in Summers's book.

JACKIE KENNEDY ONASSIS

Jackie calling Bobby Kennedy her husband comes from *America's Queen* by Sarah Bradford, as does Jackie's denunciation by the Vatican and Aristotle Onassis's proclamation that acquiring Jackie as a wife "was my last diamond on my crown." Bradford quotes Jackie as she recounts nearly drowning in 1967 during an ill-advised solo swim off the coast of Ireland in high tide and against the current—a possible death wish. Jackie wrote:

"The water was so cold that one could not hold one's fingers together. I am a very good swimmer and can swim for miles and hours, but the combination of current and cold were something I had never known. There was no one in sight to yell to.

"I was becoming exhausted, swallowing water and slipping past the spit of land, when I felt a great porpoise at my side. It was Mr. Walsh [of the Secret Service detail]. He set his shoulder against mine and together we made the spit. Then I sat on the beach coughing up sea water for half an hour while he found a poor itinerant and borrowed a blanket for me."

The secret arrangements that Onassis made with paparazzi to have an unaware Jackie photographed sunbathing nude and having sex with him on the beach are reported in Bradford's book, as is his verbal abuse of Jackie in front of esteemed guests and his denigration of Jackie to his girlfriend Maria Callas, saying "that going to bed with her was like going to bed with a corpse." Jackie's rapid aging during the Onassis years is here, too, as is her penchant, out of the public eye, for wearing the same clothes multiple days in a row. Jackie's chafing at Ari's expectation that she be a good Greek wife, "sitting at home waiting for him," is here. Her admission that she had buried her true self for Ari—"far from [my] innate self"—comes from Simon's *Touched by the Sun*.

Ari's abuse of Jackie is also reported in *The Good Son: JFK Jr. and the Mother He Loved* by Chistopher Andersen, who quotes the late controversial attorney Roy Cohn: "They were having one of their screaming matches when Ari lost his temper and hit Jackie across the face. She had a black eye, but since she wore dark glasses all the time no one suspected a thing."

Jackie's persistent nightmares about JFK's assassination come from Leaming's *Jacqueline Bouvier Kennedy Onassis*, as does the nerve damage in her neck. Of her death wish, Leaming quotes Jackie talking to Kennedy press secretary Frank Mankiewicz after Bobby had been shot: "Well, now we know death, don't we, you and I? As a matter of fact, if it weren't for the children, we'd welcome it." Her stepdaughter Christina Onassis's belief that Jackie was a black widow — "before long she will kill us all" — a belief that Christina's father, Ari, came to share, is also here.

Jackie's reawakened sexuality — Ari replacing her staid lingerie with custom-made Halston, and her viewing, in public, of the pornographic film *I Am Curious (Yellow)* — is discussed in Kitty Kelley's *Jackie Oh!*. The emergence of a Jackie O "sex doll" was reported in the Jackie-themed issue of *Confidential* magazine published in 1975, along with the story about Ari's maids selling her underwear on the black market.

Bobby Kennedy as Jackie's lover after Jack's assassination is the subject of *Bobby and Jackie: A Love Story* by C. David Heymann. He writes that in the fall of 1964, with Bobby often staying overnight at her 1040 Fifth Avenue apartment, Jackie dismissed her Secret Service detail from the 11:00 p.m. to 7:00 a.m. shift, and quotes a letter she wrote to then-secretary of the treasury C. Douglas Dillon, appearing to cover her tracks: "It's pointless for them to stand around in the cold all night in front of my apartment building." Heymann also writes that a number of Secret Service files on Jackie throughout this part of her life have vanished.

Heymann cites Ethel's absence from Bobby's campaign trail and quotes her friend Coates Redmon: "I'm certain [Ethel's] reluctance had something to do with her suspicion that Bobby and Jackie had initiated a sexual relationship. Her suspicions were well-founded... You'd go to dinner parties in New York or Washington, and people would talk. And you could see how it might all have started, and how after JFK's death they could have had a mad, morbid attraction to each other, and how this initial attachment continued to grow." Heymann quotes Franklin Roosevelt Jr., a longtime friend of JFK, Jackie, and Ari Onassis: "Everybody knew about the [Jackie–Bobby] affair," he said. "The two of them carried on like a pair of lovesick teenagers. People used to see them at Le Club, their torsos stuck together as they danced the night away."

Heymann writes that while author Peter Evans was researching his 1986 biography of Onassis, he discovered a letter Jackie wrote to Ari around 1967, as Bobby contemplated a run for president: "When death ends one dear relationship, it often creates another sweeter still... There was a time when Bobby meant more to me than life itself."

The Bobby–Jackie affair is also covered in Peter Evans's *Nemesis: Aristotle Onassis, Jackie O, and the Love Triangle That Brought Down the Kennedys,* as is Jackie's belief that if Bobby ran for president he would be killed. The night he was shot, Onassis and Jackie's friend Joan Thring called her in New York. Jackie was home at 1040 Fifth Avenue, and Thring recalled that Jackie had a psychotic episode: "Bobby was still hanging in there at that point, but [Jackie] talked about his death and about Jack's death, and the two seemed to merge in her mind. She was very distraught. It seemed to her that her country as well as her family was falling apart... She was very scared."

Ari's declaration that the widowed Jackie Kennedy needed "a small scandal to bring her alive" — and that scandal would be marrying him — is covered in Evans's

book, as is Ari's description of himself as "completely fucking ruthless." Ted Kennedy's failed attempts at negotiating a prenuptial payout for Jackie are detailed here, as is her financial adviser's opening bid to Ari of $20 million. His devaluation of Jackie in the later years of their marriage, and his summoning of her from New York for sex in order to remind Jackie of "what she was," is also here.

Jackie's work with Dr. Marianne Kris, and her shock upon learning that Kris had also treated Marilyn Monroe, comes from *Jackie: Public, Private, Secret* by J. Randy Taraborrelli.

One of the most insightful pieces about Jackie, which Jackie herself allowed her friends to cooperate with, was written by Susan Sheehan for the *New York Times* in 1970. Titled "The Happy Jackie, the Sad Jackie, the Bad Jackie, the Good Jackie," it detailed a complicated woman prone to swings of sociability and lonerism, selfishness and generosity, and what seems to be her depression, anxiety, and PTSD.

She was described, at her best, as contagiously joyful and funny; at her lowest, she slept her days away, was capricious and dismissive of others' time, needs, and wants — at heart, Black Jack's spoiled little girl who would buy everything in her sightline and literally stomp her feet if she didn't get her way. Jackie was a woman who sought friendships but had trouble, on her end, sustaining them. She was born to have become a public figure, thriving in moments of great crisis and perhaps finding some comfort in being seen by all yet known to very few.

Jackie's fundamental nature, as those who knew her told Sheehan, was self-contained and mysterious, perhaps even to herself: "Jackie's very uptight emotionally," one friend said. "Just as she can respond to the dramatic occasions but can't bring herself to deal with ordinary happenings, she isn't up to close friendships, with the weekly phone calls and lunches, the effort and the intimacy they entail."

PART NINE: HOMES FOR WAYWARD GIRLS

ROSE KENNEDY

The Kennedy matriarch kept her thoughts and feelings private; even her children struggled to understand why she behaved as she did. Her autobiography, *Times to Remember*, published in 1974, is strangely impersonal, consisting mainly of the observations and writings of others. Perhaps the most vulnerable part of the book is Rose's dedication, which used terrible nomenclature that would never be used today. She wrote in part:

"This book is dedicated to my daughter Rosemary and others like her — retarded in mind but blessed in spirit. My vision is a world where mental retardation will be overcome, where we no longer mourn with mothers of retarded children, but exult and rejoice with parents of happy, healthy youngsters."

Rose's early life as the privileged daughter of Boston mayor John "Honey Fitz" Fitzgerald is covered in *Rosemary: The Hidden Kennedy Daughter* by Kate Clifford

Larson. Her father's refusal, for purely political reasons, to forbid his smart, vivacious daughter from attending Wellesley College haunted Rose for life. Larson quotes an interview Rose gave to the historian Doris Kearns Goodwin: "My greatest regret is not having gone to Wellesley College. It is something I have felt a little sad about my whole life." Rose's attempt to leave Joe and her father's insistence that she return home to her husband and children and "go back where you belong" is also in Larson's book.

Rose's horrific home birth and the damage done to her daughter, Rosemary, is described by Larson as well, as is Rose's depression and her Catholic belief that sex, even inside of marriage, was for procreation only. Other historians as well have related this last detail: In *The Kennedys: America's Emerald Kings*, Thomas Maier writes, "After the birth of their last child, Rose demanded separate bedrooms and refused any more sex, according to historian Doris Kearns Goodwin." Her denial of the affair that Joe was conducting with movie star Gloria Swanson, of whom she writes kindly in her autobiography, is well documented here and elsewhere. That affair is the subject of its own chapter, "Gloria," in *The Sins of the Father: Joseph P. Kennedy and the Dynasty He Founded* by Ronald Kessler. A much darker side of the patriarch as not just a serial womanizer but as a rapist was reported in Evans's *Nemesis* as well as Gerald Clarke's biography *Capote: A Biography*. Capote disguised Kathleen's friend Pamela Harriman, who would become Winston Churchill's daughter-in-law, as "Lady Ina Coolbirth" in his *roman à clef Answered Prayers*. Capote maintained that it was common knowledge that Joe had raped Pamela while she was an overnight guest at Hyannis Port. In *Nemesis*, Evans writes:

"Coolbirth would describe how, when she was Kathleen Kennedy's weekend houseguest, at age eighteen, she had been raped by Kathleen's father when he slipped into her bed in the small hours." Other female friends of the Kennedy girls were told to lock their bedroom doors when staying at the Hyannis house; JFK himself would say of his father, "The ambassador has a tendency to wander at night."

In her autobiography, Rose writes of the exacting standards that she and Joe held for all their children: "Superior achievement or making the most of one's capabilities is to a very considerable degree a matter of habit. This was the reason Joe used to say to the children, 'We don't want any losers around here. In this family we want winners... Don't come in second or third — that doesn't count — but win.'"

Her distancing from her own children and her frequent travels abroad are covered in Collier and Horowitz's *The Kennedys: An American Drama* and her own autobiography. Rose's physical abuse of her children — one of the childhood traumas Jack and Jackie shared — is documented in *JFK: Reckless Youth* by Nigel Hamilton: "At first she used a ruler, kept in her sewing desk, the better, she punned, to measure the punishment. As her eldest two became more mischievous, however, she began to use wooden coat hangers, 'whacking' the children on the hands or buttocks. Coat hangers, she later explained, 'were always within reach.'"

Rose's approach to Rosemary was different. Her account of searching among top doctors for the cause of Rosemary's mental incapacities shines with maternal love but also alludes to a sense that it was all her own fault: "Joe and I looked for experts in mental deficiency, at Harvard as well as in hospitals, and I talked with some of them...They could venture certain theories to account for her condition — 'genetic accident,' 'uterine accident,' 'birth accident,' and so forth — but when I would ask, 'What can I do to help her?' there didn't seem to be much of an answer. I was frustrated and heartbroken."

Later in Rose's book, Rosemary disappears, sent off to various schools, until, she writes, "Joe and I brought the most eminent medical specialists into consultation, and the advice, finally, was that Rosemary should undergo a certain form of neurosurgery." Most historians believe that Rose had no knowledge of Joe's decision to lobotomize Rosemary; perhaps this was her way of protecting her husband in death. She nonetheless writes, "From her childhood Kick had been, in effect, our eldest daughter because of Rosemary's disability."

ROSEMARY KENNEDY

Much of my account of Rosemary's early life comes from Kate Clifford Larson's *Rosemary: The Hidden Kennedy Daughter*. Letters that Rosemary wrote to her father, mother, and family — and vice versa — are contained in *Hostage to Fortune*. Joe Kennedy's alarm at Rosemary's sexual development is noted in Maier's *The Kennedys*, as well as Larson's book: "In a household both highly sexualized on the male side and notably repressed on the female side, Rosemary's beauty was a special threat." Larson quotes Lem Billings as telling the journalist Burton Hersh that "Rosemary was 'sexually frustrated'... it was Rosemary's potential and physically obvious sexuality that her parents found dangerous."

Larson writes of the deep shame the Kennedys felt about Rosemary and their efforts to keep her hidden from all but the immediate family. That the Kennedys regarded Rosemary "a disgrace and a failure" is reported in Kessler's *The Sins of the Father*.

Joe's decision to deport his children from England as Germany prepared to attack — all but Rosemary — has been well documented, though few, if any, historians have asked: Did Joe wish his daughter dead? He certainly expressed his belief that she would be fine under a Nazi regime, one that would have exterminated Rosemary for her cognitive impairments. She writes longingly to and of her father, and of her pride in being the singled-out Kennedy child to be his companion there.

In *JFK: Reckless Youth*, Nigel Hamilton writes of suspicion as to Joe Kennedy's true motives in lobotomizing Rosemary: "Some who witnessed Joseph P. Kennedy's own behavior at home...speculated as to whether he might have sexually abused Rosemary, thus explaining her delayed outbursts" — which did not materialize until her later teenage years — "and Kennedy's guilty determination to quiet her."

Details of Rosemary's operation come from the PBS documentary *The American Experience: The Lobotomist*, about Dr. Walter J. Freeman, one of two surgeons who performed this atrocity. Also helpful were Kessler's *The Sins of the Father* and *The Missing Kennedy: Rosemary Kennedy and the Secret Bonds of Four Women* by Elizabeth Koehler-Pentacoff. Kessler writes of an interview he conducted with the other surgeon who performed Rosemary's lobotomy, Dr. James W. Watts:

"After Rosemary was mildly sedated, 'We went through the top of the head...I think she was awake. She had a mild tranquilizer. I made a surgical incision in the brain through the skull. It was near the front. It was on both sides. We just made a small incision, no more than an inch.'

"The instrument Dr. Watts used looked like a butter knife. He swung it up and down to cut brain tissue. 'We put an instrument inside,' he said. As Dr. Watts cut, [neurologist] Dr. [Walter J.] Freeman asked Rosemary questions. For example, he would ask her to recite the Lord's Prayer or sing 'God Bless America' or count backward. Her pulse became more rapid, and her blood pressure rose."

"Dr. Watts did not recall what happened to Rosemary immediately after the operation. Typically, patients are disoriented, have flattened voices, and vomit... Patients may also fumble with their genitalia or exhibit signs of euphoria."

Koehler-Pentacoff offers further details of the lobotomy: Rosemary, she writes, was given Novocain and a mild sedative. The front of her scalp was shaved and she was made to lie down with her head propped up on a sandbag. As she talked, "Dr. Watts drilled holes into each side of her prefrontal lobe. He slid tubing from a two-and-a-half-inch needle inside her brain. He then twisted 'a blunt spatula, much like a calibrated butter knife,' upward inside her brain.

"At this point, Dr. Freeman asked Rosemary to sing a song. As she sang, Dr. Watts continued to twist the 'spatula.' When she could no longer respond to their instructions, the doctors knew the lobotomy was complete."

Weeks before his death from cancer, Watts told Kessler that, in his estimation, Rosemary was not mentally impaired but rather suffered from "an agitated depression."

Koehler-Pentacoff, whose aunt helped care for Rosemary in her later years, writes of Rosemary's extreme loneliness. She writes that Rose Kennedy displayed pictures of her surviving children in color and her deceased children in black and white; Rosemary's pictures were, after the lobotomy, the latter.

"Rosemary received no visitors during the bleakest years of her life," Koehler-Pentacoff writes.

Ted Kennedy wasn't the only one traumatized by Rosemary's disappearance and the fear that if he didn't measure up, Joe would consign him to an equally terrifying fate. David Kennedy, in the throes of a drug addiction that would eventually kill him, told Collier and Horowitz about seeing his aunt Rosemary in a magazine. "She had a new pair of white shoes on and she was smiling. The thought crossed my mind that if my grandfather was alive the same thing could have happened to me that happened to her. She was an embarrassment; I am an embarrassment. She was a hindrance; I am a hindrance. As I looked at this picture, I began to hate my grandfather and all of them for having done the thing they had done to her and for doing the thing they were doing to me."

In *The Kennedy Women: The Saga of an American Family*, Laurence Leamer writes that after Rosemary was lobotomized, her mother never again included Rosemary's name in the letters she wrote to all her children: "Rosemary was gone, gone from the family letters, gone from discussions, gone."

Leamer also wrote that a nurse who had been present during Rosemary's lobotomy was so horrified that she left the profession altogether. When I contacted him after reading this, Leamer told me that he and his wife overheard this in Nashville, Tennessee, while he was working on another book. The former nurse, he said, was recounting this story to her dining companion, who seemed to have heard it many times before.

Leamer writes of one visit that Rose made circa 1949 to St. Coletta's in Wisconsin, where Rosemary would live the rest of her life: Rose "recoiled at what she saw and what her daughter had become and hardly ever traveled to Wisconsin again for two decades... When Rose arrived, her daughter turned away from her mother, wanting nothing to do with this woman who stood before her so beseechingly. Rosemary seemed to know that this was her mother, and the nuns believed that Rosemary blamed Rose for abandoning her. 'In the back of my mind is the idea that Rosemary had had this surgery and her mother didn't show up,' said Sister Margaret Ann. "And that she was taking it out on her mother...[The other nuns] said that Rosemary never accepted her."

PART TEN: REBELS

JOAN KENNEDY

The period covered in this chapter—the lead-up to Ted Kennedy's failed presidential bid in 1980—was a particularly delicate time in Joan's life: trying to stay sober, worrying that if Ted ran for president he'd be assassinated, and being kept in limbo by Ted and his advisers as his wife in name only, despite the fact that this was a role she'd have to play—to convince America their marriage was real—were he to run.

Much of the sourcing for this chapter comes from contemporaneous news reports and magazine profiles. *People* magazine's cover story on Joan in the August 7, 1978, issue (titled "Joan Kennedy Surveys Her Sober Life Alone and Exults: 'It's Not Too Late for Me'") quotes Joan on her burgeoning independence and pushing past the fear of Ted meeting a catastrophic end: "'It wouldn't be hard to imagine campaigning for Ted if he ran for president,' she says now. 'I could do a good job—if I made my own rules about where I'd go and what I'd say. So much has changed in the last year. Because of my self-confidence, I don't feel trapped in any role I don't want.'"

Ted's terrible treatment of women, the fourteen-year-old he had tried to rape, his drug and alcohol abuse, were all chronicled in *The Senator: My Ten Years with Ted Kennedy* by his former aide Richard E. Burke with William and Marilyn Hoffer. Suzannah Lessard's groundbreaking essay-slash-exposé of Ted's philandering was initially killed by *New Republic* owner Martin Peretz, but Charlie Peters at the *Washington Monthly* picked it up and made it their December cover story. Lessard's piece asserted that "this type of behavior is so classically degrading to women...at the very least, it suggests that there will be no women in positions of true power in a Kennedy administration"—just as had been true for Jack, who had no women in his executive staff. The incident in which Ted took a journalist out to see a passed-out Joan in one of their family cars is detailed in *The Kennedys* by Collier and Horowitz.

Patricia Stewart Lawford says Peter told her he had witnessed Ted Kennedy sabotage Joan's sobriety. As she told me for the *New York Post*, Peter "watched Ted spike some punch and give a glass to Joan [who] had been sober for eight years. Ted says, 'Here, have some.' And she gets picked up by the cops driving home." Marcia Chellis's *Living with the Kennedys: The Joan Kennedy Story* covers the period of Joan's life when she was asked to stump for Ted in 1980 while his team tried to crisis-manage her answers about Mary Jo Kopechne, her own subsequent alcoholism, and the state of their marriage. It also details Joan's crushing realization, once Ted withdrew from the race, that he had no interest in reconciling and had only ever been using her.

Yet Joan's star power as Ted's surrogate, her newfound feminism, and her public support of the Equal Rights Amendment were noted in much on-the-road campaign coverage, notably in "Two Wives Finding Rewards on the Campaign Trail" by Leslie Bennetts for the *New York Times*, February 24, 1980. Joan Kennedy spoke of the wage gap, the need for more childcare options for working mothers, federalized pay through Social Security for stay-at-home mothers economically dependent on their husbands, and the ERA: "It can become the means," Joan said, "by which my daughter Kara and her daughters can enjoy the choices women have been denied for generations."

Joan Kennedy made perhaps the most consequential decision of the campaign, and did so in her own best interest, when she declined to sit with Ted for an hour-long primetime interview with Roger Mudd for CBS News in September 1979. His disastrous, vague, elliptical answers — most notably to the key question, "Why do you want to be president?" — killed all hope that he would ever be elected to the Oval Office. Joan and Ted Kennedy jointly filed for divorce in 1981.

CAROLYN BESSETTE KENNEDY

Details about Carolyn's adolescence, her fractured relationship with her father, and her pattern of dating boys and men who were emotionally and psychologically abusive come from friends who wish to remain anonymous. The wedding on Cumberland Island and the advance planning has been written about in *Fairytale Interrupted: A Memoir of Life, Love, and Loss* by Rosemarie Terenzio, *What Remains: A Memoir of Fate, Friendship, and Love* by Carole Radziwill, *The Men We Became: My Friendship with John F. Kennedy Jr.* by Robert T. Littell, and *Forever Young: My Friendship with John F. Kennedy Jr.* by William "Billy" Sylvester Noonan with Robert Huber. The descriptions of the small chapel where Carolyn and John were married, which was built by slaves, comes from a research visit I took for this book.

The toast given by Carolyn's mother Ann Freeman at the rehearsal dinner, in which she expressed concern that this marriage was a grave mistake for her daughter, is recounted in Littell's memoir: "I don't remember her exact words, but she implied that she was worried for her daughter, unsure if this union was in her best interest. In hindsight, it's chilling. At the time, I was surprised at her bluntness and felt bad for John, who was visibly stung by the remarks."

Suspicion of Carolyn's motives in caring for John's terminally ill cousin Anthony was expressed by Noonan in his memoir: Noonan writes that Carolyn, on the outs with John's friends and relatives, "needed a cause célèbre...a way to survive. She found one in Anthony."

Radziwill's take is more sympathetic. In *What Remains*, she writes of Carolyn's ministrations to her husband, Anthony Radziwill, hospitalized after a harrowing surgery: "Carolyn rubs his crunchy feet. She brings back a loofah and peppermint lotion from The Body Shop. I am here, but she does the work. She holds his hand while they watch TV. She takes out her pedicure kit and soaks his feet. When we leave the hospital for a break, she never fails to bring back something for him. Anthony, I know, is uncomfortable with this level of attention. He is not the sort for this, but I don't try to change anything...I need her here, and he knows that."

Reports of the crisis both in John and Carolyn's marriage and in John's own psyche shortly before their deaths are extensive. Gillon, in particular, shed new light on John's state of mind in the weeks before the crash, writing that John had received a letter from Hachette Filipacchi Magazines, co-owner of his flailing *George* magazine, and was very upset by it. He invited Gillon over to the Tribeca apartment he shared with Carolyn to read it. Gillon writes that the letter was an all-out verbal assault on John's inability to run his own magazine, in essence calling John "lazy and stupid."

Gillon writes that Carolyn inserted herself into this conversation and lit up with rage, cursing her husband for being so passive and nonconfrontational. "Everybody fucks you, John, and you just take it!" he quotes Carolyn here, in part. "When are you going to grow some balls and start fighting back?"

Gillon writes that the combination of that letter and Carolyn's reaction led him to two conclusions: *George* would soon meet its end, and so would John and Carolyn's marriage.

The post-crash report by the National Transportation Safety Board (NTSB) found that the sole cause was pilot error. As for reports that JFK Jr. had checked weather and visibility beforehand, the NTSB finding rebukes that. "No record exists of the pilot, or a pilot using the airplane's registration number, receiving a weather briefing or filing a flight plan." JFK Jr.'s near collision with an American Airlines commercial flight making its approach to JFK International Airport is documented here, as is the condition of the plane once recovered; one of the six passenger seats was missing. The lap part of one seat belt, likely where Carolyn had been sitting, "had been cleanly cut," which would indicate that Carolyn's body did not remain intact.

The bullying of Carolyn's mother by Caroline Kennedy's husband Ed Schlossberg after the crash, and the Kennedys' disinterest in what became of Carolyn and Lauren's remains, was chronicled by Robert F. Kennedy Jr. in diaries published by the *New York Post*.

PART TWELVE: PHOENIX

JACKIE BOUVIER ONASSIS

Jackie's decision to remake herself as a working woman is chronicled in several books. Most helpful was *Jackie as Editor: The Literary Life of Jacqueline Kennedy Onassis* by Greg Lawrence, which details her career as a book editor from beginning to end, as well as the origins of her first and only piece for the *New Yorker* in 1974, and her life-long love of reading. Lawrence quotes her friend Joe Armstrong, who had served as publisher of *Rolling Stone* and *New York* magazines: "I remember being with her at the Vineyard the last summer she was there. She had just turned 64. I remember in her living room she had all these books, and she said, 'These are my other best friends.'"

Her chosen career was in some ways curious, given how much she controlled her own image and press coverage and especially her public battle with William Manchester to cancel *The Death of a President*. Manchester's son, John, shared with me a four-page handwritten letter from Jackie to Manchester, dated June 17, 1968—twelve days after Robert F. Kennedy's assassination. Her feelings toward Manchester had changed. Jackie wrote, in part:

> *Dear Bill,*
>   *When I read this spring that you were giving your support to Robert Kennedy—I was absolutely startled...*
>   *Thank you dear Bill—with all my heart—those two pathetic inadequate words—but I mean them so much—*

Her resignation from Viking over *Shall We Tell the President?* is covered in Lawrence's book, as is her willingness to bid on proposals that would be personal and painful to her. Lawrence quotes a May 14, 1980, memo Jackie wrote to a colleague about a project she hoped to land:

"MARILYN MONROE!!! Bert Stern is doing a book called 'The Last Sitting'—his 3-day photographic session with Marilyn 6 wks before she died...$50,000–$100,000 for it...Are you excited?"

Her reinvention was the cover story in *People* magazine, dated June 18, 1984. Among its revelations was her willingness to use her celebrity to land Michael Jackson's autobiography, even though Jackie found the pop star creepy. "She...works hard," wrote *People* reporter Gioia Diliberto. "She takes manuscripts to the hairdresser, Kenneth's, and home with her at night. Occasionally, visitors to her apartment find her sitting on the living-room floor, her fluffy auburn head bent over book layouts."

Jackie's work with the author Dorothy West on Martha's Vineyard is recounted in Lawrence's book as well as Taraborrelli's *Jackie*. West's resulting novel, *The Wedding*, would become an Oprah's Book Club pick and a modern classic. West, who was eighty-eight when she began working on it in earnest, dedicated the book to Jackie:

"Though there was never such a mismatched pair in appearance, we were perfect partners."

Barbara Chase-Riboud wrote about her friendship and working relationship with Jackie for *The Millions*. In "How Jackie O Helped Bring 'Sally Hemings' to Life," Chase-Riboud writes, "If . . . she hadn't nudged me to keep going and not to give up, I might have given in to victimhood and never finished what I had accidentally started, which of course resulted in the famous DNA testing by Dr. Eugene Foster that proved me right" — that Hemings had given birth to at least six of Thomas Jefferson's children while she was enslaved by him. "And Sally Hemings took on a life her own," Chase-Riboud writes, "a historical life for which I am eternally grateful."

Lost to history — until I located it in the New York Public Library's Women's Magazine Archive — was Jackie's groundbreaking cover for *Ms.* magazine's March 1979 issue, with its cover reading "Why Does This Woman Work?" "If I hadn't married," Jackie said, "I might have had a life very much like Gloria Emerson's. She is a friend who started out in Paris writing about fashion — and then ended up as a correspondent in Vietnam. The two ends of her career couldn't seem farther apart and that is the virtue of journalism. You never know where it's going to take you."

That may have been the first, and only, time that Jacqueline Kennedy Onassis publicly mused about having chosen a career over marriage — a choice she silently made, at the dawn of a new decade, for the rest of her life.

INDEX

INDEX

INDEX

INDEX

education of, 241–42

emotional outbursts of, 243, 245

Walter J. Freeman's treatment of, 246–48, 357–58n

JFK and, 157, 177, 240, 317

David Anthony Kennedy and, 175, 358n

Joseph Patrick Kennedy Sr. and, xviii, 175, 239–42, 243, 244, 245, 246–47, 248, 317, 324–25, 356–57n

Rose Fitzgerald Kennedy and, 240–42, 244–45, 317, 324, 325, 355n, 356–57n, 358n, 359n

Ted Kennedy and, 324–25, 358n

Kennedy family gatherings and, 41

lack of athleticism, 241, 244

lack of integration into home life, 244–46

lobotomy of, 246–48, 317, 324, 357–58n, 359n

loneliness of, 239, 358n

mental incapacities of, 241, 356–57n

at St. Coletta's in Wisconsin, 324, 359n

at Saint Gertrude's, 245

sexual development of, 357n

Eunice Kennedy Shriver and, 139, 239, 240, 324–25

at sleepaway camp in Massachusetts, 245

weight of, 241, 244

Kennedy, Ted (Edward Moore)

alcohol abuse of, 108, 125, 126, 135, 139, 251, 253, 260, 270, 271, 359n

Mimi Alford and, 294

Jeffrey Archer's book and, 307–8

biographies of, xiv–xv

birth of, 234

Pamela Kelley Burkley's settlement and, 173

childhood of, 131

children of, 252, 255, 323

divorce of, 255, 323, 360n

drug use of, 252, 253

emergency televised address, 120–21

father's relationship with, 131–33, 138, 358n

infidelity of, 115, 125, 128, 130–31, 134, 137, 139, 141, 251–52, 253, 255, 256, 259–62, 271, 294, 359–60n

JFK and, 133, 148

JFK Jr.'s plane crash and, 284

Joseph Patrick Kennedy II's accident and, 171, 172

Mary Richardson Kennedy's burial and, 88

Rosemary Kennedy and, 324–25, 358n

Kennedy men's protection of reputation, 107

Joan Kennedy's relationship with, 115, 125, 126–35, 136, 137–39, 140, 141, 142, 251, 252–54, 255, 256, 257, 259–62, 347–48n, 359–60n

Mary Jo Kopechne's death and, xiv, xv, 15, 105–8, 116–24, 139–40, 141, 142, 255, 258–59, 260, 270, 322–23, 346n, 347n, 360n

Mary Jo Kopechne's funeral and, 122, 140

Mary Jo Kopechne's opinion of, 115

Mediterranean trip and, 30

Jackie Kennedy Onassis's marriage to Aristotle Onassis and, 355n

plane crash of, 135–36

presidential campaign of, 251, 254, 258, 259–63, 308, 359–60n

recklessness of, 138

RFK's eulogy and, 114–15

RFK Jr.'s divorce and, 77

Senate campaign of, 133, 136–38

sexually transmitted diseases of, 252

William Kennedy Smith and, 269, 270

treatment of women, 251, 252, 359–60n

weight of, 131, 132

Kennedy, Ted (Edward Moore), Jr., 136, 142, 253, 323

Kennedy, Victoria Reggie, 284–85

Kennedy Curse, 105, 222, 227, 315, 322

Kennedy family legacy

Camelot fairy tale of, xiv, 165–66, 222, 252, 342n

women's role in, xiii, xv, xvi–xvii

Kennedys, The (2011 miniseries), xv

INDEX

ABOUT THE AUTHOR

MAUREEN CALLAHAN is an award-winning investigative journalist and the author of three previous books, including the *New York Times* bestseller *American Predator: The Hunt for the Most Meticulous Serial Killer of the 21st Century,* which was a finalist for an Edgar Award for Best Fact Crime and the winner of France's Grand Prix de Littérature Policière. Her writing has appeared in *Vanity Fair,* the *New York Times Magazine, Spin, New York Magazine,* the *New York Post,* and the *Daily Mail,* where she currently has a column. She lives in New York.